MUNICIPAL GOVERNMENT
REFERENCE SOURCES

MUNICIPAL GOVERNMENT REFERENCE SOURCES

Publications and Collections

Edited for the
**American Library Association
Government Documents Round Table**
by
**Peter Hernon, John V. Richardson,
Nancy P. Sanders, and Marjorie Shepley**

R. R. BOWKER COMPANY
New York & London   1978

Published by R. R. Bowker Company
1180 Avenue of the Americas, New York, N.Y. 10036
Copyright © 1978 by Xerox Corporation
Printed and bound in the United States of America

Library of Congress Cataloging in Publication Data
Main entry under title:

Municipal government reference sources.

   Includes index.
   1. Municipal documents—United States—Bibliography.
2. Municipal documents—United States—Library resources.
I. Hernon, Peter.   II. American Library Association.
Government Documents Round Table.
Z1223.6.A1M85   [JS13]   016.352′008′0973   78-17619
ISBN 0-8352-1003-0

CONTENTS

FOREWORD

Publication of *Municipal Government Reference Sources* will provide, for the first time, basic reference assistance to librarians and researchers concerned with municipal publications as a valuable information resource. In the past, even individual libraries, for the most part, have made no systematic effort to collect and provide access to such publications for their local constituencies. With the growing volume and importance of municipal documents relating to a wide range of social and economic problems common to urban areas across the country, the library will need to play an increasingly vital role in developing and servicing local document collections.

The lack of effective exchange of information among local governmental units on common problems and conditions, which results in widespread duplication and waste of resources, has been termed a domestic intelligence gap. Accordingly, it is encouraging to note the large number of reference sources included in this source book which provide information access to citizens of the community. The extension of interlibrary loan can be expected to reflect the increasing interdependency of local governments themselves.

Complementary to but distinct from the quarterly *Index to Current Urban Documents*, this work selects and annotates those municipal publications, libraries, and data bases which are of continuing value in filling reference requests about local government activities and functions. In addition to the editors of this guide, numerous contributors from libraries and municipal reference centers throughout the country have supported the project since its beginning. This is a tribute to the growing recognition among librarians, local government officials, and the public, of the need to utilize official publications as a means for government communication with the public.

It is my hope and conviction that many bewildered seekers after knowledge of local government activities will find this a highly usable and useful resource.

BERNARD M. FRY, Dean
Graduate Library School
Indiana University

PREFACE

Public access to municipal publications is, at best, limited. The problem is that the quantity, type, and frequency of publications at the local level varies greatly among municipalities and even within various departments and agencies of the same municipality. Materials are often published irregularly, printed in small quantities, and distributed on a very limited basis. There is little bibliographic control of municipal publishing. Although some urban areas do publish checklists of their publications, such practice is not common. Therefore, the publishing record for many cities is not preserved in a systematic or comprehensive manner. Even when the title of a particular document sought is known, locating the publication itself can be a problem. Furthermore, many municipalities do not participate in depository arrangements intended to provide centralized access to the materials published, and libraries having municipal collections may not widely publicize this fact. Such a situation must inevitably result in needless duplication of research and other investigative studies, and in underutilization of valuable resources by librarians, municipal officials, and others requiring local information.

This source guide is a cooperative, pioneering effort to identify municipal reference sources on a large scale. Under the auspices of the Task Force on Local Documents of the American Library Association's Government Documents Round Table, information was gathered by over one hundred volunteer workers under the direction of the project's editors. Concentration is on large urban areas. The arrangement is by state and, within state, by municipality. When pertinent, an overview of a given city is provided, describing special characteristics of that municipality's publishing program or distinctive features of the area's government—its history or structure. The importance of newspapers, newspaper indexes, and archival materials as municipal reference sources is emphasized by enumerating and describing, throughout, such resources and where they may be found. Specific entries follow. Most are annotated. If it is known that the document is available for distribution, the address of the issuing agency and price, if known, are given as part of the citation. For each municipality covered, special municipal collections are then listed and described. Extensive cross-references are provided throughout the volume, leading the reader from descriptive overviews to a specific document or collection.

The problems encountered by the contributors in preparing their sections underscore the need for local depository systems. It is encouraging to note that some libraries not traditionally collecting the publications of their own cities are now in the process of establishing municipal documents collections. It is also encouraging to note that some cities do have extensive publishing programs with systematic bibliographic control and good local housing of and access to the documents.

It was also heartening to note that although some libraries have not traditionally collected the publications of their own cities, their staffs, after participating in this project, became more aware of the value of the information contained therein and are now in the process of establishing municipal documents collections. Also, in at least five instances, the contributors themselves have initiated checklists for their own city's publications. One by-product of the data collection has been to show some of the innovations which might serve as models for other cities. One city, for example, has placed its newspaper index on-line and generates a daily printout for municipal government officials.

THE EDITORS

Bloomington, Indiana
March 1978

INTRODUCTION

History

The genesis of this volume was an article by Peter Hernon and Rao Aluri in the spring 1975 issue of *Government Publications Review* (Vol. 2, no. 2, pp. 127-165) entitled "Municipal Publications: A Selective Guide to 153 Cities." The editors of R. R. Bowker Company approached Peter Hernon with a proposal to produce a book-length expansion as a reference source for librarians and others who have been wrestling with the difficult problems of fulfilling municipal reference requests and acquiring municipal publications. Because of the enormous amount of data collection necessary to compile a more comprehensive work, he turned to the ALA Government Documents Round Table Task Force on Local Documents for assistance. Peter Hernon and Marjorie Shepley, coordinator of the Task Force, presented a proposal to sponsor the compilation of a municipal document reference tool to the GODORT Task Force, which agreed to assume the responsibility. After permission from the Round Table and then from the American Library Association was granted, it was agreed that all royalties from the sales of this volume would go to the Round Table.

Peter Hernon, John V. Richardson, Nancy P. Sanders, and Marjorie Shepley agreed to serve as co-editors. They organized the assignment of geographical locations to the contributing authors, composed mainly of members of the Government Documents Round Table, and data collection began in the spring of 1977. To facilitate data collection and to standardize the format in which information was received, the co-editors also devised detailed instructions and forms for the recording of the information gathered. Once the sheets were returned, the information was extensively edited and, in some cases, expanded. In certain instances, all requested information was not provided. Thus, coverage throughout the book is somewhat uneven.

Scope

The initial selection criteria for the municipalities to be covered by *Municipal Government Reference Sources* were (1) coverage by the *Index to Current Urban Documents* (described in detail later in this Introduction); and (2) population more than 100,000, or the two largest cities in the state, if none met the population criterion. In soliciting contributors for each of these cities, however, difficulty was encountered locating individuals able to cover some of the municipalities eligible for inclusion. Cities falling into this category are listed with the designation "Data not available at this time." Therefore, 167 of the approximately 200 eligible municipalities were finally included. Despite the slight reduction in the number of areas covered, the book still contains more than 2,000 entries.

The contributors were advised to emphasize the following types of sources: checklists and bibliographies listing city publications, manuals and handbooks, directories (business, public school, specialized governmental telephone books, etc.), and the municipal code (if it had a directory of city officials, organization chart, or other reference material). Furthermore, all reference publication activities of a political, social, legal, economic, scientific, or statistical nature at any level of government were to be investigated. The editors noted that any level of government might produce reference sources valuable at the municipal level (e.g., the secretary of state might produce a directory of local government officials for the entire state), and that nongovernmental or commercial sources might also enhance the understanding of municipal government. Thus, a loose-working definition of a reference source was used. The decision of which publications qualified as a *reference source* had to be left, in part, for the individual contributor to determine on the basis of the particular city's publishing record. It is very likely that pertinent sources have been excluded. Many municipal publications include sections which would qualify as reference material, while the item as a whole would not. This is especially true for statistical data.

The overlapping jurisdiction between city and county governments and their publications posed problems. In addition, many reference sources published by regional or state agencies, or private groups, collect and consolidate data on a number of municipalities. Practically speaking, the bibliography is selective—it emphasizes materials produced at the municipal level with the selective addition of publications from larger jurisdictions.

Generally, only current (1971 or later) publications were included. Exceptions to this rule were made for publications of significant historical importance.

Publications about specific municipalities by various private associations have made a significant contribution to the volume; notable among these are League of Women Voters and Chamber of Commerce publications.

Arrangement

The book is organized into sections arranged alphabetically by state with the exception of several municipal collections national in scope that appear in the beginning under "United States." Cities appear in alphabetical order under their respective state. In most cases, the state section begins with "General Publications." These are compilations published at the state level which cover several cities. Thereafter, each city is usually divided into two categories: "Publications" and "Collections." When pertinent, an overview of a given city is provided.

Publication entries are arranged alphabetically for each city, interfiled dictionary style by main entry. The entry most typically is by issuing agency, preceded by place name if that agency's title is not distinctive. Some entries are by personal author; or by distinctive title if the document does not have an issuing agency or personal author. On occasion the document appears first by place name and then title, when the issuing agency is not known and the title is not distinctive. Laws, decrees, and other acts having the force of law generally are entered under the jurisdiction with the form subheading "Ordinances, Local Laws, etc."

Basic bibliographic information (author, title, and imprint) is given and, when available, the frequency, pagination, and the price. Most entries are annotated.

The editors have attempted to provide simple, correct, and consistent entries. Extensive cross-references are provided throughout, leading the reader from descriptive overviews to a specific document or collection. The format was chosen for easy use, rather than conformity to cataloging standards. The editors, in attempting to be consistent, have also tried to avoid needless duplication of bibliographic information. There should be enough bibliographic information to locate the publication, although the editors make no claim regarding all publications' availability. When known, out-of-print items are designated as "o.p."

The second section within each city is "Collections." Generally, the entry refers to a division of a library or public agency with holdings of municipal publications. The citation includes the address and telephone number, when available, and a brief informative statement about materials, special collections, local newspaper indexing, interlibrary loan provisions, and participation in Greenwood Press's *Index to Current Urban Documents.*

Special Features

As already mentioned, the publication lists published local newspaper indexes, based on the assumption that some of the best information on municipal activities is reported in local newspapers. Users should note that this information on newspaper indexing also may be described in entries under "Collections" or as part of the overview of a given city. (*Note:* For additional coverage of newspaper indexes see Kenneth D. Sell's "A Checklist of Published Indexes to Current American Daily Newspapers," *RQ* 17 [Fall 1977]: 13–16.)

Data bases increasingly are an important source of local governmental information. These were cited when available for public access; excluded were those intended for internal use only. Citations to these data bases appear under the respective city.

Users who are interested in resources at the county level or who have only the county name and not the city name may profitably consult the Appendix. A cross-listing, alphabetically arranged by county from the county name to the city name, is provided there.

An important serial reference resource on municipal reference publications, published quarterly with an annual bound cumulated volume since 1972/73 and mentioned frequently in the body of this source guide, is the *Index to Current Urban Documents* (Westport, Connecticut: Greenwood Press, Inc.). This source guide and the *Index* are complementary, differing in their basic objectives, perspective, and intended use. The *Index* is an ongoing, current-awareness tool, aiding in bibliographic control of specific municipal publications and making available through a microfiche service delivery of many of those specific current titles listed with the service. It covers, on a regular basis, over 250 of the largest cities and counties in the United States and Canada. (*Note:* For a complete listing of cities covered by the *Index* see "Libraries, Agencies and Organizations Contributing to the Index to Current Urban Documents," *Index to Current Urban Documents* 6 [July 1977]: 111.) *Municipal Government Reference Sources* makes no attempt to comprehensively list all locally produced documents. It is prototypic, concentrating on the *kinds* of services and documents available for and about major municipalities; it is selective, citing those specific publications which primarily serve reference functions. Further, it is a finders guide, citing agencies from which to obtain those publications readily available for purchase or distribution, but more especially offering descriptions of contact points for locating not only these documents but other similar "fugitive" materials.

Our sincere gratitude is expressed to the contributors and countless other people who have supported the project since its conceptualization. To be expected in a project of this magnitude, there was difficulty in locating contributors. The editors particularly appreciate the more than 160 individuals who volunteered their time and effort. Given the current state of bibliographic control for municipal publications, these contributors performed almost heroic feats in collecting existing data; often complete citations and price information was simply not available. The editors wish to single out Anthony W. Miele, former coordinator of the Government Documents Round Table, and Nancy Cline, the present coordinator, for their encouragement, advice, and counsel.

Finally, as should be evident, the editors believe that municipal publications are important, though underutilized resources. They hope that through this pioneering effort these resources will become more accessible.

CONTRIBUTORS

ALABAMA. Anthony W. Miele, Dir., Alabama Public Library Service, Montgomery. **Joe Lloyd,** Head, Governmental Information Division, Mobile Public Library. **Elbert L. Watson,** Dir., Huntsville Public Library. **Margie P. Weisman,** Admin. Asst., Huntsville Public Library.

ALASKA. Alden M. Rollins, Documents Libn., University of Alaska Anchorage Library.

ARIZONA. Ann Berg, Governmental Reference Libn., Tucson Public Library. **Eleanor Ferrall,** Arizona Documents Collection-Hayden Library, Arizona State University, Tempe. **Kay Gregory,** Governmental Reference Library, Tucson Public Library. **Katharina Richter,** Libn., Dept. of Planning, Tucson. **Cindi Yee,** Arizona Documents Collection-Hayden Library, Arizona State University, Tempe.

ARKANSAS. Jim Hicks, Reference Libn., Central Arkansas Library System, Little Rock. **Thelma J. Wray,** Libn., Fort Smith Public Library.

CALIFORNIA. Lynda K. Adams, Libn., Government Publications Dept., General Library, University of California, Irvine. **Barbara Boyd,** Special Collections Libn., Glendale Public Library. **Kathryn Donahue,** Reference Libn., Sunnyvale Public Library. **Helen A. Dunbar,** Branch Libn., Business and Government Library, Alameda County Library System, Hayward. **Maxine Durney,** Libn., Fremont Main Library. **Carolyn Grimsley,** Senior Libn., Municipal Reference Library, Los Angeles. **Dorothy Harvey,** Head Libn., Business and Municipal Dept., Sacramento City-County Library System. **Ron Hayden,** Head, Reference Dept., Huntington Beach Public Library. **Linda Jarboe,** Reference Libn., Burbank Public Library. **Joan Kerschner,** Nevada State Library, Carson City, NV (formerly employed in California). **Robert Knepper,** Head Libn., Government Publications, Los Angeles County Public Library. **Jack Leister,** Head Libn., Institute of Governmental Studies Library, University of California, Berkeley. **Bonnie Lew,** Libn. II, Stockton/San Joaquin County Public Library. **Catherine E. Lucas,** Dir., Riverside City and County Public Library. **Kathleen Nerenberg,** Nevada State Library, Carson City, NV (formerly employed in California). **Marjorie Ng,** Libn., Association of Bay Area Governments, Berkeley. **Harold Overstreet,** Garden Grove Regional Branch, Orange County Public Library. **Mildred Pickle,** Senior Libn., Governmental Reference Library, San Diego. **Richard Ragsdale,** Senior Libn., Oakland Public Library. **Carol Slaten,** Torrance Public Library. **Sam A. Suhler,** Local History Libn., Fresno County Free Library. **Marion Vassilakos,** Head, Reference Dept., San Bernardino Public Library. **Margaret Walsh,** Libn. II, Documents Dept., San Francisco Public Library. **Dorothy Wells,** Local Documents Libn., Public Affairs Services, University of California Library. **Katy Worth,** Reference Libn., Santa Ana Public Library.

COLORADO. Esther Fromm, Libn., Greeley Public Library. **Richard E. Luce,** Coordinator for State Municipal Government Reference Services, Municipal Government Reference Center, Boulder Public Library.

CONNECTICUT. Wilbur B. Crimmin, Libn., Hartford Public Library. **Doris Goodlett,** Head, Adult Services, Stamford Public Library. **Patricia L. Joy,** Silas Bronson Library, Waterbury. **Beverly A. Loughlin,** Admin. Asst., Reference & General Reading, Hartford Public Library. **Daniel J. Palmer,** Reference Dept., New Britain Public Library. **Suzanne Rickles,** Adult Services Dept., New Haven Free Public Library.

DELAWARE. Delma H. Batton, Dir., Dover Public Library. **Benedict Prestianni,** Delaware Collection, Wilmington Institute Library. **Jean F. Trumbore,** Assoc. Reference Libn., Hugh M. Morris Library, University of Delaware, Newark.

DISTRICT OF COLUMBIA. Mary Lou Knobbe, Libn., Research Library, Metropolitan Washington Council of Governments. **Robert Schaaf,** The Library of Congress.

FLORIDA. S. J. Boldnick, Miami-Dade Public Library. **Susan Campbell,** University of Florida Library, Gainesville. **Marti Clark,** Florida Atlantic University, Boca Raton. **Margaret Duer,** Winter Park Public Library. **Frances Eubank,** John C. Pace Library, University of West Florida, Pensacola. **Phyllis Freedman,** Orlando Municipal Reference Library. **Frances Goodin,** Northwest Florida Planning and Advisory Council. **Susan E. Henderson,** Southwest Florida Regional Planning Council. **Gary Parsons,** Roux Library, Florida Southern College, Lakeland. **Amber Pavlick,** Florida Atlantic University, Boca Raton. **Phyllis Pope,** Monroe County Public Library, Key West. **Beth Pritchard,** Gulf Beaches Public Library, Madeira Beach. **Leslie Strickland,** Belle Glade Municipal Library. **Linda Lou Wiler,** Head, Reference Dept., Florida Atlantic University, Boca Raton. **Linda Wyman,** South Florida Regional Planning Council, Miami.

GEORGIA. Beverly A. Salters, Local Documents Libn., Atlanta Public Library.

HAWAII. Jean T. Kadooka-Mardfin, Dir., Municipal Reference & Records Center, Honolulu.

IDAHO. Christine L. Ellis, Reference Libn., Pocatello Public Library.

ILLINOIS. Chuck DeYoung, Rolling Prairie Library System, Decatur. **June Huizenga,** Social Science Dept., Rockford Public Library. **Joyce Johnson,** Business Science and Technology Dept., Peoria Public Library. **Yuri Nakata,** Documents Libn., Library, University of Illinois at Chicago Circle. **Edward J. Russo,** Sangamon Valley Collection, Lincoln Library, Springfield.

INDIANA. J. Louise Malcomb, Asst. Libn., Government Publications Dept., Indiana University, Bloomington. **Judith L. Violette,** Head, Reference Dept. & Government Documents Libn., Walter E. Helmke Library, Indiana University–Purdue University at Fort Wayne.

IOWA. Mary Bleser, General Documents Libn., Government Publications Dept., University of Iowa Libraries, Iowa City. **Mary McInroy,** Federal Documents Libn., Government Publications Dept., University of Iowa Libraries, Iowa City. **Eleanor Matthews,** Reference Dept., Iowa State University Library, Ames.

KANSAS. William Carmody, Head, Antioch Reference, Johnson County Library, Shawnee Mission. **Jimmie E. Hooper,** Asst. Dept. Head, Business and Technical Dept., Wichita Public Library. **Jim Muth,** Topeka Public Library.

KENTUCKY. Linda Richardson, Kenton County Public Library, Covington.

LOUISIANA. Collin B. Hamer, Jr., Head, Louisiana Division, New Orleans Public Library. **Margaret T. Lane,** Baton Rouge. **The Library Documents Department,** Louisiana State University—Shreveport.

MAINE. Compiled by the GODORT project editors.

MARYLAND. Anne W. Bledsoe, Maryland-Municipal Libn., Rockville Library. **Edward B. Hall,** Library Administrator, Public Library of Annapolis and Anne Arundel County. **Myra B. Lewis,** Head, County Services, Annapolis Area Library. **Adele Newburger,** Assoc. Dir., University of Baltimore, Baltimore Region Institutional Studies Center. **Dr. Morgan Pritchett,** Enoch Pratt Free Library, Baltimore.

MASSACHUSETTS. Ellen Coty, Reference Asst., Springfield City Library. **Barbara DiStefano,** Libn., Springfield City Library. **Nancy E. Gaudette,** Libn., Worcester Collection, Worcester Public Library. **Thelma Paine,** Head, Reference Dept., Free Public Library, New Bedford. **Marianne Pedulla,** Library Asst., Springfield City Library. **Richard Pennington,** Reference Dept., Cambridge Public Library.

MICHIGAN. Carol R. Bellinghausen, Municipal Reference Libn., The Grand Rapids Public Library. **Helga Herz,** Chief, Municipal Reference Library, Detroit Public Library.

MINNESOTA. Barb Anderson, Documents Libn., St. Paul Public Library. Jean Berglund, Library Asst. Government Publications Division, University of Minnesota, Minneapolis. Judi Devine, Library Asst., University of Minnesota Library, Minneapolis. Betty Bruce Frisbie, Special Services Libn., University of Minnesota Library, Minneapolis. Richard Hemming, Reference Libn., St. Paul Public Library. W. R. La Bissoniere, University of Minnesota Library, Minneapolis. Mary Jane Owens, Duluth Division, University of Minnesota, Duluth. Jan Schroeder, Dir., Duluth Public Library. Carolyn Sorenson, Library Asst., University of Minnesota Library, Minneapolis. Kris Vajs, Municipal Reference Libn., City of Minneapolis.

MISSISSIPPI. Harold J. Ard, Library System Dir., Jackson Metropolitan Library System.

MISSOURI. Meryl Atterberry, Coordinator, Government Documents Division, The Dept. of Higher Education, Missouri State Library, Jefferson City. Mary Bires, Reference Libn., The Pius XII Memorial Library, St. Louis University. Ann Watts, St. Louis Public Library. Assistance was also provided by the staffs of Mid-Missouri Library Network, Columbia, Kansas City Public Library, and Springfield-Greene County Public Library.

MONTANA. Harold L. Chambers, Documents Libn., Montana State Library, Helena.

NEBRASKA. M. K. Bouton, Coordinator, Central Library Network, Nebraska Library Commission, Lincoln. Susan Kling, Dept. Head, Nebraska Publications Clearinghouse, Nebraska Library Commission, Lincoln. James C. Rowling, Dir. of Technical Services, Calvin T. Ryan Library, Kearney State College. Robert Trautwein, Reference Coordinator, Lincoln City Libraries.

NEVADA. Alice Brown, Documents Libn., University of Nevada, Las Vegas. Joan Kerschner, Nevada State Library, Carson City. Richard Stegman, Reference Libn., North Las Vegas Public Library. Toby Sulenski, Reference Libn., Las Vegas City Library.

NEW HAMPSHIRE. Compiled by the GODORT project editors.

NEW JERSEY. Charles Cummings, Newark Public Library. Joan Doherty, New Jersey Room, Jersey City Public Library. Hillaire Geller, Asst. Dir., Clifton Public Library. Jaia Heymann, Drew University Library, Madison. Carol Ramsey, Somerset. Kathy Reynolds, Point Pleasant. Salvatore Stingo, Dir., Clifton Public Library. Jeremy O. Sweeton, Head Reference Libn., The Free Public Library of Elizabeth. Rhuenella Wells, Supervisor, Reference and Adult Services, Paterson Free Public Library.

NEW MEXICO. Compiled by the GODORT project editors.

NEW YORK. Michael O. Shannon, Assoc. Professor and Documents Libn., Herbert Lehman College Library, City University of New York, Bronx.

NORTH CAROLINA. Suzanne Sheldon Levy, Cataloger, North Carolina Collection, University of North Carolina Library, Chapel Hill. Mary L. Phillips, Head, Carolina Room, Public Library of Charlotte and Meckenburg County. John J. Wozny, Extension Libn., Wake County Public Libraries, Raleigh.

NORTH DAKOTA. Marilyn Guttromson, Government Services Libn., North Dakota State Library Commission, Bismarck.

OHIO. William L. Matchinski, Wyoming State Hospital Library, Box 177, Evanston, WY (formerly employed in Ohio). Sam Roshon, Head, Columbus and Ohio Division, Public Library of Columbus and Franklin County, Columbus. Earl Shumaker, Head, Government Documents Dept., Ohio University Library, Athens.

OKLAHOMA. Rosemary M. Anderson, Adult Services Libn., Lawton Public Library. Betty Jean Mathis Brown, Oklahoma Libn., Oklahoma Dept. of Libraries, Oklahoma City. Sharon Chatburn, Business and Technology Dept., Tulsa City-County Library. Bernice Jackson, Dir., Lawton Public Library.

OREGON. David J. Maack, State and Local Documents Libn., University of Washington Libraries, Seattle.

PENNSYLVANIA. Harry R. Courtright, Dauphin County Library System, Harrisburg. Clifford P. Crowes, Head, Government Publications Dept., The Free Library of Philadelphia.

Joseph Falgione, Assoc. Dir., Central Readers' Services, Carnegie Library of Pittsburgh. B. Moylan, Scranton Public Library. Hannah V. Natzke, Special Information Services Libn., Scranton Public Library. Kathryn Stephanoff, Allentown Public Library. Maria Zini, Head, Pennsylvania Division, Carnegie Library of Pittsburgh.

RHODE ISLAND. Anne Shaw, Government Publications Libn., University of Rhode Island, Kingston.

SOUTH CAROLINA. Marion Mangion, Dir. of Reference, Richland County Public Library, Columbia. Mary Bostick Toll, Documents Libn., South Carolina State Library, Columbia. Elizabeth B. Olinger, Head Libn., Greenville Technical College.

SOUTH DAKOTA. Herschel V. Anderson, State Libn., South Dakota State Library, Pierre. Jane Bramwell, City Libn., Rawlins Municipal Library, Pierre. Cynthia J. Harksen, Reference Libn., Rapid City Public Library.

TENNESSEE. Compiled by the GODORT project editors.

TEXAS. Marie B. Berry, Head Libn., History and Reference Dept., San Antonio Public Library. Walter Jeschke, Asst. Library Dir., Beaumont Public Library. Mary Meyers, Reference Libn., Houston Public Library. George Nethercutt, Fort Worth Public Library. Brenda F. Shelton Olds, Texas Legislative Reference Library, Austin. Betty Barban Sacks, Municipal Services Reference Libn., Dallas Public Library. Mary A. Sarber, Head, Southwest Reference, El Paso Public Library. Mary Kay Snell, Head, Reference Dept., Amarillo Public Library. Assistance was also provided by the staffs of the Reference Department, Irving Public Library, and La Retama Public Library, Corpus Christi.

UTAH. Alma G. Swann, Utah State Library Commission, Documents Library, Salt Lake City.

VERMONT. Charles D. Maurer, Jr., Dir., Rutland Free Library. Joan Slavin, Cataloger, Fletcher Free Library, Burlington.

VIRGINIA. Audrey Amerski, Documents Libn., Old Dominion University Library, Norfolk. Florence J. Wilson, Reference Libn., George Mason University, Fenwick Library, Fairfax.

WASHINGTON. David J. Maack, State and Local Documents Libn., University of Washington Libraries, Government Documents Center, Seattle.

WEST VIRGINIA. Lisle G. Brown, Curator of Special Collections, Marshall University, James E. Morrow Library, Huntington. Earl Shumaker, Head, Government Documents Dept., Ohio University Library, Athens, OH (formerly employed in West Virginia).

WISCONSIN. Ann Waidelich, Libn., Municipal Reference Service, Madison. Alice Alderman, State Historical Society of Wisconsin, Madison.

WYOMING. Edward W. Byers, County Libn., Laramie County Library System, Cheyenne. Martha E. Lawlor, Documents Libn., The University of Wyoming, Laramie.

UNITED STATES

General Municipal Collections

US1. International City Management Association. 1140 Connecticut Ave. N.W., Washington, D.C. 20036 (202)293-2200.
Founded in 1914, the International City Management Association (ICMA) is a professional society of city managers, county managers, and municipal administrators. The ICMA issues, among others, *Municipal Yearbook*, *Municipal Management Directory*, and *Directory of Recognized Local Governments*.

The ICMA frequently provides documents gratis if adequate copies can be obtained. If this is not possible, the association suggests that the issuing agency be contacted.

US2. National League of Cities and U.S. Conference of Mayors. 1620 Eye St. N.W., Washington, D.C. 20006 (202)293-7300/73.
The U.S. Conference of Mayors has a library with a collection of 20,000 books and 800 periodicals on urban affairs, municipal government, and city codes and reports. Both groups collect federal, state, and local documents, and produce sources such as *Urban Affairs Abstracts*.

US3. U.S. Department of Housing and Urban Development. Library and Information Division. 451 Seventh St., S.W., Washington, D.C. 20410 (202)755-6376.
As HUD is concerned with state and local activities, the library collects the publications of federal, state, and local governments. Along with the Library of Congress (see entry **US4**), it has one of the largest general collections of local documents in the United States.

US4. U.S. Library of Congress, Washington, D.C. 20540 (202)426-5000. Teletype Service: 710-822-0185.
The Library of Congress acquires for its permanent collections, in ink-print copies or in microform, the most comprehensive currently available consolidated or collected annual or biennial report, the latest revision of the city charter, code of ordinances, administrative code, codes of the major regulatory commissions, reports of the municipal courts, and opinions of city attorney or legal counsel for the following 14 cities:

Alexandria, VA	Detroit, MI	Philadelphia, PA
Atlanta, GA	Falls Church, VA	St. Louis, MO
Baltimore, MD	Houston, TX	San Francisco, CA
Boston, MA	Los Angeles, CA	Washington, DC
Chicago, IL	New York, NY	

1

If consolidated or collected annual or biennial reports are unavailable, separate reports will be acquired from the city's departments, including the municipal council.

The Library also acquires and retains for its permanent collections current publications issued by special "authorities" (e.g., housing, port, transit, water) in which any of the 14 cities participate.

The Library of Congress acquires and, when desirable, retains for its permanent collections individual publications from other cities, or comprehensive microform sets, when these publications are recommended for acquisition as containing important information on subjects of particular concern to Congress and to the federal government in general. Examples of such subjects are urban and regional land use, planning, zoning, air and water pollution, transportation, public utilities, urban geography, surveying, and mapping.

ALABAMA

General Publications

AL1. Alabama. Assembly of Community Arts Councils. *1976–77 Alabama Arts Directory.* Montgomery (P.O. Box 446, Montgomery 36101), 1975/76– . Continuously revised.
Lists board of directors of the Assembly of Community Arts Councils, members of the Alabama State Council on the Arts and Humanities, local arts councils and organizations.

AL2. Alabama. Laws, Statutes, etc. *Compiled Index to Local Laws of Autauga—Winston County, Alabama.* Montgomery: Legislative Reference Service (State Capitol), 1947– . Decennial.
The indexes to local laws are published in pamphlet form. Each county's index is prepared separately. A list of sessions laws is appended to each county index. Laws for each of the municipalities follow county laws.

BIRMINGHAM

The city of Birmingham publishes on a limited scale. Some of the major departments publish annual reports; however, there are large departments such as the park and recreation department for which there is no annual report. Most of the reference sources published are prepared by the Birmingham Regional Planning Commission and the Chamber of Commerce. **Local Newspaper Indexing:** There is no formal indexing of Birmingham newspapers; however, the Tutwiler Collection of the Birmingham Public Library (see entry **AL38**) maintains extensive newspaper clipping files providing news and editorial comment from the state's leading newspapers, with special emphasis on happenings in Birmingham, Alabama, and the South.

Publications

AL3. Alabama. University. Center for Urban Studies. *An Inventory of the Independent Boards and Agencies Serving the City of Birmingham.* Birmingham: League of Women Voters (3764 Valley Head Rd., Birmingham 35223), 1973. 62pp. $3.
This inventory, which is being revised, currently lists independent boards serving the city as of 1973. It includes only those boards for which the city has a major, if not controlling, responsibility for appointing members. It does not include purely internal management bodies such as management boards for employee plans.

AL4. Birmingham. Board of Education. *Birmingham Public Schools Directory.* (2015 Seventh Ave. N., Birmingham 35203) 1914– . Annual.
Contains school calendars and lists school personnel.

AL5. Birmingham. Chamber of Commerce. *Birmingham.* Edited by Donald A. Brown. (1914 Sixth Ave. N., Birmingham 35203) 1960– . Monthly. $9 per year.
This magazine emphasizes cultural activities but does include business activities.

AL6. Birmingham. Chamber of Commerce. *Community Organizations: A Listing of Non-Profit Clubs and Organizations in Jefferson County.* (1914 Sixth Ave. N., Birmingham 35203) Annual. $5.

AL7. Birmingham. Chamber of Commerce. *Gateway: Birmingham Transportation Directory.* (1914 Sixth Ave. N., Birmingham 35203) 1973. o.p.
Covers the primary means of moving goods and people—truck, rail, air, and water. For each means there are maps and a directory of businesses serving the Birmingham area.

AL8. Birmingham. Chamber of Commerce. *Industrial Directory: Metropolitan Birmingham.* (1914 Sixth Ave. N., Birmingham 35203) 1974– . Annual. $13.50.
A listing of products and producers in the area.

AL9. Birmingham. Chamber of Commerce. *Large Employers Directory: Metropolitan Birmingham.* (1914 Sixth Ave. N., Birmingham 35203) 1975– . Annual. $2.50.
Identifies those firms in the area that employ more than 100 persons.

AL10. Birmingham. Chamber of Commerce. *Wholesale and Distribution Directory for Metropolitan Birmingham.* (1914 Sixth Ave. N., Birmingham 35203) 1974– . Annual. $6.
Firms included within this directory are stocking wholesale distributors.

AL11. Birmingham. City Council. *City of Birmingham: The Elected Officials.* City Hall (Mayor's Office), n.d. 8pp.
This small pamphlet lists the elected officials for the city, contains biographical information on them, and lists department heads and the officials of the major boards and agencies.

AL12. Birmingham. City Council. *Summary of Proceedings.* (City Hall) 1911– . Monthly.
Gives a detailed statement of receipts and expenses of the city each month. All ordinances and resolutions adopted by the council are given and all other action is noted.

AL13. Birmingham. City Hall. *The City Hall Reporter.* Edited by Betty Jones. (Rm. 207, Birmingham 35203) 1970– . Monthly. Free.
A monthly newsletter for the employees of city government on various departments of the city. There is also a section on Birmingham history.

AL14. Birmingham. City Hall. *City Hall Building Directory.* (Birmingham 35203) 1975– . Annual.
Lists emergency telephone numbers and instructions on use of the Centrex system. The numbers for various governmental departments and subdivisions are given. Names and numbers are given for city hall employees.

AL15. Birmingham. Community Service Council Inc. *Community Resources Directory: A Guide to Human Resource Services.* . . . 1971–   . Annual. $3.50. (Available from: United Way Information Service, Suite 504, 3600 Eighth Ave. S., Birmingham 35222.)
A guide to the health, welfare, recreation, education, and planning services offered by various organizations in Jefferson, Shelby, and Walker counties.

AL16. Birmingham. Director of Finance. *Financial Report for the Fiscal Year.* City Comptroller (205 City Hall, Birmingham 35203), 1911–   . Annual.
Contains information on the following areas: combined financial statements, material on the general fund, special revenue funds, debt service funds, capital projects funds, trust and agency funds, special assessment fund, general fixed assets, general long term debt, industrial development board, and the medical clinic board. Also includes various budgetary statistics for the city as a whole.

AL17. Birmingham. Director of Finance. *Monthly Report.* City Comptroller (205 City Hall, Birmingham 35203), 1911–   . Monthly.
The financial report for the city gives a balance sheet with budget summary, general fund revenue, general fund expenditures and encumbrances, airport operation fund, federal revenue-sharing trust fund, miscellaneous board supplemental report, and a report of insurance claims released.

AL18. Birmingham. Fire Department. *A Century of Service: Birmingham Fire Department, 1872–1972.* Prepared by Jerry W. Laughlin. Birmingham: Taylor Pub. Co., 1972. 128pp.
A history of the department from its inception to its centennial year.

AL19. Birmingham. Fire Department. *Annual Report.* (1808 Seventh Ave. N., Birmingham 35203) 1922–   . Annual. Free.
Gives statistics for the department, a financial report, organization chart, the fire training bureau report, and a list of retirees and district chiefs.

AL20. Greater Birmingham Library Club. *Directory of Jefferson County Librarians. Birmingham, 1977. 35pp. $1.*

AL21. Housing Authority of the Birmingham District. *Annual Report.* (600 N. 24 St., Birmingham 35203) 1940–   . Annual.
Lists the commissioners, directors, and staff of the authority. A financial statement is given. The mayor and city council are also listed. The report discusses current building and urban renewal projects in which the city is engaged.

AL22. Birmingham. Mayor's Office. *The Government of the City of Birmingham.* (City Hall) 1970. 75pp.
This handbook to the city government attempts to explain many of the functions and operations of the various departments and independent boards. The objectives and responsibilities for each department and subdivision are outlined. An organization chart and a brief history of the city and its form of government are included.

AL23. Birmingham. Ordinances, Local Laws, etc. *The General Code of the City.* . . . Charlottesville, VA: Michie City Pub. Co., 1964–   . Quarterly. $39. (Available from: Cashier, Department of Finance, 710 20th Ave. N., Birmingham 35203.)
Contains the ordinances of a general and permanent nature.

AL24. Birmingham. Police Department. *Annual Report.* (City Hall) 1959–   .
Annual.
Gives crime statistics, the budget, a personnel profile, an organization chart,
and a section on new programs. The mayor, city council, fire chief, and deputy
chiefs are listed.

AL25. Birmingham. Public Library. *Bibliography of Birmingham, 1872–
1972.* Birmingham: Oxmoor Press, 1973. 136pp. Biennial Supplements. $10. (Available from: Public Library, 2020 Seventh Ave. N., Birmingham 35203.)
The bibliography is an attempt to list those publications significant for the study
of Birmingham and its history. It is not a listing of Birmingham imprints. It does
cover the official publications of government agencies and historical and descriptive writings about Birmingham, its people and their activities. It also includes
the writings of Birmingham authors.

AL26. Birmingham. Public Library. *Bicentennial Bibliography: A Guide to
Free and Inexpensive Material for Celebrating the Bicentennial.* (2020 Seventh
Ave. N., Birmingham 35203) 1976. 16pp. $2.
Nothing in the bibliography costs more than $5. Items are not limited to Birmingham or Alabama.

AL27. Birmingham. Public Library. Rucker Agee Map Collection. *A List of
Nineteenth Century Maps of the State of Alabama.* Birmingham: Oxmoor Press,
1973. 115pp. o.p.
The list was compiled from the holdings in the libraries in the State Archives,
Auburn University, the University of Alabama, Samford University, Mobile Public
Library, and the Birmingham Public Library. Excluded were maps of the area prior
to statehood in 1819, maps covering three or more states, and maps regularly
revised.

AL28. Birmingham. Urban League. *Black Business—Managing Personal
Finances, Buying Insurances, Investments, Help Balance the Economy
through the Black Business Guide.* (505 N. 17 St., Birmingham) 1973. 20pp. $5.
Includes all Black businessmen from professionals to blue-collar occupations.

AL29. Birmingham. Water Works Board. *The Annual Report.* (2114 First Ave.
N., Birmingham 35201) 1961–   . Annual.
Gives a financial statement and accountant's report and a ten-year summary of
revenues and expenses. The directors of the board and staff are listed.

AL30. Jefferson County. Board of Education. *Jefferson County Board of
Education Directory.* Birmingham, 1932–   . Annual. Free.
Includes an organization chart, the board calendar, the school grade ranges and
a list of county schools, their addresses, their telephone numbers, and staffs. There
are also listings of central office staff and an alphabetical list of all employees.

AL31. Jefferson County. County Commission. *Historical Facts of Jefferson
County.* Birmingham, 1974? 59pp. o.p.
The manual details the functions of the various officials, departments, and
facilities. County elected and appointed officials are listed along with their terms
of office and respective salaries. Members of the county legislative delegation are
listed with their mailing addresses.

AL32. Jefferson County. County Commission. *Jefferson County Community*

Development Program: The First Year Plan, 1973-76. Huntsville: Public Systems Inc., 1975. 82pp. o.p.
The plan includes a profile of community characteristics such as population, housing, recreation, public water, and sewers.

AL33. Jefferson County. Department of Health. *Biennial Report.* Birmingham (1912 Eighth Ave. S., Birmingham 35222), 1917- . Biennial.
Gives a fiscal report for the department, lists county health officers, and gives the reports from the various bureaus.

AL34. Jefferson County. Department of Health. Bureau of Statistics and Vital Records. *Annual Report.* Birmingham (1912 Eighth Ave. S., Birmingham 35222), 1939- . Annual.
Contains a short synopsis of vital statistics for the county.

AL35. Jefferson County. Historical Commission. *Historic Sites of Jefferson County.* Edited by Carolyn G. Satterfield. Birmingham (1321 St. N., Birmingham 35202), 1976. 166pp. $9 paperbound ($12 hardbound).
A comprehensive survey of historic sites.

AL36. Regional Planning Commission. *Directory of Local Government Officials.* Birmingham (2112 11 Ave. S., 21 Office Plaza S., Birmingham 35205), 1970- . Annual. Free.
Includes for each of the governments within the region the name, title, address, and telephone number of officials.

AL37. Regional Planning Commission. *Historic Site Survey, Jefferson County.* Birmingham (2112 11 Ave. S., 21 Office Plaza S., Birmingham 35205), 1972. 241pp. o.p.
A comprehensive inventory of the county's architectural and historic resources.

Collections

AL38. Birmingham Public Library. Tutwiler Collection. 2020 Seventh Ave. N., Birmingham 35203 (205)254-2534.
The Tutwiler Collection is the repository for city and county publications. The Department of Archives and Manuscripts presently holds the following municipal archival materials: The mayoral papers of Albert Boutwell, 1963-1967, including the files of W. C. Hamilton, executive assistant to the mayor; the mayoral papers of George Siebles, Jr., 1967-1976; the files of the city council, 1963-1974, including personal files of Councilmen George Siebles, Jr., Don Hawkins, and E. C. Overton.

HUNTSVILLE

The Huntsville-Madison County Public Library attempts to acquire all municipal publications. The Huntsville Heritage Room also houses the special archival materials pertaining to Huntsville (see entry **AL61**).

Publications

AL39. Huntsville. Chamber of Commerce. *Committee Action.* Business Research & Services Department (305 Church St., Huntsville 35801) Monthly. $1 per year.

AL40. Huntsville. Chamber of Commerce. *Huntsville Business Trends.* (305 Church St., Huntsville 35801) Monthly. $20 per year for nonmembers ($10 per year for members).
Monitors new and expanding business in the area, overviews local labor developments and local area construction, reports on area business activity.

AL41. Huntsville. Chamber of Commerce. *Membership Directory and Buyer's Guide.* Edited by John C. Meyer. (305 Church St., Huntsville 35801) Annual. $10.
Gives pertinent information about member firms and lists city and county officials.

AL42. Huntsville. Chamber of Commerce. *Update.* (305 Church St., Huntsville 35801) Monthly. $2 per year.
Reports chamber news on a regular basis.

AL43. Huntsville. Clerk-Treasurer. *Audited Financial Statements and Other Financial Information.* Huntsville: Taylto, Snyder & Co., 1976. Annual. Price range $5-10. (Available from: Clerk-Treasurer, Municipal Bldg., 308 Fountain Circle, Huntsville 35801.)

AL44. Huntsville. Clerk-Treasurer. *Annual Budget for the Fiscal Year.* (Municipal Bldg., 308 Fountain Circle, Huntsville 35801) Annual. Price range $5-10.

AL45. Huntsville. Personnel Department. *Employee Handbook.* (308 Fountain Circle, Huntsville 35801) 1976. 31pp.

AL46. Huntsville. Planning Commission. *The Huntsville Housing Market Analysis.* (Municipal Bldg., 308 Fountain Circle, Huntsville 35801) 1973. 40pp.
An assessment of the city's 1973 supply of housing as well as a limited analysis of the city's economy.

AL47. Huntsville. Planning Commission. *Huntsville's Neighborhoods: An Analysis.* (Municipal Bldg., 308 Fountain Circle, Huntsville 35801) 1973. 132pp.
A plan for the improvement of the city's neighborhoods.

AL48. Huntsville. Planning Commission. *Key Indicators of the Economy.* (Municipal Bldg., 308 Fountain Circle, Huntsville 35801) 1976. 10pp.

AL49. Huntsville. Planning Commission. *A Plan for the Present: Bikeways in Huntsville.* (Municipal Bldg., 308 Fountain Circle, Huntsville 35801) 1976. 38pp.

AL50. Huntsville. Planning Commission. *Population Estimate of the City of Huntsville by Neighborhood.* (Municipal Bldg., 308 Fountain Circle, Huntsville 35801) 1973. 56pp.
This study estimates the population living within the city by neighborhood (the planning districts).

AL51. Huntsville. Planning Commission. *Profile of the Central Business District.* (Municipal Bldg., 308 Fountain Circle, Huntsville 35801) 1975. 34pp.
This report on the central business district is the first in a series of five reports which will analyze the major sections of the city to show trends as they have occurred in the past 15 years in the areas of population characteristics, resident and population trends, housing, employment, and land use.

AL52. Huntsville. Planning Commission. *Railroad-Highway Intersection*

Safety Analysis. (Municipal Bldg., 308 Fountain Circle, Huntsville 35801) 1976. 49pp.

AL53. Huntsville. Planning Commission. *Subdivision Regulations for the City of Huntsville.* (Municipal Bldg., 308 Fountain Circle, Huntsville 35801) 1970. 29pp.

AL54. Huntsville. Planning Commission. *Unified Work Program, Fiscal Years 1977 and 1978: Huntsville Area Transportation Study.* (Municipal Bldg., 308 Fountain Circle, Huntsville 35801) Biennial.
This work outlines the transportation planning activities expected to transpire during the 1977 and 1978 fiscal years.

AL55. Huntsville. Planning Commission. *Zoning Ordinance.* (Municipal Bldg., 308 Fountain Circle, Huntsville 35801) n.d.

AL56. The Top of Alabama Regional Council of Governments. *Community Facilities Inventory.* Huntsville (350 Central Bank Bldg., Huntsville 35801), 1976. 96pp.
Presents an inventory and analysis of the city's community facilities including administrative facilities, police and fire protection, educational facilities, health, libraries, and public facilities. Standards are presented and each facility measured to determine its adequacy. Issues and problems are discussed for each facility.

AL57. The Top of Alabama Regional Council of Governments. *Summary Parks and Open Space Plan.* Huntsville (350 Central Bank Bldg., Huntsville 35801), n.d. 15pp. Free.

AL58. Urban Consultants Inc. *Central Business District Plan.* Montgomery, 1974. 74pp. (Available from: Huntsville Planning Commission, 308 Fountain Circle, Huntsville 35801.)
This report presents a development plan and a beautification program for the central business district. An inventory and analysis of existing conditions is presented along with the proposals for developing functional use areas. Alternative concepts for an overall beautification program are presented along with a design concept and typical street layouts.

AL59. Urban Consultants Inc. *Factors Affecting Development.* Montgomery, n.d. 6pp. (Available from: Huntsville Planning Commission, 308 Fountain Circle, Huntsville 35801.)

AL60. Urban Consultants Inc. *Inventory and Analysis for the Land Use Plan.* Montgomery, n.d. 119pp. (Available from: Huntsville Planning Commission, 308 Fountain Circle, Huntsville 35801.)

Collections

AL61. **Huntsville-Madison County Public Library.** Huntsville Heritage Room. P. O. Box 443, Huntsville 35804 (205)536-0023 ext. 26.
The library attempts to acquire all municipal publications. The Heritage Room also houses the special archival materials pertaining to the city. Among the vast material available are newspapers dating back to 1816, county records beginning with 1809, city directories beginning with 1909, an indexed collection of vertical file material on Huntsville, manuscripts of local people beginning in 1819, planning commission studies, financial data, Huntsvillian biographies, portraits and photographs from the 1850s, church records, and an extensive book collection. These

materials are available for use on the premises only. The Heritage Room is the only facility currently housing archival material pertaining to Huntsville. Material is also available on Madison County and surrounding counties.

MOBILE

Publications

AL62. Mobile. Board of City Commissioners. *Five-Year Program of Capital Improvements.* n.d. 30pp.
Covers capital improvements for all departments for the fiscal years 1975 to 1980.

AL63. Mobile. Board of City Commissioners. *Operating Budget for the Fiscal Year.* 1976. 65pp.
Includes the operating budget for all departments of the city for the current fiscal year.

AL64. Mobile. Board of School Commissioners. *Directory of Mobile County Public Schools.* Annual.
Contains school calendar, names of Board of School Commissioners and school personnel, and a list of schools.

AL65. Mobile. Chamber of Commerce. *Mobile: An Economic Handbook.* (P.O. Box 2187, Mobile 36601) 1971. 102pp.
Covers the history of Mobile, population of the city and county, government, area agriculture, banking, construction, building permits, city and public improvements, education, cultural and civic organizations, housing, industrial sites, air, bus, and water transportation, economic conditions and statistics.

AL66. Mobile. Chamber of Commerce. *Who's Who in the Mobile Area and Buyers' Guide.* (P.O. Box 2187, Mobile 36601) 1976. 109pp. $5.
This publication includes a brief history of Mobile and other pertinent information such as elected government officials.

AL67. Mobile. County Commission. *Mobile County Budget.* n.d.

AL68. Mobile. City Comptroller. *Annual Financial Report.* Annual.

AL69. Mobile. League of Women Voters. *This Is Mobile.* 1968. 60pp.
Information concerning city and county government structure, financing and services available to local citizens and visitors.

AL70. Mobile. Planning Commission. *Housing Demand and Need Analysis.* (City Hall) 1975. 164pp.
Covers population characteristics of city, special housing needs and problems, housing market, and recommendations.

AL71. South Alabama Regional Planning Commission. *The Economy and Population of the South Alabama Region.* Mobile (P.O. Box 1665, Mobile 36601), 1975. 120pp. $5.
Furnishes an analysis of employment, population, housing, and income in Mobile, Baldwin, and Escambia counties. Estimates project to the year 2000.

AL72. South Alabama Regional Planning Commission. *Mobile County Directory of Community Services, 1975* (with 1976 supplement). Mobile (P.O. Box 1665, Mobile 36601), 1975. 244pp.
Designed to aid senior citizens and others of Mobile County in obtaining accurate information and referral concerning the many services available.

Collections

AL73. Mobile Public Library. 701 Government St., Mobile 36602 (205)433-0483.
Each department of the city and county government issues publications as required by their department or the appropriate board of commissioners. There is no set rule whereby copies of documents are sent to the Mobile Public Library as published. However, all departments are cooperative in furnishing copies if requested. No checklist covers the publications of the city.
The Mobile Public Library sends most municipal documents to Greenwood Press for inclusion in the *Index to Current Urban Documents.* The Special Collections Division, Mobile Public Library, has some archival materials including Mobile city documents on microfilm that date back to 1824. This material may be used only in the library.

MONTGOMERY

Data not available at this time.

TUSCALOOSA

There are two main sources of reference documents for Tuscaloosa, the Tuscaloosa City Planning and Community Development Commission and the West Alabama Planning and Development Council. The publications of these two organizations cover all important facets of municipal activity. Unfortunately many of the documents are outdated at this time and have a limited usefulness. However, both agencies are preparing current documents which should become available shortly.
Local Newspaper Indexing: The reference department at the Amelia Gayle Gorgas Library, University of Alabama, selectively indexes the *Tuscaloosa News* for west Alabama news stories. The indexing was begun in January 1975. The library staff will accept queries from other cities.

Publications

AL74. Greater Tuscaloosa Chamber of Commerce. *Industrial Directory for the Greater Tuscaloosa Area.* Tuscaloosa (P.O. Box 430, Tuscaloosa 35401). Annual. $2.
The directory provides a comprehensive, alphabetical list of manufacturers, processors, wholesalers, distributors, transportation, utilities, and other large employers in the Tuscaloosa SMSA.

AL75. Profiles of Change. Detroit, MI: R. L. Polk and Co. (431 Howard St., Detroit 48231), 1975- . Annual.
This document consists of four volumes which are: Map Series; Statistical Tables; Small Area Profiles and Rank Order Reports; and Management Digest. Much of the information is presented by census tract. Statistics include information on households, housing, occupations, businesses, etc.

AL76. Tuscaloosa. City Planning Commission. *Subdivision Regulations.* (P.O. Box 2089, Tuscaloosa 35401) 1972. 24pp. Free (excluding postage). Includes all regulations governing the subdivision of land within the city.

AL77. Tuscaloosa City Schools. *Tuscaloosa City School Directory.* (1100 21 St. E., Northington Campus, Tuscaloosa 35401). Annual. Free. Covers the Board of Education and all employees of the Tuscaloosa city schools.

AL78. Tuscaloosa Community Planning and Development Commission. *Action Programs for Community Development.* Huntsville: Public Systems Inc., 1974– . Annual. Free (excluding postage). (Available from: City of Tuscaloosa, P.O. Box 2089, Tuscaloosa 35401). This publication contains a review of communitywide conditions and community development needs, issues, and priorities. It also recommends programs identified by the Community Relations Advisory Board and Community Development Advisory Group. Functional categories treated within the report are education, health, housing, human services, manpower and economic development, public safety, culture and recreation, utilities, transportation, physical environment, etc. The scope of the plan does not cover community services provided by the city or other local agencies. Instead, it deals with supplemental programs which utilize funds from sources such as the Housing and Community Development Act of 1974 and general revenue sharing.

AL79. Tuscaloosa Planning and Zoning Commission. *The Zoning Ordinance of Tuscaloosa.* 1972. 115pp. $5.

AL80. West Alabama Comprehensive Health Planning Council. *Directory of Community Services.* Tuscaloosa (P.O. Box 1488, Tuscaloosa 35401), 1972– Biennial. $2. Although this document covers several counties in west Alabama, most of the services listed in the Tuscaloosa County section are based or operate in the city of Tuscaloosa. Medical, educational, recreational, and social services are included. A majority of these services originate with the local governments or voluntary sources.

Collections

AL81. Friedman Library. 1305 Greensboro Ave., Tuscaloosa 35401 (205)759-5141. The collection at the library includes those publications issued by the Tuscaloosa Planning and Community Development Commission and those of the West Alabama Planning and Development Council which pertain to the municipal area.

ALASKA

General Publications

AK1. Alaska. Department of Economic Development, Division of Economic Enterprise. *Profiles on Alaskan Communities.* Juneau: Office of the Commissioner (Pouch EE, Juneau 99801), 1973.
The publication gives profiles on 40 Alaskan communities, including Anchorage. It has valuable statistics on population, transportation, airfields, climate, industry, education, housing, and government.

AK2. Alaska Municipal League. *Alaska Municipal League Directory.* Juneau, 1975. Annual. $3. (Available from: Alaska Municipal League, 204 N. Franklin St., Juneau 99801.)
Publication gives financial and political information about the cities and boroughs that are members of the league, plus a list of local officials.

AK3. Alaska Municipal League. *Alaska Municipal Officials Directory, 1977*. Juneau (204 N. Franklin St., Juneau 99801), 1977. 97pp. Annual.
Formerly titled *Directory of Borough and City Officials*, the publication lists local officials, tells incorporation dates, population, when elections are held, what the sales tax is, and when the local council meets.

ANCHORAGE

It is important to remember when dealing with Anchorage that from 1964 to 1976 there were two major and sometimes competing governments in the Anchorage bowl: the city of Anchorage (incorporated in 1920) and the Greater Anchorage Area Borough (comparable with a strong county government). These two published their own documents, although the borough was by far the more prolific. In 1976 they were combined into the municipality of Anchorage, which now publishes everything.

The Anchorage governments have done a creditable job of getting information into print for the public. They have been especially strong in producing, or having produced, studies bearing on the future, but weak in providing publications on the past. The emphasis, however, on future studies is well placed. Anchorage is a future, not a past. Its past is brief and preparatory; its history is only lately becoming substantial. Therefore it is no surprise that Anchorage's planning department should be the largest producer of documents in the municipal government.

Publications

AK4. Alaska Rehabilitation Association. *A Guide for the Physically Handicapped—Anchorage*. Anchorage (910 MacKay Bldg., 338 Denali St., Anchorage 99501), 1975. 42pp.
Includes a survey of public buildings in the city and standards of service for the handicapped.

AK5. Alaska. University. Arctic Environmental Information and Data Center. *Environmental Atlas of the Greater Anchorage Area Borough.* Compiled by Lidia L. Selkregg, Eugene H. Buck, et al. Anchorage (707 A St., Anchorage 99501), 1972. 112pp.
The purpose of the atlas is to summarize the physical and biological environmental factors of the Greater Anchorage Area Borough. It includes maps, tables and text.

AK6. Anchorage. *Subdivision, Street Name and Trailer Court Index.* Anchorage: Public Information Office (Pouch 6-650, Anchorage 99502), 1976. 43pp.

AK7. Anchorage Action Council. *Anchorage Blue Book.* Public Information Office (Pouch 6-650, Anchorage 99502), 1976. 156pp. $1.
A listing and description of public and private organizations and resources of all kinds available in Anchorage.

AK8. Anchorage. Chamber of Commerce. *Membership Directory and Buyer's Guide*. 1970– . Annual.

AK9. Anchorage. City Council. *Annual Budget, City of Anchorage.* Public Information Office (Pouch 6-650, Anchorage 99502), n. d. Annual.
This report offers the public a view of how the budget is scheduled to be spent. It includes a detailed breakdown of finance codes.

AK10. Anchorage. Finance Department. Comptroller Division. *Financial Report.* Public Information Office (Pouch 6-650, Anchorage 99502). Annual.
These reports show the finances of the agencies under the city government as distinguished from the borough government. The city had authority over the water, electric, and telephone utilities, the Port of Anchorage, and the museum.

AK11. Anchorage Medical Society Auxiliary. *Anchorage Volunteer Directory 1975.* 1975. 22pp. 35¢. (Available from: Mrs. William Compton, 2250 Vanderbuilt Dr., Anchorage 99504.)
List of agencies and organizations in Anchorage which function, partly or completely, with volunteer assistance.

AK12. Anchorage. Planning Department. *Community Planning News.* (Pouch 9-650, Anchorage 99502) 1972– . Monthly.
A newsletter of local governmental activities in Anchorage. It explains what the agencies are and do, what new publications are available, new construction projects, statistics, etc.

AK13. Anchorage. Yellow Cab Company. *Anchorage Area Map and Street Directory*. (2301 Spenard Rd., Anchorage 99504) 1972. 222pp.

AK14. Anchorage Telephone Utility. *Greater Anchorage Area Telephone Directory.* (600 E. 38, Anchorage 99503) Annual.
Provides the usual information about whom to call for various municipal services. It also contains a brief history of Anchorage.

AK15. Burke, Janis. *A Descriptive Bibliography of Historical Research Material in the Anchorage Area.* Anchorage: University of Alaska, 1973. 150pp. (Available from: Dr. Stephen Haycox, College of Arts and Science, University of Alaska, Anchorage 99504.)
The catalog provides descriptive listings of general historical resource materials available in libraries in Anchorage.

AK16. Greater Anchorage Area Borough. *Code of Ordinances.* Anchorage (Public Information Office, Pouch 6-650, Anchorage 99502), 1974– . 2 vols.

AK17. Greater Anchorage Area Borough. Planning Department. *Financial Report.* Anchorage (Pouch 9-650, Anchorage 99502), 1964?– . Annual.
Includes financial statements of the school district as well as governmental agencies.

AK18. Greater Anchorage Area Borough. *Inlet View, Fairview, Neighborhood Survey.* Anchorage (Public Information Office, Pouch 6-650, Anchorage 99502), 1974. 71pp.
The report contains an analysis of the population of these neighborhoods and reports their responses to questions about how the neighborhoods should be improved and developed.

AK19. Greater Anchorage Area Borough. *Land Subdivision Regulations.* Anchorage (Public Information Office, Pouch 6-650, Anchorage 99502), 1972. 38pp.

AK20. Greater Anchorage Area Borough. *Zoning Ordinance.* Anchorage (Public Information Office, Pouch 6-650, Anchorage 99502), 1976. 104pp.

AK21. Greater Anchorage Area Borough. Planning Department. *A Community Attitude Survey.* Anchorage (Public Information Office, Pouch 6-650, Anchorage 99502), 1972. 30pp.
The purpose of the study was to measure the attitudes of the residents of Anchorage toward the options that government can take in guiding future growth. Survey included questions on community appearance, the central business district, recreation, transportation, housing, future growth, education, hazardous areas, and public facilities.

AK22. Greater Anchorage Area Borough. Planning Department. *Bikeways Plan and Related Trails.* Anchorage (Public Information Office, Pouch 6-650, Anchorage 99502), 1973. 49pp.
This report offers a comprehensive study of where bike trails are and should be in Anchorage. It also provides a master plan for future growth of bikeways.

AK23. Greater Anchorage Area Borough. Planning Department. *People in Anchorage.* Anchorage (Public Information Office, Pouch 6-650, Anchorage 99502), 1972. 111pp.
Shows population growth from 1929 to 1970. It has a detailed summary of 1970 population and offers population projections.

AK24. Greater Anchorage Area Borough. Planning Department. *People in Anchorage.* Anchorage (Public Information Office, Pouch 6-650, Anchorage 99502), 1974. 63pp.
This report provides a view of past, present, and future population levels, characteristics, and distribution in the Anchorage area. (See also entry **AK23.**)

AK25. Greater Anchorage Area Borough. Planning Department. *Preliminary Comprehensive Development Plan: Greater Anchorage Area Borough.* Vol. 1: Inventory and Analysis. Anchorage (Public Information Office, Pouch 6-650, Anchorage 99502), 1973. 191pp.
Describes the Anchorage area as it existed in 1973 and gives information on topography, population, employment trends, land use, and the economy.

AK26. Greater Anchorage Area Borough. Planning Department. *Proposed Anchorage Area Metropolitan Clearinghouse Procedures Manual.* Anchorage (Public Information Office, Pouch 6-650, Anchorage 99502), 1973. 25pp.
This report explains the intent and objectives of the Anchorage Regional Clearinghouse Program as established in the planning department of the Anchorage borough by the U.S. Office of Management and Budget. This clearinghouse deals with federal grants.

AK27. Greater Anchorage Area Borough. Public Information Office. *The Blue Book.* Anchorage (Pouch 6-650, Anchorage 99502), 1975. 140pp.
A listing and description of public and private organizations and resources available in Anchorage.

AK28. Lake, Larry, editor. *All about Anchorage and Southcentral Alaska.* Salt Lake City, UT: Alaska Travel Guide (Box 21038, Salt Lake City 84121), 1974. 63pp.
The book contains an indexed street map, a hotel/motel directory, and chapters on what to see and do in Anchorage.

AK29. Player, Corrie, and Sheryl White. *Anchorage Altogether.* Anchorage: n.p. 1972. 136pp.
A homespun introduction to Anchorage with descriptions of services, housing, weather, cost of living, recreation, and idiosyncracies of living in Alaska.

AK30. Seal Enterprises Inc. *Greater Anchorage Area Directory.* Anchorage (1114 E. Fifth Ave., Anchorage 99501), 1975. $1.50.
The book is a street, telephone, personal name, and business directory of Anchorage, including Chugiak and Eagle River.

AK31. *Water for Anchorage: An Atlas of the Water Resources of the Anchorage Area, Alaska.* Anchorage: The City of Anchorage and the Greater Anchorage Area Borough (Public Information Office, Pouch 6-650, Anchorage 99502), 1972. 77pp.

Collections

AK32. Z. J. Louissac Public Library, 427 F St., Anchorage 99501 (907)264-4481.
The library attempts to collect all Anchorage documents and will provide photocopy or microfilm service for a small per page charge.

AK33. University of Alaska, Anchorage. Library. 3211 Providence Dr., Anchorage 99504 (907)272-5522.

The library attempts to collect all Anchorage documents and will provide photocopy or microfilm service for a small per page charge.

ARIZONA

Local Newspaper Indexing: Selective indexing is done by the Arizona State Library, Department of Library, Archives and Public Records for inclusion in a card file maintained in the library's Arizona Collection (see entry **AZ6**).

General Publications

AZ1. Arizona. Department of Economic Security. *Employee Wage Surveys: Maricopa County, Pima County.* Phoenix, 1976– . Annual.
Separate publications with parallel information are produced for Pima County and for Maricopa County, which are actually Arizona's two SMSAs. Wage information was gathered for 80 occupational titles within each county. Data were gathered from all wage and salary industries, with the exception of mining within Maricopa County.

AZ2. Arizona. Department of Public Instruction. *Annual Report of the Superintendent of Public Instruction.* Phoenix: Arizona Department of Education (1535 W. Jefferson St., Phoenix 85007), 1912– . Annual.
Required by state law, this annual report includes complete information on financial activities at the local and county level. Both tables and graphs present general educational statistics such as enrollment, graduations, and teachers. Detailed revenue and expenditure reports are given by county and school districts. The superintendent of public instruction also issues an annual Arizona educational directory listing information and administrative personnel for each district, arranged by county. The directory also notes state educational committees, colleges and universities, technical schools, parochial and private schools, and Bureau of Indian Affairs schools.

AZ3. Arizona. Office of Economic Planning and Development. *Arizona, USA International Trade Directory.* Phoenix (1700 W. Washington St., Rm. 505, Phoenix 85007), 1974– . Updated semiannually.
Arizona's geographical location and expanding industry provide fertile ground for expansion of international trade. This directory lists enterprises in three ways: alphabetically by company name, by SIC numbers, and by communities within which facilities are located. United States affiliates and Mexican facilities are listed under the Mexican Border Industrialization Program. Other international trade services noted are interpreters and translators, consultants, customs, and consular corps of Arizona.

AZ4. League of Arizona Cities and Towns. *Local Government Directory.* Formerly: *Directory of Arizona City & Town Officials.* Phoenix (1820 W. Washington St., Phoenix 85007), 1958– . Updated quarterly. $10.

Formerly an annual publication, the 1977 edition assumed a loose-leaf format with planned quarterly updates. City information includes address, population, incorporation date, charter adoption date, elevation, area and municipal utilities. Names, addresses, and phone numbers of the mayor, council and staff are listed, as well as the occupations of the mayor and each council member. Terms, council meeting times, and city hall hours are given. Similar information is noted for each county. The directory lists Arizona councils of governments, Congressional delegation, state legislature members, and selected state offices.

AZ5. League of Arizona Cities and Towns. *Local Government Salary and Fringe Benefit Survey.* Phoenix (1820 W. Washington St., Phoenix 85007), 1977-   . Annual. $5.
Continued in this three-part study are statistical analyses for cities and towns, for counties, and standard job descriptions. The survey outlines salary and fringe benefit schedules for supervisory, administrative, and selected benchmark positions. Municipal tables give data for individual cities in groupings by size of population. This compilation replaces two previous publications done by the league and the association on cities and towns and counties, respectively.

Collections

AZ6. Arizona State Library, Department of Library, Archives and Public Records. 1700 W. Washington St., Phoenix 85007 (602)271-3701.
Arizona municipal documents are housed in the Arizona Collection of the Department of Library, Archives and Public Records. State law requires incorporated cities to deposit annual audit reports and towns to deposit biennial audit reports with the department. The collection is extensive and particularly strong in retrospective holdings. The department's records-management division assists municipalities with records retention and conducts an active microfilming program.

AZ7. Arizona State University, Interlibrary Loan Service, University Library. Arizona State University, Tempe 85281.
The University Library recently launched an acquisitions program for Arizona municipal documents dating from 1970. All Arizona cities and towns are included. Some items are noncirculating. The library will photocopy.
    Municipal documents acquired by the University Library of Arizona State University are accessed by means of a computer-generated keyword-out-of-context (KWOC) index. Originally established as an index to state of Arizona publications, the KWOC index has been expanded into an access document for the library's Arizona Governmental Publications collection. The documents themselves are housed in an archival arrangement by issuing agency within the Government Documents section of the library. The accent is on current material, specifically from 1970.

MESA

Since 1957 Mesa has published a monthly detailed statistical review allowing for retrospective comparisons. City budgets going back to 1913 are available in the city clerk's office. The clerk's office has embarked upon a project to microfilm retrospective city publications. The Mesa Public Library has municipal documents in its Southwest Collection.

Publications

AZ8. Gruen Associates. *Mesa—1990: The General Plan.* City of Mesa (55 N. Center, Mesa 85201), 1971. 75pp.
The plan summarizes the background, research, and policy proposals to be used by the city to guide its growth. Population projections and characteristics to 1990 are listed for Mesa. The plan considers land use for residential, commercial, industrial, and agricultural needs. The projected requirements for recreational and educational facilities, dwelling units, and water and sewer facilities are noted.

AZ9. Gruen Associates. *Mesa—1990: The General Plan Implementation Guide.* City of Mesa (55 N. Center, Mesa 85201), 1971.
The guide is a series of recommendations detailing possible courses of action to implement the general plan. Elements of community design for subdivision, highways, industrial development, and community beautification are discussed. Zoning changes are recommended. A capital improvements program with methods of financing is also outlined. Tables include estimates of revenue programs and costs of public and private investments.

AZ10. Mesa. City Manager. *Data Report.* (Mesa Municipal Bldg., 55 N. Center, Mesa 85201) 1957- . Monthly.
Detailed statistical data are arranged by departments of the city. Personnel report gives totals authorized and employed by each department. City clerk's report includes permits issued and permit revenue as well as record retention and disposal figures. Municipal court and city prosecutor statistics are noted. Additional data includes public works projects, subdivisions and annexations, police activity, crime, fire calls, building permits, street maintenance, library circulation, swimming pool and golf course activity, sales tax, summary of operating revenues and statistics, refuse information, and airfield activity.

AZ11. Mesa. City Manager. *Five Year Capital Improvement Program, 1977-82.* (Mesa Municipal Bldg., 55 N. Center, Mesa 85201) 1969- .
The publication lists capital expenditures by fiscal year, by program function, and by method of financing. Project descriptions are given by method of financing. Tables are included which show bonding and borrowing capacity of the city.

AZ12. Mesa. Finance Director. *Annual Budget.* (Mesa Municipal Bldg., 55 N. Center, Mesa 85201) 1957/58- . Annual.
Mesa's budget lists current budget program goals, their cost, and financing. It includes summaries of revenues by fund and source and appropriations, details of appropriations including schedule of salary ranges, and revenue bond reserves. Program summaries note general and operational objectives as well as financial information.

AZ13. Mesa. Finance Director. *Annual Financial Report.* (Mesa Municipal Bldg., 55 N. Center, Mesa 85201) 1968/69- . Annual.
Information in the financial report of Mesa is divided into three sections. The first includes the accounting system, sources of revenue, governmental expenditure by function, revenues from utility functions and utility expenditures by function. Part 2 includes financial statements; part 3 consists of statistical tables noting fiscal information for the last ten years and property tax rates.

AZ14. Mesa. Ordinances, Local Laws, etc. *Municipal Code of the City of Mesa, Arizona.* Weiser, Idaho: Sterling Codifiers, 1958.
A listing of city officials appears on the title page. The charter of the city is included.

PHOENIX

Financial information and planning information are the strong points of the Phoenix publication program. No strong distribution or depository system has been established. The Phoenix Public Library places copies of city documents in its Arizona Room in classification order with added copies in branches and reference centers as needed.

Publications

AZ15. Phoenix. City Manager. *Annual Budget of the City of Phoenix for the Fiscal Year.* (251 W. Washington St., Phoenix 85003) 1938/39- . Annual.
Currently, the annual budget of the city of Phoenix consists of two parts: part 1 gives details of the operating budget and capital as well as schedules; part 2 includes the city manager's budget message, expenditure program summaries, budget resources estimates and budget summary tables. The table of organization, graphs, and tables illustrate part 2 material, as does a map inside the back cover showing major capital improvement construction.

AZ16. Phoenix. City Manager. *Comprehensive Capital Improvement Program 1977-82.* (251 W. Washington St., Phoenix 85003) 1970- . Annual.
The seventh annual report of the capital improvement program includes bond and federal financing sources and priority listing of projects. Capital improvements under consideration include aviation, community service centers, police protection, fire protection, street improvements, storm sewers, sanitary sewers, libraries, parks and recreation facilities, transit, municipal administration buildings, public housing, solid waste disposal, water, and urban redevelopment.

AZ17. Phoenix. City Manager. *Monthly Review, City of Phoenix, Arizona: Report of City Activities.* (251 W. Washington St., Phoenix 85003) 1953- . 4pp. Monthly.
Submitted by the city manager to the city council in compliance with the city charter, the review contains articles and photographs of current interest. A table of statistical trends gives comparative figures by decades for square miles, population, city employees, and water connections. Fiscal year to date and current month's totals are given for aircraft traffic, bus passengers, residential units, building permits, library circulation, and refuse.

AZ18. Phoenix. Finance Director. *Annual Financial Report.* (251 W. Washington St., Phoenix 85003) 1950/51- . Annual.
A graph noting the phenomenal Phoenix population and area growth since 1950 prefaces three sections of information; introductory, financial, and statistical. The letter of transmittal by the finance director highlights the year's activities. The departmental organizations chart lists title, officer, and describes functions. A statistical profile of Phoenix concludes the report.

AZ19. Phoenix Newspapers Inc. *Inside Phoenix: Phoenix, Arizona.* City of Phoenix (251 W. Washington St., Phoenix 85003) 1953- . Annual.
Over 800 questions are included in an annual random sample survey of 3,300 households within the boundaries of Maricopa County. *Inside Phoenix* reveals results of this survey compiled by areas—19 in all—which delineate cities surrounding Phoenix. The document also utilizes federal, state, academic, and commercial sources for statistics. (Information sources are noted throughout this compendium, giving leads to further research sources.) Components of the economy of

metropolitan Phoenix are revealed in sections headed population, employment, newcomer households, income, finance, housing, retail sales, and tourism.

AZ20. Phoenix. Ordinances, Local Laws, etc. *The Code of the City of Phoenix, Arizona.* City Council, 1969.
Contents limited to code and charter.

AZ21. Phoenix. Planning Department. *The Comprehensive Plan—1990: Phoenix, Arizona.* (251 W. Washington St., Phoenix 85003) 1969. 192pp.
The general pattern of proposed land uses, both public and private, necessary to serve the anticipated 1990 population of over a million persons is depicted. Elements of the plan include residential, commercial, industrial, and central Phoenix community facilities such as parks, schools, water, and refuse disposal, and transportation components.

AZ22. Scott, Harold. *Urban Sprawl in Phoenix.* Phoenix: Office of Economic Planning and Development (1700 W. Washington St., Rm. 505, Phoenix 85007) 1974. 9pp.
In June of 1974 the *Wall Street Journal* published an article entitled "Phoenix Area's Sprawl Worries City Planners but Not Its Citizenry." This paper was written to evaluate the facts and conclusions in the *Journal* article. The author supports the general facts in the *Journal* but indicates that the primary cause of urban sprawl is the strong desire of Arizonans for a low-density life-style and the resulting sprawl is an indication that people are getting what they want.

SCOTTSDALE

Access to publications of the city of Scottsdale is mainly through a public information officer who coordinates much of the publication activity. The accent within the city is on citizen involvement; publications, other than normal reports, therefore, reflect this emphasis. A municipal reference collection is shelved in the Scottsdale Public Library, and city documents are found within it as well as in the Southwest Collections. Materials are arranged by Dewey classification or in vertical files in accordance with Scottsdale Public Library procedures.

Publications

AZ23. Eisner-Stewart and Associates. *Proposed Comprehensive General Plan, Scottsdale, Arizona.* South Pasadena, CA. 1966. 294pp. 3 vols. o.p.
This basic plan was updated and revised in 1972 by Wilsey and Ham's *Scottsdale General Planning Program,* which concentrated on five specific themes: north area, circulation, central business district, fringe annexation, and development evaluation/implementation. Volume 1 of the original study is the Land Use Analysis showing forces at work on the city's physical structure. Volume 2, an Economic Base Study, delves into population, office space, transient housing–tourism, residential housing, industrial development, and revenue–cost of service analysis. The final volume, the *Comprehensive General Plan,* contains a summary. Considerations are given to existing conditions, statement of major problems, citizen committee recommendations, special consultant recommendations, and general plan recommendations.

AZ24. Scottsdale. Chamber of Commerce. *Scottsdale, Arizona: A Community Profile.* (7333 E. Main St., Scottsdale 85251) 1976-   . 4pp.

Statistics and facts have been pulled together from various sources, including the publication *Inside Phoenix* (see entry **AZ19**). Scottsdale grew from 1 square mile and 200 population in 1951 to 89,000 square miles and 80,000 population in 1975. Short entries include income, education, utilities, taxes, community services, mobility, and climate.

AZ25. Scottsdale. City Manager. *Annual Financial Plan, City of Scottsdale.* Formerly: *Annual Budget.* (3939 Civic Center Plaza, Scottsdale 85281) 1953/54- . Annual.
Publication of Scottsdale's financial plan is preceded by issuance of *Requested Budget Summary* showing city and departmental organizational structures and budget information. The plan opens with the budget message of the city manager followed by operating budgets by departments. An executive summary precedes the budget for each program.

AZ26. Scottsdale Daily Progress. *Scottsdale in Retrospect: Annual Report.* 1975- . 8pp. Annual.
An eight-page supplement to the *Scottsdale Daily Progress*, this newspaper tabloid highlights activities of municipal government. Two full pages are devoted to finances, including a statement of actual and budgeted expenses as well as revenues. Pictures of city council members and the mayor are accompanied by brief notations of their municipal activities. Illustrations abound.

AZ27. Scottsdale. Finance Director. *Annual Financial Report.* (3939 Civic Center Plaza, Scottsdale 85251) 1971/72- . Annual.
This yearly accounting of Scottsdale's finances includes a ten-year retrospective record of general revenue and tax revenues by sources, as well as expenditures by programs. Financial statements are by funds. Information on finances is augmented by miscellaneous statistical data on fire, police, recreation, voting, population, and area. An organizational chart is included.

AZ28. Scottsdale. Ordinances, Local Laws, etc. *The Charter and Revised Code of the City of Scottsdale, Arizona.* Published by order of the City Council. Phoenix: Western States Coding Service, 1972.

AZ29. *Scottsdale Town Enrichment Program, Long Range Goals and Recommendations.* Scottsdale: City of Scottsdale (3939 Civic Center Plaza, Scottsdale 85251), 1970. 103pp.
During a period of booming growth in the mid-60s Scottsdale's mayor and city council conceived the idea of citizen involvement in municipal problems, using the acronym STEP for Scottsdale Town Enrichment Program. Advisory committees of citizens were formed in the areas of public works, public utilities, public safety, parks, recreation and city beautification, civic center, libraries, museums and galleries, and airports. The committees also served as public relations groups to gain support for council decisions. In 1969 the STEP program turned its attention to long-range planning in the areas of community development, transportation, community affairs, economic development, community services, and community improvements. This document compiles the reports prepared by STEP committees in those areas. Follow-up consists of periodic city council-sponsored forums on specific problems. Individual reports are then published revealing the findings of a forum. Aging and transportation planning are among topics covered by recent forums.

TEMPE

As with other Arizona cities with expanding populations, Tempe publications stress planning for growth and financial management. Tempe gained national attention with its *Bike Survey* (see entry **AZ37**) and completes periodic citizen attitude surveys. Publications are collected in the office of the city clerk and are microfilmed. The Tempe Public Library places copies of municipal publications in its Southwest Collection and maintains a Management Library within the city hall for use of city officials.

Publications

AZ30. Hall, John S., and Michael Hutchinson. *Citizen Attitudes Towards City Services and Issues in Tempe, Arizona.* Tempe: Center for Public Affairs, Arizona State University, 1977. 36pp. $3.
The Tempe citizen attitude survey is designed to point to general areas of citizen concern, preference and priorities for city government, and to compare the responses to those from a similar survey prepared in 1969. Interviews were completed with 418 individuals selected by systematic random sampling who were 21 years or older and who had lived in Tempe for at least six months. Results are reported under the general headings of introduction, community characteristics, perceptions and images of Tempe, views toward issues and services in Tempe, and general conclusions; thereby providing city officials with base line information for policy decision making.

AZ31. Tempe. City Manager. *Annual Budget.* (31 E. Fifth St., Tempe 85281) 1962- . Annual.
Tempe's budget reflects its financial planning by department and program. The publication includes the city organizational chart, annexation, growth statistics reflecting area population, assessed valuation, summary of revenue by sources, and capital projects.

AZ32. Tempe. City Manager. *Capital Improvements Program, 1977-82.* (31 E. Fifth St., Tempe 85281) 1965- . Annual.
This annual continuation of Tempe's 1965-1971 plan lists projected improvements by programs such as water and sewers, streets and traffic signals, storm drains, parks, and library. Accompanying data includes federal aid figures.

AZ33. Tempe. Finance Director. *Annual Financial Report to the Mayor, Council & City Manager.* (31 E. Fifth St., Tempe 85281) 1967/68- . Annual.
Retrospective data, in some instances up to ten years, is available on building permits, tax revenues, expenditures, and special assessments. This report includes an organization chart, general financial data, and statistical tables.

AZ34. Tempe. Ordinances, Local Laws, etc. *The Code of the City of Tempe, Arizona: The Charter and General Ordinances of the City.* Los Angeles, CA: Michie City Publications Co., 1967.
Contents limited to code and charter.

AZ35. Tempe. Planning Department. *General Plan, 1976.* (31 E. Fifth St., Tempe 85281) 1976.
Previous analyses of Tempe's growth pattern were published in 1965-1966 (*Comprehensive Planning Program,* Van Cleve Associates) and in 1972 (*Tempe General Plan,* Eisner-Stewart and Associates). Tempe's explosive growth demanded a re-

finement of these documents. This report examines current statistics and conditions and sets goals and objectives, concentrating on the areas of land use, community facilities, and transportation.

AZ36. Tempe. Planning Department. *Statistical Report*. (31 E. Fifth St., Tempe 85281) 1976–   . Quarterly.
During the first quarter of 1977, Tempe's population grew at the rate of 386 persons per month. Updated statistics are compiled by the planning division in the areas of population, housing, census data from the 1970 and special 1975 censuses, demographics, and land use. A miscellaneous chapter includes information on annexations, commercial and industrial permits, mobile home parks, and a list of restaurants.

AZ37. Tempe. Planning Department. *The Tempe Bikeway Plan: Final Report of the Tempe Bikeway Study*. (31 E. Fifth St., Tempe 85281) 1974. $1.
Innovation marks the presentation of the *Tempe Bikeway Plan* in multicolor comic-book format. This final report of the study was preceded by: *Bike Survey* (1972), *Background* (1972), and *Preliminary Plans and Recommendations* (1973); all of which are out of print. Graphic illustrations present background material, note the four major goals, list the program's objectives and policies, map bikeway routes, and stress safety rules. Tempe's climate and the presence of a large university are factors which promote a large bicycle-riding population. The Tempe Bikeway Plan was unanimously adopted by the city council in 1973 as a supplement to the Tempe General Plan.

TUCSON

Local Newspaper Indexing: The Government Reference Library, Tucson Public Library (see entry **AZ61**) indexes articles pertaining to city and county government and urban problems. The library answers queries from researchers. Other newspaper indexes for the city: *Arizona Daily Star* Library: comprehensive; Tucson Public (Main): selective; *News Bank* includes *Arizona Daily Star.*

Publications

AZ38. Peat, Marwick, and Mitchell. *Community Environmental Analysis, TIA Master Planning Study*. Tucson: Tucson Airport Authority, 1974.

AZ39. *Tucson and Southern Arizona Metroguide*. (2nd ed.) Tucson: Metroguide Publications, 1976.

AZ40. Tucson. Accounting Division. *Annual Financial Report*. 1962–   .

AZ41. *Tucson Area Manpower Review*. Phoenix: Arizona Employment Security Commission, 1968–   .

AZ42. Tucson. Chamber of Commerce. *A Complete Analysis of the Comprehensive Planning Process Draft Report*. 1975.

AZ43. Tucson. City Manager. *Annual Budget*. 1967–   .

AZ44. Tucson. Community Development/Design Center. *An Economic Analysis of the Tucson Housing Market*. 1974.

AZ45. Tucson. Community Development/Design Center. *Tucson Parks and Recreation System: A Study and Evaluation.* 1974.

AZ46. Tucson. Comprehensive Planning Process. *The Comprehensive Plan for the City of Tucson, Pima County, the City of South Tucson and Pima Association of Governments: A Draft for Community Review.* n.d., o.p.
A preliminary draft of the Tucson Comprehensive Plan. Elements of the plan include population, environment, land use, transportation, human resources, economy, housing, and government. This huge document (over 500 pages) created a great deal of controversy in the community, and the Comprehensive Plan is at the present time in the process of being revised.

AZ47. Tucson. Comprehensive Planning Process. *The Comprehensive Plan Policies: A Physical Development Guide for Eastern Pima County.* Hearing Draft. Planning Department (P. O. Box 27210, Tucson 85726), 1977. Free.
An outgrowth of the original Comprehensive Plan draft of 1975, this document outlines proposed development policies for the Tucson urban areas.

AZ48. Tucson. Comprehensive Planning Process. Booz, Allen and Hamilton Inc. *Cost/Revenue Analysis: Four Alternative Plans for Growth.* Planning Department (P.O. Box 27210, Tucson 85726), n.d. $2.
One of the first studies of its kind, this work attempted economic impact analysis of four alternative scenarios of growth in the Tucson area: peripheral expansion, activity nodes, contained growth, and satellite cities. The study concluded that contained growth could cost 30 percent less than the peripheral expansion alternative in capital costs over the next 25 years.

AZ49. Tucson. D.A.T.E. *Tucson Industrial Directory: Manufacturers and Support Industries in the Tucson Area.* 1974–

AZ50. Tucson. Department of Budget and Research. *A Socio-economic Study of Low and Moderate Income Households.* 1976.

AZ51. Tucson. Department of Budget and Research. *Tucson Model Cities Projects: Summary Status Report.* 1975.

AZ52. Tucson. Department of Community Development. Planning Division. *Interim Concept Plan.* n.d.
The plan outlines a series of short-term policies which could be used until such time as the Comprehensive Planning Process is completed. It should be viewed as an intermediary step between the 1960 Master Plan, the General Land Use Plan, and the Comprehensive Plan now in the process of being completed. The Interim Concept Plan attempts to: (1) set forth interim policies for orderly growth and development in the Tucson urban area—84 square miles plus 3 miles urban periphery, 190 square miles; (2) improve and facilitate decision making in zoning and related land regulations; (3) provide information and recommendations for the improvement of environmental standards; and (4) establish planning priorities and policies until comprehensive plan is completed. Vol. 1: Community Inventory and Analysis. This volume gives background information on Tucson such as physical characteristics, population characteristics, economic analysis, land use, and transportation of the area. Vol. 2: Plan and Policies.

AZ53. Tucson. Ordinances, Local Laws, etc. *Charter and Ordinances of the City of Tucson.* n.p., 1883–

AZ54. Tucson. Ordinances, Local Laws, etc. *Human Relations Ordinance.* Tucson: Pima Commission on Human Relations, 1975.

AZ55. Tucson. Personnel Department. *Regional Salary and Fringe Benefits Study, 1975/76.* 1976.

AZ56. Tucson. Planning Department. *Inner City Revitalization Report.* (P.O. Box 27210, Tucson 85726) n.d.
Study of Tucson's inner city and recommendations for revitalizing the urban core. The study includes an inventory of positive factors found within the inner city area, specific policy and action recommendations for this revitalization of the inner city, and an appendix of supportive and related data.

AZ57. Tucson. Planning Department. *Tucson's Historic Districts: Criteria for Preservation and Development.* (P.O. Box 27210, Tucson 85726) n.d. Free.
This study outlines the historic development of Tucson, indicating generally the significant historic areas which still remain. Criteria are presented, both in definition and graphic form, which could be applied to new construction and redevelopment of structures within the historic districts. The Tucson Historic District Zoning Ordinance is attached.

AZ58. Tucson. Planning Department, and University of Arizona Division of Economic and Business Research. *Economic Impact Analysis: A Series of Reports.* (P.O. Box 27210, Tucson 85726) n.d. $3.
Titles of the reports in this compilation are: "An Interindustry Analysis of the Tucson Economy," "Estimates of Labor Force Participation Rates and Per Capita Incomes for Tucson S.M.S.A.," "The Interaction of Population and Economic Growths in Tucson S.M.S.A.," "Fiscal Impact Analysis: Revenue and Expenditure Methodology," and "Migration to Tucson by Persons Not Regularly in the Work Force."

AZ59. Tucson. Public Library. *Development Plan for the Tucson Public Library, 1974-84.* Compiled by Lowell Martin. 1974.

AZ60. *Tucson Today: A Market Analysis.* Tucson: First National Bank of Arizona. 1973- .

Collections

AZ61. Governmental Reference Library, Tucson Public Library. P.O. Box 27210, Tucson 85726 (602)791-4041.
Budgets, financial reports, and planning reports are circulated to city of Tucson and Pima County staff. Others may use materials in the library. The majority of the local publications in the Governmental Reference Library (GRL) relate to planning. The sources of these publications include the city planning department, the county planning department, the regional council of governments, consulting firms, and committees surveying or evaluating a particular problem or program in the area. The GRL, located in City Hall, which is part of a complex of government buildings of all jurisdictions, is used to assist city and county staff; serves as a clearinghouse for the private citizen; and acts as a liaison between outside agencies, businesses, other libraries, other communities, and government staff. The collection of the GRL includes various types of publications with information about areas similar economically, demographically, or geographically.

ARKANSAS

Local Newspaper Indexing: Shannon J. Henderson (Arkansas Polytechnic College, Russellville, Arkansas) compiles an index to the *Arkansas Gazette*. The selective index pertains to Arkansas people, events, and places.

General Publications

AR1. Arkansas Municipal League. *Arkansas Municipalities: Official Publication of the Arkansas Municipal League.* Edited by Randy Walker. Little Rock (P.O. Box 38, Little Rock 72115), 1944- . Monthly. $6 (annual).
Consists of articles about current developments in Arkansas cities and towns.

AR2. Arkansas Municipal League. *Directory of Arkansas Municipal Officials.* N. Little Rock, 1977. 64pp. Annual. $10.
Contains the names of the officials of Arkansas cities and towns.

AR3. Western Arkansas Planning and Development District. *Inventory-Directory of Health Facilities and Services.* Fort Smith, 1976. 97pp.

AR4. Western Arkansas Planning and Development District. *Land Resource Management Policy Guidance Materials for Western Arkansas.* Fort Smith, 1976. 134pp.

FORT SMITH

Publications

AR5. Fort Smith. City Hall. *Annual Budget, City of Fort Smith, Arkansas for the Year 1977.* n.p. 87pp.

AR6. Fort Smith. City Hall. *Zoning Map, City of Fort Smith, Arkansas.* n.p., n.d. 156pp.

AR7. Fort Smith. Public Schools. *Personnel Directory—Fort Smith Public Schools.* n.p., n.d. 100pp.

LITTLE ROCK

Publishing by the city of Little Rock is limited. Most of the material which is printed is that which might be required by law, such as budget and financial records, special reports that may be essential in making city decisions, and annual reports from various city departments.

Publications

AR8. Little Rock. City Hall. *Annual Budget*. (Little Rock 72201) Annual.
Depicts the general, board, and commission fund budgets for the fiscal year. Arrangement is by city department and division. Each division contains functions, goals and objectives, program contents, and budget sheet. There are organizational charts.

AR9. Little Rock. City Hall. *Annual Financial Report of the City of Little Rock, Arkansas*. Annual.
Contains the financial data for the fiscal year (financial statements of the general operations fund, financial statements of funds controlled by independent boards and commissions, and financial statistics).

AR10. Little Rock. Public Schools. *Personnel Directory*. (W. Markham and Izard, Little Rock 72201) Annual.
A directory of persons and their positions within the Little Rock Public School System.

Collections

AR11. Central Arkansas Library System. 700 Louisiana, Little Rock 72201 (501)374-7546 ext. 10.
Pamphlet material about the city is collected. Official as well as privately printed publications are acquired. The collection contains some material that dates back as far as the early 1900s. Much of the material is of an ephemeral nature but is kept because of archival usefulness. Also included in the collection are old street maps dating from 1821.

CALIFORNIA

General Publications

CA1. California. Secretary of State. *Roster of State, County, City and Township Officials.* Sacramento: (Capitol, Rm. 199, Sacramento 95814), 1945– . Annual. $2.50.

Collections

CA2. **University of California.** General Library, P.O. Box 19557, Irvine 92713 (714)833-6839. Teletype Service: (910)595-1770.
The Orange County Public Affairs Collection maintains an active acquisitions program of the basic documents of Orange County and the 26 cities in the county, as well as a number of special-purpose county governments. Included are budgets, general planning materials, organizational directories, annual reports, and special reports by governmental departments and outside consultants. In addition, there is a section of nongovernmental sources which encompasses groups and organizations active in the county. Included are economic studies of the region by major financial institutions, materials from the Irvine Company, the largest property owner in the county, and certain regional organizations in which Orange County or its elements participate (Southern California Association of Governments or the League of California Cities). A guiding principle in collection development has been to reflect the current trends in the county—rapid growth and urbanization, citizen action in local politics, environmental issues, and other related topics.

ANAHEIM

Data not available at this time.

BERKELEY

Collections

CA3. **Association of Bay Area Governments.** Hotel Claremont, Berkeley 94705 (415)841-9730.
The association, which has a library collection of master plans and other materials, advertises its publications through Greenwood Press's *Index to Current Urban Documents* and its own *ABAG Bibliography*, which lists its services and publications. For example, the association produces *Bay Area Directory: City and County Governments* (1975– , loose-leaf, $20), which is a computer-produced listing of

offices and officials. The association participates in ADLIB (Automated Data Library), a joint bibliographic project making the information resources of the association and the Metropolitan Transportation Commission available to planners, public decision-makers, and citizen groups in the San Francisco Bay Area (the system will be operative for public use by mid-1978); and in BASIS (Bay Area Spatial Information System), which will collect, maintain, and display geographic reference data by mid-1978.

CA4. **The Berkeley Public Library**. 2090 Kittredge St., Berkeley 94704 (415)644-6095. Teletype Service: (910)366-7020.
The library, which does not send documents on interlibrary loan, carries a variety of publications about Berkeley such as: *Berkeley Facts* (a statistical publication); *The People of Berkeley: Demographic Profile*; *Berkeley: Know Your Town* (prepared by the League of Women Voters of Berkeley); and the Planning Commission's *The People of Berkeley: A Policy Document* (1973).

CA5. **The Institute of Governmental Studies**. University of California, 109 Moses Hall, Berkeley 94720 (415)642-1472.
The institute has issued an accessions list, which is free to libraries, as a means of awareness about many of the official reports it receives. The material represents diverse levels of government and is available from the issuing agency. As a depository for local documents from the U.S. Bureau of the Census Library (FB3, Rm. 2450, Suitland, Maryland; mail address: Washington, D.C. 20233 (301)763-5042), the institute receives local government material which is over five years of age and for select states. Materials from the Census Bureau are available for interlibrary loan. The institute forwards health department publications to the Public Health Library, University of California, Berkeley, for retention or discarding. The library is a local document depository as authorized by the state of California.

FREMONT

Local Newspaper Indexing: The local newspaper, the *Argus*, is not indexed by either the paper itself or the Fremont Main Library. However, articles on all aspects of Fremont in the *Argus* are clipped for the local history collection of the Fremont Main Library (see entry **CA6**).

Collections

CA6. **Fremont Main Library**. Alameda County System. 39770 Paseo Padre Pkwy., Fremont 94538 (415)792-8555. Teletype Service: (910)383-0202.
The library keeps a collection of major documents of the city such as budgets, development plans, environmental impact reports, municipal and county codes, directories of business, county assessor's records, and some voting returns. The city of Fremont does not produce many documents. The library does receive copies of the most important ones along with notices of departmental public meetings and agendas for these meetings. Given the nature of this type of material, the library does not keep notices and agendas for more than several weeks. Minutes of such meetings are available from city hall. Municipal documents are kept in the library as reference material, and the availability of interlibrary loan depends on the decision of the branch head of this library. Photocopying, when possible, is available. Holdings of the local history collection are unavailable for interlibrary loan but may be photocopied at a small per page charge.

FRESNO

The city of Fresno's publications, apart from those of the city planning and inspection department and, to a somewhat lesser extent, the city's Redevelopment Agency, are largely limited to annual reports of the various city departments. The annual budgets and tax computation reports are other such regularly generated municipal publications. The planning and inspection department, on the other hand, has various neighborhood study plans and reports. Similarly, the Redevelopment Agency has periodic reports relating to urban renewal activities within the city; most of these are dated prior to 1971. Beyond the kinds of city reports already indicated, there are studies and reports issued by nonofficial sources on matters immediately concerning city officials and residents such as those of the Council of Fresno County Governments (e.g., the environmental impact report for the Fresno regional transportation plan) and various private consultative firms (e.g., Consultative Planners' environmental impact report in 1973 on commercial development in the Jayne Avenue-Interstate 5 freeway interchange).

There are no checklists of reports for official and private consultative agencies. The Fresno County Free Library (see entry **CA7**) does prepare, on a quarterly basis, bibliographies of government and government-related publications found in its Government Research Library that may be of practical use to local government planners and managers, and these quarterly lists do include some Fresno City (as well as Fresno County) documents. There are no rosters of city personnel regularly published, nor regular citywide statistical publications. The individual departments often have reports which give statistics for a given year. There is no overall city manual or handbook on governmental operations, although there are some individual departmental manuals of that sort (i.e., the Fresno Fire Department's *Manual of Operations*) as well as overviews of operations of individual departments. **Local Newspaper Indexing:** The Fresno County Free Library (see entry **CA7**) has maintained a local history index, of which entries for articles in local newspapers have comprised a major portion for many years. For the past ten years, the library staff has indexed the Fresno newspapers rather fully and broadly with items involving governmental activity from the city, county, and region.

Collections

CA7. Fresno County Free Library. 2420 Mariposa, Fresno 93721.
The cataloged Fresno area items mentioned in the overview are reference works and therefore noncirculating. There are some duplicate copies of these items that are placed in the library's Government Research Library. The library attempts to obtain all series of municipal publications from the city.

GARDEN GROVE

Data not available at this time.

GLENDALE

Publications

CA8. Glendale. Chamber of Commerce. *Glendale, Jewel City of the Verdugos: Buyer's Guide of Community Information.* n.p., n.d.

CA9. Glendale. Chamber of Commerce. Industrial Division. *Industrial Directory.* n.p., 1959–

CA10. Glendale Community Services Inc. *Articles of Incorporation of Glendale Community Services Inc.* Sacramento: Secretary of State, 1975.

CA11. Glendale. Office of the City Manager. *Service and Progress: A Bi-Monthly Report to the City Council and Citizens of Glendale.* n.p., no. 1, January 1955– .

CA12. Glendale. Planning Division. *Facts about Glendale.* 1973– .

CA13. *Glendale's Government.* n.p., n.d. 1 vol.

Collections

CA14. City of Glendale. Library Division. 222 E. Harvard St., Glendale 91205 (213)956-2030.
The Special Collections Room has city council minutes and planning commission minutes from 1971 to date. (The city clerk's office has the complete set available.) In addition, the Special Collections Room has petitions and letters of opinion by the city attorney prior to 1920.

HUNTINGTON BEACH

Collections

CA15. Huntington Beach Public Library. Information and Resource Center. 7111 Talbert Ave., Huntington Beach 92648 (714)842-4481. Teletype Service: (910)596-1741.
The library is a selective depository for city documents and reports. The staff collects municipal ordinances and zoning codes and the major reports of city departments, especially those relating to planning, finance, law, civil defense, education, recreation, and business. They keep the current agendas and minutes of all committee, board, and council meetings. The historical files are a combination of private publications, city reports, historical society reports, student research reports, and periodical articles.

LONG BEACH

Data not available at this time.

LOS ANGELES

Publications

CA16. Los Angeles. Charters. *Charter of the City of Los Angeles.* Los Angeles: Building News Inc. (3055 Overland Ave., Los Angeles 90037), 1925 with updates through 1976. $8.75 without binder ($12.28 with binder).
Basic law of the city of Los Angeles.

CA17. Los Angeles. Ordinances, Local Laws, etc. *Administrative Code.* Los Angeles: *Los Angeles Daily Journal* (210 S. Spring St., Los Angeles 90012), 1969 amended to October 1, 1976. 2 vols. $55 per set.
Codified arrangements of ordinances, rules, and regulations governing the administration of city departments.

CA18. Los Angeles. Ordinances, Local Laws, etc. *Los Angeles Municipal Code.* Los Angeles: Parker and Son Inc. (6500 Flotilla, Los Angeles), effective November 12, 1936; amended to December 31, 1976. 5 vols. $150 per set. Ordinances of the city which have been codified.

CA19. Los Angeles County. Auditor-Comptroller. *County Budget, County of Los Angeles, California.* Los Angeles: n.p. (500 W. Temple St., Los Angeles 90012). Annual.
Gives amount actually spent in the prior year and amounts requested by various departments and approved by the Board of Supervisors. Arranged by salaries and employee benefits, services and supplies, other charges and fixed assets, it gives the requirements of the special districts within the county whose affairs and funds are under supervision and control of the Board of Supervisors.

CA20. Los Angeles County. Auditor-Comptroller. *Statement of Bonded Indebtedness.* Los Angeles (500 W. Temple St., Los Angeles 90012). Annual.
This supplemental report of the Board of Supervisors includes all *ad valorem* bond issues of the county, special districts, school districts, and municipalities within the county. Noted is whether bonds issued are matured or outstanding as of the end of the calendar year. Bonds authorized, but not issued, are also listed.

CA21. Los Angeles County. Auditor-Comptroller. *Tax Payers' Guide.* Los Angeles (500 W. Temple St., Los Angeles 90012). Annual.
Provides information about tax rates and legal requirements, covering assessment of property, payment of taxes, and the various tax levies for county, school, and special districts.

CA22. Los Angeles County. Charters. *Charter of County of Los Angeles.* Compiled by John H. Larson. Los Angeles: n.p. (500 W. Temple St., Los Angeles 90012), 1976. 77pp. Irregular.
First ratified by voters of the county in 1912, this source includes all amendments through June 1976. It is annotated and gives the legislative history, cases cited, powers of the Board of Supervisors, etc.

CA23. Los Angeles County. Civil Service Commission. *Rules.* Los Angeles (222 N. Grand Ave., Rm. 585, Los Angeles 90012). Irregular. $4.25.
Covers examinations, eligibility lists, probation, transfer, leave of absence, layoff, reinstatement, performance evaluation, etc.

CA24. Los Angeles County. Ordinances, Local Laws, etc. *Administrative Code of the County of Los Angeles, State of California.* Los Angeles: n.p. (500 W. Temple St., Los Angeles 90012). Annual.
Originally adopted May 19, 1942 by the Board of Supervisors, it is revised annually. Gives the county's permanent and general administrative rules and regulations.

CA25. Los Angeles County. Ordinances, Local Laws, etc. *Salary Ordinance* (Ordinance #6222). Los Angeles (500 W. Temple St., Los Angeles 90012). Annual.
Published by fiscal year, this source gives general provisions such as working hours, vacations, severance pay, etc. It also gives salary schedules and tables of classes of positions by department (including Flood Control District and Fire Protection Districts). For each position the item number, number of employees, and title is given. Kept current by slip ordinances as amended.

CA26. Los Angeles County. Ordinances, Local Laws, etc. *Zoning Ordinance*

(Ordinance #1494). Los Angeles: County Department of Regional Planning (320 W. Temple St., Los Angeles 90012). Irregular. $5 (by mail).
Covers such matters as zoned districts, front and side yard setbacks, permits, variances, nonconforming uses and structures, etc., in the unincorporated area of the county.

CA27. Los Angeles County. Sheriff's Department. *Statistical Summary*. Los Angeles: n.p. (211 W. Temple St., Los Angeles 90012). Annual.
All types of crime-related statistics are given by divisions and by stations, including the stations of contract cities with the county, then by breakdown of reporting district within the station. It includes charts and compares statistics to the prior year giving percentage changes and projections for the coming year.

CA28. Los Angeles County. Superintendent of Schools. *Directory of the Public Schools of Los Angeles County, California.* Downey (9300 E. Imperial Hwy., Downey 90242). Annual.
Arranged alphabetically by school districts with address, telephone number, full description of boundaries, total enrollment, and roster. Subarranged by elementary, junior high, and senior high schools, it provides basic information about each school. It also has community college districts and a map.

Collections

CA29. County of Los Angeles. Public Library. 320 W. Temple St., P.O. Box 111, Los Angeles 90053.
The library serves the county of Los Angeles and 44 incorporated cities. It is in the process of compiling information on its city holdings.

CA30. Public Affairs Service/Local University Research Library. University of California. 405 Hilgard Ave., Los Angeles 90024.
The library is a local document depository as authorized by the state of California Government Code. It also receives publications from over 100 cities and counties outside California.

(See also entry **US4**).

OAKLAND

Local Newspaper Indexing: The Sociology Section of the Oakland Public Library (see entry **CA34**) selectively clips the *Oakland Tribune*, *Montclarion* and *San Francisco Chronicle* for subjects in local government and politics. The California Room of the library clips items of historical nature concerning local and state history.

Publications

CA31. Alameda County. Board of Supervisors. *Alameda County Government.* 1975. 57pp.
Explains basic organization and responsibility of the county's agencies and departments. Has organizational chart and supervisorial district map.

CA32. Oakland. City Manager. *Your City Government of Oakland.* 1971. 32pp.

Brief history and description of all departments. Includes an organizational chart, a brief directory, and vital statistics.

CA33. Oakland. League of Women Voters. *Know Your Town: A Citizen's Guide to Oakland Government*. 1976. 43pp.
First published in 1953 (revised in 1956, 1961, and 1976), this publication covers Oakland city government and regional governmental bodies in the area and has a map of council districts. In addition there is a calendar of city department meetings.

Collections

CA34. Oakland Public Library. 125 14 St., Oakland 94612 (415)273-3138. Teletype Service: (910)366-7016.
The library has publications of Oakland, Alameda County, and special districts such as East Bay Municipal Utility District and East Bay Regional Park District. There is no legal requirement that all publications of the city be filed at the library; therefore, it is often difficult to keep abreast of current publications. Oakland has in recent years reduced its publishing considerably and is reluctant to distribute free copies of materials. The library does participate in Greenwood Press's *Index to Current Urban Documents*. In addition to the sources already cited, the library has other publications which fill a reference function. These include:

1. Alameda County. Social Services Agency. *Human Services Inventory.* n.d.
2. Association of Bay Area Governments. *Bay Area Directory: City and County Governments.* n.d.
3. Oakland. Chamber of Commerce. *Directory of Officials: Oakland/Alameda County.* n.d.
4. Oakland. City Clerk. *Directory of Municipal Agencies and Officials: City of Oakland.* n.d.
5. Oakland. City Manager. *Budget Summary.* 1967/68-   .
6. Oakland. City Planning Department. *Available Publications from the Oakland City Planning Department.* 1972. 8pp.
7. Oakland. Police Department. *Weekly Crime Summary.* May 19, 1975-   .

PASADENA

Data not available at this time.

RIVERSIDE

No bibliographies or checklists of municipal publications are produced. The city releases annual budgets and occasional planning studies to the Riverside City and County Public Library (see entry **CA36**). However, there is no systematic publication program.

Publications

CA35. Riverside. League of Women Voters. *Profile: Riverside City Government.* (4255 Main St., Riverside 92501) 1972. 56pp. 50¢ (postage and mailing).
This booklet outlines the duties of elected and appointed officials as provided by the city charter and summarizes the responsibilities of city departments, advisory boards, and commissions. It also has a map of city council wards, a brief treatment of city financial procedures, and a brief history of the city.

Collections

CA36. Riverside City and County Public Library. P.O. Box 468, Riverside 92502.
The library maintains a *Press Enterprise* index for Riverside city and county history which is a selective local history index to Riverside's daily newspapers in card-file form. It covers the *Riverside Daily Press* (July 1878 to February 1973), *Daily Enterprise* (March 1973 to the present), and the *Press and Horticulturist* (1890s). Indexing includes city officials and organizations. The reference department accepts in-person and mail requests for information in the index.

SACRAMENTO

Local Newspaper Indexing: The Sacramento Public Library (see entry **CA37**) indexes the *Sacramento Bee* and the *Sacramento Union* from 1900–1937; since 1974 only Sacramento items have been indexed. A clipping file covers the years 1938 to 1973, but the file is incomplete. The library has a complete file of both newspapers on microfilm since 1855.

Collections

CA37. Sacramento Public Library. Business and Municipal Department, 828 "I" St., Sacramento 95814 (916)449-5203. Teletype Service: (910)367-0289.
About three years ago, through negotiation with city and county officials, the library was able to establish depository status for city and county documents. In addition it received publications of the Sacramento Regional Area Planning Commission. Since 1974, the library staff has established a cataloged collection of documents. Some of these are dated prior to 1974, since the library received the collections of retired city and county officials.

SAN BERNARDINO

The city of San Bernardino issues budgets, ordinances, charters, water department reports, and a statistical profile offered by the human relations department. The Redevelopment Agency has published some outstanding planning documents. Two problem areas are worthy of mention: the lack of up-to-date city personnel directories and the difficulty in getting access to air pollution and crime statistics. **Local Newspaper Indexing:** See entry **CA38**.

Collections

CA38. San Bernardino Public Library. 401 N. Arrowhead Ave., San Bernardino 92401. (714)889-0264. Teletype Service: (910)390-1145.
The staff of the library has indexed the *San Bernardino Sun* since 1965. The index covers news of local concern. Queries from other libraries will be accepted.

SAN DIEGO

Collections

CA39. Governmental Reference Library. City of San Diego. 602 County Administration Center, San Diego 92101.
The library attempts to collect all documents produced at the local level and

publishes a monthly list of acquisitions, *Timely Topics*, which includes local and state publications. Previous to 1974, the library received some documents from local governments, principally budgets and annual reports. In addition, it had many studies written in the 1950s and 1960s in preparation for various urban renewal projects. These are integrated into the local history collection. A few agencies issue annual reports, but not all, and there has been little consistency over the years. Some of the documents date back to about 1920.

All documents in the collection are for reference use only. In most cases there is only one copy. The agreement states that these documents will be made available to the public but will not circulate. However, they may be obtained on interlibrary loan for use within the borrowing library. The library has participated in Greenwood Press's *Index to Current Urban Documents* since 1972.

Much of the recent output of the local governmental agencies has consisted of environmental impact reports, including studies of regional transit, water resources, sewage disposal, parkways, airports, etc. Other types of documents are annual reports, budgets, and general plans.

SAN FRANCISCO

Local Newspaper Indexing: The *California News Index*, published by the Center for California Public Affairs (226 W. Foothill Blvd., Claremont 91711), includes the *San Francisco Examiner* and the *San Francisco Chronicle* in the list of newspapers in the state which are included in the index.

Publications

CA40. San Francisco. Board of Education. *Directory of the San Francisco Unified School District.* San Francisco Unified School District (135 Van Ness Ave., San Francisco 94102). Annual. 63pp. Free.

CA41. San Francisco. Department of Public Works. *CENTREX Telephone Directory.* San Francisco Purchasing Department (270 City Hall, San Francisco 94102). Annual. 50¢ plus tax.
A detailed listing of the telephone numbers of the city departments with a key-person index in the back.

CA42. San Francisco. Mayor. *Directory of City and County Officers.* City Hall (Rm. 200, San Francisco 94102). Annual. 10pp. Free.
The directory lists names, addresses, and telephone numbers of officers, departments, and boards.

Collections

CA43. **San Francisco Public Library.** Civic Center, San Francisco 94102.
San Francisco does not do extensive publishing. However, as the city is also a county, the library staff finds statistical data from the state and federal publications very beneficial. The outstanding feature of the reference collection is the annual reports of the various departments. The city planning department does the most publishing of documents in addition to annual reports.

(See also entry **US4**.)

SAN JOSE

Data not available at this time.

SANTA ANA

Collections

CA44. Santa Ana Public Library. 26 Civic Center Plaza, Santa Ana 92701. The library has been overcrowded for quite some time. Therefore, space for any extensive collection is not available. For this reason the library staff does not actively collect municipal documents. The University of California at Irvine is engaged in an extensive program of collecting local government documents (see entry **CA2**). The county of Orange is planning a local government resource library to be located in the courthouse adjacent to the Santa Ana Public Library. Statistical information is abundant in standard state and federal government publications, as well as county publications, which are housed in the public library. A moderate Santa Ana history collection of books and ephemera is being enlarged but does not include much documentary material.

STOCKTON

Local Newspaper Indexing: The reference staff of the Stockton/San Joaquin County Public Library (see entry **CA45**) selectively indexes the *Stockton Record* for local information. The library will accept questions from outside the library system.

Collections

CA45. Stockton/San Joaquin County Public Library. 605 N. El Dorado, Stockton 95202 (209)944-8461. Teletype Service: (510)765-6668.
Since 1971 a voluminous amount of municipal documents has been published by both city and county governmental bodies, as well as by nongovernmental and government-funded organizations. The library houses a large collection of these documents. Most recent acquisitions have been the county and city planning departments' area compilation of the U.S. Bureau of Census publications. Other collections include grand jury reports, city and county annual budgets, municipal zoning ordinances, city codes, agenda and minutes of the Board of Education (Stockton Unified School District), and the agenda and minutes of the city council.

TORRANCE

Collections

CA46. Torrance Public Library System. Civic Center Library. 3301 Torrance Blvd., Torrance 90503 (213)328-2251.
The library has environmental impact reports, city budgets, and reports of the Los Angeles County Regional Planning Commission and of the California Coastal Commission Southern Region. Documents remain in the collection for five years, after which they are discarded or returned to the publishing agency.
The Local History Collection is housed separately and includes all topics of historical nature pertinent to the city of Torrance since its founding and incorporation. These documents are retained indefinitely and, like all documents, are available for circulation.

COLORADO

General Publications

CO1. Boulder. Public Library. *Municipal Government Reference Center Catalog.* (P.O. Drawer H, Boulder 80306) 1976- . Annual. $25.
A comprehensive book catalog listing the available materials held by the Municipal Government Reference Center (see entry **CO16**). The materials listed deal mostly with local governmental topics. The catalog is available free to Colorado public libraries and at cost ($25) to other interested parties. The Municipal Government Reference Center is a specialized public source of materials on local government. The collection is unique and the most comprehensive in the state in this area.

CO2. Boulder. Public Library. *Municipal Government Reference Center Newsletter.* (P.O. Drawer H, Boulder 80306) Bimonthly.
The newsletter is a supplement to the *Municipal Government Reference Center Catalog.* It covers the most current material added to the Municipal Government Reference Center collection (see entry **CO16**).

CO3. Colorado. Department of Education. *Colorado Education Directory.* Denver, 1941?- . Annual.
A roster of educational and related groups and school districts within the state.

CO4. Colorado. Department of Education. Office of Library. *Directory of Colorado Libraries.* Denver, 1967- . Annual.
Listing of libraries, library organizations, associations, and groups.

CO5. Colorado. Department of Health. *Annual Report of Vital Statistics.* Denver (Division of Administrative Services, Records and Statistics Section, 4210 E. 11 Ave., Denver 80220), 1961- . Annual. $1.
Gives vital statistics by state, region, and county.

CO6. Colorado. Department of Health. *Demographic Profile: Colorado Planning and Management Districts.* Denver (4210 E. 11 Ave., Denver 80220), 1975. 13 vols.
Gives demographic information for each region by county. Some of the information is based on 1970 census figures while others are more current estimates.

CO7. Colorado. Department of Revenue. *Sales Tax Statistics for Counties and Selected Cities.* Denver. Quarterly.
Contains statistics for gross sales, retail sales, net sales tax, and percentage of county retail sales for all Colorado counties and selected cities.

CO8. Colorado. Division of Commerce and Development. *Colorado Community Economic Development Resource Register, Community Profiles*. Compiled by Kathy E. Scales. Denver, 1971–72. 2 vols.
Contains 82 profiles of communities giving location, climate, population, community information, transportation, distances from other communities, government and taxes, municipal bonds, labor, manufacturing firms in the immediate area, business indicators, utilities, water and waste disposal, and county indicators for the county in which the community is located.

CO9. Colorado. Division of Local Government. *Local Government Financial Compendium.* Denver, 1966–   . Annual.
Contains general government revenue activities, public enterprise activities, pension funds, general revenue sharing outlay for all Colorado counties, cities, and towns over 1,000 population.

CO10. Colorado. Division of Planning. *State, Region and County Population Projections, 1970–2000*. Denver, 1976. 154pp.

CO11. Colorado. Municipal League. *Colorado Laws Enacted in 1975 of Interest to Cities and Towns*. Wheatridge (Wheatridge 80033), 1975. 78pp. $7.
Provides municipal officials with a compilation of laws of municipal interest. There is a complete list by number, subject, and prime sponsor of all laws enacted in 1975.

CO12. Colorado. Municipal League. *Directory of Municipal and County Officials in Colorado.* Wheatridge (Wheatridge 80033), 1973–   . Annual. $12.50.
Contains listings of municipal officials in cities. A listing of county officials including El Paso is given. The Pikes Peak Area Council of Governments is given along with its officials.

CO13. Colorado State University. *County Information Service*. Ft. Collins, 1974–   . Irregular.
Statistical information by county for all Colorado cities.

CO14. Colorado University. Business Research Division. *Colorado Business Review.* Boulder, 1944–   . Monthly.
Contains labor force statistics for the state by industry for last two months and one year previous, with hours and earnings, production statistics for certain industries, bankruptcies, motor vehicle title applications, etc., for the state. Gives electric power, bank debits, and new construction statistics for 40 Colorado cities.

CO15. Colorado University. Business Research Division. *Colorado County and City Retail Sales by Standard Industrial Classification*. Boulder, 1965–   .
Quarterly and Calendar Year.
Gives state, county, and city totals for dollar amount of sales by Standard Industrial Classification for current calendar year and one year past.

Collections

CO16. Municipal Government Reference Center. Boulder Public Library. P.O. Drawer H, Boulder 80306 (303)441-3100.
The center maintains an extensive clippings file from the local newspapers related to the city and county governments. It houses over 6,000 cataloged titles, Colorado statutues and codes, 5,000 pamphlets, 200 active serials, and news clippings,

and maps (all related to local government). The center also has state and federal publications which pertain to local governmental activities. The strongest areas of the collection relate to planning, growth control, public budgeting and finance, zoning, police and corrections, personnel, management, and city/county government. These resources relate extensively to the city and county of Boulder, the Denver SMSA, and the state of Colorado.

COLORADO SPRINGS

The Pikes Peak Area Council of Governments' publications are very informative and are generally up to date. However, major gaps exist in locally and regionally published statistical information on business and industry, wages and jobs. **Local Newspaper Indexing:** The staff of the Local History Division of the Pikes Peak Regional Library (see entry **CO37**) has indexed the *Colorado Springs Gazette Telegraph* since March 23, 1872. The articles indexed pertain to city, county, and regional affairs. Those articles pertaining to state government and legislation are also indexed. The Local History Division will accept research queries from other cities as to index citations.

Publications

CO17. Colorado Springs. City Clerk. *City of Colorado Springs Council Proceedings and Department Reports.* 1909- . Monthly.
This is a summary of council proceedings and department reports. It includes a statement of revenue for a three-month period, a statement of cash report by the treasurer covering a one-month period, and a statement of comparative sales.

CO18. Colorado Springs. Comptroller. *Annual Financial Report for the Year Ended. . . .* 1901?- . Annual.
Contains a financial section giving detailed financial statements and schedules for all funds and balanced account groups. Also includes statements of general fixed assets, general long-term and other debts, and a statistical section.

CO19. Colorado Springs. Department of Public Utilities. *Annual Report.* 1908?- . Annual.
Gives financial highlights, operating revenue statistics, revenue and expenditure graphs, service rates, historical sales and income data, balance sheets, statements of income and earned equity. Includes tables.

CO20. Colorado Springs. Department of Public Utilities. Resources Planning and Development. *Water Resources and Historical Water Use for Colorado Springs.* Compiled by Jack A. McCullough. 1974. 60pp.
Gives a summary on water resources and their historical use in the city. It also has a study with tables of the available water supply, a discussion of developed and undeveloped resources and an analysis of historical water use.

CO21. Colorado Springs. Fire Department. *Annual Report.* 1953- . Annual.
Covers the alarms received and responded to, the cost of operation and maintenance, activities of the fire inspectors of the Fire Prevention Bureau, activities of the training division, and other general information.

CO22. Colorado Springs. Fire Department. Fire Alarm Division. *Activities Report.* Monthly.

Statistics on alarms answered giving locations by address and a breakdown by types of alarms.

CO23. Colorado Springs. Job Service Center. *Colorado Springs Manpower Summary*. Denver: Department of Labor and Employment, July 1975–February 1977. Monthly.
Gives statistics on the resident labor force seasonally adjusted for both El Paso and Teller counties. It also gives a summary of industrial developments and unemployment insurance activities.

CO24. Colorado Springs. League of Women Voters. *This . . . Is Colorado Springs and El Paso County.* 1970. 48pp.
Contains information on city government and departments including an organization chart. Also describes all areas of county government and the area's cooperative ventures. General information on elections, voter qualifications, and registration is given.

CO25. Colorado Springs. Planning Department. *Planning Information Report.* 1975. 81pp.
This bulletin discusses problems and possible solutions concerning transportation and land use in Colorado Springs. There are many graphs, maps, tables, and illustrations.

CO26. Colorado Springs. Police Department. *Monthly Report* and *Annual Report.* Monthly: December 1974 to date; Annual: 1967–1974.
Area crime, area activity, traffic, criminal, and administrative reports are all given in each monthly report. The annual reports include statistical data for the year.

CO27. Colorado Springs. Public Works Office and Public Affairs Office. *Guide to Development in the Colorado Springs Area.* 1974. 49pp.
This is a manual for investors, developers, and contractors. Includes illustrations and maps. Also has information on city government, land acquisition and land use, construction and building.

CO28. Colorado Springs. Regional Building Department. *Monthly Reports of Building Permits Issued.* 1968– . Monthly.
Reports of building permits issued. Includes tables.

CO29. Colorado Springs and El Paso County. City-County Health Department. *Operating Budget.* Colorado Springs: Board of Health. Annual.
The goals, objectives, revenue summaries and program reviews are given for administration, health education, child health services, nursing homes, air quality control, and other relevant areas of the health department.

CO30. Colorado Springs and El Paso County. Planning Commission. *Annual Report.* Colorado Springs: Planning Commission, 1972– . Annual.
Provides a list of members of the planning commission and planning department; discusses bills requiring subdivision regulations; and summarizes a ground water study, reports from the various committees, and a statement on the Flood Plain Zone. Also a summarization of transportation planning is given.

CO31. Colorado Springs and El Paso County. Planning Office. *El Paso County Subdivision Regulations.* Colorado Springs: Planning Department, 1972. 9pp.
Land subdivision regulations.

CO32. Pikes Peak Area Council of Governments. *Alternative Population and Employment Forecasts, El Paso County 1975-2000: Detail Report.* Colorado Springs, 1974. 74pp.
Long-range forecasts of population and employment. This report presents three alternative forecasts of population and employment for the county. The forecasts are based on alternative assumptions which lead to slow, moderate, and rapid growth.

CO33. Pikes Peak Area Council of Governments. *Annual Report.* Colorado Springs, 1975. 16pp.
Highlights activities and goals. It discusses housing, regional economic developments, growth, environmental management, human resources services, and transportation.

CO34. Pikes Peak Area Council of Governments. *Current Population Estimates Analysis Areas/Census Tracts.* Colorado Springs, 1974. 33pp.
This report estimates current population by analysis areas and census tracts for the county.

CO35. Pikes Peak Area Council of Governments. *Financial Resources: Interim Report.* Colorado Springs, 1972. 125pp.
This study is designed to determine the sources and amounts of monies available for transportation purposes in the forecast years of 1970, 1975, 1980, 1985, and 1990. Includes all functions directly or indirectly related to highway transportation such as construction, maintenance, traffic police, traffic control, and administration.

CO36. Pikes Peak Area Council of Governments. *Housing Market Analysis, Pikes Peak Region.* Colorado Springs, 1970-   . Annual.
The report analyzes the current housing situation in the county housing market area. Determinations of current housing stock and current housing needs are made based on households in the region. The level of future activity that should be reached if housing needs are to be satisfied is forecast year by year to 1980 and in a single increment from 1980 to 2000.

Collections

CO37. **Pikes Peak Regional Library. Penrose Public Library.** P.O. Box 1579, Colorado Springs 80901 (303)473-2080.
The library has all of the publications of the city planning department available as reference material.

DENVER

The greatest weakness in the city and county of Denver's publishing program is that there is no depository provision with any library or archival institution. The Denver Public Library (see entry CO64) has been collecting Denver publications since the library's inception so it has many publications from the nineteenth century as well as very current material, but the collection is not complete. **Local Newspaper Indexing:** The Western History Department of the Denver Public Library selectively indexes the *Denver Post, Rocky Mountain News, Rocky Mountain Journal,* and the *Straight Creek Journal.* Queries are accepted.

Publications

CO38. Capitol Federal Savings. *Denver Metropolitan Area Vacancy Survey for Units over One Year Old.* Denver, 1971– . Quarterly.
Gives sampling of vacancy rates by predetermined areas, and correlates this information to the various types of units and their rental range. Two other areas (Denver-Boulder and Colorado Springs) are available in separate publications.

CO39. Colorado. State Treasurer. *The Bank Book: A Consumer Guide to Banking Services; Denver Metropolitan Edition.* Compiled by Edward T. Buckingham and Joan E. Hedahl. Denver, 1976.
Compares the actual costs of savings and checking accounts in the Denver Metropolitan Area.

CO40. Colorado University. Business Research Division. *What People in Denver Earn: Where and How They Spend It.* Compiled by Gerald L. Allen and David C. Maltais. Denver: Colorado National Bank, 1975. 44pp.
Comprehensive look at the cost of living in metropolitan Denver.

CO41. *Consumer Analysis.* Denver: Denver Post (P.O. Box 1709, Denver 80201), 1956– . Annual.
A market report compiled from the results of a questionnaire answered by approximately 3,000 Denver families. Contains information on income, employment, education, and shopping habits.

CO42. Denver. Chamber of Commerce. *Greater Denver Metroguide.* 1976-77. 136pp.
Provides an overview of the greater metropolitan area for corporate executives, planners, and managers, especially for those new to the region.

CO43. Denver. Community Renewal Program. *Denver: Condition of the City.* Compiled by David R. Vokac. Denver: Planning Office, 1973. 96pp.
The study analyzes the economic basis for renewal in Denver, specifically the extent of public and private economic and financial resources which may be available to Denver for future renewal programming. Emphasis is placed on historic and current trends of Denver's economy as the basis for evaluating prospective levels of future private and governmental economic activity.

CO44. Denver. Community Renewal Program. *Denver Neighborhood Analyses, Revised and Updated with 1975 Population Estimates.* Denver: Planning Office, 1975.
Gives a demographic and social condition profile of each of Denver's 73 neighborhoods.

CO45. Denver. League of Women Voters. *Know Your Denver Government.* (2200 W. Alameda, #15, Denver 80223) 1972. 75pp.
A guide to the government and city services of Denver.

CO46. Denver. Mayor. *Mayor's Budget.* 1948– . Annual.
This is the detailed budget submitted by the mayor to the city council.

CO47. Denver. Metropolitan Study Panel. *The Denver Region Citizen-Voter: Reported Ideas and Concerns.* Compiled by Karl Flaming. 1976.
A study of Denver area voter attitudes toward government services and metropolitan government.

CO48. Denver. Metropolitan Study Panel. *Finance and Taxation.* Compiled by A. J. Mackelprang. 1976.
A finance and taxation analysis of local governments in the Denver metropolitan region. The study projects fiscal trends to the year 1980.

CO49. Denver. Metropolitan Study Panel. *The Legal Implications of a Metropolitan Form of Government.* Compiled by Alan Merson and Nick Pijoan. 1976.
A study of the legal ramifications of establishing metropolitan area government. Includes a review of home rule, regional service authority legislation, etc.

CO50. Denver. Metropolitan Study Panel. *Metropolitan Change in Denver: Past Approaches.* 1976. 25pp.
The study reviews governmental reforms in the Denver region from 1902 to 1976; the consolidation of the city and county of Denver; population increases and geographical expansion; and the resulting realization that many of the current problems require a government with metropolitan jurisdiction.

CO51. Denver. Metropolitan Study Panel. *Neighborhood Level Services.* Compiled by Gordon Von Stroh et al. 1976.
The study explores the basic concept of neighborhood organization and how it might relate to a metropolitan organization. The focuses of the project included: (1) a review of the studies and literature on the concept of neighborhood-level organizations; (2) a study of neighborhood organizations in the Denver metropolitan area; (3) an evaluation of the development of neighborhood organizations in other selected cities; and (4) the presentation of alternatives and recommendations for the Denver metropolitan region.

CO52. Denver. Planning Office. *Denver: The Core City.* Compiled by Marvin Simpson. 1974. 24pp.
Compares Denver with the contiguous counties.

CO53. Denver. Planning Office. *A Plan for Historic Preservation in Denver.* 1974. 5 vols.
Provides an inventory, survey, and procedural manuals, and program descriptions relating to the subject of historical preservation of districts, buildings, structures, sites, and objects.

CO54. Denver. Planning Office. Central Area Planning Division. *Denver Central Area Historic Buildings and Places.* 1976. 12 leaves.

CO55. Denver. Planning Office. Planning Services Division. *Population Estimate.* 1975– . Annual.

CO56. Denver. Public Schools. Board of Education. *Directory.* 1915/16– Annual.
Contains assignments, an alphabetical listing of employees, organizations, meetings, and a school calendar.

CO57. Denver. University. *Denver Metropolitan Area Consumer Price Index.* (Denver 80210) 1964?– . Quarterly.
Contains Denver metropolitan area major group and subgroup index as well as a comparison with the U.S. *Consumer Price Index* for all items and major groups.

CO58. Denver. Urban Observatory. *Denver City Spending Priorities: Opinion and Analysis.* Compiled by Charles P. Rake. 1973.

A comprehensive study of the allocation of public expenditures in the city and county of Denver. It describes public spending priorities.

CO59. Regional Council of Governments. *Clean Water Program*. Denver, 1976. 31pp.

CO60. Regional Council of Governments. *COG Notations: A Report on Program Activities*. Denver, 1972– . Monthly.
Often includes population and economic statistics and trends.

CO61. Regional Council of Governments. *The Denver Regional Capital Improvement Program*. Denver, 1975. 3 vols.

CO62. Regional Council of Governments. *Metropolitan Water Requirements and Resources 1975-2000*. Compiled by the Denver Water Department. Denver, 1975. 3 vols.
Covers the water suppliers and distribution agencies.

CO63. Western Interstate Commission for Higher Education. Resource Development. Internship Program. *A Social-Economic Profile of the Denver Region*. Compiled by Joan Bassert. Boulder, 1975. 165pp.

Collections

CO64. **Denver Public Library.** 1357 Broadway, Denver 80203 (303)573-5152 ext. 220.
The Government Publications Division of the library is a regional depository for U.S. government publications. It also maintains a collection of Colorado state publications, Denver city and county government publications, and regional publications from agencies in which Colorado or Denver are members. The state, regional, and most of the Denver collections are fully cataloged. Since 1971, Denver publications have been included in the *Index to Current Urban Documents* published by Greenwood Press.

PUEBLO

Local Newspaper Indexing: The staff of the Pueblo Regional Library (see entry CO74) selectively indexes the *Star-Journal* and *Pueblo Chieftain* and will accept queries.

Publications

CO65. Comi, Gladys R. *The Last Ten Years: A History of the Pueblo Regional Planning Commission*. Pueblo Regional Planning Commission (1 City Hall Pl., Pueblo 81003), 1970. 27pp.

CO66. Dahlin, Donald C., and Jay M. Newberger. *The Youth Services Systems in Pueblo County*. Pueblo: Pueblo Area Council of Governments (1 City Hall Pl., Pueblo 81003), 1973. 101pp.

CO67. Pueblo Area Council of Governments. Human Resources Commission. *Inventory of Human Resources*. 3rd ed. (1 City Hall Pl., Pueblo 81003) 1976. 231pp. $5.

This is an inventory of 214 human service agencies, organizations, clubs, and associations in the Pueblo area.

CO68. Pueblo Area Council of Governments. Regional Planning Commission. *An Analysis of the Market for Public Housing in Pueblo as of January 1, 1972.* (1 City Hall Pl., Pueblo 81003) 1972. 32pp.

CO69. Pueblo Area Council of Governments. Regional Planning Commission. *Pueblo Design Quarterly.* (1 City Hall Pl., Pueblo 81003) 1973. Free.
The existing three issues, which were prepared in magazine format, cover landscape design for Pueblo citizens, architecture in Pueblo, and facts about Pueblo.

CO70. Pueblo Area Council of Governments. Regional Planning Commission. *Pueblo Regional Fact Book.* (1 City Hall Pl., Pueblo 81003) 1961. 106pp.
Intended as a reference volume for public officials and others. Stress is on factual data covering population, housing, land use, climate, water and minerals, energy resources, transportation, and the economy.

CO71. Pueblo Manpower Area Planning Council. *Labor Market Analysis of Pueblo.* Compiled by Walt Speckman. Pueblo: Human Resources Commission (1 City Hall Pl., Pueblo 81003), 1973. 42pp.

CO72. Pueblo Regional Library. *Catalog of the Western Research Collection.* (100 E. Abriendo Ave., Pueblo 81004) 1976. 301pp. Free.
A catalog of the items in the collection.

CO73. Pueblo. School District 60. *Directory.* (Public Relations Office, 102 W. Orman, Pueblo 81004). Annual. Free.

Collections

CO74. *Pueblo Regional Library.* 100 E. Abriendo Ave., Pueblo 81004 (303) 544-1940.
Local Newspaper Indexing: The library staff selectively indexes the *Star-Journal* and *Pueblo Chieftain*, and will accept queries.

CONNECTICUT

General Publications

CT1. Connecticut. Department of Commerce. *Connecticut Market Data.* Hartford (210 Washington St., Hartford 06106). Annual. $5.
Covers marketing data including income, population, retail trade, media, employment, housing, motor vehicles, and regional planning.

CT2. Connecticut. Development Commission. *Community Monographs.* Hartford, 1970- . (Available from: Connecticut Development Commission, Department of Commerce, 210 Washington St., Hartford 06106.)
Concise, general introduction to each town or city covered. It includes information on location, climate, topography, government, taxation, housing, education, labor statistics, planning and zoning, local media, banking and finance, etc. Each report is compiled by the town covered.

CT3. *Connecticut Manufacturing Directory.* Hartford: Connecticut Labor Department (200 Folly Brook Blvd., Wethersfield 06109), 1973. $5.
Lists all manufacturing firms and workshops (laundries and dry cleaning, auto repair shops, etc.). Name, address, and brief description of products are given.

CT4. Connecticut Public Expenditure Council Inc. *Municipal Budgets in Connecticut.* Hartford (21 Lewis St., Hartford 06103), 1975/76- . Annual?
Statistical comparison of the budgets of most Connecticut municipalities. It gives the sources of revenue and a breakdown of expenditures in broad categories. Additional information includes property tax data, school enrollment, form of government, area, and number of miles of town roads.

CT5. Connecticut. State Department of Education. *Connecticut Education Directory.* Hartford (Box 2219, Hartford 06115). Annual.
Lists address, telephone number, and administrator for all schools; public, private, and special on all levels of education in the state. Also included are city and state boards and their staff members.

CT6. Connecticut. Secretary of State. *Register and Manual.* Hartford, 1977. 902pp. Annual.
Gives public officials, regional planning agencies, regional councils of governments, regional transit districts, and town chairmen and vice-chairmen of both political parties. It also has information about state newspapers, radio and television stations, associations, societies, hospitals, and election statistics.

CT7. State Industrial Directories Corp. *Connecticut State Industrial Directory*. New York, NY: (2 Penn Plaza, New York 10001). Annual.
Lists all industrial corporations in the state and information such as their address, employee and plant data, and product description.

BRIDGEPORT

Data not available at this time.

HARTFORD

Local Newspaper Indexing: Since 1945 the Hartford Public Library (see entry CT17) has maintained a Highlight Index of the *Hartford Courant* and the *Hartford Times;* the latter ceased publication in October 1976. Inquiries are welcome.

Publications

CT8. Greater Hartford. Chamber of Commerce. *Greater Hartford Economic Facts*. Hartford (250 Constitution Plaza, Hartford 06103), 1976.
This resource provides information on the economy of the greater Hartford area. It covers labor, markets, services, transportation, central city, and environment.

CT9. Hartford. City Hall. *City of Hartford Directory of City Officials.* (550 Main St., Hartford 06103) 1973.
Lists the departments, commissions, and other agencies of Hartford's municipal government. Also included are a list of the mayors of Hartford from 1784, when the city was incorporated, until 1973, with the dates of their terms of office; and a list of the clerks of the city of Hartford, with the dates that they assumed office.

CT10. The Hartford Courant. *Where to Get Help in Greater Hartford*. (285 Broad St., Hartford 06105) n.d. 31pp. Updated edition in progress. Free.
This pamphlet lists social service agencies available to local residents. A map is also included for aid in locating the services.

CT11. Hartford. Court of Common Council. *Journal of the Court of Common Council of the City of Hartford.* City Clerk (550 Main St., Hartford 06103), n.d.
The *Journal*, the official record of the activities of the Hartford Court of Common Council, records the proceedings of the regular and special sessions of the council. Council discussion and action on ordinances, proposals, amendments, proclamations, resolutions, hearings, committee reports, and other municipal activities are contained in the *Journal.*

CT12. Hartford. Department of Health, Division on Aging. *Directory of Elderly Aid*. City Court of Common Council (550 Main St., Hartford 06103), 1973? $5.
Acquaints senior citizens of Hartford with the federal, state, local, public, and private agencies in the area.

CT13. Hartford. Human Relations Commission. *Minority Registry of Construction Services.* Vol. 2. (550 Main St., Hartford 06103) 1973.
This registry comprises a comprehensive listing of minority and construction-related services in the region. Also listed are agencies able to provide assistance to minority contractors, community and other resource agencies and firms.

CT14. Hartford. Public Schools. *Directory, 1973-1974.* (249 High St., Hartford 06103) 1974. Irregular.
Lists personnel by area of specialization or department, and by schools. Also included are the names and addresses of the Board of Education members; lists of schools, centers, and school-related programs with addresses and telephone numbers; and a telephone directory for central administrative personnel.

CT15. La Casa de Puerto Rico. *A Study of Educational Opportunities for the Spanish-Speaking in Hartford.* Compiled by Adriana Falcon. Hartford: Lincoln Institute (University of Hartford, 26 Trowbridge St., Cambridge, MA 02138), 1978. 78pp.
This report addresses the subject of education for Spanish-speaking individuals in Hartford. Gives figures on the number and distribution of Spanish-speaking students in Hartford schools, describes their problems, and makes recommendations for meeting the problems. The section on vocational-technical education gives enrollment figures for schools statewide, and suggests ways to increase the Spanish-speaking enrollment in these schools. The sections on adult education and higher education identify and evaluate opportunities for the Spanish-speaking community of Hartford in these areas, and conclude with recommendations for improvements.

CT16. Southern New England Telephone Company. *Market Report: The Hartford Area, 1977-1978.* (227 Church St., New Haven 06506) Annual.
The report is a compilation of facts and figures useful for business or industries considering locating in the Hartford area. Data furnished include retail sales receipts, number of building permits, employment figures, description of transportation facilities, visitor attractions, etc. The last section comprises a listing of industries located in the area.

Collections

CT17. The Hartford Public Library. 500 Main St., Hartford 06103 (203)525-9121.
The Hartford Public Library presently receives a number of annual reports from various city departments. The Court of Common Council's *Annual Budget,* the City Manager's *Annual Report,* and the Finance Department's *Financial Report* are three such valuable resources. A July 5, 1977 directive issued by the Hartford city manager, which instructs all city departments to forward four copies of any and all public materials to the library, should strengthen the library's municipal documents collection. In addition, it will enable the library to participate in Greenwood Press's *Index to Current Urban Documents.* The weakness which exists is that information is outdated rather quickly. Also, due to financial limitations, publication of valuable resources is often interrupted or dropped. For example, the latest *Public School Directory* was issued in 1973. The public library updates information by pencil correcting certain reference resources and by daily indexing of the local newspaper.

NEW HAVEN

Local Newspaper Indexing: The New Haven Free Public Library (see entry CT24) has been indexing the *New Haven Register* and the *New Haven Journal-Courier* since 1965. The index concentrates on city and state politics and government, education, business, crime, local biography, community affairs, special events, etc. There is a large clipping file covering the period prior to 1965, with the local papers available on microfilm from 1954.

Publications

CT18. New Haven. *City Yearbook.* New Haven: n.p., 1871–1952. o.p.
Abstracts city department and agency reports to the mayors from 1871 to 1952.

CT19. New Haven. *Manual of the City Government, New Haven, Conn.*
New Haven: Town Clerk (Hall of Records, Rm. 307, 200 Orange St., New Haven 06510), 1940– . Annual. Free.
Contains names and addresses of major city officials and employees, list of city departments and their heads, and city boards and their members.

CT20. New Haven. *Annual Reports of the City Boards and Agencies.* New Haven: n.p. Annual. Free. (Available from: the reporting agencies.)
Each city agency and department is required to file a report of its activities for the preceding year with the mayor in January. Copies are also to be filed with the public library, but there are large gaps in the library's collection. Its most complete holdings relate to the police and fire departments, and housing and redevelopment departments.

CT21. New Haven. Board of Aldermen. *Journal of the Board of Aldermen of the City of New Haven.* 1889– . Annual. Free. (Available from: Town Clerk, Hall of Records, Rm. 307, 200 Orange St., New Haven 06510.)
Contains minutes of the meetings of the New Haven Board of Aldermen, the city's legislative body.

CT22. New Haven. Board of Finance. *Budget, City of New Haven, Conn.*
1958– . Annual. Free.
Detailed breakdown of allocations to city agencies.

CT23. New Haven. Greater New Haven Chamber of Commerce. *Economic Profile and Industrial Directory of South Central Connecticut.* (195 Church St., New Haven 06510) Annual. $7.
Directory of business and economic trends for the New Haven SMSA. It includes population, economic trends, media in the area, a list of manufacturers in the county, a census of county business, etc.

Collections

CT24. New Haven Free Public Library. 133 Elm St., New Haven 06510 (203)562-0151 ext. 1302.
The library collects documents, records, and general history of the city of New Haven.

STAMFORD

Each of the city agencies and commissions issues an annual report to the mayor that ranges from a simple letter to a published report. Minutes of major city boards are kept on file at the town clerk's office, and minutes of the Board of Education and Board of Representatives are kept at the Ferguson Library (see entry **CT31**). The library attempts to acquire all town and city documents; however, as only one copy is often published, obtaining a file copy for the library is sometimes difficult. **Local Newspaper Indexing:** The *Advocate*, Stamford's daily newspaper, is not indexed. The staff of the Ferguson Library (see entry **CT31**) clips and selectively subject categories the newspaper items for a local file. The Ferguson Library also maintains a card file index to the obituary notices appearing in the *Advocate*.

Publications

CT25. Stamford Area Commerce and Industry Association. *A Directory of Industry and Corporations of Southwestern Connecticut.* Edited by Thais E. Morgan. (1 Landmark Sq., Stamford 06901) Annual.
A list of manufacturing-service firms in southwestern Connecticut.

CT26. Stamford Genealogical Society. *Connecticut Ancestry.* (P.O. Box 249, Stamford 06904) 1958– . Quarterly. $7 annually.
This publication deals with Stamford's local history and the genealogy of many of its families.

CT27. Stamford. League of Women Voters. *They Represent Us.* (P.O. Box 3402, Stamford 06905) Annual.
A listing of all city boards, commissions, appointed and elected officials, and all state and federal elected officials that represent Stamford. Phone numbers and dates of terms are also given.

CT28. Stamford. League of Women Voters. *This Is Stamford.* Annual. Free.
A brief description of all city boards and agencies, schools, hospitals, and public services. A brief city history and organization chart are also given.

CT29. Taxation Board of the City of Stamford. *Real Estate on the Grand List.* (429 Atlantic St., Stamford 06901) Annual.
Gives the assigned value for taxation of all property in the city.

CT30. Voluntary Action Center of S.W. Fairfield County. *VAC Guide to Community Services.* Stamford: Stamford Junior League, n.d. Free.
A listing of all groups and agencies that provide community services. It covers such areas as legal services, personal and social services, housing, and employment services.

Collections

CT31. The Ferguson Library. 96 Broad St., Stamford 06901 (203)325-4354. The library has the minutes of Board of Representatives and Board of Education. Municipal documents are part of the reference collection and do not circulate.

WATERBURY

Local Newspaper Indexing: Since 1976 the Silas Bronson Library (see entry **CT56**) has indexed the local newspapers on a selective basis, concentrating on municipal events and activities. The library staff will accept index citation inquiries. Comprehensive indexing is done by the newspaper librarian at the *Waterbury Republican-American* for the newspaper staff.

Publications

CT32. Central Naugatuck Valley Regional Planning Agency. *Annual Report 1975-76: Regional Transportation Planning Program.* (20 E. Main St., Waterbury 06702) 1976. 25pp.
The report describes accomplishments of the program over the past year, future aims, and the various organizations involved in the transportation planning process, maps showing the location of locally approved transportation projects, general characteristics of the region, and a description of its transportation system.

CT33. Central Naugatuck Valley Regional Planning Agency. *Base to Unit Three! Base to Unit Three! The Waterbury Mini Transit Service: 1972-1975.* (20 E. Main St., Waterbury 06702) 1975. 41pp.
This document contains a history of the Waterbury Model Neighborhood Mini Transit Service since its inception in 1972. The report indicates the typical user, destination, and the patterns of travel within the city.

CT34. Central Naugatuck Valley Regional Planning Agency. *Child Care: A Parents' Guide for the CNVR: 1976.* (20 E. Main St., Waterbury 06702) 1976. 81pp.
This guide provides a complete listing of all State Department of Health licensed child care centers in the Central Naugatuck Valley Regional Planning Agency.

CT35. Central Naugatuck Valley Regional Planning Agency. *Communications Element.* (20 E. Main St., Waterbury 06702) 1975. 22pp.
This report highlights the major characteristics and trends of the media serving the region and its municipalities.

CT36. Central Naugatuck Valley Regional Planning Agency. *Criminal Justice Element.* (20 E. Main St., Waterbury 06702) 1975. 68pp.
This report is a compilation of police, court, and correctional program data on the amount of crime, rate of crime, cost of crime, location of crime, disposition of offenders, and the recidivism rate for the region and its municipalities. The tables present information on past trends and current conditions as well as an analysis of critical crime problems in the region.

CT37. Central Naugatuck Valley Regional Planning Agency. *Economic Development: 1976.* (20 E. Main St., Waterbury 06702) 1975. 45pp.
This document contains a detailed analysis of trends in employment, industrial location, commercial sales, and manpower. Areas of potential economic growth are discussed.

CT38. Central Naugatuck Valley Regional Planning Agency. *Education Element: 1975.* (20 E. Main St., Waterbury 06702) 1975. 35pp.
This document contains a detailed analysis of educational resources and expenditures in relation to demographic trends and financial capacity. The report presents an overview of trends in education and its financing.

CT39. Central Naugatuck Valley Regional Planning Agency. *Equal Opportunity.* (20 E. Main St., Waterbury 06702) 1975. 27pp.
The report is a compilation of pertinent federal and state employment and housing laws prohibiting discrimination in the region and its municipalities. The report also discusses municipal zoning, sewerage, building requirements, and public transit as they affect the opportunities of residents within the region.

CT40. Central Naugatuck Valley Regional Planning Agency. *Fire Prevention and Suppression.* (20 E. Main St., Waterbury 06702) 1975. 42pp.
This report is a compilation of fire statistics for the region and its municipalities. The tables present information on past trends, current problem areas, and the manpower and water resources of the region's municipalities.

CT41. Central Naugatuck Valley Regional Planning Agency. *Historic Landmarks and Programs for Preservation.* (20 E. Main St., Waterbury 06702) 1976. 54pp.
This report lists the historic resources of the National Register, Connecticut Historical Commission, and localities as they pertain to the region. A detailed inventory of methods of preservation, their costs and benefits, and regional goals, objectives, and policies is also given.

CT42. Central Naugatuck Valley Regional Planning Agency. *Housing Element: 1975.* (20 E. Main St., Waterbury 06702) 1975. 133pp.
This document examines the region's present housing situation, identifies regional housing problems and needs, and sets forth policies to address these issues. The report also contains an analysis of demographic, social and economic characteristics and trends of the region's population and presents population projections for the region and its municipalities. Finally, a descriptive inventory of currently funded federal and state housing programs and income eligibility requirements for those programs is presented in the appendices.

CT43. Central Naugatuck Valley Regional Planning Agency. *Manpower Report for the Waterbury Labor Market Area (WLMA): 1975.* (20 E. Main St., Waterbury 06702) 1975. 69pp.
This report presents an analysis of employment and unemployment trends in the WLMA. It contains a description of the general characteristics of the Waterbury labor market area labor force, the geographic boundaries of the labor market area and an inventory of existing manpower planning and training programs in the region.

CT44. Central Naugatuck Valley Regional Planning Agency. *Profile of the Central Naugatuck Valley Region: 1970-74.* (20 E. Main St., Waterbury 06702) 1976. 34pp.
The report is a compilation of post-census population, employment, and housing data. The tables provide information on the general trends in the region and its municipalities since 1970 when the last census was taken. Data in the report come from various federal, state, and local sources.

CT45. Central Naugatuck Valley Regional Planning Agency. *Social Services Element: 1975.* (20 E. Main St., Waterbury 06702) 1975. 25pp.
This report contains a brief discussion of the development of the social services system and an overview of the major issues in social services. A series of indicators of regional needs are given and efforts being made to improve the system.

CT46. Central Naugatuck Valley Regional Planning Agency. *Some Answers to Your Questions about Septic Systems.* 1974. 23pp.
A series of five questions commonly raised by the municipal commissions and officials involved with land use development concerning septic systems are answered in the light of a recent research publication, *Longevity of Septic Systems in Connecticut Soils* (Bulletin 747, June 1974, by David E. Hill and Charles R. Frink of the Connecticut Experiment Station, New Haven).

CT47. Central Naugatuck Valley Regional Planning Agency. *A Statistical Packet for the Central Naugatuck Valley Region: 1975.* (20 E. Main St., Waterbury 06702) 1975. 42pp.
This report is a compilation of selected population and housing data for the region and its municipalities. The tables present information on past trends and current conditions.

CT48. Central Naugatuck Valley Regional Planning Agency. *Zoning in the CNVR.* (20 E. Main St., Waterbury 06702) 1971. 117pp.
This report summarizes existing zoning plans and regulations in the region. Included are local regulations governing the use of residential, commercial, industrial, and special land uses.

CT49. *Direction: A Directory of Community Services.* Edited by Michael DeLeo. Waterbury: The Waterbury Foundation. 1976. 75pp. o.p.
The booklet, arranged alphabetically by subject, lists community service organizations and agencies in the greater Waterbury area.

CT50. Southern New England Telephone Company. *Market Report: The Waterbury-Cheshire Area 1977-78.* (333 Meadow St., Waterbury 06702) 1977. 127pp.
The report covers Waterbury and surrounding towns. It includes many facts and figures on the area's economic picture, employment and unemployment statistics, building permits, housing units, commuting patterns, educational facilities, industrial and business growth, and downtown redevelopment. For each municipality brief information is given on the form of government, population, tax rate, educational facilities, expenditures, community services, recreational facilities, churches, media, and transportation. A list of manufacturers and their products is also included.

CT51. Waterbury. Board of Aldermen. *Journal of the Board of Aldermen of the City of Waterbury.* Annual. (Available from: City Clerk's Office, City Hall, Waterbury 06702.)
The publication includes minutes of all Board of Aldermen meetings.

CT52. Waterbury. City Clerk's Office. *Budget of the City of Waterbury.* (City Hall, Waterbury 06702) 1977. $1.
Includes estimates of the expenses, liabilities, and resources of the city for the current fiscal year as submitted to and approved by the Board of Finance and Board of Aldermen. All city departmental budgets are included.

CT53. Waterbury. Comptroller. *Financial Report of the City for Fiscal Year Ending December 31, 1974.* 1974. 236pp.
Includes certification of the financial report of the city of Waterbury by the city auditor, plus a report of an independent audit firm.

CT54. Waterbury. Ordinances, Local Laws, etc. *The Charter and Related Laws of the City of Waterbury,* published by order of the City, 1967. (Supplementary revisions are issued every two years.) Charlottesville, VA: Michie City Pub. Co., 1967 642pp. $35. (Available from: City Clerk's Office, City Hall, Waterbury 06702.)
Codification of the general ordinances of the city. It is updated to include all charter amendments and ordinance changes.

CT55. Waterbury. Youth Service System. *Services for Youth in the City of Waterbury, 1976.* (YMCA, 136 W. Main St., Waterbury 06702) 1976. 46pp. Semi-annual.

The directory lists all programs and services available to Waterbury youth under the age of 18. The format is a loose-leaf binder.

Collections

CT56. Silas Bronson Library. 267 Grand St., Waterbury 06702 (203)755-2218. The main city documents held are *The Charter and Related Laws of the City of Waterbury* (see entry **CT54**) and *Journal of the Board of Aldermen* (see entry **CT51**). There are no municipally produced bibliographies or checklists on Waterbury documents. Annual reports of the various city departments are available at the Silas Bronson Library and the city clerk's office. A directory of city officials is available from the mayor's office and at the library. There is no organizational chart.

The Bronson Library attempts to acquire all current municipal publications and has in its collection documents pertaining to local government as far back as the late 1880s. Interlibrary loan of the materials may be restricted in some cases due to the scarcity of certain documents (photocopy service is available at a small, per page charge with a minimum charge of $1). The most prolific publisher, at present, is the Central Naugatuck Valley Regional Planning Agency which serves the greater Waterbury area.

DELAWARE

General Publications

DE1. Delaware. Department of Public Instruction. *Directory of Delaware Schools.* (Dover 19901) 1914– . Annual. $5.
Names of Boards of Education members, administrators of each school district, and each school are given as well as names and addresses of all public and private schools, special schools and services, and colleges.

DE2. Delaware. State Planning Office. *Delaware Statistical Abstract.* (Thomas Collins Bldg., Dover 19901) 1973– . Annual. $5.
Statistics are given for the state and in some cases by county or by school district. While not specifically for each city, the publication acts as an index to the kinds of statistics being collected by each state office.

DE3. Delaware. University. Library. Reference Department. *Bibliography of Delaware: 1960–1974.* Newark: Hugh M. Morris Library, University of Delaware, 1976. 226pp. $5. (Available from: Bookstore, University of Delaware, Newark 19711.)
This compilation supplements Henry Clay Reed's and Marion B. Reed's *A Bibliography of Delaware* (University of Delaware Press, 1966), indexes Delaware periodicals for their Delaware content, and lists all dissertations and theses completed on Delaware topics. City and state serial publications were not included but special studies on particular problems were.

DE4. Reed, Henry Clay, and Marion Bjornson, compilers. *A Bibliography of Delaware through 1960.* Newark: University of Delaware Press, 1966. 196pp. $9.50. (Available from: Bookstore, University of Delaware, Newark 19711.)
This bibliography is an important checklist for documents published by Delaware cities. All items listed may be found in the collections of libraries within the state.

NEWARK

Newark, a small city, does not publish reference books but is included in several that have been published for the state as a whole. The City of Newark Technical Library (see entry **DE7**) has the only complete holdings of recent materials.

The Wilmington newspapers are good sources of information for Newark and for the entire state. A clipping file by subject since 1955 has been kept by the News Journal Company Library (831 Orange Street, Wilmington). Additional sources of information are the League of Women Voters of Newark (913 Pickett Lane, Newark) and the Newark Chamber of Commerce (250 E. Main St., Newark). The College of Urban Affairs and Public Policy at the University of Delaware (see entry **DE9**) has completed studies for a number of local governments in the state and should also be contacted.

Publications

DE5. Newark. League of Women Voters. *This Is Greater Newark.* (913 Pickett Lane, Newark 19711) 1975. 32pp. Free.
Intended as a guide for the Newark citizen, this booklet describes all city services giving telephone numbers of persons to contact. There is a brief explanation of the city budget, the tax calendar, and voter registration. Sections are also included for human and social services, medical services, schools, and leisure activities. A new edition is scheduled for publication in spring 1978.

DE6. *Your Newark City Government.* City of Newark (P.O. Box 390, Newark 19711), 1972- . Quarterly. Free.
This city newsletter provides timely information on city problems and achievements, parks and recreation schedules, recycling days, and the like. Fiscal data are given along with information on capital budget improvements.

Collections

DE7. City of Newark Technical Library. Municipal Bldg., 220 Elkton Rd., Newark 19711 (302)366-7095.
The library has the major city publications and a collection of books and magazines which contain material on the government and its activities. City documents are supplied for Greenwood Press's *Index to Current Urban Documents.* Many city publications are mimeographed for internal use. Documents felt to be of interest to other cities are supplied annually to Greenwood Press.

DE8. University of Delaware. Hugh M. Morris Library. Newark 19711 (302) 738-2236. Teletype Service: (510)666-0850.
The library has historic holdings for Newark but few current municipal documents.

DE9. University of Delaware. College of Urban Affairs and Public Policy. Department Library, Newark 19711 (302)738-2394.
While the purpose of this library is to serve the College of Urban Affairs and Public Policy, others are permitted to use the collection and to borrow material. The collection for Newark includes studies done by the college in cooperation with the city, some city documents, and papers written by urban affairs students on Newark issues. Most items were written since 1960. Other local governments in the state are represented in the collection. Publications prepared by the college may be purchased.

WILMINGTON

Local Newspaper Indexing: The Wilmington Institute Library (see entry **DE19**) selectively indexes the Wilmington *Morning News,* the city's morning newspaper. The library will accept queries from researchers in other cities as to index citations.

Publications

DE10. Delaware. Department of Labor. *The Wilmington Labor Area: Employment, Hours, and Earnings.* Dover. November, 1960- . Monthly.
This publication discusses labor conditions in the city and the statistics from the

U.S. Department of Labor. Included are monthly statistics on Wilmington manufacturing and labor turnover.

DE11. Delaware. League of Local Governments. *Directory of Delaware's Local Government Officials.* (P.O. Box 484, 134 E. Water St., Dover 19901) 1976. 32pp. Updated periodically. $25.
Lists the name, address, and home telephone number of the mayor, council members, city clerk, and city solicitor.

DE12. Delaware State Chamber of Commerce Inc. *Synopsis of New Castle Council Meetings, Wilmington City Council Meetings and Status Reports of Legislation of Both Councils.* (1102 West St., Wilmington 19801) Weekly.
In this loose-leaf binder each week's county and city council meetings are reported. The synopses are arranged in two ways: first, each ordinance is discussed according to subject. This is followed by a compilation of the current status and legislative history of the proposed ordinances and resolutions under consideration.

DE13. Greater Wilmington. League of Women Voters. *How Wilmington Serves You.* Wilmington, 1976. 43pp.
This handbook describes the organization of the city government, the function and purpose of each agency, agency addresses and telephone numbers, and all the different services and special programs sponsored by the city.

DE14. New Castle County. Department of Elections. *City of Wilmington Street Directory.* Wilmington, n.d. 40pp.
Lists all the streets in the city and tells which election district, state representative district, state senate district, county council district, and city council district to which each street belongs.

DE15. Wilmington. *Annual Budget: City of Wilmington.* Wilmington: n.p., 1967– . Annual.
This work contains the budget of each agency that comprises the municipal government. Included is the amount allocated for salaries for each position within each agency, and the mayor's budget message.

Wilmington City Council. See entry **DE12**.

DE16. Wilmington. *Report of Audit of the City of Wilmington.* Wilmington: n.p., Vol. 1, 1907– . Annual.
Lists the financial information of each of the areas that the city is responsible for (i.e., utilities and public safety). Also included are the city's schedule of investments and bond interest obligations.

DE17. Wilmington. Division of Social and Human Development. *A Profile of Wilmington: A Compilation and Interpretation of 1970 Census Data.* n.d. 134pp.
This statistical analysis of the different residential neighborhoods of Wilmington is based on the 1970 census. A statistical breakdown by race, sex, and age is given. Among the topics covered in each neighborhood are population, household relationships, school enrollment, occupation, family income, and cost of housing.

DE18. Wilmington. Ordinances, Local Laws, etc. *City of Wilmington Code: Charter, Related Laws and the General Ordinances.* 2 vols. Charlottesville, VA: Michie City Pub. Co., 1969.

The charter of the city as well as city ordinances are given. At the end of the second volume, there is a subject index to the code of ordinances.

Collections

DE19. Wilmington Institute Library. Tenth and Market Sts., Wilmington 19801 (302)656-3131.
The library attempts to collect as many municipal documents as it can. The documents, which are kept with the local history materials, do not circulate. However, there are photocopy services available for a small per page charge.

DISTRICT OF COLUMBIA

Local Newspaper Indexing: The Washington Division of the D.C. Public Library (see entry **DC10**) clips material on the city government and files it by subject. The *Washington Post* is indexed by Bell and Howell Company (Micro Photo Division, Old Mansfield Road, Wooster, OH 44691).

Publications

DC1. District of Columbia. Department of Economic Development. *Directory of Public Data Sources for Areas below City Level.* Washington, DC: Office of the Mayor, 1973. 190pp. $2.75.

DC2. District of Columbia. Executive Office of the Mayor-Commissioner. Office of the Executive Secretary. *Government of the District of Columbia Departmental and Agency Fact Sheet.* Washington, DC, 1972. 186pp.
This describes 40 official departments and gives an overview of local government. For each department there is a statement of purpose, general status, and leadership; and a concise summary of activities, problems, plans, major operational facilities, etc.

DC3. Metropolitan Washington Council of Governments. *Directory of Special Transportation Services in the Metropolitan Washington Area.* (Metropolitan Information Center, 1225 Connecticut Ave. N.W., Washington, DC 20036) 1975. 75pp. Free.
This directory (updated edition available shortly) is intended to assist those individuals with special needs (e.g., handicapped or the elderly) to find the agency necessary to provide the transportation services they require.

DC4. Metropolitan Washington Council of Governments. *Governments of the Washington Metropolitan Area.* (Metropolitan Information Center, 1225 Connecticut Ave. N.W., Washington, DC 20036) 1968-   . Irregular.
Outlines the major local governmental functions and their relationship to the District of Columbia. This manual also describes local governments and gives city hall addresses, legal bases, general government responsibilities, other local agencies, and organization charts. Other parts of the work explain intergovernmental organizations and list state agencies with identical functions.

DC5. Metropolitan Washington Council of Governments. *Guide to Social Services Directories in the Washington Metropolitan Area.* (Metropolitan Information Center, 1225 Connecticut Ave. N.W., Washington, DC 20036) 1976. 90pp. $3.
Covers available directories which provide data on social services available to residents of the DC area.

DC6. Metropolitan Washington Council of Governments. *Major Centers of Employment—1976 (Map).* (Metropolitan Information Center, 1225 Connecticut Ave. N.W., Washington, DC 20036) 1976. Free.
It is to be updated every two years and to identify major employment centers in the area.

DC7. Metropolitan Washington Council of Governments. *Metropolitan Washington Areawide Local Government Job Vacancy List.* (Metropolitan Information Center, 1225 Connecticut Ave. N.W., Washington, DC 20036) Monthly. $1 per issue. Contact persons are identified for available jobs.

DC8. Metropolitan Washington Council of Governments. *Metropolitan Washington Directory of Nursing Homes and Related Facilities for the Aged.* (Metropolitan Information Center, 1225 Connecticut Ave. N.W., Washington, DC 20036) 1975. 35pp. $1.
Lists the facilities and their addresses, telephone numbers, and bed capacities. The Metropolitan Washington Council of Governments also issues *Metropolitan Washington Directory of Nursing Homes Certified for Participation in Medicare and Medicaid Programs* (1975, 23pp, $1).

DC9. Metropolitan Washington Council of Governments. *Metropolitan Washington Regional Directory.* (Metropolitan Information Center, 1225 Connecticut Ave. N.W., Washington, DC 20036) Annual with periodic updates. Free.
The directory covers elected officials (their names, titles, addresses, and office telephone numbers) and members of the Virginia and Maryland legislatures, of the United States Congress, and of regional organizations. The directory also gives meeting schedules for local governments and population estimates for the area.

Collections

DC10. D.C. Public Library. Washingtoniana Division. 901 G St., Washington, DC 20001 (202)727-1213.
The library has an extensive collection of local documents. The Municipal Reference Library for District of Columbia has been subsumed by the D.C. Public Library.

DC11. Metropolitan Washington Council of Governments. 1225 Connecticut Avenue N.W., Washington, DC 20036 (202)223-6800.
The Metropolitan Washington Council of Governments (COG) has a research library, map library, and information center. The Research Library collects local documents needed by the staff and lists them in *COG Wheel,* a bimonthly, annotated bibliography. The library also collects all of the city and county codes.
   The Map Library collects current and retrospective maps for the District of Columbia, Prince George's County, Montgomery County, Alexandria County, Arlington County, Fairfax County, Loudoun County, and Prince William County. These maps pertain to subjects such as land use and transportation. Maps in the collection are available for public use; only those produced by COG are available for sale or reproduction. The Map Library has a computer printout of its holdings, which is arranged by geographic area, subject, scale, and author. The section listing maps produced by COG is available by special request for $5 per copy.
   The Information Center serves two functions: sale and distribution of COG publications and answering questions (by phone, mail, and walk-in customers) concerning any level of government. Only when a customer needs in-depth information or research material is a referral made to the Research Library. The Information Center collects local documents on a smaller scale than the Research Library. Their

collection consists of directories, statistical reports, and informational or promotional type items such as summer park programs and adult education courses. The Information Center issues *Publications Metropolitan Washington Council of Governments*, which lists the publications and provides other information.

In summary, the Council of Governments, which was established in 1957, is concerned with all aspects of metropolitan development and regional planning. It is the areawide organization of the government officials located in the region's major cities and counties, and members of the Maryland and Virginia legislatures, and the U.S. Congress.

(See also entry **US4**.)

FLORIDA

General Publications

FL1. Brown, Arnetta. *Our Florida Government.* Lakeland: League of Women Voters of Florida (1035-S S. Florida Ave., Lakeland 33803), 1977. 28pp. $1.
Brief chapters on elections and local government. It includes municipalities with pie charts of revenue and expenditures at county and municipal levels. Most local leagues have studies available of their cities and/or counties. The publication dates, sizes, and prices vary from place to place.

FL2. Florida Atlantic University. Library. *FAU-FIU Joint Center for Environmental and Urban Problems* (KWIC Index). Compiled by Elaine Kelly. (Boca Raton 33431) 1976. 248pp.
Listing of materials on the urban and environmental areas including federal, state, and local government documents; maps; periodicals and major works in the field.

FL3. Florida Atlantic University. Library. *Florida State Document KWIC Index.* Edited by Elaine Kelly. (Boca Raton 33431) 1976. 407pp. Annual. (Available from: Department of State, Florida State Library, Tallahassee 32304.)
Contains a complete cumulative listing by key title words in context of all Florida depository materials maintained at Florida Atlantic University Library. Municipal, county, and quasi-official state publications are excluded but many local plans, reports, and statistics are included in Florida state documents.

FL4. Florida Atlantic University. Library. *Municipal Documents Index.* Edited by Linda Wiler. (Reference Department, Boca Raton 33431) 1974. 50pp.
Contains a listing of municipal, county, and quasi-official state publications maintained in the library.

FL5. Florida. Chamber of Commerce. *Who's What in Florida Government.* (P.O. Box 5497, Tallahassee 32301) 1977. 44pp.
List of top executives in Florida government such as legislators, governor, and cabinet members, and supreme court justices.

FL6. *The Florida Handbook.* Compiled by Allen Morris. Tallahassee: The Peninsular Pub. Co. (P.O. Box 5078, Tallahassee 32301), 1947/48-   . Annual.
Contains facts and figures about the state government, sights, history, counties, cities, and other topics.

FL7. *The Florida Industries Guide '75: A Directory of Florida Industries with Products Classified by SIC Codes.* Orlando: McHenry Pub. Co. (P.O. Box 935, Orlando 32801), 1975. 184pp. Annual.

FL8. Goodin, Frances, editor. *Bibliographic Data by Region and County.* Panama City: Northwest Florida Planning and Advisory Council (521-B W. Highway 98, Panama City 32401), 1976. 50pp.
Listing by county and region of documents published in the 13 counties of northwest Florida.

FL9. *Regional Directory '76.* Fort Myers: Southwest Florida Regional Planning Council (2121 W. First St., Fort Myers 33901), 1976. 54pp.
Basic directory of the southwest Florida region. Gives names, telephone numbers, and addresses of officials in the counties of Charlotte, Collier, Glades, Hendry, Lee, and Sarasota; it also covers the major cities in the area. Also included are county and circuit court judges, state senators and representatives, planning agency members, state district officers, and state and federal government agencies.

FL10. Tallahassee. Division of State Planning. Department of Administration. *A Bibliography: Florida's Planning Documents.* (Tallahassee 32304) n.d.
Listing of Florida's planning documents giving bibliographic data.

Collections

FL11. Florida Atlantic University. Boca Raton 33431 (305)395-5100. Teletype Service: (510)953-7532.
Collection contains materials from local governments in the state. The majority of materials are planning reports and codes. The FAU-FIU Joint Center for Environmental and Urban problems, a part of Florida Atlantic University, has a basic library of urban and environmental material which includes federal, state, and local government documents, maps, periodicals, and major works in the field. (See also entries **FL2, FL3,** and **FL4.**) It is also a member of the Inter-University Consortium for Political Research.

FL12. Northwest Florida Planning and Advisory Council. P.O. Drawer 71, Panama City 32401 (904)785-9581.
The council has a medium-sized collection covering the northwestern part of the state.

South Florida Regional Planning Council. See entry **FL17.**

FL13. Southwest Florida Regional Planning Council. 2121 W. First St., Fort Myers 33901 (813)334-7382.
The planning research library of the council includes approximately 300 publications specifically related to the counties and municipalities within the region.

FL14. University of Florida Libraries. Gainesville 32611 (904)392-6001. Teletype Service: (810)825-6320.
The University of Florida Urban and Regional Research and Documentation Laboratory, established in 1972, is a HUD 701 depository library, containing approximately 15,000 comprehensive planning reports. It is estimated that the laboratory holds 20 percent of the HUD 701 comprehensive planning reports published by cities, counties, regions, and states. While the collection covers the entire United States, emphasis has been placed on obtaining Florida documents.

West Florida Regional Planning Council Library. See entry **FL29.**

FORT LAUDERDALE

Fort Lauderdale, a growing community, has all the governmental agencies of some of the largest cities in the country. It has been experimenting with various governmental forms and many studies have been written on the area. Each department produces many documents each year on planning, annual reports, and other topics.

HIALEAH

Data not available at this time.

HOLLYWOOD

Data not available at this time.

JACKSONVILLE

Jacksonville, the largest city in the state, has many overlapping governmental areas. The region, county, and city all have their own divisions and publications. There is no centralized source for materials although the public library and the City Information Agency do try to keep track of part of the publications. Some items are also incorporated into Greenwood Press's *Index to Current Urban Documents.*

MIAMI

The city of Miami and metropolitan Dade County regularly issue financial and statistical reports of the various departments. In addition, special reports on departmental activities and major studies on specific topics (water quality, rapid transit, etc.) are available. All of these items are covered by Greenwood Press's *Index to Current Urban Documents.* Local Newspaper Indexing: The Miami-Dade Public Library (see entry **FL16**) clips all local newspapers and 22 Sunday Florida newspapers for Florida-related articles. Letter queries are accepted.

Publications

FL15. Metropolitan Dade County. Planning Department. *Publications.* Miami (900 Brickell Plaza, 909 S.E. First Ave., Miami 33131), 1976. 7pp.
Listing of countywide plans and studies, small-area and neighborhood studies, and the publications of the Research Division.

Collections

FL16. Miami-Dade Public Library. One Biscayne Blvd., Miami 33132 (305) 579-5001.
The large collection of publications covers the entire state with emphasis on Miami and metropolitan Dade County. Interlibrary loan is not provided for material listed in Greenwood Press's *Index to Current Urban Documents.* All city of Miami and metropolitan Dade County documents in the library's collection have been included in *Index to Current Urban Documents*, excepting city code, county code, city directories, departmental telephone directory, minutes of city commission meetings, and minutes of county commission meetings.

FL17. South Florida Regional Planning Council. 1515 N.W. 167 St., Suite 429, Miami 33169 (305)621-5871.
The large collection covers south Florida including Dade, Broward, and Monroe counties. It relates to planning, urban studies, environment, housing, criminal justice, economics, transportation, public services, land use, and coastal zone management. Supplementing the bound volumes are over 100 periodicals including technical journals, newsletters of public agencies and interest groups, and reports of city, county, state, and federal agencies which provide current planning information. In the future, all council maps will be placed in a storage and retrieval system and indexed in the card catalog. Although not a lending library, the continuously expanding facility is open for in-office use.

ORLANDO

The Municipal Reference Library (see entry **FL19**), a city documents depository, located in the Orlando City Hall, contains materials published by and about the city. Major emphasis is on municipal, county, and regional documents, whether codes or charters, annual reports, in-house studies and reports, or consultants' studies. Ephemeral material, particularly as it may pertain to local government (Orlando, Orange, Orange-Seminole, and Osceola counties) is also kept.

Publications

FL18. Human Services Council of Orange County. *Information and Referral Center.* Orlando: Information and Referral Center (215 E. Jackson St., Orlando 32801), 1975- .

Collections

FL19. Municipal Reference Library. City Hall, 400 S. Orange, Orlando 32801 (305)849-2249.
The library collects city and some county publications.

PENSACOLA

The publications of Pensacola appear in the form of annual reports, codes, directories, budgets, financial statements, and special reports. Some of these are issued by ad hoc committees from both city and county. Reports from local citizens' groups involved in public affairs are published on occasion. In recent years, the city-county planning commission (which developed into a regional planning council to cover Sub-State Planning District 1) has promulgated a significant number of documents of local interest. The proceedings of the City Council of Pensacola and the Board of County Commissioners of Escambia County are not published.

Publications

FL20. Eubank, Frances Anne, compiler. *Escambia, Santa Rosa and Okaloosa Counties: A Checklist of Selected Research,1965-1975.* Pensacola: John C. Pace Library (Pensacola 32504). 55pp.
Updates *Metropolitan Pensacola: A Checklist of Selected Documents, 1963-1973,* which includes Okaloosa County, thereby completing bibliographic coverage for Sub-State Planning District 1. This update includes official publications, planning

documents prepared for governmental units, regional surveys, theses, and other research of civic interest published within the past decade. Each report is described in brief form together with its location within the John C. Pace Library (see entry **FL25**).

FL21. Eubank, Frances Anne, compiler. *Metropolitan Pensacola: A Checklist of Selected Documents, 1963-1973.* Pensacola: John C. Pace Library, 1973. 18pp. This checklist includes those reports and publications that relate to Escambia County, Pensacola, and Santa Rosa County. It describes each item and gives its location in the John C. Pace Library at the University of West Florida (see entry **FL25**).

FL22. Pensacola. Ordinances, Local Laws, etc. *Code of the City of Pensacola.* Vols. 1 & 2. Spencerport, NY: General Code Pub. Co., 1968.

FL23. Services, James Albert, compiler. *A Bibliography of West Florida.* Pensacola: n.p., 1974. 3 vols. 1393pp.
Lists printed works relating to Pensacola and western Florida. The first two volumes of this work cover the period 1935-1971; the third volume provides an index. A supplement is in progress. Processed, mimeographed, and typed documents such as technical reports, theses, and dissertations are included in addition to printed books, journal articles, pamphlets, and ephemeral material. Effort is made to cite all major works published through 1940; materials of a later date are presented selectively.

Collections

FL24. Pensacola Department of Community Design and Planning Library. 233 E. Gregory St., Pensacola 32501 (904)436-4294.
The library has a small collection of plans and financial reports covering the local area.

FL25. University of West Florida. John C. Pace Library. Pensacola 32504 (904) 476-9500. Teletype Service: (510)737-7957.
The library has approximately 2,000 documents relating primarily to Pensacola and the western counties.

FL26. Pensacola Junior College. 1000 College Blvd., Pensacola 32504 (904) 476-5410.
The library has a small collection covering Pensacola.

FL27. *The Pensacola News-Journal Library.* 101 E. Romana St., Pensacola 32501 (904)433-0041, ext. 234.
An index to clippings of the *Pensacola News-Journal* from 1950 to the present is available. The approach is principally by subject.

FL28. West Florida Regional Library. Headquarters: Pensacola Public Library, 200 W. Gregory St., Pensacola 32501 (904)438-5479.
The library collects early volumes of census, particularly those of the Florida panhandle, Alabama, and Georgia for genealogical research.

FL29. West Florida Regional Planning Council Library. 106 S. Reus St., Pensacola 32501 (904)434-1026.
Municipal publications relating to planning and redevelopment from all over the

country are available from about 1965 to the present. A card file is provided for anyone who wishes to use it. Maps are a specialty.

ST. PETERSBURG

Data not available at this time.

TALLAHASSEE

Tallahassee, the center of state government and the clearinghouse for state documents, is an active legislative community. The local government is, as a result, somewhat overwhelmed by the state operation. It does produce its own set of local documents (annual reports, budgets, etc.), which are available from the departments' publishing and through Greenwood Press's *Index to Current Urban Documents.*

TAMPA

The Tampa-St. Petersburg area is very active in regional planning activities. Comprehensive reports have been made on everything from busing of the elderly to waste disposal. The Tampa Bay Regional Planning Council is the hub of this activity. Also, each city in the area takes an active part in producing reports and other such documents.

Publications

FL30. Greater Tampa. Chamber of Commerce. Committee of 100. *Directory of Tampa Industries.* Tampa (801 E. Kennedy Blvd., Tampa 33602), 1973. 40pp. $3.

Collections

FL31. **University of South Florida.** Library. Tampa 33620 (813)974-2729. Teletype Service: (810)876-0601.
The library has a small collection of municipal documents covering the Tampa area.

GEORGIA

General Publications

GA1. Association County Commissioners of Georgia. *Foundations of Government—The Georgia Counties.* (Suite 1124, Carnegie Bldg., Atlanta 30303) 1976. 175pp. $7.50.
This book gives historical notes and anecdotes about the Georgia counties. It is a collection of facts about each county's founding and its current condition, though it is by no means a definitive history of every county. The book hopes to give a better understanding of the county in relation to its citizens and to the whole structure of government.

GA2. Clark College. Southern Center for Studies in Public Policy. *Georgia Guide for Elected Officials.* 3rd ed. Edited by Willie J. Woods. (Clark College, Atlanta 30314) 1976. 208pp.
The guide is an annual catalog of governmental structures and personnel. It is aimed at providing essential services to Georgia's elected officials. As a catalog, the guide contains chapters on the city of Atlanta, the state of Georgia, federal government, attorneys and physicians, news media, and a miscellaneous section. Within these chapters is found detailed information on departments and office holders at the various governmental levels.

GA3. Georgia Department of Human Resources. *Directory of Mental Health Services, 1975.* Atlanta, 1975. 107pp.
The directory provides a complete listing of public agency mental health and mental retardation services in Georgia. It includes programs serving clients with mental or emotional problems, mental retardation problems, drug abuse related problems, and alcohol abuse related problems.

ATLANTA

Atlanta's departments and agencies publish extensively. There is no checklist of city publications, making bibliographic control difficult. Atlanta Public Library (see entry **GA48**) is trying to ease this situation by cataloging all local documents and thereby making them more readily available. Most of the reference sources published cover the day-to-day functioning of the city's government. The majority of the publications can be borrowed on interlibrary loan from Atlanta Public Library. Atlanta Public Library contributes to Greenwood Press's *Index to Current Urban Documents.* Only the very latest of publications are sent to Greenwood.

Some archival material is available, but it is limited. Atlanta Public Library became a municipal collector in 1972, making the majority of information available current in nature. **Local Newspaper Indexing:** The Atlanta Public Library (see entry **GA48**) indexes the *Atlanta Journal*, the evening paper. Indexing is done by the staff of the General Reference Department of the Central Library. The indexing is selective as it pertains to Georgia and Atlanta. Very limited searching can be handled by the indexing staff. The *Fulton County Daily Reporter* also covers news of import on the government scene. This is held by the library, but is not indexed.

Publications

GA4. Atlanta. Bureau of Planning. *How to Do Neighborhood Planning*. (68 Mitchell St., Atlanta 30303) 1974. 28pp.
This booklet is designed to serve as a technical guide to neighborhoods which are developing comprehensive plans. It describes and illustrates for the reader a step-by-step process for comprehensive neighborhood planning and stresses the importance of neighborhood planning committees to prepare and carry out planning activities for their neighborhoods.

GA5. Atlanta. Bureau of Planning. *Interaction: A Summary of Citizen Opinions and Neighborhood Plans*. (68 Mitchell St., Atlanta 30303) 1975. 87pp.
This booklet is a composite of suggestions and recommendations offered to the Bureau of Planning for neighborhood planning and citizen involvement in the planning process. Neighborhood plans for specific areas are included as are city-wide plans. Also given is a map of planning units for Atlanta's neighborhoods.

GA6. Atlanta. Bureau of Police Services. *History of the Atlanta Police Department*. Atlanta: Policemen's Relief Association, 1976. 68pp.
This document serves as a brief chronicle of the Department of Police of Atlanta. There had never been a line of record made before of this department of the city government and all the data had to be secured from old citizens whose memories could recall the facts that were sought. The study covers "three epochs" in the history of the police department: The days of the antebellum marshals; the organization of the police board; the present system.

GA7. Atlanta. Charter Commission. *City Charter, City of Atlanta, Approved by General Assembly and Signed by the Governor, March 1973*. 1973. 100pp.
The charter of the city of Atlanta reincorporates the city in the counties of Fulton and DeKalb. A bill of rights is provided for in the charter. Also provided for by the charter are the name, powers, and corporate limits of the city; the government of the city; the officials and employees thereof; the qualifications, oath, powers, and duties of said officials; their compensation and terms of office; the organization and administration of said city; the election and removal of city officers; the establishment of a municipal court; a system for finance and fiscal matters; municipal services and regulatory functions; an electoral system for first officials and a system of severability. In summary the charter governs all aspects of municipal life.

GA8. Atlanta Clean City Commission. *Resource Guide of the Clean City Commission*. (178 Pryor St. S.W., Atlanta 30303) 1976. Various paging.
Provides "how to" information for individuals wanting to conduct workshops and informational briefings, and developing project plans on combatting litter. Some information contained in the guide includes general overviews of committee plans and commission goals.

GA9. Atlanta Criminal Justice Coordinating Council, Crime Analysis Team. *Directory of Criminal Justice Agencies Serving the Atlanta Community*. (96 Mitchell St. S.W., Atlanta 30303) 1977. 65pp.
Law enforcement agencies, the courts, probation, parole, correctional services, the

juvenile justice system, community-based services, and criminal justice planning agencies are examined in this directory. Given information includes names of agencies, names of persons involved with respective agencies, phone numbers, addresses, and jurisdictions if appropriate.

GA10. Atlanta Criminal Justice Coordinating Council, Crime Analysis Team. *1976 Local Criminal Justice Master Plan.* (96 Mitchell St. S.W., Atlanta 30303) 1975. 487pp.
The 1976 Local Criminal Justice Master Plan is a blueprint for achieving the goals of crime reduction and system improvement in the quality of justice. The plan covers the criminal justice system which serves the city of Atlanta and Fulton and DeKalb counties. The system's components are police courts, corrections, and juvenile and community crime prevention. The plan includes a statistical abstract, a compilation of issue papers and a section on administration and evaluation.

GA11. Atlanta. Department of Budget and Planning. Bureau of Planning. *1977 City of Atlanta Comprehensive Development Plan.* (City of Atlanta, 700 City Hall, Atlanta 30303) 1977. Annual.
The 1977 City of Atlanta Comprehensive Development Plan is a compilation of the city's goals, objectives, policies, and program-projects for the period 1977–1991. The plan is segmented into functional categories of urban development and neighborhood preservation, transportation, economic development, human development, recreation and cultural opportunities, environmental protection and enhancements, protection of persons and property, and general government, and time elements of one-, five-, and fifteen-year improvements.

GA12. Atlanta. Department of Community and Human Development. *Heart of Atlanta Shopping District Study: A Plan to Regenerate Atlanta's Historic Business District.* Atlanta: Bureau of Housing and Human Development (148 Cain St. N.E., Suite 901, Atlanta 30303), 1977. 80pp.
The purpose of this study is to identify the forces of decline and regeneration in the old downtown and the conditions for its regeneration. One outcome of the planning process was the identification of actions that might be undertaken by the city of Atlanta, Fulton County, MARTA, area property owners, area merchants, and Central Atlanta Progress Inc., in order to fulfill the several conditions for regeneration. This report is concerned with the lower downtown area—the original commercial heart of Atlanta. The heart of Atlanta shopping district functions as a major regional shopping center serving a large segment of the city's population as well as downtown workers. The district is at an important crossroads in its history. Age and obsolescence are taking their toll. A coordinated public-private action program is vitally needed to rescue the district from the effects of past destructive forces.

GA13. Atlanta. Department of Planning. *Atlanta Urban Framework Plan.* (68 Mitchell St., Atlanta 30303) 1973. 41pp.
The objective of the plan was twofold: (1) To identify how the city can best accommodate the MARTA rapid transit system and its facilities into an existing land-use fabric; and (2) to identify where and how the rapid transit system should be used as a catalyst to stimulate future growth and development. The plan produces a graphic citywide concept plan which represents the refinement or urban framework goals. It also presents a set of goals, objectives, and policy statements. These will in turn support a land use and transportation pattern based on optimizing the rapid transit system.

GA14. Atlanta. Department of Planning. *Central Atlanta: Opportunities and Responses.* (68 Mitchell St., Atlanta 30303) 1971. 62pp.

This publication is a sub-area transportation study, focused on that area of the Atlanta metropolitan area within the railroad-built line. For the first time, the area was subjected to detailed economic, transportation, planning, and urban design analysis. This report summarizes the findings of that examination, as well as the conclusion and recommendations flowing from them. The primary emphasis has been placed on proposals for increasing access to the central area and improving circulation of vehicles, people, and goods within the core of the metropolitan area.

GA15. Atlanta. Department of Planning. *Changing Atlanta: Population and Housing.* (68 Mitchell St., Atlanta 30303) 1973. 40pp.
Trends in the housing stock and population of the city of Atlanta, Georgia, between 1960 and 1970 are examined in this report. Base data came from the 1960 and 1970 Census of Population and Housing, the City of Atlanta Department of Planning's PLAN File, and records maintained by the Department of Building Inspector of the city. Trends are presented for the age, race, income, geographic distribution, and density of the poulation; and quantity, degree of overcrowding, type of occupancy, and cost of housing as well as minority opportunity for housing.

GA16. Atlanta. Ordinances, Local Laws, etc. *Charter, Related Laws and Code of Ordinances, Atlanta, Georgia.* Tallahassee, FL: Municipal Code Corp., 1965. 3 vols.
This publication is a compilation of laws governing the citizenry of the city of Atlanta. It is updated by regular supplements. The ordinances in the code have been classified as to subject matter. The chapters have been arranged in alphabetical order, and the various sections in each chapter have been catchlined to facilitate usage. An organizational chart is not included but is available.

GA17. Atlanta Public Library. *Atlanta's Neighborhoods: A Demographic Description of 181 Neighborhoods Organized According to Twelve Council Districts.* 1975. 2 vols.
This compilation of neighborhood profiles is an effort to supply to residents, elected officials, and professionals the means to communicate more effectively on problems and possibilities for the city in general and neighborhoods in particular. Information given for a specific neighborhood includes population, age, employment, transportation-mode to work, education, income, economic dependency, housing, family characteristics, and crime.

GA18. Atlanta Public Schools. *The Development of the Public Secondary Schools of Atlanta, Georgia, 1845-1936.* (Office of School System Historian) 1974. 247pp.
The purpose of this study is to locate, assemble, and make available significant facts concerning the development of public secondary education in Atlanta, Georgia, from 1870-1937. The problem involved in this study has three main divisions which may be stated as follows: (1) To trace the development of public secondary education in Atlanta, Georgia, from 1870-1937, by discovering, organizing, interpreting, and presenting important facts in this development; (2) to trace some of the changes which have taken place in the organization and administration of the white and black public secondary schools of Atlanta; and (3) to present appropriate conclusions which may be of value to those whose responsibility is to administer a public secondary school program in a metropolitan city.

GA19. Atlanta Public Schools. *From Ivy Street to Kennedy Center: Centennial History of the Atlanta Public School System.* Atlanta, 1972. 477pp.
This book is intended to be an administrative and internal history of the Atlanta Public School System as it reached the hundredth year of operation. It attempts to describe

the evaluation and development of public education in the city of Atlanta, the development of administrative policies, the creations and revisions of an instructional program, the construction and modification of physical facilities, and the continuous search for teachers and administrative personnel necessary to devise and implement proper methods of teaching the students enrolled in these programs and facilities.

GA20. Atlanta Regional Commission. *Analysis of Zoning Trends in Metropolitan Atlanta.* (Suite 200, 230 Peachtree St., Atlanta 30303) 1973. 50pp.
The primary purpose of this report is to identify and analyze regional zoning trends. It can also be used by local governments in a general reassessment of capital improvement budgets in terms of emerging trends. For the purpose of this report, information on rezoning activity has been grouped by seven land-use categories including low density residential, medium density residential, high density residential, planned unit development, commercial, office-institutional, and industrial. Maps have been prepared for each of these groupings showing rezoning activity by year, land-lot location, and the amount of land involved in terms of general acreage groupings. The maps in this report include the 1970 base-year zoning.

GA21. Atlanta Regional Commission. *The Atlanta Area Family Planning Program.* (Suite 200, 230 Peachtree St., Atlanta 30303) 1972. 20pp.
This publication discusses what is being done in Atlanta about family planning. Information in the work includes the number of active patients by agency, agencies in the metropolitan area, clinic resources, and human resources.

GA22. Atlanta Regional Commission. *Atlanta Impact Program, Master Plan.* Vol. 1. (Suite 200, 230 Peachtree St., Atlanta 30303) n.d. Various paging.
The *Master Plan* is a multipurpose document. Its primary function is that of a decision-making tool. Volume 1 of the *Master Plan* contains an identification of the crime specific problems; the program goals, subgoals, and objectives; the plan implementation; and the grant administration process. Volume 1 also contains chapters dealing with the four major areas of concern, i.e., police, courts, corrections, and community security. Each chapter contains a summary of any funded project in the particular area.

GA23. Atlanta Regional Commission. *The Atlantic Region: Framework for the Future.* (Suite 200, 230 Peachtree St., Atlanta 30303) 1974. 19pp.
This report explains briefly the growth predicted for the region over the next 25 years, the problems that can accompany such growth, and the commission's legal responsibility for producing a long-range, comprehensive guide for the region's development. Also described is the process for preparing a regional development plan, including the strategy of evaluating alternative approaches to the region's future.

GA24. Atlanta Regional Commission. *Atlanta Region Transportation Plan: Effective Use of the Existing System. A Transportation Systems Management Plan.* (Suite 200, 230 Peachtree St., Atlanta 30303) 1976. 39pp.
This document presents a plan which outlines short-range, low-cost transportation policies and specific projects to be implemented in the Atlanta region.

GA25. Atlanta Regional Commission. *The Atlanta Regional Commission Regional Housing Plan.* (Suite 200, 230 Peachtree St., Atlanta 30303) 1976. 139pp. Free.
Based on the adopted goals and objectives, continuing and formalized citizen participation, responses to surveys conducted by ARC in conjunction with other planning

activities, and plans adopted in other functional areas, such as water, sewer, transportation, land use, and the environment. the Atlanta Regional Commission adopted a Regional Housing Plan. The components of the plan are policies, strategies for implementation of the policies, and suggested design criteria for use where appropriate. The regional housing policies are of several types: (1) policies which ARC can use in its advisory role to local governments and others; (2) policies which local governments can implement; and (3) policies which should be reflected in every appropriate governmental action in the Atlanta region.

GA26. Atlanta Regional Commission. *The Bicycle: A Plan and Program for Its Use As a Mode of Transportation and Recreation.* (Suite 200, 230 Peachtree St., Atlanta 30303) 1973. 70pp.
The principal objectives of this study were the following:

1. To assess current bicycle trends both in the nation and in the Atlanta metropolitan area
2. To develop a conceptual bicycle facility plan for the region that would identify those corridors and areas with the greatest potentials for bicycle facilities
3. To select and evaluate alternative types of bicycle facilities that might be provided.
4. To determine the most significant potential funding sources for initiating new bicycle programs and constructing bicycle facilities
5. To research legal constraints to constructing new bicycle facilities
6. To suggest educational and registration programs that would reduce bicycling accidents and thievery.

This report summarizes the basic trends and policy issues regarding bicycle facility development and bicycling programs in the Atlanta metropolitan area.

GA27. Atlanta Regional Commission. *Census Tract Street Index Guide.* (Suite 200, 230 Peachtree St., Atlanta 30303) 1977. 247pp. $15.
The file covers the seven counties of Clayton, Cobb, DeKalb, Douglas, Fulton, Gwinnett, and Rockdale circa 1970-1975. Some areas are more current than others. The publication is updated quarterly. Given information includes the street name, house numbers included, 1970 tract number, 1980 tract number, the zip code, and the city.

GA28. Atlanta Regional Commission. *Comparative Revenue Study of the Atlanta Metropolitan Area.* (Suite 200, 230 Peachtree St., Atlanta 30303) 1973. 81pp.
The study assesses local governments in the metropolitan Atlanta area regarding their revenue programs. The study then compares these programs according to both degree and variety of resources used. The study analyzes each revenue source and provides a measure of the municipality's and county's use of that source. In cases where the cities and counties are ranked, the jurisdiction can compare itself to similar governments in the area regarding a particular source. The study examines three fundamental revenue producers—the property tax, revenues derived from utilities, and business taxes and license fees. Each of these resources is explained and then revenues received from or rates for the resources are displayed.

GA29. Atlanta Regional Commission. *Comprehensive Health Plan.* (Suite 200, 230 Peachtree St., Atlanta 30303) 1975. 462pp.
This first edition of the Atlanta region's Comprehensive Health Plan is intended to provide the initial, brief survey of the health system, its strengths and shortcomings, its problems and some possible solutions, and the community's priorities in improv-

ing the system. In order that the health of the citizens of the region may reach the highest possible level, the plan makes a number of general and specific recommendations for meeting the needs of the community by aiding the development of the health system in an orderly and cost-effective manner.

GA30. Atlanta Regional Commission. *Construction Codes in the Atlanta Metropolitan Area: A Survey of Current Practices.* (Suite 200, 230 Peachtree St., Atlanta 30303) 1974. 67pp.
Presented in this report are the results of a survey of local practices relating to the adoption and enforcement of construction codes in the Atlanta metropolitan area. Forty-four cities and seven counties participated in this survey. To guide and govern construction activity, to ensure that consumers and other citizens are protected, and to make and maintain minimum construction standards, local officials have adopted and enforced a variety of regulatory codes and ordinances. This report summarizes the codes-related activities currently being undertaken by jurisdictions in this seven-county area.

GA31. Atlanta Regional Commission. *Criminal Justice 1973.* (Suite 200, 230 Peachtree St., Atlanta 30303) 1973. 171pp.
This document consists of an action program which is concerned with the most pressing needs of the criminal justice system. The solutions proposed herein constitute a statement of goals which are reasonable and attainable, and which could result in measurable, positive alleviation of some of the severest problems in the criminal justice system. Covered in this publication are the criminal justice planning methodology; 1973 action program covering prevention, juvenile delinquency, police, courts, corrections, civil disorders, organized crime, research and development; 1973 priorities; and related programs. The planning guide should remain relatively static from year to year. It should be modified, however, to reflect the impact of new state or federal programs, changes in LEAA guidelines, and changes in the environment.

GA32. Atlanta Regional Commission. *Health Facts, Metropolitan Atlanta Region,* 2nd ed. (Suite 200, 230 Peachtree St., Atlanta 30303) 1973. 42pp.
This publication is statistical in nature. Covered herein are: health status indicators, i.e., birth and death rates, infant and maternal mortality, causes of death, suicide and homicide; environmental quality indicators, i.e., water pollution and air pollution; health facilities and services, i.e., licensed hospitals and number of beds, average hospital occupancy, beds in use, nursing homes and beds; and health manpower, i.e., doctors, nurses, dentists.

GA33. Atlanta Regional Commission. *Hospital Development Guide.* Vol. 1. (Suite 200, 230 Peachtree St., Atlanta 30303) 1973. 113pp.
The *Hospital Development Guide* is a document intended for immediate and continued use in a community in which the planning and construction of new hospitals and modifications to existing hospitals is a constant and active process. Topics covered by the guide include direction, assets, needs, past and future trends, priorities, anticipated problems, and the best methods of implementation.

GA34. Atlanta Regional Commission. *Human Resources Handbook.* 2nd ed. (230 Peachtree St., Suite 200, Atlanta 30303) 1975. 227pp. $1.
The handbook is intended to serve as a source of information for both the decision-maker and private citizens interested in targeting centers of interest and activity in the seven-county region. Organizational data herein includes: officers, members, how often the group meets, and where.

GA35. Atlanta Regional Commission. *Local Government Officials of the Atlanta Region.* (Suite 200, 230 Peachtree St., Atlanta 30303) 1977. 80pp. $1.
This publication is a current directory of municipal officials of local governments within the Atlanta metropolitan area. Information included for each municipality is the address of the seat of government, officials of the local government with address and phone number, staff of said government, meeting time, and election date.

GA36. Atlanta Regional Commission. *1976 Population and Housing.* (Suite 200, 230 Peachtree St., Atlanta 30303) 1960-   . Annual. $1. (From 1950-1959, issued by Metropolitan Planning Commission.)
This report presents the ARC's 1976 estimates of population and housing for the seven counties, the 49 municipalities, and the 243 census tracts which comprise the commission jurisdiction. The basis for the publication is to supply essential information for analysis and projection of growth trends which provide a support for projections, regional planning studies, and policy recommendations.

GA37. Atlanta Regional Commission. *Regional Development Plan.* (Suite 200, 230 Peachtree St., Atlanta 30303) 1976. 84pp. Free.
The Atlanta Regional Development Plan is an expression of how the Atlanta region should grow and change in order to achieve the region's goals for the future. It has several important characteristics. (1) The plan is long range in outlook; studies were made and policies recommended for a 25-year period. (2) The plan is general in nature, therefore providing a framework for more detailed decision-making at the regional and local levels. (3) It is part of an ongoing planning process; other regional development plans have preceded this one and others will follow as needed. (4) The plan is not comprehensive by itself, but taken together with other detailed plans, such as water resources, housing, and transportation, provides a comprehensive growth policy for the Atlanta region.

GA38. Atlanta Regional Commission. *Regional Housing Opportunities Near Rapid Transit Stations.* (Suite 200, 230 Peachtree St., Atlanta 30303) 1973. 122pp.
This study analyzes housing opportunities at various proposed MARTA station locations and the surrounding area within a 2,500 foot radius. This study is not an inventory of existing housing but rather an identification of present vacant land suitable for residential development. Several factors considered are goals devised by individual and local governments, site characteristics of the areas around the station locations and their influence as a stimulus or deterrent to residential development and housing goals and objectives adopted by ARC.

GA39. Atlanta Regional Commission. *Water Supply Plan for the Atlanta Region.* (Suite 200, 230 Peachtree St., Atlanta 30303) 1976. 43pp. Free.
The plan is intended to provide a framework for water supply and water resource decisions and is designed to be consistent with the ARC-adopted Regional Development Plan (RDP). The RDP itself consists of policies based on natural features and other land-use policies and improvements. Forecasts were prepared of the most likely regional distribution of population, employment, and land use. The basic objective of the plan is to provide high-quality water to the people and businesses of the region in the quantity needed to serve the activities anticipated in the RDP.

GA40. Atlanta-Fulton County League of Women Voters. *Facts, Political Directory, 1975-76, City of Atlanta and Fulton County Including Metropolitan Councils, etc.* (1182 W. Peachtree St. N.W., Rm. 209, Atlanta 30309) 1974-1976. Annual. $1.50.
An annual political directory of municipal officials in the Atlanta and Fulton County

governments, this publication briefly surveys each position within the government. Given information includes position, term, salary, and duties.

GA41. Metropolitan Atlanta Crime Commission Inc. *Metro Atlanta Crime Statistics 1973-75.* (75 Marietta St. N.W., Atlanta 30303) 1976. 16pp.
The purpose of this report is to serve as a reference source for law enforcement executive, criminal justice planners, and citizens to aid in planning, budgeting, and administering crime prevention and control activities. It was prepared and based on the Uniform Crime Reporting System of the FBI. The crimes included on this report are murder, forceable rape, robbery, aggravated assault, burglary, larceny, theft, and motor vehicle theft. The data presented includes criminal attempts as well as actual perpetrated offenses. The publication covers law enforcement agencies in the seven-county metropolitan area.

GA42. Research Atlanta. *The Criminal Justice System in the City of Atlanta, Georgia: An Overview.* (52 Fairlie St. N.W., Atlanta 30303) 1974. 33pp. $1.60.
This paper presents an overview of the criminal justice system in the city of Atlanta. It describes the events from point of arrest following the commission of a crime, through the judicial and correctional processes. This description is designed to (1) identify the decision-making points for entry and exit from the system; (2) emphasize the high degree to which the police, courts, and correctional responsibilities are interrelated; and (3) outline the problems that occur in the operation of this system and to suggest alternatives that both the public and their policy-makers might consider to correct them. The paper discusses the responsibilities at the local, state, and federal governmental levels to formulate policy in the criminal justice system. The primary emphasis is on describing the decision-making process for individual cases by identifying the various decision-makers and critical decision points.

GA43. Research Atlanta. *Governmental Reorganization in Atlanta, Executive Summary.* (52 Fairlie St. N.W., Atlanta 30303) 1975. 71pp.
The purpose of this report is to provide factual information on various governmental and financial reorganization plans to legislators, local government officials, community leaders, and the public at large. The report assesses the fiscal impact, legal constraints, and general implications of four proposals: (1) Atlanta-Fulton County consolidation plans; (2) annexation by the city of Sandy Springs, Fulton Industrial District, or both areas; (3) Fulton-DeKalb consolidation; and (4) limited consolidation under seven-county government structure. In addition, the report assesses the likely impact of three financial reorganization plans: (1) taxation of unincorporated Fulton separately for municipal-type services; (2) Fulton County revenue sharing; and (3) metropolitan area tax base sharing program.

GA44. Research Atlanta. *The Local Option Sales and Income Taxes: A Comparative Analysis.* (52 Fairlie St. N.W., Atlanta 30303) 1975. 51pp.
The adequacy of the property tax as the primary means of financing local government operations in Georgia has been steadily declining in recent years. In addition, the popularity among taxpayers, as indicated by recent opinion polls, is at one of its lowest points in history. As a result, the General Assembly in its 1975 legislative session enacted a 1 percent local option sales tax, which, in turn, activated a 1 percent local option income tax passed a year earlier. With this action, local governments were effectively granted the prospect of more diversified revenue structures, stronger, more responsive tax bases, property tax relief, and a more equitable distribution of tax burdens both within and among jurisdictions. Because the laws stipulate that only one of the two taxes may be levied by any one government and that the authority to levy is contingent upon the approval of a jurisdiction's voters, local

governments in the Atlanta metropolitan area must decide which tax is most appropriate. The purpose of this paper is to provide area policy-makers and the public with the information necessary to make such a decision.

GA45. Research Atlanta. *The Plan of Improvement: An Analysis of Services in the City of Atlanta and Fulton County.* (52 Fairlie St. N.W., Atlanta 30303) 1974. 81pp.
This report was written in response to the need for a comprehensive review of the provisions of the Plan of Improvement (1950–1952), the current allocation of service responsibilities between Fulton County and the city of Atlanta, and some alternative solutions to the problems. The report includes three major sections: (1) background on the plan, its goals, major provisions, and initial implementing legislation; (2) problems with the plan over the years, including the annexation failures, fiscal disparities, and division-of-service responsibilities; (3) service provision today on a service-by-service basis. The analysis also includes a detailed fiscal breakdown of county expenditures and an examination of services for alternative methods of delivery.

GA46. Research Atlanta. *Reveue Sharing in Atlanta and Fulton County.* (52 Fairlie St. N.W., Atlanta 30303).
This report is a financial analysis of general and special revenue sharing and its impact on Atlanta and Fulton County, Georgia. The analysis includes local government policy implications created by changes in federal funding. The report is written in two parts—general and special revenue sharing. The general revenue sharing chapter documents the amount of funds coming to Atlanta and Fulton County from fiscal year 1972 through 1976 and the local policy implications of this change in funding. The special revenue sharing chapter documents the amount of SRS funds that would be received by Atlanta and Fulton county.

GA47. Research Atlanta. *School Desegregation in Metro Atlanta, 1954–1973.* (52 Fairlie St. N.W., Atlanta 30303) 1973. 63pp. $2.
This report is intended to be a factual analysis of desegregation data. Section 1 contains historical information on school desegregation in metropolitan Atlanta. Included are details of various school desegregation suits as well as information concerning the extent of desegregation. Section 2 is an analysis of desegregation in metropolitan Atlanta schools for the 1972–1973 school year. Section 3 covers private school enrollment and racial composition. Comparisons to public school enrollment and information on future expansion potential of area private schools are also included.

Collections

GA48. Atlanta Public Library. Central Branch. 10 Pryor St., Atlanta 30303 (404)688-4636, ext. 203/204.
The Atlanta Public Library's municipal collection is one of current materials. There are some documents of historic nature, these being annual reports for the city and various agencies of city government. The Atlanta Public Library was designated a local documents depository in 1972. The library is by ordinance required to house two copies of every publication published by city departments for public use. Local documents are defined as publications issued by or contracted for local government agencies in the Atlanta metropolitan area. Publications which are issued come from various city departments, e.g., police, fire, personnel, etc. These documents consist of annual reports, minutes of meetings, special reports, etc. Publications contracted for are documents from agencies affiliated with the government but not of the

government. Agencies which are included are Metropolitan Atlanta Rapid Transit
Authority (MARTA), Atlanta Regional Commission (ARC), etc. The library's local
documents cover municipal finance, housing, health, transportation, parks and
recreation, police, fire, personnel, crime, etc., for the city of Atlanta and vicinity.
The library also maintains a collection of city ordinances and resolutions and is the
only local agency with these publications readily available for public use.

Atlanta Public Library has a computer data base system housed in the Government Information Center of APL Central Branch. The system deals with two programs known as CPIS (Community Participation Information System) and CPRG
(Community Participation Report Generator). CPIS is of interest to any city of Atlanta department or agency that deals with community organizations. The purpose of
CPIS is to facilitate communication between city government and community organizations in the conviction that this is a prerequisite to effective community and
citizen participation in government. Essentially, CPIS is a computer file of community
organizations. The information maintained on each organization includes type and
areas of special interest, geographic areas, publications, contact persons and
addresses, etc. There are procedures to input and correct information and methods
of retrieving the information selectively in a useful format and on a timely basis
through the use of CPRG.

CPIS is available both to citizens and the government of Atlanta. Inquiries into
single organizations may be made, where available, through a video terminal con-
nected to the city of Atlanta computer network. Paper listings of the file are avail-
abile regularly. Special reports or address labels are available upon request to city
departments and agencies.

(See also entry **US4**.)

COLUMBUS

Data not available at this time.

MACON

Data not available at this time.

SAVANNAH

Data not available at this time.

HAWAII

HONOLULU

The city and county of Honolulu is the capital city of the state of Hawaii and a publisher of local government documents ranging from short information leaflets to substantial, comprehensive studies and technical reports. Local documents are deposited in the Municipal Reference Library of the Municipal Reference and Records Center (see entry HI8). The library's *A List of Publications in the Municipal Reference Library Issued by or for Honolulu City Agencies through June 30, 1972* (1973) (see entry HI4), and its *Supplement, Covering Publications Received through 1976* (1977) (see entry HI5), provide the most comprehensive reference source to publications of the city and county of Honolulu. Publications are generally available free of charge from the issuing agency. Some publications are sold by the Purchasing Division of the finance department. The cumulative lists of 1973 and 1977 are updated by the Municipal Reference Library's quarterly list, *Honolulu Hale* (see entry HI3). Interlibrary loan is not available outside the island of Oahu (i.e., the city and county of Honolulu).

Publications of local government are also collected by other libraries in Honolulu such as the Hawaii State Library's Hawaiian Room, and the University of Hawaii's Special Hawaiian Collection. The Hawaii State Library is Honolulu's public library. It produces the indexes to the two daily newspapers, the *Honolulu Advertiser* and the *Honolulu Star-Bulletin*. The Hawaii State Library would be able to handle inquiries referred to it from other libraries. The Hawaii State Library is not affiliated with the city and county government or the Municipal Reference Library of the Municipal Reference and Records Center.

A minimum reference collection for the city and county of Honolulu should include at least the following: (1) *Revised Charter of the City and County of Honolulu, 1973;* (2) Annual reports of departments and agencies of the city and county of Honolulu; (3) *Executive Program and Budget: Summary* (for revenues and expenditures); and (4) *Finance Director's Annual Financial Report* (includes an organizational chart for city and county). **Local Newspaper Indexing:** The Office of Library Services (Department of Education, State of Hawaii) publishes indexes to the *Honolulu Advertiser* and *Honolulu Star-Bulletin*. Indexes for 1929-1967 were published in 1968; 1968-1969 supplements were published in 1970; thereafter there have been annual indexes. The latest index in the Municipal Reference Library is for 1975, which was published in 1976. Queries for sale copies as well as index citations should be addressed to: Hawaii State Library, Punchbowl and King Sts., Honolulu 96813.

Publications

HI1. Hawaii. Legislative Reference Bureau. *Cumulative Checklist of State and County Government Publications.* Honolulu (State Capitol, Rm. 004, Honolulu 96813), July 1973. 37pp.
Final issue of the checklist. In 1973 the legislature mandated that the state archivist maintain a central index of government studies. This listing gathers the library's acquisitions for half of 1973.

HI2. Hawaii. Legislative Reference Bureau. *Directory of State, County, and Federal Officials* (Supplement to *Guide to Government in Hawaii* . . . as of September 30, 1975). Compiled by Jon T. Okudara and Deborah Ching. Honolulu (State Capitol, Rm. 004, Honolulu 96813), 1975. 122pp. (loose-leaf). $1.
This directory contains a listing of members of the state legislature, administrators of the state executive branch and the officials elected and appointed to the county governments (from the city and county of Honolulu, of Kauai, and of Maui). It also lists members of the Hawaii congressional delegates and administrators in federal departments in Hawaii.

HI3. Honolulu. Municipal Reference & Records Center. Municipal Reference Library. *Honolulu Hale.* (558 S. King St., City Hall Annex, Honolulu 96813) 1964–
Quarterly. Free.
This bibliography lists all publications by and about the city and county of Honolulu which are received in the Municipal Reference Library. These items listed were cumulated for *A List of Publications in the Municipal Reference Library Issued by or for Honolulu City Agencies through June 30, 1972* (1973) and its *Supplement . . . through 1976* (1977).

HI4. Honolulu. Municipal Reference & Records Center. *A List of Publications in the Municipal Reference Library Issued by or for Honolulu City Agencies through June 30, 1972*. 1973. 82pp. Free (limited supply available).

HI5. Honolulu. Municipal Reference & Records Center. *A List of Publications in the Municipal Reference Library Issued by or for Honolulu City Agencies through June 30, 1972. Supplement, Covering Publications Received through 1976.* (558 S. King St., City Hall Annex, Honolulu 96813) 1977. 30pp. Free.
Occasionally the bibliography lists older publications because the library had just acquired them.

HI6. Honolulu. Municipal Reference & Records Center. Municipal Reference Library. *Municipal Library Bookshelf.* (558 S. King St., City Hall Annex, Honolulu 96813) 1948– . Monthly. Free.
A selective listing of those publications newly acquired by the library.

HI7. Mitsuba Publishing Co. *Directory of Government Services, State of Hawaii, City and County of Honolulu.* Honolulu (7548 Huialoha St., Honolulu 96825), 1975 and supplement (1975). $2.50 (supplement also $2.50).

Collections

HI8. **Municipal Reference & Records Center.** Municipal Reference Library. City Hall Annex, 558 S. King St., Honolulu 96813 (818)523-4577.

The library serves the research needs of the employees, administrators, consultants, and members of boards and commissions, of the city and county of Honolulu. The library maintains a comprehensive collection pertaining to all areas of municipal government concerns. Established in 1929, the library has tried to acquire all city documents produced by or for city agencies and departments. This includes such publications as the mayor's annual reports, city budgets (operating and capital improvement programs), directories, and environmental impact statements. Since 1974 the Municipal Reference Library has been an official city depository for three copies of each city document. The library participates in Greenwood Press's *Index to Current Urban Documents* and most of Honolulu's publications since 1971 are available from Greenwood Press in microfiche format.

IDAHO

General Publications

ID1. Duncombe, Herbert, et al. *Handbook for Elected City Officials in Idaho.* Moscow: University of Idaho (Bureau of Public Affairs Research, Moscow 83843), 1971. 102pp. $7.
The purpose of the handbook is to acquaint newly elected city officials with their duties and authority, and services offered.

ID2. University of Idaho. Bureau of Public Affairs Research. *Handbook for City Finance Officers in Idaho.* 2nd ed. Moscow, 1972. 76pp. $5.95.
This publication, prepared by the staff of the Association of Idaho Cities with the assistance of the City Clerks and Fiscal Officers Association, outlines the responsibilities and duties of city finance officers.

BOISE

Data not available at this time.

POCATELLO

Publications

ID3. Griffin, Carl, and Paul Tamminen. *Guide to Community Resources.* Pocatello: Southeastern Idaho Community Action Agency Inc. (Information Center, 1356 N. Main, Pocatello 83201), 1974. $2.
This publication is a guide to nonprofit services in a six-county area. It is useful in determining the agency to meet a particular need.

ID4. Pocatello. *Operating Budget.* Pocatello: City. Annual. Not sold.
Details the financial workings of the city and the services provided.

ID5. Pocatello. Chamber of Commerce. *Pocatello Industrial Survey: Planned Growth at the Crossroads of Idaho's Interstates.* Los Angeles, CA: Kingsbacher Murphy Co., 1973. Not sold.
An overview of the community, its facilities and institutions; labor and employment in Pocatello and the surrounding five-county area; financial institutions; utilities; taxes; transportation; buildings; and production material.

ID6. Pocatello. City Council. *City of Pocatello Agenda: Regular City Council Meeting.* Pocatello: City Council (209 E. Lewis, Pocatello 83201) Printed every two weeks following council meetings. Not sold.
Minutes of the regular city council meetings are printed and distributed to the various city departments.

ID7. Pocatello. League of Women Voters. *Know Your Town Pocatello, Idaho.* 1976. 47pp. $2.
This general history of the town and government is well illustrated. Voter requirements and election procedures are enumerated as a special feature.

ID8. Pocatello. Public School District #25. *Change and Consistency: A Progress Report of School District #25, 1963-1973.* (Education Center, 3115 Pole Line Rd., Pocatello 83201) 1973. 20pp. $2.
Contains numerous photographs of new construction since 1962. Goals of the school district are listed on the back page. Major financial functions of the Board of Trustees are enumerated. There is a financial comparison outlook over the ten-year period.

ID9. Pocatello. Public School District #25. *Comprehensive District Needs Assessment.* (Education Center, 3115 Pole Line Rd., Pocatello 83201) 1973. $1.50.
Lists members of the Board of Trustees, Quality Assurance (Steering) Committee, and Needs Assessment Task Force. The report also summaries the results of a questionnaire concerning needs assessment.

ID10. Pocatello. Public School District #25. *Policy and Procedure Handbook.* (Education Center, 3115 Pole Line Rd., Pocatello 83201) 1975- . Not sold.
The handbook contains policy and procedure for community relations, Board of Trustees, school officials, and students.

ID11. Purce, J. Michael, compiler. *Southwest Idaho Council of Governments: Human Services, Region V.* Pocatello: Southeast Idaho Council of Governments (Outreach Coordinator, P.O. Box 4169, Pocatello 83201), 1977- . $3.
The guide is not comprehensive even for the agencies covered.

Collections

ID12. Pocatello Public Library. 812 E. Clark, Pocatello 83201 (208)232-1263.
The library has the majority of materials collectable from city government. In addition to the sources listed in the Pocatello section, there are commission and board minutes and interdepartmental publications. Minutes are kept but are not printed for distribution. Interdepartmental publications can be used for grant-writing purposes at the request of the appropriate department.

ILLINOIS

General Publications

IL1. Center for the Study of Middle-Size Cities. *Recent Publications: An Annotated Bibliography.* Springfield: Sangamon State University (Springfield 62708), December, 1976– . 4pp. Irregular. Free.
Catalog of publications available through the agency (founded 1974). The center is based at the university and is charged with the study of middle-sized cities in general and Illinois' middle-size cities in particular. Publications stress demographic profiles and focus on the quality of life and government in the cities.

IL2. Illinois State Library. *Guide to Statistics in Illinois State Documents.* Compiled by Mary Redmond. Springfield, 1976. 259pp.
Modeled after the Directory of Federal Statistics for States issued by the U.S. Bureau of the Census, this is an excellent guide to statistics covering a wide variety of subjects—population, vital statistics, income and earnings, labor and employment, day care, transportation, etc. Included in the entries are subjects, tabular detail (kinds of statistical breakdowns available) frequency, coverage, and titles of publications in which statistical data may be found.

IL3. *Illinois Voters Handbook: For Citizens, Students and Public Officials.* Chicago: League of Women Voters of Illinois (67 East Madison St., Chicago 60603), 1976. 268pp. $3.95.
The handbook provides basic information about the various types of governmental agencies in Illinois as well as descriptions of the qualifications and duties of public officials at all levels. A lengthy chapter on the Illinois court system provides a clear explanation of Chicago judicial procedures.

CHICAGO

The Chicago Municipal Reference Library (see entry **IL18**) has the largest collection of local government publications in the city of Chicago. It publishes checklists and other bibliographic aids to assist librarians in the city. **Local Newspaper Indexing:** The Chicago Municipal Reference Library (see entry **IL18**) has maintained a newspaper clipping file since 1956, with clippings from the Chicago daily newspapers and some neighborhood papers.

Publications

IL4. Chicago Association of Commerce and Industry, Research and Statistics Division. *Community Area Data Book for the City of Chicago: 1970 Census*

Data by 75 Community Areas. (130 S. Michigan Ave., Chicago 60603) 1974. 620pp. Irregular. $10.
Based on 1970 tapes for the city of Chicago, this publication includes the breakdown of census data by community area. Since the statistics included are based on raw data only, the compilation lacks the analyses and historical data on community areas found in the *Local Community Fact Book* (see entry **IL17**) of earlier years.

IL5. Chicago Association of Commerce and Industry. Governmental Affairs Division. *Legislative Directory, with Listings of Illinois, Cook County and Chicago Public Officials.* (130 S. Michigan Ave., Chicago 60603), 1959/60?- . 84pp. Irregular. $6.30.
The directory provides a listing of all officials on the local, state, and federal levels, who have jurisdiction over the city of Chicago. Maps of Chicago wards, and Illinois congressional and legislative districts are included.

IL6. Chicago. League of Women Voters. *The Key to Our Local Government: Chicago, Cook County Metropolitan Area.* Chicago: Citizens' Information Service (67 E. Madison St., Chicago 60603), 1st ed. 1960, 2nd ed. 1966, 3rd ed. 1972; new edition in process. 234pp. Irregular. $2.25.
Written in easily read style aimed at voters, the concerned citizen, and students of government, this publication is designed primarily to open a door to local governmental activities. Contents are arranged by broad topics including, for example, organization, finance, education and recreation, courts and the administration of justice, environmental quality, political parties and elections. Included are maps of the wards, Cook County legislative districts and the Cook County congressional districts. For the junior high school level and above, this publication will serve a useful reference source. A detailed index facilitates access.

IL7. Civic Federation. *Annual Study of Debts, Taxes, Assessments of the Major Chicago Governments.* (29 E. Madison St., Chicago 60606), No. 1- (1933-   ). Unpaged. Annual. Free.
A very useful document that gathers together financial data for the various local governments which have jurisdiction over the city of Chicago, this study is unique in its depth and length of coverage.

IL8. Municipal Reference Library. *Checklist of Publications Issued by the City of Chicago.* (Rm. 1004, City Hall, Chicago 60602), Vol. 1, 1958-   . Unpaged. Quarterly.
This is a very useful checklist which can serve as an acquisition tool. A list of documents received from other local governments is also included in each issue.

IL9. Municipal Reference Library. *Facts about Chicago, 1976.* (Rm. 1004, City Hall, Chicago 60602) 1976. 5pp. Annual.
This is a leaflet giving statistical information about Chicago. Population, vital statistics, geography, weather, government, budget, police, school enrollment are some of the topics covered.

IL10. Municipal Reference Library. *The Government of the City of Chicago: A Guide to Its Structure and Function with a Directory of Officers.* (Rm. 1004, City Hall, Chicago 60602) 1976. 28pp. Irregular, with supplements. 55¢ (including postage).
A brief but useful guide to Chicago city government describing functions of the various units. Important features are a list of current members of the city council,

an organization chart, a history of the municipal flag of Chicago, the corporate seal of Chicago, and the official flower. A selected bibliography is included.

IL11. Municipal Reference Library. *Historical Information about Chicago.* (Rm. 1004, City Hall, Chicago 60602) 1975. 26pp. 55¢ (including postage).
This history of Chicago emphasizes the city's corporate development, with attention given to accomplishments in the area of public works. Brief histories of the Chicago police and fire departments are also included.

IL12. Municipal Reference Library. *The Mayors of Chicago: A Chronological List.* Compiled by Florence E. Johnson. (Rm. 1004, City Hall, Chicago 60602) 1962. Unpaged. Updated after each mayoral election. 25¢ (including postage).
This chronological listing of mayors includes their political affiliation, terms of office, dates of election, and birth and death dates.

IL13. Municipal Reference Library. *Recent Additions, Municipal Reference Library.* (Rm. 1004, City Hall, Chicago 60602) Vol. 1, 1958– . Monthly.
This is a list of titles added to the collection of the Municipal Reference Library. Titles are listed by subject with full bibliographic citation, including OCLC numbers.

IL14. Municipal Reference Library. *Recent Additions, Police Branch Library.* (Rm. 1004, City Hall, Chicago 60602) Vol. 1, 1968. 608pp. Bimonthly.
Arranged by subject with full bibliographic citations, this is a list of titles added to the Police Branch Library of the Chicago Municipal Reference Library. This list is useful as an acquisition tool for selected materials on law enforcement.

IL15. *Olcott's Land Values: Blue Book of Chicago.* Chicago: G. C. Olcott & Company (111 W. Washington St., Rm. 1142, Chicago 60602), 1900-1976– . Annual. $26.
Anyone interested in assessing neighborhoods in the Chicago metropolitan area will find this blue book valuable. It gives information on zoning provisions, class of buildings, and land values. An index to streets refers to detailed maps of areas. Schools are also indexed and located on maps. Predominant nationalities are also indicated on the maps.

IL16. Rather, Ernest R. *Chicago Negro Almanac and Reference Book.* Chicago: Negro Almanac Publishing Co. (5100 S. Cornell, Chicago 60615), 1972. 256pp.
The most comprehensive Who's Who to Blacks in Chicago, the almanac includes biographical information on selected Blacks as well as lists of names, i.e., Chicago Negro judges, Negro librarians, established Negro churches, etc.

IL17. University of Chicago. *Local Community Fact Book: Chicago Metropolitan Area.* Edited by Evelyn M. Kitagawa and Karl E. Taeuber. Chicago: University of Chicago (Chicago Community Inventory), 1963. 345pp.
To fulfill the "need for a convenient compilation of a variety of information on local communities within the [Chicago] metropolitan area," this compilation gives detailed analyses of census data relating to local communities. An excellent history of each community is included in the 1960 edition. For statistical data by community areas for 1970, see *Community Area Data Book* (entry **IL4**).

Collections

IL18. Chicago Municipal Reference Library. Rm. 1004, City Hall, 121 N. LaSalle St., Chicago, 60602, (312)744-4992.

The primary function of the Chicago Municipal Reference Library, established in 1901, is to serve the city of Chicago departments and agencies, but it also serves as a public reference library. The collections cover the subject areas of concern to municipal government. Special strengths include all aspects of Chicago; law enforcement and criminal justice, housing, public finance, urban affairs, and urban planning. For the city of Chicago the collection includes all published departmental reports from 1871 to date; *Proceedings of the City Council*, 1865 to date; *Municipal Code*, 1837 to date; and election returns for the city, 1892 to date (on aperture cards). Special collections include a local newspaper clipping file, begun in 1956 and now grown to 81 legal-sized filing drawers; community area information, Chicago campaign literature from 1902 to date; and a Chicago street name file giving origins and changes in street names.

(See also entry **US4**.)

PEORIA

Data not available at this time.

ROCKFORD

Local documents are published by the city of Rockford, Winnebago County, the park district, sanitary district, school district, airport, library, City-County Planning Commission, Mass Transit District, Rock Valley Metropolitan Council (planning for Winnebago County, Illinois, and Rock County, Wisconsin), Comprehensive Health Planning of Northwest Illinois, Rockford School of Medicine, Rockford Area Chamber of Commerce, United Way Services, Winnebago County Council on Aging, American Association of University Women, League of Women Voters, and numerous other agencies.

A great deal of publishing has been done by the local planning agencies. Annual reports and budgets are not available from some of the special taxing districts. Also it is difficult to obtain many of the older documents published by local agencies. **Local Newspaper Indexing**: The Rockford Public Library (see entry **IL35**) does not maintain an index but has an extensive selective collection of articles of lasting historical interest in a clipping file on the city and county arranged by subject and in chronological order. Selection is done by Jan Stokes of the library.

Publications

IL19. City-County Planning Commission. *County of Winnebago Capital Improvements Program, 1977–1982.* Rockford (425 E. State St., Rockford 61104), 1976. 23pp. Updated annually. $1.
This report updates the proposed schedule of public works and related equipment to be built or purchased by local governments during the following six years. All future projects are listed in order of construction priority together with cost estimates and anticipated means of financing.

IL20. City-County Planning Commission. *East Side Rockford Fact Book, West Side Fact Book, Southwest Rockford Fact Book.* Rockford (425 E. State St., Rockford 61104), 1976. $2.
These reports inventory and analyze existing land use, residential structural conditions, community facilities and socioeconomic characteristics. The studies have been developed to help determine projects and funding for community development programs.

IL21. City-County Planning Commission. *Housing Fact Book.* Rockford (425 E. State St., Rockford 61104), 1974. 61pp. $2.
This document is one of a series of technical reports prepared as a part of the Housing Study for Rockford-Winnebago County. It contains much statistical data on population and housing characteristics as well as analytical material and recommendations.

IL22. City-County Planning Commission. *The Neighborhood Analysis Fact Book.* Rockford (425 E. State St., Rockford 61104), 1974. 104pp. $1.50.
Through use of the 1970 census of population, the report provides profiles of neighborhoods in Rockford and Winnebago County, Illinois. The profiles analyze physical, socioeconomic, and demographic variables at the neighborhood level. Variables include population, density, poverty families, family income, employment, schooling, age and value of housing, plumbing facilities, overcrowded housing, rentals, population under 18, automobiles, and welfare. It also analyzes noncensus data such as police calls and admissions to mental health zone center. One section of the report measures interrelationships between variables. The final section includes the part of a community health survey dealing with environmental health conditions.

IL23. City-County Planning Commission. *Plan for Parks and Open Spaces in Winnebago County.* Rockford (425 E. State St., Rockford 61104), 1973. 90pp. $1.50.
This report is a segment of the Comprehensive Plan for Winnebago County. It provides a framework for development of parks and open spaces. Goals, policies, and priorities are presented, and park and open space needs and resources are analyzed. Appendixes include an inventory of public and private parks, natural areas, and open space; a listing of potential reservoir sites; and an inventory of public and private schools in the Rockford urban area.

IL24. Rockford. Chamber of Commerce. *Facts, Figures, Features.* (815 E. State St., Rockford 61101) n.d. Continuously updated. 50pp. Available free of charge to businesses interested in investing in the community and on interlibrary loan from Rockford Public Library.
This publication is a detailed statistical analysis of the Rockford area, designed to meet the information needs of businesses interested in investing in the community.

IL25. Rockford. Chamber of Commerce. *Rockford Area Manufacturers Directory.* (815 E. State St., Rockford 61101) 1976. 90pp. Updated biannually. $5.
This directory lists 525 manufacturing firms in Rockford and Winnebago County. Officers, employment, and products are shown for most firms.

IL26. Rockford. Chamber of Commerce. *Rockford Metro-Guide.* (815 E. State St., Rockford 61101) September 1977. Approx. 100pp. Updated biannually.
The guide will contain information of particular interest to new residents of the Rockford area. Included will be facts on housing, recreation, shopping, health, education, and transportation. Contains a city locator guide map.

IL27. Rockford. League of Women Voters, and American Association of University Women, Rockford Branch. *The Government Guide to Winnebago County and Rockford, Illinois.* Rockford (2929 N. Main, Rockford 61103), 1976. 76pp. $1.50.

This booklet includes basic information on governmental structure and officials of the county as well as communities and special districts within the county. It also includes information on elections and a short history of the county. Brief bibliography.

IL28. Rockford. School of Medicine, Office of Community Health Research. *Community Health Survey: Summary.* (1601 Parkview Ave., Rockford 61101) 1973. 248pp. Free (limited number of copies).
The report provides a summary of health statistics and information gained from a consumer survey of Winnebago and Boone counties, Illinois. It summarizes physical, environmental, and mental health characteristics. Results are based on responses from 1,700 households.

IL29. Rockford. School of Medicine, Office of Community Health Research. *Seven Counties Regional Health Survey: Summary Report.* (1601 Parkview Ave., Rockford 61101) 1973. 302pp. Free (limited number of copies).
The report surveys physical, environmental, and mental health in a seven-county region of northwest Illinois. It is essentially similar to the Community Health Survey conducted in Winnebago and Boone counties.

IL30. Rockford. School of Medicine. Office of Community Health Research. *Survey of Health Manpower, Resources and Education.* 4 vols. (1601 Parkview Ave., Rockford 61101) 1973. 499pp. Free (limited number of copies).
The survey is a comprehensive analysis of practitioners and agencies dealing with the health of the people of northwest Illinois. It examines the extent, needs, and trends of health personnel and facilities in the area.

IL31. United Way Services. *United Way Directory of Service Agencies and Associations.* Rockford (304 N. Main, Rockford 61101), 1976. 90pp. Updated semiannually. $2.50.
This directory of service agencies in the Rockford area is arranged alphabetically by agencies. Each entry includes address, phone number, main contact person, and a paragraph explaining the purposes and services of the agency. The index is arranged by broad service categories.

IL32. Webster, Ernest, and Marilee McSweeney. *Whole Rockford Catalog: A Handbook for Daily Living.* Rockford: Rockford Public Library, 1974. 46pp. Copies no longer available for purchase.
This handbook in its easy-to-read format and language, was designed to provide information to meet daily needs. Individual chapters inform the reader of agencies and resources available in crisis situations and in problems involving discrimination and civil rights, education, employment, family problems, recreation, housing, medical problems, money, and transportation. There are indexes by subject, agency name, and individual.

IL33. Winnebago County Council on Aging. *Guide to Senior Services in Winnebago County.* Rockford (212 N. Main, Rockford 61101), 1976. 66pp. $2.
The directory is designed to provide access to the senior citizen service network and to help the professional who is not in constant contact with that system. The entry for each agency details functions of the agency, cost of its services, accessibility to the handicapped, and bus line proximity. The detailed table of contents is color coded to provide easy and rapid accessibility to directory contents. There is also a subject index.

IL34. Winnebago County Council on Aging and Rockford School of Medicine, Office for Community Health Research. *An Assessment of the Health Status and Health Needs of the Elderly of Winnebago County, Illinois: A Summary Report.* Edited by Dennis A. Frate and Dennis Haffron. Rockford: Winnebago County Council on Aging or Rockford Public Library, 1976. 64pp. Available on loan. This report is a summary of health and health-related data on the elderly of Winnebago County. The survey was conducted by means of a questionnaire, and the seniors to whom it was mailed were selected randomly from the council's mailing list. Six hundred and one individuals age 60 years and older resided in the 459 households responding. Data in the report includes marital status, ethnicity, income levels and sources, housing characteristics, physician and hospital visits, medical problems, food allowance, disability, club membership, and health expenditures.

Collections

IL35. Rockford Public Library. 215 N. Wyman St., Rockford 61101 (815)965-6731. Teletype service in process of changing.
The library has the Rockford-Winnebago County Ordinances, the complete publications of the City-County Planning Commission and the Mass Transit District as well as the area health care studies done by the Rockford School of Medicine and Comprehensive Health Planning of Northwest Illinois. The library is a state document depository, and much local data is available in state documents on deposit at the library. Microfiche of the tapes of the 1970 census of Illinois provide extensive census data on the area. A special nine-month library project, Planning and Progress Information Services, indexed sources of local data and statistics, and the files of this project remain very useful.

SPRINGFIELD

Springfield city offices produce most of their reference works in the form of continuations. These are minutes, annual reports, and so forth. In addition to continuations, many departments issue irregular reports on various topics. Distribution copies are usually available for a few months only . The Springfield-Sangamon County Regional Planning Commission produces the greatest quantity of individual reports.
No department offers a catalog of publications available, nor is there a centralized distribution point. The Lincoln Library's (Springfield's Public Library) Sangamon Valley Collection (see entry **IL41**) has copies of most items printed after 1973. **Local Newspaper Indexing:** The *Illinois State Journal*, Springfield, is indexed by name only to 1860. Index available at Illinois State Historical Library, Springfield 62701. Current issues of the *Journal* are indexed by obituaries only. Information available at the Lincoln Library (see entry **IL41**). Queries accepted.

Publications

IL36. Capital City Railroad Relocation Authority. *Preliminary Corridor Report.* Edited by Harland Bartholomew and Associates. Springfield, 1975. 133pp. (Available on interlibrary loan from: Sangamon Valley Collection, Lincoln Library, 326 S. Seventh St., Springfield 62701.)
Railroad relocation has been a popular subject in the Springfield area since the early 1900s. Finally, in the 1960s, the CCRRA was formed to implement the project. This report contains much more than the title would suggest. The authority is con-

cerned with all forms of local transportation in relation to the railroads. This mammoth work contains maps, letters, suggestions, etc., as background for the project which will not be completed for another ten years. It provides much insight into the city politically, culturally, geographically, and historically.

IL37. Harrison, Shelby M. *The Springfield Survey: Social Conditions in an American City.* 3 vols. New York: The Russell Sage Foundation, 1918. (Available from: Lincoln Library, 326 S. Seventh St., Springfield 62701).
Historically, one of the best works for studying the make-up of the community. Nothing of its kind has been attempted since. The foundation explored every facet of city life, good and bad. It focuses on all types of social problems found in Springfield. It is the swan song of Springfield's reform years.

IL38. Springfield. Department of Accounts and Finances. *City of Springfield, Illinois Financial Report.* (Rm. 210, Municipal Bldg., Springfield, 62701) 1950/51– date. Annual.
This work offers an in-depth assessment of the city's current financial condition. This is Springfield's official account book. All city departments are covered, even though each may publish a separate report. No index, but a well organized table of contents is useful for scanning. A "Facts about Springfield" section gives a current report on city progress. Although written in a flattering manner, it does contain many important facts.

IL39. Springfield. League of Women Voters. *The Citizens' Guide to Sangamon County.* (330 S. Sixth St., Springfield 62701) 1975. 77pp. $1.50.
A compendium of facts useful for dealing with all city and county offices. Better than anything published by either government. This publication includes the only known *published* chart of city government organization.

IL40. West, Myron Howard. *City Plan of the City of Springfield, Illinois.* . . . Springfield: City Council, 1925. 93pp. (Available on interlibrary loan from: Sangamon Valley Collection, Lincoln Library, 326 S. Seventh St., Springfield 62701.)
A grandiose plan intended to change the face of Springfield, this plan was adopted in 1925. It is important chiefly for the zoning changes implemented. It reflects on the city's problems which resulted during its rapid growth in the preceding 50 years.

Collections

IL41. Lincoln Library. Springfield's Public Library. 326 S. Seventh St., Springfield 62701 (217)753-4910.
Lincoln Library's Sangamon Valley Collection is building a comprehensive collection of city documents and complementary materials. All current items are added to the collection which contains records dating back to the 1850s. The Sangamon Valley staff attempts to answer any question relating to Springfield and the surrounding area. If the information is not found in this library, other community resources will be utilized. In short the Lincoln Library's Sangamon Valley Collection will attempt to locate any city information.

INDIANA

General Publications

IN1. City Securities Corporation. *Financial Facts on All Indiana Taxing Units*. Indianapolis (400 Circle Tower, Indianapolis 46204) 1961– . Annual. Free.
Arranged by county, each section begins with a narrative description of the county, noting especially the principal industries, the net assessed valuation and the county bonded by indebtedness. Data for each taxing unit (townships, school, corporations, etc.) includes current figures for general obligation bonds, veterans and common school loans, revenue bonded debt, net assessed valuation, and total tax rate. There is no index.

IN2. Commission for the Handicapped in Indiana. *Directory of Services for the Handicapped in Indiana, 1976.* Indianapolis (State Board of Health, 1330 W. Michigan St., Indianapolis 46206), 183pp. Irregular. Free.
This is a general guide to the services available in Indiana from agencies and organizations offering direct or referral services to handicapped individuals. It is arranged alphabetically by the name of the agency or institution but there are also two appendixes which include an alphabetical index and a service area (subject) index. Each entry provides the address, telephone number, administrative officer, type of organization (i.e., private or public), general purpose, persons served, application procedure, financial foundation, and local offices. This is only a guide to these agencies and does not constitute endorsement by the commission.

IN3. Indiana. Commission on the Aged and Aging; State Board of Health; and Indiana Senior Citizens Association Inc. *Directory of Indiana Senior (Citizens) Centers*. 3rd ed. Title varies: 1964 and 1971, *Directory of Services for the Aging*. Indianapolis: Indiana State Board of Health, 1975. 16pp. Irregular. Free. (Available from: Indiana Senior Citizens Association Inc., 215 N. Senate Ave., Indianapolis 46202.)
The cooperation of two state agencies and one independent association produced this directory of centers serving senior citizens. There are two sections in the directory. The first lists the area agencies on aging, giving complete name, director, address, telephone number, and area number which corresponds to the map that follows the list. The second part lists by area, then alphabetically by county, the various centers and clubs serving senior citizens. The complete name, address. and telephone number are given for each center, plus the name of its director and the size of its membership.

IN4. Indiana. Department of Mental Health. Statistics Office. *County Statistics: Fiscal Year 1975.* Indianapolis (5 Indiana Sq., Indianapolis 46204), 1975. 31pp. Annual. Free.

Statistics, organized alphabetically by county, are given on persons being served by the state mental hospitals, mental health clinics, and other developmental disabilities hospitals. Data is provided on the number of hospital admissions, patients, discharges, and terminations. Patients are identified by county of residence. Admissions and discharges are given by basis for admission and by rates per 1,000 county population of county of legal residence.

IN5. Indiana. Department of Public Instruction. *Indiana School Directory, 1976–1977.* Indiana School Officials. Indianapolis (227 State House, Indianapolis 46204) 122pp. Annual $2.50.
Directory information for the various school systems, both state and local, is listed in this publication. The first section is primarily devoted to state agencies and various state-operated schools, such as vocational-technical schools and state mental schools. The remaining listings are mainly for local school corporations. Public schools are listed in alphabetical sequence and provide the principal's name, address, telephone number, and school enrollment. This information is repeated when schools are presented alphabetically by county. Public school superintendent's names are given alphabetically with directory information. Two other sections that are particularly helpful as a local reference tool are: private and parochial schools in county sequence and publishers and school house suppliers. All sections are easy to use.

IN6. Indiana. Department of Public Welfare. *Semi-Annual Statistical Report: July–December, 1976.* Indianapolis (Rm. 701, State Office Bldg., Indianapolis 46204), 1976. 239pp. Semiannually. Free.
The Department of Public Welfare publishes factual information concerning welfare programs in Indiana by county in this semiannual publication. Since 1936 the publication has changed content due to the many changes in welfare programs. However, it has continued to present data on major welfare programs, cases, and costs. Some of the most interesting tables include food stamp participation for counties by race, medicaid expenditures by county, cost of programs by counties showing participation of federal, state, and county funds, and the use of the county welfare dollar. Several maps and illustrations are provided. Comparison figures for various years are given for some of the statistics in the July–December issue.

IN7. Indiana. Employment Security Division. Research and Statistics Section. *Occupational Wage Survey, 1968, 1970, 1972.* Indianapolis (10 N. Senate Ave., Indianapolis 46204), 1976. Unpaged. Irregular. Free.
Some basic population statistics are given in this survey but its primary purpose is to examine occupational demand. The occupations surveyed are those most common to the manufacturing industries in firms participating, classified on a uniform basis as determined in the survey questionnaire. The data presented are number of employees, and amount of earnings, including cost-of-living bonuses, and incentive pay (overtime is excluded) by occupation. This is a current source of employment statistics.

IN8. Indiana. Employment Security Division. Research Statistics Section. *Profile of Economic Regions: Region 13, 1972.* Indianapolis (10 N. Senate Ave., Indianapolis 46204), 1976. 13pp. Irregular. Free.
Although the Employment Security Division publishes these regional profiles, they provide much more than employment statistics. Statistically, they give population, commuting patterns, employment, industrial firms and employment, occupations of numerical significance, and occupational demands. These profiles

are a good resource when a larger area of information is needed than is available from most local sources and many other state or federal compilations.

IN9. Indiana Farm Bureau Inc. *County Government, Statistical Report: Handbook for Farm Bureau Local Affairs Committees and Local Public Officials.* Indianapolis (Legislative Department, 130 E. Washington St., Indianapolis 46204), 1976. 77pp. Annual.
A wealth of statistical material is provided in this publication primarily for the purpose of comparing county expenditures and appropriations. A most useful table is the one on salary figures for the officials and staff. All tables are heavily footnoted indicating any special circumstances needed in comparisons. There is an extensive narrative, explaining the general essence of county government which includes a summary of various county regulations. Two examples are issuance of bonds and the functions of the county cemetery commissions.

IN10. Indiana. State Board of Accounts. Statistical Department. *Roster of State and Local Officials of the State of Indiana.* Indianapolis (912 State Office Bldg., Indianapolis 46204), 1976. 129pp. Annual. Free.
This is a most useful compilation of names and addresses of state and local officials. The roster currently includes eight parts of which three are devoted to state officials and agencies including the legislative and judicial branches. Part 4 identifies federal officials. The remaining parts are devoted to local officials including county sheriffs, school clerks, town clerk-treasurers, and township assessors and trustees. Political affiliation and length of terms are indicated for elected officials. Also given are township population from the latest U.S. census, county seats, and various maps illustrating congressoinal districts, judicial circuits, etc. As an added benefit, the roster cites relevant sectons of the Indiana code. The one drawback to the roster that should be mentioned is that there is no functional or name index. Although state agencies are arranged by the key word of the exact name of the department, without some knowledge of the agencies, the roster is difficult to use. A name index would be particularly helpful in verifying what office a specific person holds.

IN11. Indiana. State Board of Health. *Indiana Vital Statistics, 1975.* Indianapolis: State Board of Health, Public Health Statistics (1330 W. Michigan St., Indianapolis 46204), 1976. 57pp. Annual. Free.
By not only covering the state and the counties, but by also including the major cities in the presentation of statistical data, this publication is an invaluable resource tool. Like most compilations of vital statistics, it includes deaths and their leading causes, death rates, birth rates, births, stillbirths, and marriages, among others. Additional tables on infant deaths, premature births, illegitimate births and rates are available upon request but not included in this volume. The tables are easy to use and include the information necessary for reference. The major drawback of this publication is its late issuance which, because of compilation of statistics, cannot be improved.

IN12. Indiana. State Board of Health, Division of Hospital and Institutional Services. *Directory of Indiana Hospitals, 1955, 1958, 1962.* Indianapolis (1330 W. Michigan St., Indianapolis 46206), 1977. 41pp. Annual. Free.
Divided into two sections, the 1977 Directory of Indiana Hospitals provides a list of hospitals in Indiana by county. Section 1 lists general and allied special hospitals, while section 2 covers psychiatric hospitals, retardation and development disabilities hospitals and community health centers, each type listed separately.

Entries are listed alphabetically within each county and include name of facility, address, telephone number, administrator's name and, when relevant, the name of the medical officer. A list of the members of the Hospital Licensing Council and their addresses is also included. An index by name of facility is also available.

IN13. Indiana. State Board of Health, and Health Facilities Council. *Indiana Licensed Health Facilities: Directory.* Indianapolis (1330 W. Michigan St., Indianapolis 46206), 1976. 31 pp. Annual. Free.
This directory provides a listing of the health facilities in Indiana by county. The complete name of the facility, capacity classification, address, telephone number, and the name of the administrator are given. There is also an alphabetical index by name of the facility. Although the directory specifically states that the facility should be contacted regarding available services, it does give a general classification of services (i.e., comprehensive nursing, residential and boarding home for the aged) through an identification code.

IN14. Indiana. State Chamber of Commerce. *Here's Your Indiana Government.* 17th ed. Indianapolis (201 Board of Trade Bldg., Indianapolis 46204), 1975. 16 pp. Irregular. $1.75.
Although this is primarily a guide to state government, it does cover the basic organization of local government as required by the state law. It provides a description and full explanation of the various responsibilities and functions of counties, townships, towns, cities, and special districts including water and sanitary districts and election districts. It provides organization charts for the various classed cities and for Indianapolis. Besides an historical section on the state, there is also a part describing the origins of the counties. A copy of the current state constitution is located at the end. The subject index makes this guide easy to use. This is a standard reference tool which continues to be a major contribution to any library needing Indiana information.

IN15. Indiana. State Chamber of Commerce. *The Indiana Industrial Directory.* 17th ed. Indianapolis (2nd Floor, Board of Trade Bldg., Indianapolis 46204), 1976/1977. 379 pp. Biennial. $20.
Commercial concerns and business establishments of the communities in the state of Indiana are presented in this statewide guide. The three major sections are the civic encyclopedia, which lists industries by community and also gives general facts about the community such as location, population, and zip code; the buyer's guide, which identifies industries by product; and the alphabetical index. Also included in the directory are a few maps of bus routes and a listing of county seats.

IN16. Indiana. State Highway Commission. *Directory of Indiana State, County, and City Officials Responsible for Road and Street Work, 1974.* Compiled by D. G. Shurig. Lafayette: Purdue University (West Lafayette 47907), 1977. 28 pp. Annual. Free.
Although this directory is primarily concerned with officials involved with road and street responsibilities, it also includes major county officials plus many city officials, such as mayor, chief of police, and engineers. It identifies the engineers and managers of the six state highway districts as well as officials of the State Highway Commission, Toll Road Commission, and various associations. This directory duplicates to a great degree the information contained in the Roster of State and Local Officials (see entry **IN10**) issued by the Indiana State Board of Accounts. However, it lists several officers which are excluded from the roster, making it

worthwhile in locating lesser-used addresses for reference and acquisition purposes.

IN17. Indiana. State Library. *Statistics of Indiana Libraries, 1975.* Indianapolis 46204), 62pp. Annual. Free.
The State Library compiles this publication which is quite useful in locating both statistical information and services but also serves as a directory since it lists both the location of the libraries and the librarian in charge. The statistics given include population served, date organized, original financial base, book and nonbook holdings, and financial data, such as book expenditures and number of personnel. Information is given for public and nonpublic, county, city, academic, and special libraries. A locational map is provided with a key by name of library. Statistics for public libraries are based on calendar year; other libraries on fiscal year.

IN18. Indiana. State Planning Services Agency. *Indiana Fact Book.* Indianapolis (3rd Floor, Harrison Bldg, 143 W. Market, Indianapolis 46204), 1976. 325pp. Irregular.
The *Indiana Fact Book* is a compilation of statistical tables on a wide range of subjects for the state of Indiana and its various communities. Much of the information is presented either by county or by the eleven SMSAs. Tables are arranged by broad subject sections, which consist of demographic, economic, social, environmental, and governmental data, and are then broken down into more specific subject areas such as manufacturing, poverty and welfare, and land use. The extent to which the data is analyzed by state, region, county, of SMSA varies, but all tables are clearly cited for use in obtaining more specific details. Maps of counties, principal cities, planning and developmental regions, and SMSAs are included. Some comparative data for various years is presented and a general description of development is contained for the state in the introduction. Although the tables are arranged by subject, an index with cross-reference would be a welcome addition.

IN19. Indiana. State Planning Services Agency. *Social Indicators.* Indianapolis (3rd Floor, Harrison Bldg., 143 W. Market, Indianapolis 46204), n.d. Unpaged.
This volume presents both bibliographic and statistical informaton that presents Indiana's social development. Phase 1 is entitled "A bibliographical index of relevant materials for state social and human services planners" and was completed in 1974. It critically annotates reports applicable to Indiana's level of social and human services or the social accounting process. The reports are arranged by spheres of interest, such as methodology and historical development. The materials included are books, government documents, and periodical articles, published from 1955 to 1974. Phase 2 of the volume is statistical and is entitled "A study in comparative descriptive indicators for the state of Indiana." It was prepared in June 1975. Almost all the data is by county, but some city information and statistics are given. Types of material included are buying power, numbers of marriages and divorces, religious participation, and death rates. Data are 1967 or later. Data sources of tables are well cited making this tool more useful. Although the list of tables is descriptive, an index is definitely needed to ease access to many valuable tables.

IN20. Indiana State Teachers Association. Research Service. *Local Salary Schedule Compilation: Indiana School Corporation.* Indianapolis (150 W. Market St. 46204), 1976. Unpaged. Annual.

Arranged by county, this reference tool provides the local salary schedules for each school corporation in Indiana. Salaries are given for teachers, showing the influence of experience and educational attainment. The tables also relate the salary to the length of school term. Any other special information relative to salary is noted. Also included are the minimum salary schedules passed by the state of Indiana in 1967 and basic educational requirements for teachers in Indiana. This is especially helpful for people looking into comparisons of school systems or evaluating employment conditions.

Collections

IN21. Indiana University. Bloomington Library. Tenth and Jordan Sts., Bloomington 47401. (812)337-6924. Teletype Service: TWX, (810)351-1386.
The IU Library, Government Publications Department, collects and maintains a file of municipal publications for cities and counties in Indiana and the major metropolitan areas across the United States. These files are far from comprehensive but support local demands and interests. It also collects official publications of states of the United States, foreign governments, and international governmental organizations. The collection is a depository for U.S. documents, receiving most reports issued by the U.S. Bureau of the Census as well as the numerous other offices of the federal government. It is also a depository for state of Indiana documents, collecting these documents as comprehensively as possible.

IN22. INDIRS (Indiana Information Retrieval System). Division of Research. Graduate School of Business, Indiana University, Bloomington 47401.
INDIRS is a major computer information system operated chiefly for the citizens of Indiana by the Indiana Division at the Indiana State Library. However, the system is accessed throughout the state at numerous locatons in public libraries, schools, and businesses. The system is continually expanding its capabilities but for the most part it contains information on social, political, cultural, economic, and general activities of the state, its counties, economic regions, cities, and the eleven SMSAs that include Indiana counties. Sources of the governmental statistics are primarily from federal, state, and local agencies but other sources may be included if the information is reliable. Since the system is currently operating on an experimental basis and is supported by a federal grant, the costs for its use may vary in time. Further information may be obtained by contacting the INDIRS program manager. A manual describing the data is available for $20 and may be ordered from the Division of Research.

EVANSVILLE

Besides annual reports of the various departments, the largest percentage of the publishing done by the city of Evansville is planning documents or studies. Nongovernmental agencies publish the majority of reference resources which include directories, economic statistics, and organizatonal charts of government. The publications are usually available free; for priced items, the issuing agency should be contacted. Materials may be borrowed, except for certain items classified as reference, from the Evansville Public Library and Vanderburgh County Public Library (see entry **IN29**), the Indiana State Library, and the Indiana University Library, Government Publications Department (see entry **IN21**). **Local Newspaper Indexing:** The Evansville Public Library (see **IN29**) has indexed the *Evansville Press*, *Evansville Courier*, and the *Sunday Courier-Press* since 1972, and before this a clipping file was maintained.

Publications

IN23. Evansville. League of Woman Voters. *Focus on Evansville.* 1967. 83pp. Irregular. (For further information contact: Julie Oberhelman, 3513 Aspen Dr., Evansville 47711.)
This is a summary of the functions and services of Evansville area officials. It gives no statistics but does describe the levels of government and their responsibilities. At the beginning there is a directory of officials. Also included is a brief history of the city, as well as a cultural view of the present Evansville. A good subject index and a map of the general area are included.

IN24. Evansville. Redevelopment Commission. *Twenty Years of Progress: Urban Renewal, Evansville, Indiana.* (Rm. 327, City-County Administration Bldg., Evansville 47708), n.d. 40pp.
This report is primarily concerned with the progress of Evansville's urban renewal projects from 1953 through 1973. The reason for including it as a resource tool is that it also provides a roster of the present and former officials concerned with urban renewal. Again covering the period 1953–1973, it lists mayors, redevelopment trustees and commissioners, and executive directors. There are some statistics provided concerning the expenditures, land area affected, and persons relocated for individual urban renewal projects.

IN25. Metropolitan Evansville Chamber of Commerce. *Evansville-Vanderburgh County, Indiana: Profile with Facts and Figures about Mid-America's Growth Center on the Ohio River, 1968.* 3rd ed. Evansville (Securities Bldg., Evansville 47708), 1971. Folder. Irregular. Free.
This small folder contains a large amount of factual information on the Evansville area often needed for quick reference. The information consists of, among others, land area, altitude, latitude, driving distance to major surrounding cities, climate, and population. Also contained is information and listings on local taxes, income level, industries employing 100 or more, educational, cultural, and medical centers, and agricultural developments. Brief glimpses into the Evansville area local government and its early economy are presented. Some of the statistics include comparison data for various dates going back to 1961.

IN26. Metropolitan Evansville Chamber of Commerce. *Metropolitan Evansville Economic Trends: A Ten-Year Study, 1961–1970.* Evansville (Southern Securities Bldg., Evansville 47708), n.d. 6pp. Free.
This statistical compilation provides basic descriptive data covering Evansville, Vanderburgh County, as well as some information for the Evansville SMSA. Information is given on the number of conventions plus the revenue they yield, new car and truck sales, banking deposits and debts, utility sales, building permits, and employment from various state and local sources. Figures from the 1970 U.S. Census of Population and Housing are also provided, giving population by census.

IN27. Real Estate Research Corporation. *Economic Market Analysis Study: Evansville Neighborhood Development Program.* St. Louis, MO (411 N. Seventh St., St. Louis, 63101), 1971. 205pp. Addendum.
This report was prepared for the Evansville Redevelopment Commission as a planning report for future development projects. However, it is a most useful tool since the research completed for the report provides statistical information, current and projected. Data is included on office space, parking, retail and whole-

sale sales, income, and population, among others. There is a special analysis of the central business area and the Beverly Heights area. Several detailed maps and illustrations are provided that are unavailable elsewhere. Accurate citation of the sources used appear throughout the publication as well as a critique of relevant studies (annotated bibliography) which is attached in the addendum.

IN28. Sprinkles, Dallas W. *The History of Evansville Blacks.* Evansville: Mid-American Enterprises. 1974. 123pp. $3.50.
This historical view of the Black community of Evansville is basically arranged by subject area, but with some chronological order. Since most of the material for the book was obtained orally, much of the early information is general but impressively interesting. It identifies several prominent Black leaders and groups of importance and provides descriptions for each. Newspaper accounts are given in several instances and there are some good photographs of places and people. Two sections of interest are "Black First" and "Black Publications." Although general organization is confusing for specific reference work, for general reading the book is of great value.

Collections

IN29. Evansville Public Library and Vanderburgh County Public Library. 22 S.E. Fifth Street, Evansville 47708 (812)425-2621. Teletype Service: TWX, (810) 353-0580.
The Adult Information Department of the Evansville Public Library and Vanderburgh County Public Library collects and stores as many of the local publications as possible including local histories, laws, and annual reports.

FORT WAYNE

Reference materials for the Fort Wayne area are for the most part nonexistent or at any rate inaccessible. The few important publications that do exist are often marred for reference use by the lack of an index or footnotes. A major problem is one of bibliographic control. There is no central collection agency. The public library (see entry **IN52**) has a municipal documents collection dating from the nineteenth century, but it is far from complete and there is no catalog to it. The newer library at Indiana University-Purdue University at Fort Wayne (see entry **IN53**) also collects municipal documents and accepts the responsibility of sending them to the *Index to Current Urban Documents.* But this collection, too, is far from complete. Other collections of documents are housing in various offices where there is little public access.

The weakness of the Fort Wayne municipal reference publications is obvious: (1) there is a need for a retrospective and then current and ongoing checklist of official local government publications; (2) there is a need for an index to the major Fort Wayne newspapers, both current and retrospective; (3) there is a need for a source-book of local municipal information (this is accomplished partly by the *Human Services Directory* (see **IN51**) and partly by *Your Local Government* (see entry **IN32**) so one knows where to go or what publications to consult for local crime statistics, tax rates, retail sales or any other current information; (4) there is a need for a biographic directory of community leaders; (5) there is a need for a directory of members of government advisory boards and councils; and (6) there is a need for an annual report both for the city and for the county. The situation improves each year, however, partly because of the demand for local information by local and regional planning agencies.

Publications

IN30. Allen County. Auditor's Office. *Financial Report.* Fort Wayne (City-County Bldg., 1 Main St., Fort Wayne 46802). Annual. Free.
Lists county receipts and disimbursements, tax rates in townships, towns and cities in Allen County (with comparisons to selected earlier years), welfare receipts and disimbursements by township, county indebtedness, an abstract of net taxable property and taxes levied, and distribution of taxes for the city of Fort Wayne. In addition to statistical data, the report provides the names and addresses of all county and township elected officials.

IN31. Allen County. League of Women Voters. *Your Government Officials, January 1977–1979.* Rev. ed. Fort Wayne (3001 Fairfield Ave., Fort Wayne 46807), 1977. Unpaged. Free.
Information provided in this publication includes name, address, party affiliation, salary, and term for officials elected locally to national, state, county, and city offices. At the county and city level, appointed officials are also listed. Also included are state and local judges and addresses of local school systems. Tips for communicating with these officials are offered. There is no index. Much of this information is also available in the *Roster of State and Local Officials* (see entry **IN10**), issued by the Indiana State Board of Accounts.

IN32. Allen County. League of Women Voters. *Your Local Government: A Guide to the Government of Fort Wayne and Allen County, Indiana.* Fort Wayne (3001 Fairfield Ave., Fort Wayne 46807), 1977. Unpaged. $1.
Your Local Government attempts to explain the complex interrelationships between the duties and responsibilities of the advisory boards, the elected and the appointed officials in each department of government, as well as the administrative organization of such local institutions as the library and the public schools. Information was gleaned through interviews, Indiana statutes, and other published sources. Charts, including government organization charts, and maps complement the text. Included in this booklet is a Bibliography of Sources of Information on Fort Wayne and Allen County, 90 percent of which is a checklist of local documents for the period 1970–1976. This is a publication of the Indiana State Chamber of Commerce. An index is provided.

IN33. *Fort Wayne (Allen County, Indiana) City Directory.* Taylor, MI: R. L. Polk and Company (6400 Monroe Blvd., P.O. Box 500, Taylor 48180), 1976. Unpaged. $85.
One of the standard city directories issued for major cities across the country, it is arranged in four parts: (1) the buyer's guide and classified business directory, (2) alphabetical directory (of personal names), (3) street directory of householders and businesses, and (4) numerical telephone directory. Information is gathered by a door-to-door citywide canvas. A companion directory, *Fort Wayne Suburban (Allen County) Directory*, performs the same function for the county areas outside the city limits.

IN34. Fort Wayne Community Schools. *Statistical Report.* (1230 S. Clinton St., Fort Wayne 46802) Unpaged. Annual. Free.
This annual report of the Fort Wayne Community Schools provides names, terms, and photos of school board members and the names and addresses of school facilities. Also provided are summary statistics on enrollment and enrollment trends, on income and expenditures, on employment, and on the adult education and special education programs. In addition the proposed budget and calendar for the ap-

proaching year are included. Omitted are the names of school officials and administrators. The publication is not indexed.

IN35. Fort Wayne. Comptroller. *City of Fort Wayne Comptroller's Annual Report.* (One Main St., Fort Wayne 46802) Unpaged. Annual. Free.
The comptroller's *Annual Report* details by department and by function the receipts and disbursements of the city's funds during the year. It closely parallels the budget in both arrangement and coverage. There is no index.

IN36. Fort Wayne Horizons Council. *Fort Wayne, Indiana, Data Book.* (Chamber of Commerce Bldg., 826 Ewing St., Fort Wayne 46802) 1977. Unpaged. $20.
The Data Book primarily includes social and economic data for the city of Fort Wayne but also includes Allen County and the Fort Wayne SMSA. With the exception of the statistics taken from the 1970 U.S. Census of Population and Housing or from the 1972 economic censuses, the information is current as of 1976. Few historical statistics are given. Issued in loose-leaf form, the Data Book is divided into eight major sections. Statistical data only is provided in the following sections: dynamic economic, population, employment, taxes, and manufacturing. In addition to statistical data the following sections provide short, narrative descriptions and lists of community facilities: transportation, utilities, and community resources. Sources of data are indicated. There is no bibliography or index. The Horizons Council plans to update the material, but they do not know when or how often.

IN37. Fort Wayne. Mayor's Office. *Civil City Budget, Fort Wayne, Indiana.* (One Main St., Fort Wayne 46802) Unpaged. Annual. Free.
The city's budget requests are enumerated department by department. The following items are covered where applicable: personal services, contractual services, supplies, materials, current charges, current obligations, and properties. There is no index and no apparent order to the entries. The city comptroller's report details the actual expenditures.

IN38. Fort Wayne Newspapers Inc. *Fort Wayne: Indiana's $3 Billion Golden Zone Market.* (National Advertising Dept., 600 W. Main St., Fort Wayne 46802) 1975. 27pp. Biennial. Free.
This booklet describes the marketing situation and the market potential for Fort Wayne and the surrounding area. Statistics, with sources, are provided on a variety of topics including population, housing, retail sales, newspaper circulation, and banking debits, clearings, deposits, and savings. In addition there are lists of test market organizations operating in the city, of food brokers, of major warehousing operations, and of manufacturers employing 50 or more people. A shopping center directory lists the stores in each of the shopping centers in the county. There is no index.

IN39. Fort Wayne. Personnel Office. *Centrex Index.* (City-County Bldg., One Main St., Fort Wayne 46802) 1976. 40pp. $1.
This telephone directory is divided into four sections: (1) civil-city and city utilities departments, (2) county offices, (3) court house offices, and (4) contact employees. The first three sections are arranged by government and subsection. Heads of departments or sections are listed with room number and Centrex number. There is no index.

IN40. Greater Fort Wayne Chamber of Commerce. *Directory of Organizations: Fort Wayne, Indiana.* Fort Wayne (Chamber of Commerce Bldg., 826 Ewing St., Fort Wayne 46802), 1971. 23pp.

This is an alphabetical list of service, professional, and social organizations in the city. The name and address of the club president and secretary (as of 1971) and the month of the election of officers are given. There is no index by name or subject. The *Human Services Directory* (issued by the United Way of Allen County) covers the service organizations included in this directory more thoroughly.

IN41. Greater Fort Wayne Chamber of Commerce. Economic and Business Developmental Department. *Principal Industries of Fort Wayne, Indiana.* Fort Wayne (826 Ewing St., Fort Wayne 46802), August 1976. 23pp. $6.
The 350 principal industries in the Fort Wayne area are listed alphabetically. Criteria for inclusion are not given. Information provided for each entry are address, product, president, telephone number, and an employment symbol. If the firm exports or imports products, this is also indicated. There is no index. The *Indiana Industrial Directory* (see entry IN15), issued by the Indiana State Chamber of Commerce, provides similar information.

IN42. Greater Fort Wayne Chamber of Commerce. Economic and Business Development Department. *Ten Year Business Indicators: Fort Wayne, Indiana— Ten Year Business Trends.* Fort Wayne (826 Ewing St., Fort Wayne 46802), 1970. 5pp.
Covering the years 1960 through 1969, the business indicators are statistics on air traffic, automobile sales and registration, building permits, conventions, employment, finance, income, population, households, postal receipts, property valuation, rail traffic, retail sales, school enrollment, tax rates, utilities, and vital statistics. Most figures are for Allen County, and sources are not given. A supplement issued in 1975 covers the years 1970 through 1974. Similar data is currently incorporated into the publication *Fort Wayne, Indiana, Data Book* (see entry IN36).

IN43. Indiana University-Purdue University at Fort Wayne. Walter E. Helmke Library. *Sources of Information about Fort Wayne and Allen County.* Compiled by Judith L. Violette. (2101 E. Coliseum Blvd., Fort Wayne 46802) 1977. 11pp. Free.
This is a checklist of documents issued by the city of Fort Wayne, by Allen County, and by regional agencies during the period 1970 through 1976. Several nondocument reference publications are listed as well. The bibliography is divided into the following sections: (1) directories, (2) local government finances, (3) local government officials, (4) planning documents, (5) schools, (6) statistical information, and (7) miscellaneous government reports and studies. There is no index.

IN44. Northeastern Indiana Regional Coordinating Council. *Community Facilities, an Inventory.* n.p. Winter 1976.
This is an inventory of art galleries, fairgrounds, golf courses, hospitals, recreation centers, and other buildings or areas which exist for the benefit of the community. Covered are facilities in existence in 1976 in Allen, Adams, Dekalb, and Wells counties (the Fort Wayne SMSA). There are, however, several important omissions. Arrangement is by county and then by type of facility. For each entry, only names and addresses are given and there is no index.

IN45. Planning Department and City Planning Association Inc. *Fort Wayne, Indiana, Economic and Demographic Data Book. Community Renewal Program: Indiana R-89 (CR),* May 1972.
Using data provided primarily by the 1970 U.S. Census of Population and Housing and partly by local government agencies, the compilers of this book have summarized the data and developed tables, charts, and census tract maps to depict data graphically and to show trends. Besides population and housing data, there is infor-

mation on the labor force and employment, on income, and on miscellaneous other topics such as park lands, airline passengers, and tax rates. Paging and an index would make this more useful.

IN46. Public Library of Fort Wayne and Allen County. *Roster of Officials of the City of Fort Wayne, Indiana.* (900 Webster St., Fort Wayne 46802) 1976. 146pp. $3. Elected and appointed officials (including members of boards and commissions) of the city government are listed here by function. The years 1940–1976 are covered primarily; but all mayors, city clerks, fire chiefs, and chiefs of police are listed from the incorporation of the city in 1840. Also all trustees of the public schools and of the public library are named. Sources are given, and enabling legislation is provided for many city offices. A name index would improve this publication.

IN47. Public Library of Fort Wayne and Allen County. *Statistical Abstract, 1966.* (900 Webster St., Fort Wayne 46802) 1966. 118pp. Local statistics are difficult to collect and this publication represents a major effort to bring together historical data about the city of Fort Wayne and Allen County. Statistics are grouped into the following categories: vital statistics, government, economics, transportation, communications and utilities, education, religion and welfare, culture, and recreation. In addition to statistics, important events and people in the city's history are listed and there are short histories and descriptions of Fort Wayne's cultural organizations. Of special note is a section on the newspaper publishing history of the city. Unfortunately the sources of information are not given and there is no index.

IN48. *Spotlight on Fort Wayne.* Fort Wayne: O'Toole Inc. (1200 Anthony Wayne Bank Bldg., Fort Wayne 46802), 1962. Unpaged. Monthly. $6 per year. What to see, where to go, and what to do are spotlighted and promoted in this publication. Each issue includes an annotated list of Fort Wayne area restaurants, a calendar of events, and a list and map of area shopping centers.

IN49. Taxpayers Research Association. *Allen County Budget Book, 1974– 1977.* Fort Wayne (826 Ewing St., Fort Wayne 46802), 1977. 102pp. Free. Comparisons of budgeted figures and actual data are given for each department of county government, for the township assessors, and for the courts. There is a table of contents (called "index"), but there is no actual index. Figures for most departments are presented in three major categories: personnel services, contractual services, and supplies. These categories are then further detailed.

IN50. Taxpayers Research Association. *Fort Wayne Civil City Budget Book, Budgets and Expenditures 1973 through July 1, 1976.* Fort Wayne (826 Ewing St., Fort Wayne 46802), 1977. 76pp. Free. Comparisons of budgeted and actual figures for each department of the city government are presented. There is no index, but there is a table of contents which is helpful since there is no particular order to the arrangement of the departments. For each department, data is presented for personnel services, for contractual services, and for supplies.

IN51. United Way of Allen County. *Human Services Directory.* Fort Wayne (227 E. Washington Blvd., Fort Wayne 46802), 1974. Updated irregularly. $8 (plus $1 mailing). Included in this unique directory are "primarily agencies, organizations or institutions which are voluntary nonprofit organizations with an established board of directors, or publicly financed services administered within a local county, state, or federal department or jurisdiction." (Preface). The directory is divided into four distinct, but interrelated sections: Section 1, an index of agencies and Section 2, a problem index (from "abused and mistreated individuals" to "zoning") relate to Section 3, Agency Descriptions, giving for each agency the address, description of services and a UWASIS code. This code refers to Section 4, the Service Identification System, an outline of community services defined under six major goal areas and based on the United Way of America Service Identification System (UWASIS). The format thus allows access for quick reference and for detailed program planning.

Collections

IN52. Public Library of Fort Wayne and Allen County. 900 Webster St., Fort Wayne 46802 (219)424-7241, ext. 216. Teletype Service: TWX (800)332-1409.
The public library, established in 1894, is one of the largest in Indiana and is known nationally for its fine genealogy collection. The collection is particularly strong in local history. The library is nearly a full depository for federal documents (since 1896) and since 1973 has received Indiana state documents for deposit. The vertical files are extensive and many of the local documents are maintained here. The Indiana collection is an important resource of local community development.

IN53. Indiana University-Purdue University at Fort Wayne. Walter E. Helmke Library. 2101 E. Coliseum Blvd., Fort Wayne 46805 (219)482-5887. Teletype Service: TWX (800)332-1409
The library at Indiana University-Purdue University at Fort Wayne was established in 1964. The strongest collections are in business, science, and general bibliography. Local and state documents are collected selectively. The library is a select depository for U.S. documents.

GARY

Gary publishes several annual reports and some planning documents which provides information on the city to some extent. Nongovernmental organizations have published a few resources which give statistical and directory information from a local source; otherwise federal and state sources must be relied on. Documents may be borrowed, except for certain reference items from the Indiana State Library and Indiana University—Bloomington, Government Publications Department. The materials at the Gary Public Library may be requested through interlibrary loan but photocopies only will be sent at a small per page charge. **Local Newspaper Indexing:** An index completed by the WPA covers 1906 to 1939 and is available for use in the Gary Public Library (see entry **IN55**). It covers several Gary newspapers including the *Gary Post Tribune*. This paper is also subject accessed through a clipping file of the public library, which began with the late 1950s.

Publications

IN54. Gary. Comptroller. *Annual Report.* (Comptroller's Office, 401 Broadway, Gary 46402) 1976. 54pp. Annual.
Even though annual reports are not commonly thought of as reference tools, this report of the comptroller of the city of Gary qualifies since it contains not only the annual statistics of the expenditures and receipts of the city, but also the official directory. The official directory lists the officers, including the members of the common council and the Board of Public Works and Safety. However, it fails to list all departments nor does it provide the addresses of their offices. The comptroller's report includes a statement of appropriations and disbursements by department, giving the amount spent on salaries and wages, traveling expenses, etc.

Collections

IN55. Gary Public Library. 220 W. Fifth Ave., Gary 46202 (219)886-2484. Teletype Service: TWX (810)698-2526.
The Indiana collection which includes most of the local municipal documents does not circulate. Photocopies can be provided at a small per page charge. The library collects the annual reports for the city departments, various planning and development reports, and has a major collection of local histories of Gary and Indiana.

HAMMOND

Hammond is not an extensive publisher of reference tools on the city but does publish annual reports, council minutes, and some planning reports which can serve as an access to the basic information on the city. Nongovernmental organizations do publish the basic reference resource tools giving directory and statistical information. The Hammond Public Library has collected the local newspapers plus a microfilm copy since 1906, but no index is available. The library has classified most of the local material as reference but some may be sent through interlibrary loan. These materials may also be borrowed from the Indiana State Library and the Indiana University Library, Government Publications Department.

Publications

IN56. Hammond. Chamber of Commerce. *Hammond, Indiana.* Chicago, IL: Windsor Publishers, 1971. 59pp. Irregular. $2. (Available from: Hammond Chamber of Commerce, 429 Fayette St., Hammond 46320.)
The publications provide the standard information needed for a reference guide to the city of Hammond. The basic statistics on population, area, climate, retail sales, and income are presented as well as a table giving driving time from Hammond to various points of interest in the Chicago region. The narrative descriptions of the city's social, cultural, and economic aspects are informative and concise. This includes a brief general history of the city and provides glimpses into the governmental structure and into the local media. Advertisements are scattered throughout the publication which has both advantages and disadvantages depending on the use of the publication. A most helpful section, especially for newcomers in the area is the "where to find it" directory located at the end of the publication and arranged by broad subjects.

IN57. Hammond Area. League of Women Voters. *Local Government Directory of Hammond, Indiana.* Hammond (Mrs. R. L. Kandalec, 6642 Kentucky Ave., Hammond 46323), 1977. 23pp. 50¢ ($1 if mailed).
By including some statistical and organizational information, this directory provides an exceptional reference resource for Hammond. A complete list of city officers provides not only the name of the officials, some staff and directory information but also gives salary information, political affiliation, and terms of each official. Notes of salary policies are included, such as for longevity and overtime pay in certain departments or for nonelected officials. A section on the Hammond Public Schools serves as an education directory, since the names of officials, principals, P.T.A. officers, and others are given as well as salary scales for teachers. County, township, state, and national senatorial officials follows, listing names, addresses, telephone numbers, and political affiliation. Democratic and Republican committee persons are listed by precinct.

IN58. Hughes-Neidigh Associates. *Park and Open Space Plan, Hammond, Indiana; Final Report—April, 1975.* Mishawaka: Hughes-Neidigh Associates Planning Consultants (100 Center Complex, P.O. Box 1009, Mishawaka 46544), 1975. 61 pp.
The Park and Open Space Plan for Hammond examines the area's resources and needs for planning the future of Hammond's recreational facilities. The plan itself is also included. The major resource aspect of this publication is that it inventories Hammond's geology, topography, soils, climate, land use, and population. Several color-coded maps and other illustrations show aspects of this inventory. Some citations to the U.S. Census are not given in full but all have some source given, many completed specifically for this study. Descriptions of current parks and recreational facilities are brief but well done for this purpose. It could serve many uses in providing reference to a variety of patrons.

Collections

IN59. **Hammond Public Library.** 564 State St., P.O. Box 889, Reference and Interlibrary Loan Department, Hammond, 46320 (219)931-5100.
Municipal documents are mainly classified reference and thus do not circulate on interlibrary loan. However, photocopies may be requested for a small per page charge. The library has a special collection of the Calumet region history and collects most of the public documents from the Hammond area. These are primarily annual reports and planning documents. Hammond Public Library neither prepares an index nor maintains a clipping file. However, the library does have the *Hammond Times* (now known as the *Times*) on microfilm and does maintain a file of the newspaper's photographs since there is no morgue at the *Times*. This file is arranged by subject and has been collected since 1962.

INDIANAPOLIS

Because of the many recent changes occuring in the Indianapolis area and the continuing growth of the area both demographically and economically in the past ten years, the publishing by and about the city has increased at a rate incomparable to most cities its size. Due to this, there are numerous duplications in publication efforts and an acknowledged need for bibliographic control. According to Mayor William Hudnut, improvements in these areas and in an arrangement for some kind of depository system will be sought in the near future. Currently, the six Unigov departments, through their public information officers, do report publications of documents to the mayor's office, and many independent corporations and county-level offices sometimes notify that office even though there is no compulsion to do so. Current publications cover the most basic reference needs particularly on economic development, governmental structure, and basic directories to local officials and organizations. Statistics are readily available and with the ever increasing capabilities of the computer system INDIRS (see entry IN22), statistics will become more easily located and convenient to use. Publications vary in price, but some are provided free; the issuing agency should be contacted. Many of the publications are available for interlibrary loan either from the Indianapolis-Marion Public Library, the State Library, or Indiana University-Bloomington Library, Government Publications Department. **Local Newspaper Indexing:** The Indiana Division at the Indiana State Library indexes the two Indianapolis daily newspapers selectively and may be used by the public for research. The newspapers themselves index extensively, but for the most part, these indexes are closed to the public.

Publications

IN60. Community Services Council of Metropolitan Indianapolis Inc. *A Characterization of Poverty in Marion County.* Indianapolis (English Foundation Bldg., 615 N. Alabama St., Indianapolis 46204), 1972. 51pp.
By gathering numerous statistics and information into one publication, the Community Service Council has provided a useful resource tool for the Indianapolis community. The data and a great deal of the narrative is compiled from various reports of the U.S. Census Bureau, but having the information in one handy location is quite valuable. Data for the Indianapolis area is analyzed by township and census tract, giving breakdowns by age, race, and income. Shaded maps illustrating distribution of poverty in the area are included. Census sources should have been specifically cited to increase the usefulness of this publication.

IN61. Hungness, Carl, editor. *The Indianapolis 500 Yearbook.* Speedway: Carl Hungness & Associates (Box 24308, Speedway 46224), 1975. 223pp. Annual.
This publication describes the major activities of the Indianapolis 500 automobile race and provides a pictorial and detailed look at the many persons involved in this event. Biographies are given for the drivers, their spouses, and other major individuals who participate in the activities, but descriptions are also given on sponsors, broadcasters, and photographers. Track records and other statistics have been tabulated. There are sections dealing with historical aspects of the race and the old-timers of past races. The publication is not a typical resource tool, often appearing to be more publicity and glamour than a compilation of information on the race. An index by subject and individual's names would be a great addition.

IN62. Indiana Heartland Coordinating Commission. *PARC 600 Regional Development: An Analysis of Employment Trends in the Heartland Region, 1964-1974.* Indianapolis (7212 N. Shadeland, Suite 120, Indianapolis 46250), 1976. 49pp. & App.
The Indiana Heartland Coordinating Commission which frequently publishes numerous reports on the area concerning water resources but ranging in other subjects, published this report on employment trends. It provides several statistics on employment and the general economy of the Indianapolis area and the surrounding counties of Boone, Hamilton, Hancock, Hendricks, Johnson, Marion, Morgan, and Shelby. Methodology for the analysis is explained and sources of the statistics are given, but no citations are included for each individual table. Numerous detailed charts and groups are presented.

IN63. Indiana Heartland Coordinating Commission. *Regional Directory: Governmental and Service Agencies in the Heartland Region.* Indianapolis (7212 N. Shadeland, Suite 120, Indianapolis 46250), 1976. 25pp. Irregular. Free.
This directory lists both governmental and nongovernmental service agencies in the Indianapolis-Marion County area, including the surrounding counties of Boone, Hamilton, Hancock, Hendricks, Johnson, Morgan, and Shelby. It is arranged by level of coverage, i.e., national, state, regional, and local organizations. Organizations are presented alphabetically by name within these levels and directory information as well as the name of the official in charge is given.

IN64. Indianapolis Black Business Directory Committee. *The Black Business Directory.* Indianapolis: Indianapolis Urban League Business Development Center (3326 N. Clifton St., Indianapolis 46208), 1973.
This directory provides the basic information needed in locating the services of the 766 Black businesses in Indianapolis. It gives name of business, address, telephone number, owner, and the type of business in alphabetical order by name of business

but also includes this information in the second section which is by broad subject areas. Although this duplicates the information, it is useful for quick reference. Some other information is included when available including years the business has been in operation and number of employees. A short list of government agencies which are of particular interest to the directory's purpose is given.

IN65. Indianapolis. Department of Metropolitan Development, Division of Planning and Zoning. *Areawide Socio-Economic Forecasts, 1975-1985. U.P.P. 520/ Work Paper No. 1; Transportation Research and Procedure Development.* (2041 City-County Bldg., Indianapolis 46204)
Normally a work paper would not classify as a resource tool, but this paper provides projections in five-year intervals on most vital statistics of the Indianapolis Regional Transportation and Development Study area. This area consists of Marion County and parts of Hamilton and Johnson counties. The purpose of this document is to provide projections of population, housing, employment, school enrollment, and automobile registrations in order to do long-range planning for future needs in the area of transportation. Several tables of data are given. Most are derived from U.S. Census studies but many include descriptions of methodology used in doing the forecasts and other explanations of needs and future land use developments.

IN66. Indianapolis. Department of Metropolitan Development, Division of Planning and Zoning. *Neighborhood Organizations; Notification of Petitions.* (2041 City-County Bldg., Indianapolis 46204) 1973. 16pp. Free.
This is primarily a roster of service-oriented community organizations of the Indianapolis-Marion County area, effective January 1 to December 31, 1974. The correct name of the major officer or executive, address, and telephone number are given. The major advantage to this directory is that it designates the area covered by the organizations by giving street boundaries covered. Used with other directories, such as the *Orange Pages* (see entry **IN67**) or the *Indianapolis Services Identification System: Directory of Community Resources* (see entry **IN72**), this can be quite useful.

IN67. Indianapolis. Department of Metropolitan Development, Division of Planning and Zoning. *The Orange Pages: A Directory of Local Government Services.* (2122 City-Council Bldg., Indianapolis 46208) 1975. 145pp.
This consumer-type directory to the services and service-oriented organizations located in Indianapolis and the Indianapolis metropolitan area is arranged specifically for the easy use of citizens. It is arranged by problem areas or very basic subject areas about which citizens might most likely need assistance in locating relevant information. For instance, a few of the subject areas covered are drug problems, noise problems, rat control, and zoning. Cross-references are given throughout the directory. For each list of agencies, there is an introductory paragraph explaining particular points and giving hints about obtaining information including the right agency to contact. An index to agencies and a more detailed subject index are presented at the end of the directory as well as an organization chart of the consolidated government for Indianapolis-Marion County and a couple of maps on government coverage and councilmanic districts. On the back cover, emergency numbers for fire, police, ambulance, poison control, and suicide are listed for the various township or city areas.

IN68. Indianapolis. Department of Metropolitan Development. Division of Planning and Zoning. *Small Area Socio-Economic Forecasts for the Year 2000 by Traffic Analysis Zones, U.P.P. 522/Work Paper 2; Transportation Research and Procedure Development.* 2nd ed. (2041 City-County Bldg., Indianapolis, 46204) 1975. 79pp. & App.

As its predecessor, Areawide Socio-Economic Forecasts, 1975–1995, this second work paper presents statistics and projected statistics on the Indianapolis area but breaks them down by sector, district, and zone levels. Socioeconomic variables are examined primarily for use in transportation planning but can be used for several other purposes. Among others, these include school enrollment, housing, and employment. Methods used in disaggregating the data are explained. The appendixes include revised and corrected data from the earlier work paper and some addition information. Most of the statistical material is presented in tables, but a few maps are included. Citations of sources used are usually complete, noting that much of the data is from unpublished material.

IN69. Indianapolis. Department of Metropolitan Development: Division of Planning and Zoning, and Department of Administration, Community Service Program. *400 Community Services: Need Identification Mechanisms for Indianapolis Community Services.* (2041 City-County Bldg., Indianapolis 46204) 1974. 201pp. The purpose of this study was to review recent efforts in need assessments of human services in the Indianapolis area and to synthesize those studies conducted primarily by the Department of Metropolitan Development. The true value lies in the fact that it identifies studies and presents a description of their content. Each description or annotation explains the rationale, methods of data collection and analysis, projections of need, constraints (such as in funding), and the final use of these projections. It is not comprehensive but does present analysis of 34 studies which represent the major survey methods employed or that were available in completed form at the time of publication. This is a most needed document since it provides evaluation of the numerous needs assessment activities and at the same time gives a selected bibliography of these studies.

IN70. Indianapolis. League of Women Voters. *UNIGOV: What It Is—What It Isn't.* Indianapolis: Chamber of Commerce, 1972. 29pp. 50¢. (Available from: League of Women Voters of Indianapolis, 3620 N. Meridian St., Indianapolis 46208.) Since the consolidation of the governments of Indianapolis and Marion County in 1970, there have been numerous questions as to what is and what isn't handled by the UNIGOV offices and what remains in the realm of city and county officials. This small book provides the basic answers to these questions but also details the resulting government structure. It defines the geographic areas included in UNIGOV, lists the various UNIGOV offices, briefly describes their individual functions, and explains that this consolidation does not mean complete federation. An organizational chart of the consolidation government for Indianapolis and Marion County and a map of city-county council districts are included.

IN71. Indianapolis Power and Light Company. *Data On: Indianapolis.* (25 Monument Circle, P.O. Box 1595, Indianapolis 46204) Unpaged. Irregular. Most of the basic community statistics are gathered together in this databook making access to these figures quite convenient. The source of the statistics are from various levels of government: state, federal, and local agencies. Aspects include are primarily on economics, labor, utilities, banking, transportation, and industry. Coverage is mainly 1970 but there are some comparison figures given for 1960 as well as projections when available. Most of the material is presented in tables but a narrative description as well as maps are provided. Although an index would improve these publications, the table of contents is quite adequate for most purposes.

IN72. *Indianapolis Services Identification System: Directory of Community Resources.* Indianapolis: Community Services Council of Metropolitan Indianapolis Inc. (615 N. Alabama St., Indianapolis 46204), n.d. 526pp. This comprehensive directory to the public and private human services organizations in the Marion County area uses the Indianapolis Service Identification System to classify these agencies. Part 1 consists of the major listing, alphabetized by official name of the agency and providing address, telephone, hours, director, brief description of the agency's function, and the primary and secondary ISIS programs. There are numerous cross-references throughout this section but there is also an alphabetical agency index. Part 2 contains several types of subject indexes, classified target clientele listing, classified ISIS program listing and a fold-out ISIS chart. This most useful tool for reference and address verification in acquisition use would be a must for libraries needing information on the Indianapolis area.

IN73. Indianapolis-Marion County Public Library. *Authors of Indianapolis and Marion County.* Indianapolis (40 E. St. Clair St., Indianapolis 46204), 1973. 43pp.
This is a well-done compilation of authors of the Indianapolis area. There is a short biography for each author which includes full name, birth/death dates, birthplace, when the author resided in Indianapolis, and the names and copyright dates of published works. The book is conveniently divided into two sections, but fiction, history, and other nonscientific areas seem to be stressed. Local historians would find the book particularly interesting.

IN74. Marion County Criminal Justice Coordinating Council. *1976 Annual Action Plan.* Indianapolis (Rm. 1441 City-County Bldg., Indianapolis 46204), 1976. Unpaged. Annual; Semiannual.
Although not published as a reference tool per se, this plan analyzes the Indianapolis area's crime programs and problems through the use of U.S. Census material and other statistics. It is made up of four sections. First, a descriptive analysis of the existing criminal justice systems and available resources are given and the different agencies' functions and actual work responsibilities are explored. It includes statistics on case loads and various court statistics. Secton 2 is a profile of the Marion Couinty area's high crime incidence and law enforcement activity, which includes demographic, socioeconomic, housing, health, and educational statistics. Section 3 presents the multiyear plan itself, while Section 4 provides program support data, i.e., funding approaches. There are numerous tables and maps included as well as a general organizational chart of the government of Indianapolis.

Collections

IN75. Indianapolis-Marion County Public Library. 40 E. St. Clair St., Indianapolis 46204 (317)635-5662.
The Indianapolis-Marion County Public Library has a major collection of publications from Indianapolis and Marion County, including annual reports, ordinances, and planning reports. Most of the municipal documents are classified as reference; photocopies can be requested for a per page charge.

SOUTH BEND

The city of South Bend is gradually increasing the extent of its publishing. For the most part, the publishing currently comprises annual reports and some planning documents which provide some good reference information. Publications are indexed in *Index to Current Urban Documents.* Most of the statistical and directory resources are published by nongovernmental agencies. *Local Newspaper Indexing:* The History and Travel Department of the South Bend Public Library (see entry **IN81**) has indexed the *South Bend Tribune* since January 1976. A clipping file was maintained before this. Both are available to students and researchers at the library. The newspaper also indexes, but its indexes are for the most part closed to the public.

Publications

IN76. Fraught, Jim D. *Social and Economic Conditions of the Spanish Origin in South Bend: Report No. 1, Census of Population.* Notre Dame: University of Notre Dame (Centro De Estudios Chicanos, P.O. Box 543, Notre Dame 46556), 1974. 122pp.
This report was prepared for the Centro De Estudios Chicanos E Investigacione Sociales at the University of Notre Dame and represents the latest available study on the people of Spanish origin for any city in Indiana. Many of the statistics are from U.S. Census Bureau reports but other data were gathered specifically for this report and present much more detail than previously published. The data are primarily on population, migration, and economic and educational status. Also included are sections dealing with the social mobility from farm labor to other occupations and local politicians' views of Mexican-American problems in South Bend. Data are 1970 to 1973, depending upon availability. The table of contents and lists of tables are descriptive, but an index by subject would have been useful.

IN77. *Market Data: '74/'75.* South Bend: the *South Bend Tribune* (South Bend 46601), 1974. 48pp. Irregular.
The *South Bend Tribune* publishes this compilation of statistics which deals with almost every aspect of the socioeconomic conditions of the South Bend area. Like most statistical publications, it covers population, employment and industry, income, and retail sales. However, this publication examines a broader area and explores a wider range of subject areas. Some of these include media coverage, giving the distribution of not only the *Tribune*, but also of the *Chicago Sun-Times*, *Chicago Tribune*, and the *Chicago Daily News*. There are several comparisons made between South Bend and nearby cities, such as La Porte and Goshen. Most tables are cited, clearly showing that the majority of information came from the U.S. Census Bureau's reports.

IN78. South Bend. Comptroller. *Comptroller's Report: City of South Bend.* (South Bend 46601) 1973. 89pp.
The outstanding aspect of this publication is that it includes a list of elected city officials, noted as incomplete but fairly extensive, and an organization chart of the governmental structure. The listing of officials would be more helpful if office addresses were included. The organization chart is quite useful and also notes if an official is elected or appointed. The comptroller's report section provides tables on the expenditures and receipts from the city of South Bend's various funds, the state of appropriations, and disimbursements of the individual departments. The report also contains four other departmental annual reports.

IN79. South Bend Public Library. History and Travel Department. *Selected List: Civic, Fraternal and Social Organizations, South Bend, Indiana, 1976–1977.* (122 W. Wayne St., South Bend 46601) 1976. Annual. Free.
Arranged by broad subject areas, this directory provides information to the local service organizations in South Bend. The presiding officer and secretary, mailing address, and telephone number are provided. Organizations are listed in the *Encyclopedia of Associations*, 9th edition. An alphabetical index is included. Another quite useful section for clubs and organizations is the one on "Suggested readings for club members" listing basic materials on parliamentary procedures, fund-

raising, planning, and general information for the clubs and organizations. This would be particularly helpful to persons not familiar with the South Bend area.

IN80. United Community Services of St. Joseph County. *Directory of Health, Welfare, and Recreation Services.* Edited by Mildred A. Higgins. South Bend (120 S. Taylor St., South Bend 46601), 1970. 61 pp. Free.
The primary purpose of this directory is to make information on the various health, welfare, and recreation agencies available to citizens of the South Bend-St. Joseph County area. It includes agencies which are members of the United Community Services but also gives independent private agencies and publicly supported programs. The directory is arranged alphabetically by standard subject headings but the alphabetical index of agencies makes this useful. The following information is given for each agency entry: name of agency, address, telephone number, regular office hours, and the geographical area served.

Collections

IN81. South Bend Public Library. 122 W. Wayne St., South Bend 46601 (219) 288-4413. Teletype Service: TWX (810)299-2593.
The South Bend Public Library attempts to maintain a collection of all municipal and county documents in its local history collection of the History and Travel Department. All materials may be made available on interlibrary loan either for borrowing or for copying. The South Bend Public Library has collected materials concerning the local area since its founding in 1888 and currently attempts to locate these items comprehensively.

IOWA

General Publications

IA1. Iowa. Department of Public Instruction. *Iowa Educational Directory.* Des Moines (Information Services, Grimes State Office Bldg., Des Moines 50319). Annual.
The arrangement is by school district and then by individual school.

IA2. Iowa. Development Commission. *Statistical Profile of Iowa: Industry, Agriculture, Travel, Foreign Export, Economic and Social Data.* Des Moines (Resource and Support Division, 250 Jewett Bldg., Des Moines 50309), 1970- . Annual.

IA3. Iowa. Office for Planning and Programming, Division of Municipal Affairs. *Directory, Areawide Planning Organizations, State of Iowa.* Des Moines (523 E. 12 St., Des Moines 50319), 1974/75- . Annual. Free.
This HUD-funded directory covers planning districts and organizations. Maps are included for the planning districts, and a statewide summary is given for both organizational process and organizational structure for Iowa's planning organizations.

IA4. League of Iowa Municipalities. *Directory of Iowa Municipal Officials.* Des Moines (444 Insurance Exchange Bldg., Des Moines 50309), 1972?- . Biennial (with off-year updates). $22.50.
Computerized list of elected and appointed officials and employees furnished to the league by city clerks.

IA5. Northwestern Banker. *Iowa Bank Directory.* Des Moines (306 15 St., Des Moines 50309), 1892- . Annual. $8.
Lists members of banking associations, committees, and various other associations. It also gives Iowa banks.

CEDAR RAPIDS

Cedar Rapids publications are not systematically collected in any one office in the city. The city clerk's office collects and microforms city council proceedings and selected annual reports from city departments. A subject index to city council proceedings goes back to 1908, and the proceedings are on microfilm, through the latest complete year. Each city department has charge of its own publications, and no effort is made to keep either a list of all city publications or a listing within each department of what the department has published. Publications may be requested from the issuing office and are usually free of charge, when copies are available. The city clerk's office will copy items for a small per page charge. Local Newspaper In-

dexing: The Cedar Rapids Public Library (see entry IA16) indexes the *Cedar Rapids Gazette*, which prints city council minutes in each Tuesday's paper, on 3 x 5-inch cards filed in the reference area. The index file, begun in 1946, was very selective at first and remained so until the late 1960s, when more articles were included. The indexing is still selective, with an emphasis on Cedar Rapids news. National news is included only when it concerns Cedar Rapids. The 1883-1908 *Gazette* index is currently being compiled at the library and consists of three files headed "Iowa," "Linn County," and "Cedar Rapids." An organizations drawer, a spin-off from the *Gazette* index, is kept current by clippings from the newspaper naming local organizations and their officers.

Publications

IA6. Cedar Rapids. City Council. *Proceedings of the City Council of the City of Cedar Rapids.* 1908- . Monthly.
The proceedings are printed weekly in the *Cedar Rapids Gazette*, as of August 1975. The city clerk's office collects each month's weekly proceedings, adds budget information, resolutions approved, other city actions, and a subject index and publishes a limited number of copies of the monthly proceedings. The Cedar Rapids Public Library keeps these proceedings for the public to examine, and there are copies in the city clerk's office (none, however, for distribution). The monthly proceedings include a current directory of city officials and commission members. Subject access to council proceedings back to 1908 is available in the city clerk's office, as are the microfilms of the proceedings themselves.

IA7. Cedar Rapids. Community Schools. Information Services. *Directory.* Cedar Rapids: Educational Service Center (346 Second Ave. S.W., Cedar Rapids 52404), 1970?- . Free.
Lists members of the Board of Education, educational associations and organizations, the Educational Service Center, and the schools. There is also a precinct map for the school district.

IA8. Cedar Rapids. Department of Social Planning. *Information on City Services.* 1976. 4pp. Irregular? Free. (Available from: CETA Information Office, City Hall, Cedar Rapids 52401.)
Lists city departments and parks, and answers basic questions concerning the responsibilities of specific departments.

IA9. Cedar Rapids. Fire Department. *Cedar Rapids Street Directory.* 1973?- . Annual. 50¢. (Available from: City Clerk's Office, City Hall, Cedar Rapids 52401.)
Streets are listed alphabetically within sections of the city.

IA10. Cedar Rapids-Marion. Chamber of Commerce. *General Survey (Cedar Rapids, Iowa): Demographic, Economic, Retail, Wholesale, Manufacturing, Liveability, and Transportation.* Cedar Rapids (127 Third St. N.E., Cedar Rapids 52401), 1956- . Annual. Free.
This publication is produced for distribution to commercial and industrial firms expressing interest in the Cedar Rapids area. It is a composite of statistical information culled from various publications and nonstatistical information, which is usually compiled by the Chamber of Commerce. There is an appended list of manufacturers in the Cedar Rapids area.

IA11. Cedar Rapids-Marion. League of Women Voters. *Cedar Rapids-Marion 1977 Political Directory.* Cedar Rapids (YWCA Bldg., 318 Fifth St. S.E., Cedar Rapids 52401), 1948- . Annual. Free.

This pamphlet lists and describes state legislative districts for the area, school board representatives, and voter registration information.

IA12. Cedar Rapids-Marion. League of Women Voters. *Know Your Community.* Cedar Rapids, (YWCA Bldg., 318 Fifth St. S.E., Cedar Rapids 52401) 1975. 28pp. Irregular. Free.
This small pamphlet includes historical background of the area, a voter's guide, and organizational charts on county and city governments. The human services section deals mostly with Linn County services available. Parks and cultural facilities are also described.

IA13. Linn County. Health Center. Information and Referral Service. *Directory of Human Resources for Linn County.* Cedar Rapids (400 Third Ave. S.E., Cedar Rapids 52401), 1975–   . Rev. ed. (with annual updates). $3 for complete directory ($1 for update and 75¢ for postage).
A guide to agencies and services in Linn County.

IA14. Linn County. Regional Planning Commission. *Publications List.* Cedar Rapids (6th Floor, City Hall, Cedar Rapids 52401), 1977. 1pp. Irregular? Free.
This sheet lists regional planning projects completed or in progress. It is not a complete list of all publications but reflects those still available on request from the commission.

IA15. Linn County. Regional Planning Commission. *Summary Report of Population, Economic, Traffic and Financial Information for the Linn County, Iowa Region.* Cedar Rapids (6th Floor, City Hall, Cedar Rapids 52401), 1970. 103 leaves. Free.
Both historical and current statistics are emphasized in the population section of the report.

Collections

IA16. **Cedar Rapids Public Library.** 428 Third Ave. S.E., Cedar Rapids 52401 (319)398-5123. Teletype Service: (910)525-1336.
City council minutes are permanently retained, but the city documents are kept on a current only basis. There is no attempt made on the public library's part to collect or house all publications emanating from city hall.

DAVENPORT

The city of Davenport has a number of directories: school directories, city directories, manufacturers' directories, and directories of services offered in the area. Not all of these are published by the city, but they fill many of the information needs of a citizenry spread over a large geographic area. The city publishing efforts are mainly directed toward the traditional government publishing such as city minutes, financial reports, zoning, and municipal codes. One of the most prolific agencies in the city is the Department of Community Development, which prepares a number of analytical and statistical planning reports on such varied topics as the housing situation, the capital improvements program, and the city plan.

The city has no checklist or bibliography of its publications. In fact, it is difficult to research municipal activity unless one visits each department individually or consults the documents collection at the Davenport Public Library—a collection that has gaps because there is only a loose depository arrangement with city offices. Another problem to keep in mind is the intergovernmental relationships among Davenport, Rock Island, Moline, Illinois, and Iowa. As a result, the search for informational resources may extend beyond Davenport. **Local Newspaper Indexing:** The Davenport Public Library (see entry IA28) has been selectively indexing the *Quad City*

Times and its predecessors for the past 30 years. The indexing is by very general subject topics. The library cannot handle out-of-city requests about information in the index.

Publications

IA17. Bi-State Metropolitan Planning Commission. *Study of Regional Data Systems.* Rock Island, IL (1504 Third Ave., Rock Island, IL 61201), 1976.
The Planning Commission coordinates several different data systems for the quad-city area of Iowa and Illinois. In this document various data systems are presented. In many cases, these are only available for internal use, but the Bi-State Planning Commission can provide up-to-date information on accessibility and costs.

IA18. Davenport. Chamber of Commerce. *Industrial Directory, Davenport-Bettendorf, Iowa.* (404 Main St., Davenport 52801) 1974. 11pp. $1.50.

IA19. Davenport. City Clerk. *Operating Budget, City of Davenport.* City Clerk's Office (City Hall, 226 W. Fourth St., Davenport 52801). Annual. Free.
In addition to budget information, this publication presents a directory of principal city officials and council members. Departmental purposes and functions are also given.

IA20. Davenport. City Hall. *Your City Government at Work—Who, What, When, Where, How. . . .* (226 W. Fourth St., Davenport 52801) 1966? 11pp. Free.
Presents the history of the city, analysis of the form of government, and an organizational chart.

IA21. Davenport. Community School District. *1976-1977 Directory, Davenport Community Schools.* (Administration Bldg., 1001 Harrison St., Davenport 52803) 1964/65- . Annual.
This document, intended for employees of the school system, includes a school calendar, financial report, history of the school system, etc.

IA22. Davenport. Department of Community Development. *Davenport, Iowa Comprehensive Plan: Background Report.* (City Hall, 226 W. Fourth St., Davenport 52801) 1976. 154pp. Free.
The report emphasizes the most current data on population, the economy, transportation, land use, education, and many other topics.

IA23. Davenport. Department of Community Development. *Total Housing Inventory System (T.H.I.S.) Davenport, Iowa.* (City Hall, 226 W. Fourth St., Davenport 52801) 1975. 52pp. Free.
This HUD 701 project report describes the computer data base for current information on housing, land, and building use. The file provides a record by address on all structures in the city as of 1972. The printed report presents aggregate data by census tract, but the agency has more detailed data available. Inquiries should be directed to the department. The agency plans to update the survey information soon.

IA24. *Quad-City Directory of Manufacturers.* Rock Island, IL: Quad-City Development Group (406 First National Bank Bldg., Rock Island, IL 61201), 1977? 100pp. $5.
The directory provides information on companies in Rock Island County, Illinois, and Scott County, Iowa, which can be classified as manufacturing concerns by Standard Industrial Classification codes.

IA25. Scott County. League of Women Voters. *Directory of Local Officials—Scott County, Davenport and Bettendorf.* Davenport: Voter Service (Sheila Fretwell, 2155 W. 30 St., Davenport 52804), in preparation.

IA26. Voluntary Action Center of Rock Island and Scott Counties. *Directory of Services: Health, Welfare, Educational, Recreational and Cultural Services for the People of the Quad-Cities Area* (cover title: *Directory of Human Services for the People of Rock Island and Scott Counties*). 2nd ed. Rock Island, IL (639 38 St., Rock Island, IL 61201), 1976?
This is a community resource directory for the area which includes both private and governmental agencies.

Collections

IA27. City of Davenport. City Hall. 226 W. Fourth St., Davenport 52801 (319) 324-2111.
The city clerk's office has the official council proceedings which visitors may consult.

IA28. Davenport Public Library. 321 Main St., Davenport 52801 (319) 326-7832. Teletype Service: (910)520-2665.
The library is the only place in the city that maintains a somewhat systematic archival collection of municipal documents. This is also the only place in the area where the public can consult older financial reports of the city, various directories of the area, as well as the index to the *Quad City Times.*

DES MOINES

The city of Des Moines publishes extensive information which is used in the financial planning and operation of the city. The key documents are performance goals and objectives (program budget), overall program design, capital improvements program and budget, monthly financial quarterly activity reports, and the operating budget. The Overall Program Design was used as part of the application materials submitted for the "All-American City" designation awarded to Des Moines.
The plan commission is working on a comprehensive plan for 1990/2000 (physical development plan). Several elements of it (public parks and open space plan, and population) have been published. The Comprehensive Plan for 1980 is currently in effect, but there are no more available copies.
In recent years, because of financial considerations, very few city departments have issued annual reports. An abbreviated annual report in the form of a calendar is published. It lists the meetings of the city council, commissions and boards, displays an organizational chart, and gives brief explanations of the functions of the city departments.
Other publications of interest concern the model-cities program, published by the Office of Community Development; the annual report of the Des Moines Low-Rent Housing Agency; and a survey of significant architecture of the city conducted by the Plan and Zoning Commission. The Des Moines Independent Community School District is a completely independent governmental entity. The documents containing the information needed to run the system (i.e., the operating budget, policy and procedures manuals, and directory of school personnel) are published annually. A history of the Des Moines Public Schools was published as a bicentennial project.
Local Newspaper Indexing: The Public Library of Des Moines (see entry IA36) maintains a subject index for the *Des Moines Register* and *Tribune.* Articles of state and local interest are indexed. The library will accept queries. The Reference Department, Iowa State University Library, Ames, also indexes the *Des Moines Register.*

Publications

IA29. Des Moines. City Manager. *Annual Calendar Report.* (E. First and Locust Sts., Des Moines 50307) 1972-   . Annual.
The cale⁓   , which is an abbreviated annual report, has an organizational chart.

IA30. Des Moines. Independent Community School District. Board of Education. *Directory.* (1800 Grand Ave., Des Moines 50307) 1914-   . Annual.
Lists the schools and their employees.

IA31. Des Moines. Independent Community School District. Office of Community Relations. *Statistical Handbook.* Compiled by the Department of Administrative Services. (1800 Grand Ave., Des Moines 50307) 1964-   . Annual.
Includes data on school enrollment, employees, physical plant, and finances.

IA32. Des Moines. Mayor's Ad Hoc Task Force on Drug Abuse Programming. *Directory of Drug Abuse Services.* (E. First and Locust Sts., Des Moines 50309) 1975.

IA33. Des Moines. Office of Community Development. *Des Moines Community Development Program: Handbook.* (E. First and Locust Sts., Des Moines 50309) 1972.

IA34. Greater Des Moines United Way. Planning Division. *Human Resources Directory: Greater Des Moines Area.* Des Moines (750 Sixth Ave., Des Moines 50309), 1972.
Lists agencies and emergency services.

Collections

IA35. Drake University. 25 St. and University Ave., Des Moines 50311.
The university has collections of the principal municipal publications, both retrospective and current in nature.

IA36. Public Library of Des Moines. 100 Locust St., Des Moines 50309 (515) 283-4152.
City and state publications are shelved in the Iowa Collection. Unless there is a second copy, they must be used in the library and do not circulate on interlibrary loan. The library has an extensive retrospective and current collection of municipal and school publications. Although the city clerk has a list of all the publications of the city of Des Moines, there is no central location where they can be obtained. Because there is an ordinance making the public library the depository for certain key publications, such as the budget, the library has the most complete collection of the city's publications. Annual reports of the city, the assessor, the Department of Finance, Board of Water Works Trustees, Low Rent Housing Agency, and the operating budget of the city are forwarded to Greenwood Press for inclusion in their *Index to Current Urban Documents.*

IA37. The State Library of Iowa. Historical Bldg., 12 and Grand Sts., Des Moines 50319.
The library has collections of the principal municipal publications, both retrospective and current in nature.

KANSAS

KANSAS CITY

Data not available at this time.

OVERLAND PARK

Local Newspaper Indexing: The Johnson County Library (see entry **KS10**) indexes the Johnson County page of the *Kansas City Star and Times* and maintains this index from 1973 to the present in the reference department of the Antioch branch.

Publications

KS1. Overland Park. City Manager. *Overland Park Quarterly Report.* n.p. (8500 Santa Fe Dr., Shawnee Mission 66212), 1974– . Free.
This quarterly newsletter is mailed to residents of the city of Overland Park. The emphasis is on providing relatively simple presentations of the city's finances, on explaining city ordinances, on spotlighting departments such as the police, and on listing achievements and signs of progress in the city. Each issue carries the names, districts, addresses, and phone numbers of the mayor and city council members. The newsletter is a well-done effort. It is attractive, informative, both for established residents who follow local government activities and for newcomers to this mobile and transient community.

KS2. Overland Park. City Manager. *Annual Budget.* (8500 Santa Fe Dr., Shawnee Mission 66212). Annual. Free.
The annual budget for the city is prepared by the city manager and presented to the mayor and council for deliberation and approval. The budget follows a basic outline from year to year: the first section deals with sources of revenue, the second with expenditures from the general fund, the third with expenditures from the special funds. Although the exact length varies from year to year, the budget normally runs about 40 pages.

KS3. Overland Park. Ordinances, Local Laws, etc. *Overland Park Municipal Code.* City Clerk (8500 Santa Fe Dr., Shawnee Mission 66212), n.d. Updated irregularly.
The Overland Park code was begun with the incorporation of the city in 1961. The code is in a loose-leaf format, with changes inserted in the appropriate section. The updating is done irregularly through the city clerks office. The code itself is kept to a limited number of copies, for the purpose of efficient updating. A copy of a section of an ordinance however is readily obtainable from either the city or the Johnson County Library (see entry **KS10**).

KS4. Overland Park. Park and Recreation Department. *Citizens Recreational Survey Report.* (8500 Santa Fe Dr., Shawnee Mission 66212) 1975. 84pp.
This study reports the findings of a survey conducted by the city park and recreation department of the recreational needs and desires of the residents. The methodology and questionnaires are reproduced as well as the data compiled. this study was produced as a part of the project to plan the physical facilities of the park system and the program activities to take place in them.

KS5. Overland Park. Park and Recreation Department. *Parks Development Plan of Existing Sites for the City of Overland Park, Kansas.* (City of Overland Park, 8500 Santa Fe Dr., Shawnee Mission 66212) 1974. 71pp.
This study was prepared in conjunction with a new site park development plan presented by Kellenberg & Co., released at the same time. This deals with the further development of park lands owned by the city at the time of the study.

KS6. Richard H. Kellenberg & Co. *Land Use Intensity—Overland Park, Kansas.* Kansas City, MO: Kellenberg & Co., (1920 Swift, N. Kansas City, MO 64116), 1972. 9+pp.
This document was prepared to supplement the plans put forth in the previous year in the Master Development Plan. It suggests land use intensities for the southern sections of the city, which at this time were only lightly developed. The study includes maps and graphs indicating the desired intensity.

KS7. Richard H. Kellenberg & Co. *A Master Development Plan for Overland Park, Kansas.* Kansas City, MO: Kellenberg & Co. (1920 Swift, N. Kansas City, MO 64116), 1971. 73pp.
This study was prepared to serve as a guide to the development of the southern sections of the city, which were newly annexed in 1971. The intent was to propose a series of arterial streets and other transportation facilities which would allow for a flexible pattern of growth in both business and residential sectors. The consultants recommended that their suggestions be used as a forecast of physical needs for growth in an orderly and functional manner. This was the second master development plan for the city. The first was prepared in the early 1960s and copies of this are not available at this time.

KS8. Richard H. Kellenberg & Co. *Parks Development Plan for the City of Overland Park, Kansas.* Kansas City, MO: Kellenberg & Co. (City of Overland Park, 8500 Santa Fe Dr., Shawnee Mission 66212), 1968. 41pp.
This is the original plan prepared for the city to push for the passage of a bond issue for recreational facilities. The study demonstrated the city to be very inadequate by national standards in parks and other recreational facilities. It pointed out what could be done with money raised from the bond revenue. The initial thrust of the program is toward neighborhood park space.

KS9. Richard H. Kellenberg & Co. *Parks Development Plan for the City of Overland Park, Kansas.* Kansas City, MO: Kellenberg & Co. (City of Overland Park, 8500 Santa Fe Dr., Shawnee Mission 66212), 1974. 30pp.
The second park development plan prepared for the city takes into account the enormous growth in population and land area in the six years since the previous study, as well as the professionalization of the recreations department of the city. This study projects the needs of the community for the years 1974 through 1980. This study was published simultaneously with a development plan for existing park sites prepared by the city parks and recreation department.

Collections

KS10. Johnson County Library. P.O. 2901, 8700 W. 63, Shawnee Mission 66201 (913)831-1550.

Johnson County Library is the only library which maintains a collection of Overland Park city documents, as well as those of other municipalities in this area. Due to the fragmented political makeup of Johnson County, which is a mixture of small, suburban municipalities, undeveloped farmland, and small cities, information on the activities of government is difficult to come by. The Johnson County Library subscribes to all municipal newsletters in the county and has tried to gather a complete set of all municipal ordinances in the county. The city of Overland Park is the largest of the cities in the county and also has the most extensive information and publication program. The Johnson County Library has copies of almost all Overland Park publications. All others are accessible through the city's public information officer.

TOPEKA

Local Newspaper Indexing: Topeka Public Library (see entry **KS18**) is indexing the local newspapers, the *Topeka Daily Capital* and the *Topeka State Journal*. It is selective indexing—important items dealing with Topeka and Shawnee County. The state of Kansas is not included unless it involves Topeka or Shawnee in some way. Obituaries are indexed. The years 1971 through 1974 are completed. The years following 1974 are in various states of completion (except for the obituaries which are much more current). The library can do limited research for patrons—by mail.

Publications

KS11. Topeka. City Commission. *City of Topeka, Annual Report, Department of Finance & Revenue.*

KS12. Topeka. City Commission. *City of Topeka, Kansas Annual Operating Budget.*

KS13. Topeka. Fire Department. *Annual Report.*
Statistical and informational annual report of the fire department.

KS14. Topeka. City Commission. *The Code of the City of Topeka.* n.d.
Contains the general ordinances of the city of Topeka.

KS15. Topeka. Police Department. *Annual Report.*
Pictorial and statistical information about the police department for the previous year.

KS16. Topeka. Public Schools. *Topeka Public Schools Directory.*
Directory listing public schools in Topeka, official organization, the Board of Education, and assignment of personnel.

KS17. Topeka and Shawnee County. Health Department. *Annual Report.* Topeka.
Pictorial and statistical information about the city-county health department.

Collections

KS18. Topeka Public Library. 1515 W. Tenth, Topeka 66604 (913)233-2040. The Topeka Public Library municipal documents collection is in the formative stages, with only the preliminary steps yet completed. Discussions are underway with city officials to establish an informal depository system.

WICHITA

Publications

KS19. Arthur D. Little Inc. *Wichita: The Potential for Office and Service Industry Operations, Report to Wichita Area Chamber of Commerce.* San Francisco, CA: Arthur D. Little Inc., 1971. 30pp. (Available from: Wichita Area Chamber of Commerce, 350 W. Douglas, Wichita 67202.)
The study, prepared for the Wichita Chamber of Commerce, cites the factors important to the development of service industries. Wichita is compared to several other major cities for cost of living, employment structure, and other relevant measures.

KS20. Ayres, Daniel. *Community Services Directory.* Wichita: Horde Inc. (2040 Westridge, Wichita 67203), 1973. 67pp. $1.
Directory of community service organizations with their addresses, telephone numbers, and type of service offered.

KS21. Department of Community Development. CDA Office of Research and Evaluation. *Sedgwick County Annual Enumeration and Socio-Economic Survey.* Langston, Kitch and Associates Inc. (455 N. Main, Wichita 67202), 1969–1974. 142pp.

KS22. Kansas Department of Human Resources, Division of Staff Services. *Annual Planning Report, March 1977, Wichita, Kansas Standard Metropolitan Statistical Area.* (P.O. Box 877, Wichita 67202) 1977. 20pp.
Contains historical and current labor force data for the Wichita SMSA. The information was designed to aid local business and industry in manpower planning.

KS23. Kansas Department of Labor Employment Security Division. Wichita Job Service Center. *Area Manpower Review, October 1975. Wichita, Kansas Area Standard Metropolitan Statistical Area.* Wichita: Wichita Job Opportunity Center (P.O. Box 877, Wichita 67202), 1975. 41pp. Semiannual.
Analyzes labor market information for the Wichita Standard Metropolitan Statistical Area. Includes information for manpower and community planners, educators, antipoverty organizations, local and state officials, business labor, and community leaders.

KS24. United States Department of Labor, Bureau of Labor Statistics. *Area Wage Survey: Wichita, Kansas Metropolitan Area, April 1976.* Washington, DC: United States Government Printing Office, 1976. 24pp. $55.
The report includes the results of an April 1976 survey of occupational earnings in the Wichita, Kansas Standard Metropolitan Statistical Area.

KS25. Wichita Area Chamber of Commerce. *Clubs and Organizations Directory.* (350 W. Douglas Ave., Wichita 67202), 23pp. Annual. $5.

Lists clubs and organizations in the Wichita area with their addresses, telephone numbers, and presidents.

KS26. Wichita Area Chamber of Commerce. *Directory of Job Shops, Wichita, Kansas Area.* (350 W. Douglas, Wichita 67202) 95pp.
Provides a listing of job shops in Wichita and locales within ten air miles, and their capabilities.

KS27. Wichita Area Chamber of Commerce. *Manufacturers Directory.* (350 W. Douglas, Wichita 67202) 1975-76. 94pp. Biennial.
Directory of Wichita manufacturing firms, arranged both alphabetically and by Standard Industrial Classification. Indicates firms address, telephone number, products, SIC code, number of employees, and one main officer.

KS28. Wichita Area Chamber of Commerce. *Wage and Fringe Benefit Survey 1974.* (350 W. Douglas, Wichita, 67202) 1974.
The study summarizes wage and fringe benefit statistics for Wichita. It is designed to provide an overview for companies contemplating the establishment of offices in the area.

KS29. Wichita Area Chamber of Commerce. *Wichita.* (Formerly: *Wichita Trends and Wichita Week*) (350 W. Douglas, Wichita 67202) Vol. 42, No. 26, July 8, 1965- .
Bimonthly. $6 year.
Carries articles on life in Wichita, area personalities, local institutions and information of interest to local residents and businessmen.

KS30. Wichita Area Chamber of Commerce. *The Wichita Area Chamber of Commerce Business and Professional Directory.* (350 W. Douglas, Wichita 67202) 1976. 130pp. Biennial.
Contains Chamber of Commerce membership roster and local buyer's guide arranged according to product. Provides addresses and telephone numbers for firms included.

KS31. Wichita Area Chamber of Commerce. *Wichita Area Economic Facts.* (350 W. Douglas, Wichita 67202) 1973.
A comprehensive community economic analysis designed to stimulate the interest of potential residents.

KS32. Wichita. United Way Planning Department. *Directory of Community Services.* (212 N. Market, Wichita 67202) 1976. 237pp.
A list of services available in Sedgewick County, including address and telephone number, purpose, and services rendered, eligibility, application procedure, fees, hours, and source of funds.

KS33. Wichita-Sedgewick County Metropolitan Area Planning Department. *The Housing Situation in Wichita, 1970-71.* (455 N. Main, Wichita 67202) 1971.
Specifies housing needs in Wichita.

KS34. Wichita-Sedgewick County Metropolitan Area Planning Department. *1970 Decennial Census Fact Book: Central Plains Tri-County Planning Area.* (455 N. Main, Wichita 67202) 1973.
Assesses the area's strengths, weaknesses, opportunities, problems, and possible solutions.

KS35. Wichita-Sedgewick County Metropolitan Area Planning Department. *Wichita Profile 1970.* (455 N. Main, Wichita 67202), 36pp.
Presents demographic, economic, and housing data collected in Wichita during the 1970 census. Data gathered from other sources is also drawn upon. Data is presented in a series of multicolored maps, dividing Wichita by census tract.

KS36. Wichita State University. Gerontology Center. *Resource Directory.* (1845 Fairmount, Wichita 67208) 1977.
Lists faculty, library, and other gerontology service resources in the Wichita-Sedgewick County area.

Collections

KS37. Wichita Public Library. 223 S. Main, Wichita 67202 (316)265-5281.
The library currently houses the local history collection for the city of Wichita, containing photographs and written material collected by the local historian, William Ellington.

KENTUCKY

General Publications

KY1. Carroll, Julian. *The Kentucky Executive Budget, 1976–78.* Frankfort: Governor's Office, 1976. 577pp. Biennial.
The report provides appropriations for counties and schools.

KY2. Fulmer, John L. *Development Potentials for Kentucky Counties with Related Statistics.* Lexington: University of Kentucky, Bureau of Business Research, 1966. 220pp.
Covers population, employment, manufacturing, agriculture, income, and educational data.

KY3. Haynes, Nathaniel. *County Government in Kentucky.* Rev. ed. Frankfort: Legislative Research Committee, 1976. 164pp.
A fiscal and regulatory breakdown of duties, appointments, etc. of county court systems, taxing systems, and general government.

KY4. Hill, Jerry D. *Climate of Kentucky.* Lexington: University of Kentucky, College of Agriculture, n.d. 89pp.
Covers all forms of weather data for the state, with tabular breakdown by specific localities.

KY5. Kentucky. Committee on Human Rights. *Kentucky Directory of Black Elected Officials.* Frankfort, 1972– .
Includes biographical sketches and makes comparisons with the rest of the nation.

KY6. Kentucky. Department of Commerce. *Industrial Resources, Northern Kentucky.* Frankfort (Capital Plaza Office Tower, Frankfort 40601), 1971. 37pp.
Profiles the northern part of the state and emphasizes present and potential industrial growth.

KY7. Kentucky. Department of Commerce. *Kentucky Deskbook of Economic Statistics.* Frankfort (Capital Plaza Office Tower, Frankfort 40601), 1963– . Annual.
Economic data (income, agriculture, retail, etc.) for the entire state. The data are broken down by county.

KY8. Kentucky. Department of Commerce. *Kentucky Directory of Manufacturers.* Frankfort (Capital Plaza Office Tower, Frankfort 40601), 1957– . Annual. $15.
The manufacturers are broken down by city.

KY9. Kentucky. Department of Public Information. *Kentucky News Media Directory.* Frankfort, Annual. (Available from: South Central Bell State Public Relations Office, P.O. Box 538, Louisville 40201.)
Includes newspapers, radio, and television media sources, college news sources, wire services, and associations listed by community.

KY10. Kentucky. Legislative Research Committee. *Duties of Elected County Officials.* Rev. ed. Frankfort, 1972. 123pp.
Arranged by individual office, this publication profiles the officials, their background, qualifications, and duties.

KY11. Northern Kentucky Area Development District. *Northern Kentucky Senior Services Directory.* Florence. Annual.
Complete listing of educational, housing, health care, social service, and other organizations serving the elderly. It includes hours, contact person, address, etc.

COVINGTON

Covington provides directory and statistical information primarily relating to revenue, labor, and urban renewal. Because of the city's close proximity to, and inclusion in the SMSA of Cincinnati, researchers can find pertinent information on Covington in the publications pertinent to northern Kentucky and southwestern Ohio. **Local Newspaper Indexing:** The Kenton County Public Library (see **KY20**) is in the process of indexing for the nineteenth century; the staff hopes to complete the indexing by June 1978. The indexing is comprehensive for local information. Queries from outside the area will not be accepted.

Publications

KY12. Community Chest. Council of the Cincinnati Area. *Directory of Community Services.* Cincinnati, OH: (2400 Reading Rd., Cincinnati 45202), 1972. 224pp. Irregular. $6.50.
Descriptive list of social and governmental service agencies in greater Cincinnati area including Boone, Campbell, and Kenton counties.

KY13. Covington. Mayor's Office. *General Fund Budget.* Office of City Manager (City-County Bldg., Covington 41011), n.d.
This publication contains the operating budget by department.

KY14. Covington. League of Women Voters. *Gateway to Kenton County: Handbook about Kenton County, Kentucky.* 1968. 36pp. o.p.
A good overview of Kenton County including history, government, county services, highways, etc.

KY15. Covington. Ordinances, Local Laws, etc. *Code of the City of Covington, Kentucky: General Ordinances of the City.* Washington DC: n.p., 1974. 736pp.
Administrative and general ordinances of the city.

KY16. Northern Kentucky Area Planning Commission. *City of Covington Financial Analysis.* Newport (11 and Lowell, Newport 41071), 1966. 73pp.
Includes the city, school system, and sanitation districts. Analyzes accounting, budget, bonds, auditing, and revenue.

KY17. Northern Kentucky Area Planning Commission. *Neighborhood Analysis, Covington.* Newport, 1969. 510pp.
A detailed analysis of the neighborhood structure of Covington including population, housing, crime, etc.

KY18. Northern Kentucky Chamber of Commerce. *Organization Directory.* Covington: (223 Scott, Covington 41011). Annual. $1.25.
Listing of all major professional organizations, service clubs, and interest groups in the area. Social service organizations, however, are excluded.

KY19. Northern Kentucky Chamber of Commerce. *Street and Highway Directory: Northern Kentucky Area.* Covington (223 Scott, Covington 41011). Irregular. $1.
Complete breakdown by city of streets in separately indexed map form.

Collections

KY20. **Kenton County Public Library.** Fifth and Scott, Covington 41011 (606) 292-2363. Teletype Service: (810)541-8518.
The library collects local history and genealogy extensively.

LEXINGTON

Data not available at this time.

LOUISVILLE

Data not available at this time.

LOUISIANA

General Publications

LA1. *Louisiana Almanac, 1975-1976.* Gretna: Pelican Publishing Company Inc. (630 Burmaster St., Gretna 70053), 1975. Annual. $5.95.
This book contains a variety of information, historical and practical, about the state of Louisiana. The population section includes basic data from the 1970 (and earlier) U.S. censuses as well as recent population estimates. A section on Louisiana parishes and cities contains summaries of charter provisions, a brief directory of officials, detailed statistics on port activities, basic data profile, and brief discussions of a number of city facilities. Various tables include statistics for parishes such as schools, number of registered voters, sales and other tax amounts, religious affiliations, and vital statistics. Some excerpts of the Louisiana Roster of Officials are included. There is a reprint of the 1974 Louisiana Constitution which contains provisions dealing specifically with municipal corporations. Publications of the almanac dates back to 1949. Much of the data is collected from other sources so that the current edition does contain a good deal of outdated information. There is a new edition in preparation.

LA2. Louisiana. Department of Commerce and Industry. *Louisiana Directory of Manufacturers.* Baton Rouge (P.O. Box 44185, Baton Rouge 70804), 1942-1975. 127pp. Irregular (biennially, usually). $10. Title varies: 1942, *Industrial Directory, State of Louisiana.* 1947-1951, *Louisiana Industrial Directory.* Cover Title, 1954, *Louisiana Directory of Manufacturers.*
Part 2 is an alphabetical listing of the cities and towns of the state and the industries located in each. Following each manufacturer's name these items of information appear: address; name of principal official at the plant; date of establishment; the SIC numbers of the products manufactured in Louisiana, along with specific product descriptions; information reflecting normal employment and areas of distribution; purchasing agent's name when available, and business telephone number.

LA3. Louisiana. Department of Public Works. *Directory of Louisiana Cities, Towns and Villages.* Baton Rouge (P.O. Box 44155, Baton Rouge 70804), 1961-1976. 167pp. Irregular. Free.
The directory was compiled from data utilized in producing the 1976 bicentennial edition of the official map of the state of Louisiana, along with records of the Bureau of the Census and U.S. Postal Service. Every community indicated on the official map is included in a listing, first in alphabetical order, and secondly in order by parishes. The 1970 census populations are included.

LA4. Louisiana. Department of Public Works. *Directory of Basic Data for Local and Regional Areas (Project No. CPA-LA-06-48-1023).* Prepared by Ed Reed

Organization. Baton Rouge (P.O. Box 44155, Baton Rouge 70804), June 1974. 86pp. Free.

"Basic data of Louisiana parishes and planning districts relating to population growth, population distribution, employment, income, and other areas designed to formulate profiles of local areas. Intended to provide local planners with raw data as an aid to future planning." (From bibliographic data sheet.) Key words from bibliographic data sheet: population trends 1940-1970; population distribution 1940-1970; racial, urban and rural; income and employment 1960-1970; industry and commerce 1970; finance and taxation 1960-1970; agriculture 1959-1969; recreation 1970; health 1970; education 1960-1970.

LA5. Louisiana. Department of State. *Municipal Election Information.* Baton Rouge: Secretary of State (P.O. Box 44125, Baton Rouge 70804). Annual. Free.
Chronological tables for municipal elections and the primary and general elections giving beginning dates and deadlines to be observed by election officials (with citations to the revised statutes). The pamphlet has been checked and approved by the attorney general. Published prior to the year to which it applies.

LA6. Louisiana. Department of State. *Roster of Officials.* Baton Rouge: Secretary of State (P.O. Box 44125, Baton Rouge 70804), 1975. 247pp. Irregular (biennially, usually). $2.50.
The roster has a section on municipal officials arranged alphabetically by locality and including zip code, population, parish, and the names of the mayor, chief of police, and councilman. The form of government is indicated by a symbol.

LA7. Louisiana Municipal Association. *Directory of Louisiana Municipal Officials, 1977.* Baton Rouge (5615 Corporate Blvd., Suite 3B, Baton Rouge 70808), 1977. 40pp. Irregular (biennially, usually). $15.
Arranged alphabetically by town or city. Lists officials with a code number to identify each. Also has financial information—budget, property assessment, millage, as well as services such as sewerage, ambulance, etc.

LA8. Louisiana. State Department of Education. *Louisiana School Directory, Session 1975-76.* Baton Rouge (P.O. Box 44064, Baton Rouge 70804), 1975. Annual.
Listings arranged by city include (1) art galleries, museums, public buildings, and historical sites, (2) proprietory schools, and (3) flight training schools. Listings of public schools and nonpublic schools are arranged by parish, with the city indicated in the address of the school.

LA9. University of New Orleans. Division of Business and Economic Research. *Statistical Abstract of Louisiana,* 5th ed. 1974. Compiled by James Bobo and Jesse M. Charlton, Jr. New Orleans (College of Business Administration, University of New Orleans, Lakefront, New Orleans 70122), 1965- . 441pp. Irregular (biennially, usually). $4.50.
The statistical information in the abstract was taken from diverse sources. Most tables are divided by parish; however, some are arranged by city. Tables include labor force and employment, general manufacturing statistics, average electricity used, selected housing data, retail trade, and wholesale trade.

Collections

Many municipal document holdings of various Louisiana libraries can be found in: *Louisiana Union Catalog (and index) 1973.* Compiled by Louisiana Library Association, Louisiana Union Catalog Committee. Southern Microfilm Corporation,

1975. 1 vol. (loose-leaf folder). $45. (Available from: Norma Durand, Dupre Library, University of Southwestern Louisiana, Lafayette, LA 70501.)

LA10. Louisiana State Library. 760 Riverside N., P.O. Box 131, Baton Rouge 70821 (504)389-6651. Teletype Service: (510)993-3539.
The Louisiana Division has an outstanding history and state document collection of about 40,000 cataloged items (most state documents are not cataloged).

BATON ROUGE
Publications

LA11. East Baton Rouge Parish. City-Parish Planning Commission. *Special Census, 1974.* Baton Rouge (805 St. Louis St., Baton Rouge 70802), April 1974. 23pp. Free.
Census by tracts showing population (age, race, sex) employment, income, occupation, and housing.

LA12. East Baton Rouge Parish. Louisiana Council on the Aging. *Council on Aging Directory.* Edited by Sandra C. Shallcross. East Baton Rouge Council on the Aging (1961 Government St., Baton Rouge 70806), 1974. 214pp. $1.50.
Alphabetical list of agencies in Baton Rouge that serve the aging, educationally, medically, socially, and financially. Detailed information about each agency is given. Indexed under type of service.

NEW ORLEANS

There is no agency regulating the overall printing by the city government. Each department publishes an annual report, with the length and content of each varying. Several departments also publish a number of surveys and special reports. Such documents of the City Planning Commission have in past years been useful in identifying and cataloging historic areas, in producing statistical information about the city, and in illustrating long-range developments. The Regional Planning Commission has performed a similar function for the metropolitan area. These publications have not been included in the list of documents either because of their specializations or because they date prior to 1971.

A number of publications relate primarily to interdepartmental matters. They are not designed for use by the public but the researcher who is aware of their existence can gain useful information from them. The city archives receives most of the publications from most of the city departments. In addition to published documents, several departments also submit photocopies of the minutes of monthly meetings and of monthly statistical reports. Copies of city ordinances are regularly deposited in the archives which has indexes that are updated periodically. **Local Newspaper Indexing:** The *New Orleans Times-Picayune* has been indexed since 1972 by Bell & Howell, Wooster, OH; their indexing of city government activities is quite extensive. The New Orleans Public Library (see entry **LA36**) has its own card file index dating 1804-1964 for news articles and 1804-1972 for obituary notices. Both files contain numerous gaps. Neither is being extended beyond end dates although some of the gaps in the obituary file are being filled in. The library will check either file on request. Total number of cards in the files surpasses one million.

Publications

LA13. Board of Commissioners of the Port of New Orleans. *1977 Annual Directory.* New Orleans (Public Relations Department, 2600 International Trade Mart, New Orleans 70160), 1977. Annual. Free.

The Board of Commissioners is a state agency which regulates the operations of the port. This directory is an annual publication serving as an introduction to the port and its services. There is a brief description of the board's organization and functions along with descriptions of various public and private bodies active in the affairs of the port. Port-related businesses are listed by category, and a number of advertisements are printed in the directory. Several maps of the port are reproduced and several statistical graphs and tables are included. A good deal of public relations-type material is compiled in this report but there is also a good deal of useful, straightforward information. The Board of Commissioners also issues an annual report and monthly *Port Record*.

LA14. Bobo, James R. *The New Orleans Economy: Pro Bono Publico?* New Orleans: University of New Orleans (Division of Business and Economic Research, New Orleans 70122), 1975. 135pp. $5.50.

This report is a detailed critical analysis of the economy of New Orleans and the metropolitan area. The basic presentation is narrative but there are numerous charts, tables, and maps providing statistical support for the text. Dr. Bobo briefly traces the area's economic development from 1954–1970 and then deals more fully with the period 1970–1975. He describes a picture of continuing economic stagnation following the boom of the space era. A particular emphasis is placed on the problems resulting from it. Dr. Bobo is especially critical of the failure of the economic powers in the city to admit the problems and to make a concerted effort to educate the community and to seek the type of drastic solutions that he believes to be necessary. A concluding chapter summarizes his findings and offers basic suggestions for action.

LA15. Bureau of Governmental Research. (various publications.) (1308 Richards Bldg., New Orleans 70112) n.d.

The BGR is ". . . a non-profit, non-political, independent fact-finding organization of citizens dedicated to the improvement of the several governments operating in the Greater New Orleans Area." The Bureau of Government Research issues position papers on issues before the various governing bodies. Regular papers on budgets, bond issues, and other elections are standard. Because of the wide variety and brevity of these reports, the BGR does not write up individual items but advises researchers of the existence of this source. Copies of papers and reports will be sent on request if available. Often there is a nominal charge although in some cases a larger report will require larger payments.

LA16. Mayor's Council on Economics. *Metropolitan New Orleans Urban Affairs Bibliography.* New Orleans: Office of Policy Planning and Analysis (Rm. 8E08, City Hall, New Orleans 70112), August 1975. 68pp. Free.

This bibliography is based on a 1968 compilation by the Urban Studies Center at Tulane University. It includes books, articles, and other publications from private and university sources as well as city government documents. Works included date from the 1950s to 1975. It was intended to be updated annually, but the first update is still awaited. The compilers explain that the new edition will contain many more entries and it is taking a longer time than anticipated to put it together. Materials are divided into several categories, e.g., finance and economy, health, and planning. Each listing includes the source reporting the item. Unfortunately, many

of the documents are available in more than one location and the listing makes
no note of this. This is the only item which can be included in the category of "Government and Non-Governmental Checklists and Bibliographies."

LA17. Mayor's Criminal Justice Coordinating Council. *City of New Orleans
1975 Crime Analysis.* New Orleans, 1976. 102pp.
Introductory pages describe the functions of the CJCC, list its members and the
members of its staff, and describe the purpose of the report, i.e., to provide a "comprehensive crime picture for the city." It is designed for use by law enforcement
and criminal justice agencies. General crime statistics are published for the years
1965-1975. Charts and maps are used to indicate the zones in the city which have
the greatest incidence of crime. This is close in tabular form with a narrative section for each of the eight police districts. An attempt is made to correlate crime
with the factors used to establish an index of blight in the city. Separate sections
deal with the problem of juvenile crime and with a subjective analysis of crime and
its impact on the citizenry. An appendix includes definitions of the crimes investigated as well as the factors contributing to the blight index.

LA18. New Orleans. Chief Administrative Office. *Operating Budget for Calendar and Fiscal Year 1977.* December 1, 1976. Annual.
This is the city's operating budget as adopted by the city council. Tables include
projected revenue by source for 1977-1981, projected expenditures for the same
period by department, comparative statements of revenues between 1976 and
1977, and a number of other breakdowns and analyses to illustrate the budgeting portion of the government. This section is followed by a departmental listing
which includes budget summaries and then breakdown by subdivisions within
each department. Both expenditures and source of revenues are shown and classified by type. Accompanying these budget statements are descriptions of the
program objectives for each division. Personnel summaries are included, and a
chart of salary ranges is provided. The volume also contains an organizational
report. These operating budgets have been published yearly since 1955 with the
ones through 1975 being multivolumed. The 1971-1975 operating budgets are
currently available through Greenwood Press. The 1976 and 1977 budgets will
be included in the next shipment to them.

LA19. New Orleans. Chief Administrative Office. *A Report on the State of
the City.* September 4, 1974. 38pp.
This report is the text of a speech presented by Chief Administrative Officer, Richard Kernion. It is an overview of what the city government accomplished in 1974
along with a statement of goals for the future. Subjects covered include governmental finance, equal opportunity, criminal justice, economic development, public
safety, and human resources. Some of these broad categories are broken down
into their component aspects. The format is to identify and describe problems and
to illustrate the programs designed to deal with them. As the report was originally
given orally, only general information is included. There are no detailed statistical
tables to illustrate progress in a problem area nor are there any detailed descriptions of the organization or operation of specific departments. The report does
identify areas of interest to the researcher who can then go to the individual department for additional information. Available from Greenwood Press.

LA20. New Orleans. City Council. *The Code of the City of New Orleans,
Louisiana.* (City Hall, New Orleans 70112) 1956. 1,000pp. $50 (plus $10 for 4
quarterly revisions).

The 1956 codification of city ordinances was the first in 60 years. The present code is updated quarterly by inserting loose-leaf revisions into the binder. It contains all ordinances of a "general and permanent nature" but omits code published separately, such as the building code, fire prevention code, and comprehensive zoning ordinance. Chapters are arranged alphabetically by subject. A subject index provides cross-references, and a comparative table identifies the original ordinances affecting the code since 1968. Chapters deal with general subjects such as health and sanitation, elections, and miscellaneous offenses, but some are devoted to specific bodies including the Fink Asylum and the Edward Wisner Donation Advisory Committee. Some chapters go into great detail, such as the one which deals with motor vehicles and traffic, listing one-way streets and no-parking zones.

LA21. New Orleans. City Council. *Home Rule Charter of the City of New Orleans.* (City Hall, New Orleans 70112) 1954. 99pp. $3.
In 1950 the state legislature provided for the creation of home rule municipal governments in Louisiana. The present charter was adopted shortly thereafter. It contains ten articles entitled: incorporation and form of government; powers; the council; executive branch; executive branch—unattached boards and commissions; financial administrative procedures; financing street improvement; department of civil service; general provisions; and schedule. The articles on the executive branches are broken down by the various departments and boards, outlining the powers and duties of each. It contains amendments through 1966. The charter is the legal foundation of the city government—the various codes of ordinances reflect the more changeable legislative aspects. A charter revision committee has been at work for over a year and has produced a draft charter dated February 18, 1977. This document provides for a reorganization of the executive branch, eliminating some departments and placing their duties and powers under control of the mayor's office. Another major change deals with enlarging the membership of the city council. Both of these changes will meet with opposition so it may be some time before the city votes on the new plan.

LA22. New Orleans. City Planning Commission. *Capital Budget and Capital Improvement Program, 1977-1981.* (City Hall, New Orleans 70112). Annual. Free.
The recent capital budget reports provide a vivid picture of the city's needs and also of the financial problems which are making it impossible to meet these needs. Prefatory comments explore the extent of the money shortages and the overall effects that they have on the city's capital development. The remainder of the budget report consists of departmental requests for capital expenditures along with the recommendations of the Planning Commission relative to each request. There is a table showing each program, the projected cost, the commission action on the request, and the effect, if any, that it will have on the city's operating budget. The tables are followed by brief descriptions of the project along with the reasons for the action taken by the Planning Commission.

LA23. New Orleans. Department of Finance. *Annual Financial Report.* (Rm. 3E05, City Hall, New Orleans 70112) 1975. Annual. Free.
This report includes a complete financial statement for the city of New Orleans. Balance sheets and statements of revenues, expenditures, etc., are given for the general fund, special revenue funds, capital projects funds, enterprise funds, trust and agency funds, and special assessment funds. Also included are additional tables relative to the city's financial basis, an organizational chart, brief facts about city government, and highlights of the year for the finance department. These re-

ports date back to 1853 as the annual report of the comptroller. Reports for 1970–1975 are available from Greenwood Press.

LA24. New Orleans. Department of Health. *Ecological Inventory of the City of New Orleans.* 1972. 181pp.
This document was produced through cooperation among the city health department, Tulane University Medical Center, and the U.S. Public Health Service. It is intended as a preliminary catalog of environmental assets and liabilities to be used to assess the effects of environmental control programs. The data is derived from the 1970 census and from various city departments and private agencies. A summary description of the city is followed by sections on ecology, population, economics, use patterns, and community facilities. Information is provided by both narrative and tabular means. A good deal of statistics are presented according to planning districts (i.e., neighborhood groups). The section on community facilities includes descriptions of city government, both topically and by department. The entire report is a convenient grouping together of a diversity of information.

LA25. New Orleans. League of Women Voters. *What's What in New Orleans Government: A Citizen's Guide.* (1636 Toleclano, New Orleans 70115) 1969. 63pp. o.p.
This is a handy guide to the organization and activity of the New Orleans government. It includes a department-by-department breakdown giving information on the head of each, the legal organizations, the budget (in 1969), and a statement on the department's functions. All charter-established agencies are included along with a number of other bodies which have official or semiofficial control over city activities. An organizational chart is included. A section on the budget outlines budgetary procedures and gives 1969 figures. There is also a section which discusses city government by subjects including recreation and culture, education, health, and sanitation, and welfare services, etc. A final section provides information for voters. The study is indexed. A revision is in progress and is expected to be available before September. The league has not yet established a price for the new guide. Part of the delay is due to a current charter revision.

LA26. New Orleans. Office of Policy Planning and Analysis. *An Analysis of Blight in the City of New Orleans.* (Rm. 8E10, City Hall, New Orleans 70112) November 1974. 184pp. Free.
This report was a response to the 1974 Housing and Community Development Act. It first defines blight and then establishes a means of measuring blight within neighborhood units. An extensive methodological section deals with the problem of measurement. Most of the data comes from the 1970 census and includes such factors as poverty rate, overcrowding, and immature birth rate. These indicators were used to form a blight index with neighborhoods ranked as critical, very severe, severe, endangered, safe, and good. The blight index and individual indicators are described in table form and in map form. Also investigated are several non-census indicators: crime, environment, fire protection, lighting, and recreational open space. Methodological statements on these indicators is included. Each neighborhood is evaluated separately according to the various indicators. A more recent blight index, based on 1974 data, has been issued, but a copy has not yet been received by the office.

LA27. New Orleans. Office of Policy Planning and Analysis. *The New Orleans Economic Outlook through 1980.* Compiled by Marjorie Fox Larson. (Rm. 8E10, City Hall, New Orleans 70112) April 26, 1976. 76pp. Free.

This report forecasts the New Orleans economy through 1981 and for comparison purposes includes a forecast of the national economy. These forecasts are described in narrative form with tables to further illustrate them. An evaluation of previous national and local forecasts is included. Local indicators are gross local product, business activity, civilian labor force, employment, unemployment rate, personal income, port cargo, department store sales, building contracts, electric consumption, demand deposit debts, banking activity, welfare, and food stamps. These are reviewed for the previous 12 years in order to explain the forecast. Similar national indicators are also reviewed for the past 12 years. Both reviews take the form of tables and graphs.

LA28. New Orleans. Office of Policy Planning and Analysis. *A Socio-Economic Profile of New Orleans and Its Neighborhoods.* (Rm. 8E10, City Hall, New Orleans 70112) December 1974. 633pp.
The report is based primarily on the 1970 census but also includes data provided by city departments of health, recreation, and police. The subject areas treated are demography, family structure, education, income and employment, housing and transportation, health, crime and delinquency, recreation, and citizen attitudes. Citywide data is presented in a narrative section. Following this is a breakdown by 20 planning units called neighborhood groups. Data for these divisions is presented in both narrative and tabular form. A large appendix includes tables for each of the 63 neighborhood groups. The 24-page section on citizen attitudes is based on random sample surveys conducted in 1973. It discusses both citywide and neighborhood concerns and includes a detailed description of the shortcomings of the survey.

New Orleans. Ordinances, Local Laws, etc. See entry **LA20.**

LA29. New Orleans. Public Relations Office. *Directory of City Departments and Officials.* (City Hall, New Orleans 70112) 1975. 32pp. Free.
This directory lists by department and by divisions within a department the elected, appointed, and civil service officials of the city. City Hall room numbers (or other addresses if not located in City Hall) are given along with telephone numbers. Also included are parochial and judicial offices and a number of frequently called non-government agencies.

LA30. New Orleans Public Schools. *Directory, New Orleans Public Schools, 1976-1977.* Orleans Parish School Board (4100 Touro, New Orleans 70112), 1976. Annual. $5.
This directory lists all employees of the school board, teachers, administrators, clerical, and custodial workers, etc. Addresses and telephone numbers of schools and administrative units are given. A separate entry for each school lists the boundaries of the school attendance district, names of all teachers, their professional degrees, and teaching fields. There is also an alphabetical listing of staff. The directory includes no organizational charts or any other explanation of the relationships between the various units listed, nor is there any description of a particular unit's activity.

LA31. New Orleans Public Schools. Division of Finance and Planning, Department of Research and Evaluation. *Facts and Finances 1976-1977.* Orleans Parish School Board (4100 Touro, New Orleans 70112), 1976. Annual. Free.
This is a statistical profile of the public school system in New Orleans. It includes names of school board members, supervisory staff members, and an organizational chart. Information provided includes enrollment by school and by grade

within each school, data on special education services, revenues and expenditures systemwide, teachers' salaries, number of teachers and other staff, non-teaching positions and salaries, and food service operations. This data is given in table form. Also included is information on the city's property tax structure, number of births in the city, and school calendars. Some of the tables also include breakdowns by race. Some tables include data from previous years, as far back as 1962-1963. There is no narrative section discussing goals or achievements of the school system.

LA32. New Orleans Total Community Action. *Profile of Poverty in New Orleans.* Compiled by the Department of Program Development. April 1973. 42pp.
Based on data from the 1970 census, this report details the extent of poverty in New Orleans and investigates the factors accompanying it. It contains a number of tables and charts showing overall percentages of people in the poverty classification as well as showing breakdowns by race, sex, age, etc. Census tract maps are reproduced with color coding to indicate the percent of families below poverty level, percentage of welfare recipients, unemployment percentage, etc. The various conditions accompanying poverty are explored in textual and graphic form. One section specifically concerns crime as a product of poverty. No solutions to the problem are offered here. The purpose of the report is to define the problem as a first step in finding a solution.

LA33. New Orleans. Volunteer and Information Agency. *Directory of Social Welfare and Related Services for Orleans, Jefferson, St. Bernard, and Saint Tammany Parishes.* (211 Camp St., New Orleans 70130) 1974. 304pp. $10.
This triennial publication provides resource information for the entire metropolitan area. It includes a wide range of services, both governmental and private. Among the listings under New Orleans itself are Alcohol Safety Action Program, Community Improvement Agency, health department, housing authority, police department, and public library. Each listing gives address, phone numbr, top officials, a statement of purposes and service, territory served, information on admission and application, fees, and source of support. There is an alphabetical table of contents and an index by type of service rendered. The directory is updated periodically by mimeographed revision sheets.

LA34. Public Affairs Research Council of Louisiana Inc. *Statistical Profile of Orleans Parish.* Baton Rouge (P.O. Box 3118, Baton Rouge 70812), 1973. 7pp. 50¢.
The PAR is a private, nonprofit research organization devoted to improving Louisiana government through public enlightenment. This pamphlet is part of a statewide series. Orleans Parish and the city of New Orleans have the same boundaries. Tables present data on population, 1950-1970, by ward, race, age, sex, education, income, welfare assistance, housing, employment, severance tax collections, and property tax assessments. Several tables compare New Orleans with the state as a whole. There is a brief narrative historical sketch, but not material on city government.

LA35. Regional Planning Commission for Jefferson, Orleans, and St. Bernard Parishes. *History of Regional Growth.* New Orleans, November 1974. 101pp.
This study traces the historical development of the New Orleans area focusing on the trends that continue to influence local planning. Recent trends in population, transportation, and the economy are discussed along with implications for the future. Maps of the region are reproduced, some of them showing projected

developments. While dating from before 1971, the work contains a good deal of information not gathered together elsewhere. It is the type of general reference that for the most part is lacking in the official publications of the area.

Collections

LA36. News Orleans Public Library, Louisiana Division. 219 Loyola Ave., New Orleans 70140 (504)586-4912/13/14. Teletype Service: (810)951-5320.
The Louisiana Division of the library houses the New Orleans city archives. City departments are directed by the city code and by memorandum of the chief administrative offices to forward copies of all reports, surveys, etc., to the archives. Most do cooperate. In addition to these official channels the archives receives city documents from sources such as the Bureau of Governmental Research and the architectural firm of Curtes and Davis. A rich source of otherwise unavailable material are the papers of the mayor which come to the archives at the end of his term of office. Often included in this source are special reports to the mayor which did not receive other circulation. The archives also includes manuscript material dating back to 1769 when the department was created by the Spanish governing body, the Cabildo. These documents are being microfilmed in a continuing filming operation with the division. Microfilms are available through interlibrary loan. A separate card catalog is maintained for the archives materials. Descriptive subject headings are assigned to each document as it is cataloged. The cataloging system was devised by the archives staff and employs letters to designate the issuing agency and numbers to identify the type of record. The division has participated in Greenwood Press's *Index to Current Urban Documents* since its beginning. Documents dating back to 1970 are available through Greenwood Press.

SHREVEPORT

Collections

LA37. Louisiana State University in Shreveport Library, 8515 Youree Dr., Shreveport 71106 (318)865-7121, ext. 203.
Most of the municipal publications and related material are stored in the Louisiana Collection, a restricted area. Shreveport Department of Finance, annual receipts, 1972, Department of Public Safety receipts, 1971 to date and monthly supplements can be found in this collection. Other examples include Community Buildings Report, Tourism Plan, and Historic Sites Inventory. *Historical Summary of Shreveport Fire Department—Monograph;* The League of Women Voters of Shreveport, Louisiana, *What Makes It Tick?;* and *Measuring Potential for the Quality of Life: A Research Study,* are some miscellaneous items to be found in the library. Microfilmed copies of city council minutes and Caddo Police Jury minutes are also in the archives collection.

MAINE

General Publications

ME1. *Maine Register, State Yearbook, and Legislative Manual.* Portland: Tower Pub. Co. (335 Forest Ave., Portland 04101). Annual. $38.
This state bluebook is a guide to personnel and organization for government at the state, county, and municipal levels.

ME2. Maine. Secretary of State. *State of Maine State and County Officers.* Augusta (State Capitol, Augusta 04330), n.d.
This publication, which covers the county level of government, lists judges, court clerks, treasurers, sheriffs, and other key officials.

AUGUSTA

Publications

ME3. Augusta. City Manager. *Annual Report for the Year Ended. . . .* Annual. An organization chart for the city government is found in the report.

LEWISTON

Data not available at this time.

PORTLAND

Local Newspaper Indexing: The Portland Public Library (see entry ME6) maintains a card file for the *Portland Herald*, *Portland Evening Express*, and *Maine Sunday Telegram*. The staff will accept requests for information contained in these newspapers.

Publications

ME4. Portland. City Manager. *Budget/Work Program for the Fiscal Year.* n.d. This publication, which covers the municipal programs, contains the program objectives of municipal agencies and projects. It also has an organization chart of city government.

ME5. Portland. Finance Department. *Financial Report.* Annual.

Collections

ME6. Portland Public Library. Baxter Library, 619 Congress St., Portland 04101 (207)773-4761.
The library collects publications of the city but they are not available on interlibrary loan. Incidentally, the executive department (208 City Hall, Portland 04111) will make available a listing of city officials.

MARYLAND

General Publications

MD1. Health and Welfare Council of Central Maryland Inc. *Directory of Community Services in Maryland.* Baltimore (Directory Office, 428 E. Preston St., Baltimore 21202), 1975. 476pp. Triennial. $8.50.
This directory is a listing of about 1,800 organizations and agencies which are generally operated by private, nonprofit corporations or governmentally sponsored ones. All have a major concern for the sponsorship or operation of a continuing program of services to Maryland residents in the areas of health, education, recreation, employment, welfare, and corrections. Arranged alphabetically, each entry provides the address, telephone number, name of executive, a short description of function, and source of funding. The information is obtained from the organizations. Indexes are geographical, alphabetical, and by subject.

MD2. Maryland. Department of Economic and Community Development. *Directory of Maryland Manufacturers 1976-77.* Annapolis (2525 Riva Rd., Annapolis 21401), 1977. Biennial.
This directory includes a list of manufacturers alphabetically by city as well as an alphabetical listing for the entire state. There is a list of manufacturers by 39 categories with page reference to major listing which is by cities. There is also an alphabetical index by products and a listing of the Standard Industrial Classification numbers. There is a cities and counties cross-index. Major entries are by city and include the date firm was founded, number of male and female employees, and product manufactured as well as the address and name of principal owner.

MD3. Maryland. Department of Economic and Community Development. *Directory of Science Resources for Maryland 1976-1977.* Annapolis, 1976. 230pp. Biennial.
The Maryland businesses included in this directory are classified as research and development, or service to research. Within each major category firms are arranged alphabetically and assigned control numbers. When available, entries include total employees and number of professional employees as well as year firm was established in Maryland. A principal activities locator and geographic locator make it possible to locate all firms in cities throughout the state and includes a number of entries under Rockville.

MD4. Maryland. Department of Education. *Directory of Public Education— State of Maryland.* Baltimore (P.O. Box 8717, Baltimore-Washington International Airport, Baltimore 21240), 1971/72-   .Annual.
The information in this directory for the state of Maryland includes state education

personnel; members of local boards of education; the local superintendents of schools; the principals, the administrative and supervisory staffs of schools; and the trustees of those public libraries which are state-aided. Two of the sections of this book are listings of elementary schools by name of school and secondary schools by name of school. These two sections are more broadly arranged by counties so that one can find, for example, an alphabetical list of elementary schools in Anne Arundel County. Included in the book is an organization chart of the state department of Education.

MD5. Maryland. Department of Education. *Maryland Nonpublic Schools Approved by the State Superintendent of Schools.* Baltimore (P.O. Box 8717, Baltimore-Washington International Airport, Baltimore 21240), 1950-   . Annual.
This directory is an official listing of elementary and secondary schools, nursery schools, kindergartens, tutoring schools, and education institutions for the handicapped in the state of Maryland. Arranged in three parts, the first part is an alphabetical listing of the schools and includes information about enrollment figures, addresses, sex of students accepted, and classification of grade level. The second part is a geographical index to the schools included, and the third section is an alphabetical listing by name of school with the main division by type of school.

MD6. Maryland Municipal League. *Directory of Maryland Municipal Officials 1976-1977.* Annapolis (76 Maryland Ave., Annapolis 21401), 1976. 39pp. Biennial. $3.
This directory includes a municipal listing by counties in Maryland, and an alphabetical listing with address, telephone, meeting dates of governing bodies, names of the municipal elected officials, and key administrative employees.

MD7. Maryland Municipal League. *Survey of Municipal Government Services in Maryland.* Annapolis (76 Maryland Ave., Annapolis 21401), 1976. 118pp. $7.50.
Based on the responses of 79 municipalities, this book provides a variety of general reference material to municipal officials. Five main sections are broken down as follows: (1) general municipal government—finance, licensing and regulations, general operations; (2) community development—planning and zoning, housing, recreation; (3) transportation—taxis, buses, parking, airports; (4) public safety—police services, fire services, animal control; and (5) public works—street openings, maintenance, street trees, public utilities. Each section has a narrative summary followed by individual city data.

MD8. Maryland. Technical Advisory Service. *Compensation Plans of Maryland Counties and Municipalities.* College Park (Division of Behavioral and Social Sciences, University of Maryland, College Park 20742), 1977. Vol. 1: 261pp.; Vol. 2: 195pp. Vol. 1: $15. Vol. 2: $5.
The purpose of this publication is to provide current information on compensation plans in use by local governments in Maryland. The coverage of salaries for as many positions as possible was the goal of the author. Other information is also given; for example, population figures are included. Volume 1 consists of the salaries of local government employees from the mayor down to a clerk-typist. The information provided in this reference was compiled from questionnaires sent to 150 cities (80 cities responded). Volume 1 also has a section on labor relations and fringe benefits in the public sector of Maryland. Volume 2 is a compilation of statistics concerning the salaries of government employees of the metropolitan counties and Baltimore.

Collections

MD9. Enoch Pratt Free Library. 400 Cathedral St., Baltimore 21201 (301) 396-5468.
The documents collection in the Maryland Department has publications of the governments of the state of Maryland, Maryland counties, and Maryland cities as well as studies done by consultant firms for these governments. The collection includes annual reports, planning studies and surveys (e.g., housing, transportation, population, etc.), newsletters and bulletins for specific city, county, and state agencies, ordinances and local laws, and ephemera (explanatory brochures to explain the function of an agency, make people aware of a service offered, or help with a specific problem). Interlibrary loan requests should be made through the local library and addressed to Maryland Interlibrary Loan Organization (MILO).

ANNAPOLIS

The municipal publications of Annapolis are not overabundant. For the most part, the city does not publish documents but prints a minimal number of copies as they are needed. Those items that are annually or regularly written serve to provide a picture of the activities of the local government. A gap in reference service exists in the lack of indexing for the local newspaper, the *Evening Capital*, and in the lack of an organization chart in the city code. Files of the newspaper dating to 1827 are stored on microfilm at the Maryland Hall of Records in Annapolis.

Publications

MD10. *Annapolis (Anne Arundel County, Maryland) City Directory; Including Edgewater.* Richmond, VA: R. L. Polk Co. (2910 W. Clay St., P.O. Box 27546, Richmond, VA 23261), 1956- . Annual. $75.

MD11. Annapolis. Department of Planning and Zoning. *Annapolis Housing Data Inventory, 1970.* Compiled by H. Grant DeHart. (166 Duke of Gloucester St., Annapolis 21041) 1971. 62pp.
In this report, Mr. DeHart identifies the city's housing needs and those population groups with the greatest housing needs. He also lists those geographic areas in the city with the greatest housing problems, and identifies both public and private housing resources. Overall, this study is an identification of housing data currently available (i.e., in 1971). Provided are those city, county, and state agencies that have information on housing, a bibliography of housing reports relating to Annapolis, and sources of unpublished housing-related data. This is an excellent source of bibliographic information on housing in Annapolis.

MD12. Annapolis. Department of Planning and Zoning. *Annapolis, Maryland Housing Element 1971-1973.* Compiled by H. Grant DeHart. (166 Duke of Gloucester St., Annapolis 21041) 1973. 30pp.
In this study, Mr. DeHart identifies housing problems in Annapolis in terms of supply, condition, and social problems. He gives the obstacles to better housing, suggests preliminary housing objectives for the purpose of planning, and describes previous and future planning activities as well as implemented actions. A bonus to this report is a section that provides rental fees for Annapolis apartment buildings in 1968.

MD13. Annapolis. Department of Planning and Zoning. *Annual Report for 1975.* (166 Duke of Gloucester St., Annapolis 21401) 1976. Annual.

The annual report lists and summarizes the activities and projects of this agency for the past year. Subjects included are: studies undertaken; city statistics for population, housing, and employment; maps available for either review or distribution; documents available; lists and maps of development activities in Annapolis; and recommendations for improving the planning process.

MD14. Annapolis. Department of Planning and Zoning. *An Environmental Action Strategy: Annapolis, Maryland.* Compiled by Murphy Williams, (166 Duke of Gloucester St., Annapolis 21041) 1974. 114pp.
This report is an attempt to provide the residents of Annapolis with information that will allow for the planning of an environmental action strategy. Discussed are environmental improvements possible through various local public official agencies, how the city's code might be made more effective to handle environmental problems, and possible measures for dealing with problems. The three problems on which the report focuses are storm water pollution, soil erosion, and the loss of natural land features—all of which have an immediate impact on Annapolis' environment.

MD15. Annapolis. Department of Planning and Zoning. *The Non-White Housing Market in Annapolis.* Compiled by H. Grant Dehart. (166 Duke of Gloucester St., Annapolis 21041) 1971. 34pp.
Mr. DeHart provides an investigation of market potential and need for housing by nonwhite households in Annapolis as of April 1971. He has attempted to identify the quantity of housing that would be needed to house all nonwhite households existing in Annapolis in adequate housing. Provided in the report are figures on population, housing, and income for nonwhites. The information is based on 1970 census data; projected income figures are from 1960 census data.

MD16. Annapolis. Department of Planning and Zoning. *Proposed Comprehensive Plan for the City of Annapolis, Maryland—Preliminary.* Compiled by Murphy Williams, Urban Planning and Housing Consultants. (166 Duke of Gloucester St., Annapolis 21401) 1974. 158pp.
This report is a review and a revision of the 1962 comprehensive master plan for Annapolis. It provides basic data such as special analyses of population trends and housing needs, assessment of economic trends and land use requirements for projected development, and inventory of current land use. Also included is the consideration of public policy issues such as growth policies, conservation of natural environmental quality, community facility needs, and housing program initiatives. The document's data are supplemented with charts, maps, and tables.

MD17. Annapolis. Department of Planning and Zoning. *Public Awareness of Housing Discrimination: A Strategy for Future Action.* By Elizabeth Shirey. Edited by H. Grant Dehart. 1971. 16pp.
Ms. Shirey discusses the need to make the public aware of the effects of racial discrimination in housing and to develop plans that can be used to gain more public acceptance of racially integrated neighborhoods. Included in this report is a summary of segregated housing problems in Annapolis. Also, Ms. Shirey ponders the importance of community awareness, planning and programming strategies, local activities going on in the early 1970s to inform the public, and methods of increasing public awareness.

MD18. Annapolis. Department of Transportation. *Annapolis Transportation Study, January 1977.* Compiled by Peat, Marwick, and Mitchell. Baltimore: Department of Transportation (Baltimore 21201), 1977. 273pp.
This is a study of the county transportation system, the metropolitan transportation

system, the downtown transportation system, and the bicycle and pedestrian system. The report provides in-depth research into traffic patterns, roadways, shuttle buses, bikeways, and pedestrian paths in both Annapolis and Anne Arundel County. Well illustrated with charts, tables, and maps, the study makes suggestions for immediate action. Not covered in this report is air transportation. There is a 29-page volume available which is the executive summary to this report.

MD19. Annapolis. Office of the Mayor. *Report for the Fiscal Year Ended June 30, 1976.* Compiled by McGraw & Simmons Professional Association. (Municipal Bldg., Annapolis 21401) 1976. Annual. 55pp.
A report of the yearly audit of various funds and balanced account groups of the mayor and aldermen of Annapolis.

MD20. Annapolis. Office of the Mayor. *State of the City, January 17, 1977.* (Municipal Bldg., Annapolis 21401) 1977. 9pp. Annual.
An annual message from the mayor to his constituents, this address is a discussion of the accomplishments and disappointments of the administration for the past year. In this message, the mayor also introduces his goals and hopes for the new year. This is an excellent summary of the major concerns of Annapolis municipal government within a given year.

MD21. Annapolis. Office of the Mayor and Aldermen. *Approved Budget for the City of Annapolis, Maryland July 1, 1976 to June 30, 1977.* (Municipal Bldg., Annapolis 21401), 1976. 17pp. Annual.
In this publication are comparative figures for the budget for Annapolis for fiscal years 1974–1975, 1975–1976, and 1976–1977. It is also an in-depth coverage of the finances of the city.

MD22. Annapolis. Ordinances, Local Laws, etc. *The Code of the City of Annapolis, Maryland: The Charter and the General Ordinances.* Charlottesville, VA: Michie City Publishers, 1969. 536pp.
The charter and the laws of the city of Annapolis are found in this city code. Chapters are arranged alphabetically and there is an analysis preceding each chapter which can serve as an index. At the end of the volume is an overall index. Footnotes throughout the code refer to related state law as well as to other areas of city law. The boundaries to the city and to the wards are described in detail. An organization chart has not been included. The code is supplemented regularly.

MD23. Anne Arundel County. Council of Community Services. *Directory of Community Services of Anne Arundel County.* Annapolis (P.O. Box 1968, Annapolis 21404), 1976. 157pp. Biennial. $3.
This compilation of official, voluntary, and service-oriented agencies in Anne Arundel County gives descriptions of approximately 500 groups. Arranged alphabetically by agency, there are also pages devoted to officials and commissions of Annapolis, of Anne Arundel County, and of Maryland. Each entry provides an address, a phone number, the name of the group's president, a brief summary of the group's purpose, and their source of funds. The directory also lists schools and churches in the county. Index is by subject.

MD24. Anne Arundel County. League of Women Voters. *Arundel Voter.* Annapolis (5 State Circle, Annapolis 21401). Monthly. 15pp.
The league's newsletter, this publication provides background information on issues of current interest, announces meetings, hearings, etc., on local and state levels, and discusses a variety of problems, legislation, and news on the local, state, and national levels. It is a good source for those who are interested in discovering what

issues the membership considers currently important. The league also produces the League of Women *Voters' Guide* before all elections. This is an excellent guide to biographical information on the candidates as well as a source to the election issues.

MD25. Anne Arundel County. Office of Economic Development. *Industrial and Commercial Inventory of Business Enterprises in Anne Arundel County.* Annapolis (Annapolis 21401), 1976. 161pp.
This source is a catalog of 1,753 industrial and commercial establishments located in Anne Arundel County. It is arranged in three sections: an alphabetic firm listing by company name with entries providing street address, mailing address, year the firm was established in the county, number of employees, SIC number, description of product or service; a listing by geographic location—each town in the county followed by a list of all businesses in that town; and a listing of firms by SIC number. Easy access to information regarding businesses in Annapolis is provided by this reference.

MD26. Anne Arundel County. Office of Planning and Zoning. *Population and Statistical Data.* Annapolis (Arundel Center, Annapolis 21404), 1973. 66pp. $5.
The purpose of this publication is to provide statistics about Anne Arundel County and the towns in that county to government agencies, civic groups, and individual citizens. Included in this document are population statistics and projections for Annapolis, nearby towns, and the county; county census data covering population characteristics, social characteristics, education, employment, and occupation; census data for places in the county, including Annapolis with information on zoning, land use, census, and church memberships; census tract data.

MD27. Stewart Directories Inc. *Anne Arundel County Criss-Cross Directory.* Baltimore (304 W. Chesapeake Ave., Baltimore 21204), 1956-   . Annual.
Useful as a supplement to the Annapolis City Directory (see entry **MD10**), the criss-cross directory is composed of four parts: (1) a zip code map and a set of street locator maps of the county, (2) alphabetical list of streets showing names and phone numbers of residents by house number, (3) a directory of major office and public buildings and apartment buildings giving street addresses plus census information about the county, and (4) a numerical section that lists telephone numbers numerically showing names of phone subscribers. The criss-cross is published with information from the telephone company; therefore, if a resident has an unlisted phone number, neither the address nor phone number will appear in this directory.

Collections

MD28. Annapolis Area Public Library. Interlibrary Loan Department, 1410 W. St., Annapolis 21401 (301)224-7501.
Polk City Directories, Stewart Criss-Cross Directories, and local telephone books are an important part of the Annapolis collection. These directories have been accumulated for the last 20 years and the phone books for the last 50 years. The library attempts to gather all city documents of current importance.

BALTIMORE

Local Newspaper Indexing: Partial indexing of Baltimore newspapers is done by putting clippings under Library of Congress subject headings in Maryland Department vertical file in the Enoch Pratt Free Library (see entry **MD9**). The headings also include names of people, places, and organizations. The department also has a query file, in part as a cross-reference to the vertical file (commonly indexed from specific headings to general headings).

Publications

MD29. Baltimore. Board of Supervisors of Elections. *Map of Baltimore City Showing Boundaries of Precincts, Wards and . . . Districts, 1898-1975*. n.p. 1975. Irregular.
Three maps, one each for councilmanic districts, legislative districts, and congressional districts. Latest edition, 1975, is 15" × 18½" with no scale given. In editions prior to 1954 not all three governmental election districts were included.

MD30. Baltimore. Bureau of the Budget and Management Research. *Administrative Manual*. n.p. 2 vol. Annual. 1970-   . Title and issuing agency vary from 1957-1969.
This how-to manual for Baltimore city government is loose-leaf, with supplementary update pages. It includes procedures (for ordering supplies, record keeping, etc.), personnel policies, etc. Not included are job description sheets and number and names of jobs organized by name of agency. Although the index is comprehensive, there is no table of contents.

MD31. Baltimore. Bureau of the Budget and Management Research. *Budget in Brief*. n.p. 1966/67-1976/77.
This budget is the *final* budget for each year. It includes two circle graph overviews of the Baltimore City budget dollar; "where it comes from" and "how it is used." It has a table of contents but no index. Earlier issues of the city budget are entered under: Board of Estimates. *The Ordinance of Estimates for the Year. . . .*

MD32. Baltimore. Bureau of the Budget and Management Research. *Departmental Budget Requests and Board of Estimates Recommendations*. n.p. 1967/68; 1971/72-1977/78.
(The budgets for the last two years have been issued in two volumes, the second containing "capital project detail.") This budget represents the second stage of the budget planning process. It has a table of contents and an index. It is difficult to use without some training in accounting and finance.

MD33. Baltimore. Bureau of the Budget and Management Research. *Departmental Budget Requests and the Department of Finance Recommendations*. n.p. 1972/73; 1976/77-1977/78.
(The budgets for the last two years have been issued in two volumes, the second containing "capital project detail.") This budget represents the first published stage of the budget planning process. It has a table of contents and an index. It is difficult to use without some training in accounting and finance.

MD34. Baltimore. City Council. *Journal of Proceedings*. n.p. 1828-   .
The proceedings are bound and indexed through 1968/69, the Second Councilmanic Year of the Session of 1967/1971. The more recent unbound proceedings are indexed through the Fourth Councilmanic Year 1970/71. The time lag between the council meeting and date received is about three or four weeks.

MD35. Baltimore. Department of Finance. *Annual Financial Report of the City of Baltimore*. n.p.
Annual report of the city treasurer and the commissioners of finance to the mayor and the members of the city council for the fiscal year ending June 30, 1966-

1975/76. Among the statements included are cash receipts, cash disbursements, loans, and bonded debts. There is a comprehensive table of contents but no index.

MD36. Baltimore. Department of Legislative Reference. *Baltimore Municipal Handbook, 1974.* Edited by Elizabeth T. Clark. n.p. 1974. 152pp. Supplement July 1975. (13pp.) Revised edition, 1977.
A brief description of each Baltimore city department is given with a list of the high-ranking members of each. City councilmen are listed with a map of each council-manic district. Also included are an organization chart for Baltimore City government and a description of the court system. The lists of names are not often updated.

MD37. Baltimore. Department of Legislative Reference. *Legislative Reference Bulletin.* n.p. Setember 1968– .
This selected list includes books, reports, periodicals, and municipal documents. The municipal documents include Baltimore and other U.S. cities. Reports from state agencies are listed, but few from other Maryland towns or counties. No indexes or annotations are included.

MD38. Baltimore. Department of Planning. *Baltimore's Automated Information Systems Inventory: A Report to the Department of Planning.* Compiled by W. Theodore Durr, Elaine Loebner, and Jeff Coleman. Baltimore Region Institutional Studies Center (847 N. Howard St., Baltimore 21201), 1977 (rev. ed.). 85pp.
The city of Baltimore utilizes an automated information system centered on, but not exclusive to, finance and personnel administration. The information environment in Baltimore is dynamic in the sense that minor innovations are constantly introduced; it is static in the sense that major changes indicating growth and better utilization are called for but not anticipated by the city's leadership. This survey is, in effect, a time capsule which portrays Baltimore's automated information systems as of summer 1975. Files of documentation are available at the Baltimore Region Institutional Studies Center (BRISC) (see entry **MD47**). Fifteen different categories of operations systems exist serving about 50 different purposes. The systems are described by department, bureau, and service. A major need exists for control and management development. While administrative capacity to generate, organize, store, retrieve, and analyze data bases is adequate for present needs, projected demands in the near future indicate that much attention should be paid to disseminating information to a broader community; predicting the cost to automated information management of implementing proposed legislation; and to focusing on the degree to which coordination between manual and automated systems might be facilitated.

MD39. Baltimore. League of Women Voters. *The Voter.* (From 1948 through May 1964 called *Newsletter;* June 1964–July 1965 called *The Voter;* August 1965–August 1973 called the *Baltimore Voter;* September 1973 to date, *The Voter.*) n.p. Information herein includes lists of area meetings (includlng non-LWV) on political issues, brief accounts of recent meetings, brief analyses of issues of interest and issues on which action should be taken.

MD40. Baltimore. League of Women Voters. *Voters Guide.* n.p. 1950– .
Herein are contained interviews with candidates giving their answers to a slate of questions asked of each, and annotations of city ballot questions, giving brief summary of what a vote for and a vote against signifies.

MD41. Baltimore. Mayor. *City of Baltimore Annual Report Fiscal Year.* n.p. 1976– .

This first combined annual report for all city agencies includes narrative information with statistics woven in. Capsule financial data is given. The report has no index and an inadequate table of contents. It is too brief for anyone wanting more
than a summary statement about each agency. It will be harder to get in-depth
information about city departments in the future.

MD42. Baltimore. Mayor and City Council. *Real Estate Tax Assessments,
Baltimore.* n.p. 1935–1975. Biennial.
Published in cooperation with the Greater Baltimore Board of Realtors. Properties
are listed alphabetically by street address with house numbers listed chronologically by even numbers and odd numbers. Listings include the size of the lot, the
lot number, in whose name the lot is assessed, and the amount of the assessment
for improvements. It is usually received toward the end of the biennial odd year.
It has no index.

MD43. Baltimore. Municipal Telephone Exchange. *Municipal Telephone
Directory.* n.p. Published since 1930 with the following frequencies: 1930–1940
biennial; 1941; 1944/45–1967/68 annual for most years; 1970 with 1972 supplement; 1973, 1974, 1976. Latest issue 1977, 42pp.
Earlier issues included a listing by departments indicating locations and high-
ranking staff of each. The issues for 1970 and later list staff members and departments separately. A building code is given which must be checked against a key.

MD44. Baltimore. Ordinances, Local Laws, etc. *Baltimore City Code* (1966
ed.) *Containing the General Ordinances of the Mayor and City Council of
Baltimore, Maryland,* in force on April 1, 1966. . . . Edited by Carl N. Everstine,
Director, State Department of Legislative Reference. Baltimore: King Brothers
Inc., 1966.
Contents: Vol. 1: articles 1–30 (general); vol. 2: article 31 (transit and traffic); vol.
3: article 32 (building regulations). A supplement for each volume, citing ordinances enacted through December 9, 1971 is inserted. A new edition for 1977 is
being printed in two volumes.

MD45. Baltimore. Ordinances, Local Laws, etc. *Charter of Baltimore City,
1964 Revision with Amendments to July 1, 1973. Supplement:* with amendments to January 1, 1977. Compiled and indexed by the Baltimore City Department of Legislative Reference. n.p. 166pp.

MD46. Baltimore. Ordinances, Local Laws, etc. *Ordinances and Resolutions of the Mayor and City Council.* n.p. 1977.
These ordinances are numbered by date of passage during each quadrennial
term of the city council. The beginning of each councilmanic year is the Thursday
after the first Monday in December (according to the current *Charter of Baltimore
City*). As of July 1977 the ordinances are indexed and bound through councilmanic year 1974/75. The Enoch Pratt Free Library (see entry **MD9**) has the more
recent ordinances in unbound form without an index. The time lag between date
of passage and date received is usually about ten days.

Collections

MD47. **University of Baltimore.** Baltimore Region Institutional Studies Center (BRISC). 847 N. Howard St., Baltimore 21201 (301)727-6350.
The Baltimore Region Institutional Studies Center performs an essentially archival
function of collecting, preserving, and making accessible the operating files of

organizations and agencies active in the metropolitan area. The local regional source records deposited at BRISC provide a nucleus of primary source material for those involved in urban research. A unique feature is use of the computer to integrate the collections conceptually while maintaining them physically intact as received, thus retaining full integrity of provenance. The collections contain a wealth of urban social, economic, and planning informaton ranging generally from late nineteenth through the twentieth centuries, with bulk dates post-1930. Holdings include records of such agencies as the Chamber of Commerce of Metropolitan Baltimore, Baltimore City Planning Department, Baltimore Criminal Justice Commission, Citizens' Planning and Housing Association, the Greater Baltimore Committee, Maryland Council for Social Concern, Planned Parenthood, Regional Planning Council, League of Women Voters, and the Urban Conservatory. Twenty-three collections are presently held, with more anticipated. Records must be used on the premises, with duplication available.

The Baltimore Region Institutional Studies Center's ARCHON (ARCHives ONline) is an information system designed to facilitate research of the holdings maintained at the center. Its three major components are (1) a descriptive subsystem for abstracting subject, qualifier, geographic, and chronological information; (2) a set of computer programs to organize and maintain this information in a data bank; and (3) an on-line, interactive search system to query the data bank. The combination of computerized search and controlled vocabulary description is the basis for a system of search services and finding aids to individual file units. The on-line search system accepts descriptors, qualifiers, geocodes, and time elements as input, and produces citations to primary source records. The citations are tailored to individual research needs. The data record includes the following elements: descriptor elements; record group; series; box; file unit; item identification (where applicable). A variety of printed indexes and thesauri are produced. BRISC data bases are accessible on application to the Information Manager, (301)727-6350, ext. 420. Fees are not currently being charged but a fee schedule may be established.

(See also entry US4).

ROCKVILLE

The city of Rockville has not maintained or published a list of its current or former publications or legal documents. The city's growth has paralleled that of Montgomery County, Maryland—a major suburb of Washington, D.C. Its nonpartisan government was named an All-American City in 1976 for the third time, and its operations have been citizen-oriented for the past two decades. In the late 1950s, the city initiated studies of its future needs and from that period to the present has commissioned studies for its water and sewer requirements, its housing, its transportation, its human services, and the future of its business community. Many of these studies are part of an uncataloged collection in Maryland-Municipal Reference (see entry MD75). In addition to its role as the major city in Montgomery County with its own government powers, Rockville is also the county seat and a participating jurisdiction of the Metropolitan Washington Council of Governments. Social, economic, and financial statistics appear in most Montgomery County and Council of Government documents. Early census information dating from 1790 is available on microfilm at Maryland-Municipal Reference, Rockville Library. Rockville has not officially published its election statistics, but the results are published in local newspapers and are available as part of the formal record in the Office of the City Clerk, Maryland at Vinson, City Hall, Rockville.

Publications

MD48. Henningson, Durham and Richardson of Maryland Inc. *Metro Transit Impact Study, Rockville, Maryland (Draft)*. Rockville, 1975. 200pp.
This consultant report provides a comprehensive analysis of the impact of the proposed "metro" subway system on the city of Rockville and very specifically to its two station sites, Rockville and Twinbrook. The analysis focuses first on the social, land use, and transportation effects and then turns to the very specific impacts around the two stations showing vehicle access, traffic, parking, esthetic, land use, community, and social impacts. Twenty-seven exhibits are listed and ten are included in the study. Twenty-three supporting tables provide basic data on parking and traffic as well as carbon monoxide concentrations and noise levels, etc. Appendixes include a list of 32 selected references, back-up data, a chronology of metro planning and reprints of county council and Washington Metropolitan Area Transit Authority resolutions.

MD49. Maccallum, Donald J. *Juvenile Delinquency in Rockville, Maryland: An Analysis of the Problem and a Proposal for Delinquency Prevention*. Rockville: United Church Center, 1969. 43pp.
This paper describes the nature and incidence of juvenile delinquency in Rockville in 1967 and proposes a program to prevent future delinquency.

MD50. Malloy, Mary Gordon, and Jane Sween. *A Selective Guide to the Historic Records of Montgomery County, Maryland*. Rockville: Montgomery County Department of Public Libraries, 1974. 36pp. $1.
This guide is designed to expedite searches and research in local history. (The city of Rockville is also the county seat of Montgomery County, Maryland). The guide covers the location and systems of indexing land records, wills, guardianship, marriage, divorce, and naturalization papers as well as court minutes, corporation records, assessment records, and registers of physicians and surgeons. The guide also explains where to write for birth and death records and enumerates the original source records for the county available in the Maryland Hall of Records. This is one of the publications put out during the bicentennial and is valuable for genealogists working on Montgomery County family histories.

MD51. *Polk's Rockville City Directory*. Richmond, VA: R. L. Polk and Co. (2910 W. Clay St., P.O. Box 27546, Richmond, VA 23261), 1958–
Polk's Rockville City Directory includes a buyer's guide and classified business directory, an alphabetical directory listing name, address, name of spouse, occupation, name of employer, as well as street directory of householders and businesses, and a numerical telephone directory.

MD52. Public Administration Service. *A Personnel System for the City of Rockville*. Chicago, IL, 1962. 50+pp.
A landmark study prepared by the Public Administration Service, a consulting and research firm. It contains proposed position classification and compensation plans for the civil service of the city of Rockville. Suggested amendments to the personnel ordinance and regulations and a proposed resolution for adopting the plans are also included.

MD53. Real Estate Research Corporation. *Land Utilization and Marketability Study Mid-City Urban Renewal Area, Rockville, Maryland*. Rockville, 1962. 150pp.

A landmark study, this document is the first comprehensive market and feasibility survey of the mid-city urban renewal area in Rockville. Prepared in 1962, it provides extensive data about Rockville and surrounding areas and the future potential for revitalizing the central business district. Much of the supporting data is based on the period between 1950 and 1960 providing information for later comparative studies. It is particularly strong in its inventory of existing professional and commercial land uses in Rockville as well as housing values and buying habits. The 94-page narrative is interspersed with charts and maps. The last 56 pages are charts and tabulated results of surveys. Very few copies are available, but the study may be borrowed on interlibrary loan from Maryland-Municipal Reference, Rockville Regional Library (see entry **MD75**).

MD54. Rockville. *Class Specifications, Rockville.* n.p. 1973. 300pp.
This city government personnel document includes an alphabetical index of class titles as well as a job description for each personnel classificatoin. The job descriptions cover the nature of work, examples of duties, desirable knowledge, abilities and skills, and desirable training and experience..

MD55. Rockville. *Red Gate Farm: Summary of Planning and Financing Proposal.* n.p. October 29, 1971. 34pp.
This report contains a summary of the proposals from earlier studies for the use of a large tract of farm land purchased by the city. A variety of proposals including an 18-hole golf course, tennis, ice skating, bowling facilties, and bike trails are reviewed with estimated construction and maintenance costs and revenue potentials. The earlier studies were: Rockville Department of Recreation, *A Report on the Need of Three Major Recreation Facilities* (February 1963); Rockville City Manager, *Municipal Swimming Pool Feasibility Report* (December 1964); Rockville Department of Recreation, *Municipal Golf Course Report* (January 1969); Rockville Mayor and Council, *Staff Report on Proposed Recreation Facilities and Land Use Alternatives—Red Gate Farm* (December 1969).

MD56. Rockville. Ad Hoc Committee to Review CATV. *Final Report: CATV in Rockville: A Report by the Mayor and Council's Committee on CATV.* 1973. 42pp. (Available from: City of Rockville, Maryland, at Vinson, Rockville 20850.)
This report describes the development of cable television and its future potential in Rockville. Sections explore service capabilities and recommended configuration for a system as well as the costs and potential revenues and ownership. Appendixes provide cost and revenue estimates, technical specifications, and a bibliography.

MD57. Rockville. Chamber of Commerce. *Community Guide Bicentennial Edition 1976.* (Executive Director, Rockville Chamber of Commerce, P.O. Box 173, Rockville 20850) 1976. 91pp. $1.
The Chamber of Commerce Community Guide includes an alphabetical listing of chamber members, a classified listing of member firms and professional member firms. Its contents include lists of clubs, organizations, civic groups, churches and synagogues, day care centers, parks, playgrounds, shopping centers, schools, and sites to visit as well as information about housing, transportation, and medical facilities.

MD58. Rockville. City Manager. *All American City 1976-1977, FY 1978 Proposed Budget by Programs.* 1977-   . (1974, Budget by Programs.). Annual.
The proposed operating budget is a program budget covering executive management, community development, administrative services, recreation and leisure

time, transportation, human resources, environment, and health and safety. This document provides expenditure by fund and area for 1976 and 1977 and estimates for 1978 as well as providing supplementary information on the assessable base, tax rate, and tax yield. The document also includes recently adopted salary schedules. Very complete table of contents, but no index.

MD59. Rockville. City Manager. *Annual Report, City of Rockville, Maryland Fiscal Year 1976.* (Maryland at Vinson, Rockville 20850) 1954/55- .
The annual report for the fiscal year 1976 reviews the major accomplishments by program category and outlines the plans and priorities of the mayor and council. The brief descriptions of goals and concise listing of all programs provide a quick overall look at the city of Rockville in 1976. The first annual report of the city's activities in 1954/55 provided a directory of city officials, a list of offices to call for a variety of city services, and eight bar charts of water, sewer, and street construction projects. The early report also included brief accounts of recreation programs and administrative services. There are pictures of the elected officials and key appointed officials. Although there is no index, the topic headings provide quick access to content. Very useful as a source of basic information on the activities of the city government and its fiscal health.

MD60. Rockville. Department of Planning. *State of Rockville Report.* 1974. 115pp. (Very few copies are available, but copies may be borrowed through interlibrary loan from Maryland-Municipal Reference, Rockville Regional Library, 99 Maryland Ave., Rockville 20850.)
The report is a comprehensive social and economic profile of the city of Rockville prepared by the city's planning department. The narrative is supported by charts or graphs throughout. The report includes an analysis of the population characteristics, the pattern of growth from 1950 to 1980, the housing quality and stock, educational levels, employment, and recreational activities, as well as the quality of the environment, together with the services provided by the city government. The report focuses on the role of the city government in the life of the community and the city's relationship with the state and county (Montgomery). An organization chart of the city government is part of the text. This report is used by students constantly. It is more comprehensive than the annual reports and the source information which footnote the charts lead students to other references which are also available in the collection.

MD61. Rockville. Department of Planning. *Town Center Background Report March 1977.* 1977. 176pp.
This staff report presents background information on the central business district of Rockville. The first portion tells of the revitalization efforts in the town center as well as the problems which have developed. The body of the report presents planning and development choices and an inventory of developed and underdeveloped land. The last portion discusses the potentials for the town center. There are five appendixes with information about the chronology of the urban renewal project, pertinent excerpts from the earlier marketability study, land use survey and coding methodology, and transportation design improvements data.

MD62. Rockville. Department of Recreation and Parks. *Maintenance Profile Report 1961 through 1980.* 1971. 20pp.
This report relates labor costs to acres of parkland, the number of recreation buildings, the recreation activities, and miles of right-of-way. The report is designed to provide the mayor and council of the city with facts and projected growth patterns as they relate to recreation facility needs. Useful to students in recreation administration.

MD63. Rockville. Department of Urban Renewal. *Housing Assistance Plan: Community Development Block Grant.* 1975. 18pp.
The Housing Assistance Plan for Rockville was approved and adopted by HUD, February 24, 1975. It contains a survey of housing goals as well as a review of target areas. The exhibits included maps and charts, and the plan ends with a bibliography and list of data sources.

MD64. Rockville. Director of Finance. *Annual Financial Report Fiscal Year Ended June 30, 1975.* 1962/63- . Annual.
A detailed and comprehensive statement of the expenditures of the city for the year ending June 30, 1975, as well as a statement of all revenues received by source. A statistical section contains charts with comparative information annually from 1966 through 1975. Report of independent auditor is included.

MD65. Rockville. Historic District Commission. *Annual Report.* 1977- Annual.
This brief document is a status report on the activities of the Historic District Commission. It includes a review of continuing projects, states the need for preservation guidelines, and concludes with a description of its effort to move the historic B. and O. Railroad station to an appropriate location.

MD66. Rockville. Human Relations Commission. *Equal Opportunity in Housing in Rockville: A Report to the Mayor and Council.* 1966. 90pp.
This committee report presents the extent of the housing problems in Rockville in regard to racial discrimination and explores the status of fair housing legislation. It summarizes the provisions of the proposed Rockville ordinance on fair housing and concludes with a formal recommendation to the mayor and council. Appendixes include the opinion of the city attorney on the ordinance and copies of pertinent federal legislation.

MD67. Rockville. Human Relations Study Group. *Human Relations in the City of Rockville: A Report by the Human Relations Study Group.* 1964. 58pp.
The Human Relations Study Group reviewed the role of the city government in coping with social changes in Rockville. The group summarizes employment opportunities, housing, education, justice, and public accommodations, and provides recommendations for future action. The report included five exhibits as supporting data for its recommendations.

MD68. Rockville. Mayor and Council. *City of Rockville Citizen's Handbook.* 1966- . 32pp. Irregular. Free.
This handbook briefly summarizes the history and development of the city of Rockville and describes the form of government, its relationship to other governmental agencies, its registration and election procedures, the municipal services it provides, and the local and state taxes, as well as benefits of city residence, location of churches, hospitals, libraries, newspapers, schools, and transportation. It is an attractive, brief, and concise booklet for residents of the city.

MD69. Rockville. Mayor and Council. *Minutes and Agenda.* 1921- . Holdings: 1921-74 available in microform at City Hall; 1971- available in loose-leaf format at Maryland Municipal Reference.
The minutes cover reports from the city manager, nomination and confirmation of appointments, contracts awarded on capital projects, memoranda of agreements authorized, ordinances and resolutions introduced, discussed, amended, passed, or defeated. The proceedings cover work sessions on proposed ordinances and replies to communications from state and county governments, as

well as summaries of citizen forums which are a part of the structure of each meeting.

MD70. Rockville. Ordinances, Local Laws, etc. *Laws of the City of Rockville, Maryland*. (Loose-leaf) n.p. n.d.
This loose-leaf publication contains the Rockville City Charter, the local laws and ordinances, and the regulations adopted by the mayor and council which are currently in force. The city is incorporated and exercises all the powers granted under Article 66B of the Maryland Annotated Code. The volume is updated regularly.

MD71. Rockville. Planning Commission. *Capital Improvements Program 1977-1982*. 1963/69- . Annual.
This legal document describes the long-range building and construction programs of the city government. Revised and adopted annually, it provides detailed project descriptions and funding over a six-year period. The projects are listed and the estimated costs projected by program areas, i.e., executive management, community and economic development, administrative services, recreation and leisure time, transportation, human resources, environment, and health and safety. The CIP analyzes sources of funding and estimated tax rates.

MD72. Rockville. Planning Commission. *Master Plan for the City of Rockville: A Revision of the Master Plan Adopted September 22, 1960*. Addendum Issued September 13, 1972. Amended, March 1973. (1960 Master Plan: Urban Assistance Planning Project 701, Maryland P-2.) 1970 (73). 103pp.
This planning document as amended is a revision of a plan adopted on September 22, 1960. Contents include the community goals, the history of land use development in the city and region and the planning process. In addition to inventories of land use, zoning, housing, parks and recreation, sewer and water facilities, schools, and transportation, the report also includes the maximum expansion limits and the commercial and industrial potentials. A fiscal analysis and land use map are included. The 1973 amendment is attached to the back and describes the changes concisely.

MD73. Smith, Wilbur and Associates, Consulting Engineers and Planners. *Feasibility of an Intra-City Bus System in Rockville*. Rockville, 1973. 43pp.
This is a technical and economic study which explores the feasibility of establishing and operating an intracity bus system. The contents includes possible routes, the estimated patronage, the equipment needs, alternative fare proposals, and schedules. There are maps and charts.

MD74. Thompson, Noma. *Western Gateway to the National Capital (Rockville)*. Washington, DC: Stewart Printing Co., 1949. 122pp.
A brief history of Rockville which focuses on the land grants, Rockville as a hamlet, Rockville as a city and as the county seat. The publication also provides brief histories of the city's local institutions, roads, public utilities, hospitals and sanitariums, churches, courts, schools, etc. The history concludes with sketches of the congressional airport and the first television station in operation in the period from 1900 to 1930. There is no table of contents and only a short index.

Collections

MD75. Maryland-Municipal Reference. Rockville Regional Library, Montgomery County Public Library System, 99 Maryland Ave., Rockville 20850 (301)-279-1966. Teletype Service: (710)828-0220.
The Maryland-Municipal Reference collection at the Rockville Regional Library,

not only attempts to acquire reference and circulating copies of all regular city publications but also any special studies prepared by consultants under contract. An extensive collection of archival materials is available, both in print or on microfilm, for use in the library or for photocopying.

The special collection also includes 45 recorded tapes and transcripts focused on the political, social, and economic history of the county prepared by the Montgomery County League of Women Voters and the Montgomery County Historical Society. Since Rockville is the historic and governmental hub of the county, Rockville residents are included.

For the bicentennial, photocopies were made of all historic maps of Montgomery County and western Maryland in the Library of Congress map collection and donated to the local history collection of the library. These maps have been indexed by geographic location, by date published, and by type. Recent zoning, land use, topographic, geologic, and highway maps have been added to the historic collection and are similarly indexed.

Under its charter, the city of Rockville has its own planning, zoning, and taxing powers, but the area surrounding the city is under the jurisdiction of the county. This collection includes historic runs of the planning and legal documents of Montgomery and the state of Maryland.

MASSACHUSETTS

General Publications

MA1. Massachusetts. Department of Commerce and Development. *Commerce Digest.* Boston (State Office Bldg., Government Center, 100 Cambridge St., Boston 02202), 1959– . Monthly. Free.
The coverage of the business situation for communities is extensive and includes individual companies, business indicators, and economic trends.

MA2. Massachusetts. Department of Commerce and Development. *Monographs.* Boston (State Office Bldg., Government Center, 100 Cambridge St., Boston 02202), 1964. Irregular. Free.

MA3. Massachusetts. Secretary of the Commonwealth. *City and Town Clerks.* Boston (State House, Boston 02133), 1976. 12pp. Irregular. Free.

BOSTON

Publications

MA4. Boston. Administrative Services Department. *Index of City Services.* n.p., 1972. 31pp.

MA5. Boston. Conservation Commission. *Directory of Environmental Groups.* n.p., December 1971. 24pp.

MA6. Boston. Mayor. *City Record; Official Chronicle, Municipal Affairs.* Weekly. Index.

MA7. Boston. Public Schools. *Personnel Directory of the Public Schools of the City of Boston.* n.d.

MA8. Boston. School Committee. *Directory of the Public Schools of the City of Boston.* 1972. 618pp.

Collections

MA9. **Boston Public Library.** 666 Boylston St., P.O. Box 217, Boston 02117 (617)536-5400, ext. 295. TWX (710)321-0513.
The public library attempts to collect all official Boston publications and selective publications from other cities in the state. The collection, which is basically non-

circulating, contains historical as well as current materials. Incidentally, it should be noted that the Office of the Boston Bicentennial has produced materials promoting the city and its history.

(See also entry **US4**.)

CAMBRIDGE

The city of Cambridge publishes a wide variety of documents covering the many diverse activities of the city and its government. There is no checklist for these documents. **Local Newspaper Indexing:** Since 1975 the Reference Department, Cambridge Public Library (see entry **MA12**) has been indexing comprehensively the local newspaper, the *Cambridge Chronicle*.

Publications

MA10. Cambridge. Department of Budget and Personnel. *Annual Budget, 1976-1977*. (City Hall, 795 Massachusetts Ave., Cambridge 02139) 1942–   . 188pp. Annual. Free.
This publication is divided into six parts: the budget message, summaries, financial plan, service programs, public investments, and appropriation orders. The budget, which includes totals from the two previous fiscal years for comparison, is indexed and detailed.

MA11. Cambridge. Department of Budget and Personnel. *Annual Report, 1975-1976*. (City Hall, 795 Massachusetts Ave., Cambridge 02139) 1942–   . 24pp. Annual. Free.
This report outlines in short articles what each division of the Cambridge city government has done in the previous year. It also contains information such as the vital statistics for the city and lists the names of the department heads and various personnel from different departments. The report, which includes illustrations and charts, is addressed to the citizens of the city and is submitted to them by the city manager.

Collections

MA12. Cambridge Public Library. 449 Broadway, Cambridge, MA 02138 (617)876-5005, ext. 91.
The major municipal collections are located at the Cambridge Public Library, Cambridge City Hall (Microfilming Division), and Harvard University (Littauer Library). The public library is the major depository of city publications. Besides having the annual reports and annual budgets which date back to 1942, the library owns the annual documents which encompass the years 1846 to 1942. The library has a good collection of genealogical records and local histories, and participates in Greenwood Press's *Index to Current Urban Documents*.

NEW BEDFORD

Data not available at this time.

SPRINGFIELD

Local Newspaper Indexing: The *Springfield Union*, the *Daily News*, and the *Sunday Republican* are indexed by the Springfield City Library (see entry **MA27**) as of 1976. There are selective indexes for the *Springfield Republican* from 1899 to 1903 and the *Springfield Union* from 1912 to 1918, 1920–1923, and 1935 to 1941. Queries will be accepted.

Publications

MA13. The Community Council of Greater Springfield Inc. *Priorities 1977.* Springfield (1618 Main St., Springfield 01103), March 1977. 127pp. Irregular. Free.
Final report of the Joint Priority Study Committee established by the Community Council and the human services department of the city of Springfield. Includes areas of concern singled out for attention, medical needs, overview of services, service needs cited by agencies, number of agencies with staff speaking foreign languages, and geographic location of services.

MA14. The Junior League of Springfield, Massachusetts Inc. *Community Services Directory.* (254 Worthington St., Springfield 01103) 1975. 144pp. Irregular. $1.50.
Nonprofit agencies and organizations which offer a direct, regular service to the general public, or which have planning and action programs for the benefit of the entire community are listed.

MA15. Plouffe, William C., and Kirtland H. Olson. *Summary of Operations and Procedures, Building Department, City of Springfield.* September 1971. 37pp. Irregular. (Available from: Office of Code Development, Department of Community Affairs, Commonwealth of Massachusetts, Boston, or Building Dept., City Hall, Court St., Springfield 01103.)
A survey of the operations of the building department including job descriptions, sample permits, statistics, records, and procedures.

MA16. Springfield Area. League of Women Voters. *Springfield Area Handbook.* 1972. 54pp. Irregular. (No permanent address. Officers' names can be obtained from the Springfield City Library.)
A survey of Springfield and bordering communities. Includes government departments, chart of city organization, cultural and recreational facilities, judicial system, and a description of Hampden County government. Brief descriptions of Agawam, West Springfield, Chicopee, Ludlow, Wilbraham, East Longmeadow, and Longmeadow are included.

MA17. Springfield. City Planning Department. *Capital Improvements Program 1 January 1973-30 June 1978, Springfield, Massachusetts.* (City Hall, Court St., Springfield 01103) February 7, 1973. 23pp. Free.

MA18. Springfield. City Planning Department. *Neighborhood Analysis.* (Administrative Bldg., Court St., Springfield 01103). Irregular. Not for sale.
A series of ten reports done on the identifiable neighborhoods of the city. Areas of study include population, housing, community facilities, land use, and public improvements. Information is largely statistical and based on the 1970 U.S. Census data.

MA19. Springfield. City Planning Department. *Report to the City Council on the Status of Subsidized Housing in the City of Springfield, MA Phase I.* (City Hall, Court St., Springfield 01103) April 5, 1972. 5pp. Irregular. Free.
Survey of subsidized housing in the city, with maps and statistics.

MA20. Springfield. City Planning Department. *Springfield Planning Department's Library of Community Reports.* (City Hall, Court St., Springfield 01103) April 1970. 25pp. Irregular. Free.

MA21. Springfield. Department of Police. *Springfield Police Department Equal Employment Opportunity Plan.* (130 Pearl St., Springfield) 1974. Irregular. Free.

MA22. Springfield. Historic District Study Committee. *Final Report Historic District Study Committee.* 46pp. with appendix. Irregular. Free.

MA23. Springfield. Ordinances, Local Laws, etc. *Revised Ordinances of the City of Springfield, Massachusetts.* Charlottesville, VA: Michie City Publishing Co., 1963. 440pp. Irregular. (Available from: City Clerk's Office, Administrative Bldg., Court St., Springfield 01103.)
The first revision and codification of the general ordinances since 1956. It contains the charter (Plan A of the General Laws), those ordinances of a general and permanent nature passed prior to July 1, 1963, as were found desirable for retention, except those expressly saved from repeal, and rules and regulations of the Board of Park Commissioners. It also has a table showing the disposition of ordinances passed subsequent to 1905, lists of special acts applying to the city which are not printed in the volume, and a list of acts which were required by law to be accepted. Ordinances are in the process of revision and may be consulted at the city clerk's office.

MA24. Springfield. Park and Recreation Department. *Park and Recreation Department Services—Program Facilities* (Forest Park, Springfield 01108) 25pp. Irregular. Free.
Survey of facilities, programs, and services offered by the park department as well as an outline of the department's staff.

MA25. Springfield. Planning Department for Springfield Redevelopment Authority. *Reconnaissance Report for the Model Neighborhood Development Program.* (73 State St., Springfield 01103) January 1973. 21pp. Irregular. Free.
Survey of people, land, buildings, transportation, and public facilities of the model neighborhood development area. It includes maps, charts, and statistics.

MA26. Springfield. School Department. *Directory of the Public Schools, Springfield, Massachusetts.* (195 State St., Springfield 01103) October 1976. 181pp. Annual. Free.
Includes school calendar; school committee members; staff of the central office; staffs of the elementary, junior high, and senior high schools; teachers of special subjects; vision and hearing testers; unassigned staff members; evening adult schools; federal programs; employees on leave of absence; committees; school organizations; health department; alphabetical list of employees of the public school system; and Springfield public school system telephone numbers and addresses.

Collections

MA27. Springfield City Library. 220 State St., Springfield 01103 (413)739-3871, ext. 6/7.
The library attempts to obtain all municipal publications. Selected materials in the collection date back to 1852 and are available for use in the Local History Room.

Though the library does not have a complete collection of municipal publications, the staff attempts to acquire them as they receive requests or otherwise learn of their publication. At present, the library has many current reports of the planning department and the school department, fewer by police, city council, etc.

WORCESTER

Worcester is not a large publisher. There is no checklist of publications, although it is possible to identify many of them through the calendar of the city council meetings. Publications are available from the publishing agency. Two copies of most publicly available items are sent to the Worcester Public Library (see entry MA35) for public use and inclusion in Greenwood Press's *Index to Current Urban Documents*. Material dealing with the city is published by regional, county, and state agencies.

Publications

MA28. U.S. Department of Labor. Bureau of Labor Statistics. *Area Wage Survey, Worcester, Massachusetts, Metropolitan Area.* Washington, DC: Government Printing Office. 31pp. Annual.
This item contains the results of a survey of occupational earnings and supplementary wage benefits in the Worcester SMSA.

MA29. Worcester. [*Annual Reports of the Several City Departments for the Calendar Year Ending. . . .*] 1848/49- . Annual.
Compilation of annual reports from Worcester's city agencies. These contain summaries of the departments, operations, and statistical data. The public library has the annual reports from 1848/49 to date available for use within the library.

MA30. Worcester. City Council. *Manual of the City Council.* Worcester: n.p., 1890- . Biennial.
This booklet lists all city officers and members of the various committees. It also provides statistical data such as school enrollment, population, and valuation. The rules of the city council are included.

MA31. Worcester. League of Women Voters. *Here's Worcester.* Worcester (P.O. Box 988, Worcester 01601), 1969. 101pp. Irregular.
An overview of the city with special attention paid to governmental agencies and structures. It is in the process of being updated.

MA32. Worcester. Office of the City Manager. *City of Worcester Organizational Structure, Goals and Objectives.* Worcester: n.p., 1977. Irregular.
Departments are arranged chronologically by department budget number. Goals and objectives precede the organizational charts.

MA33. Worcester. Ordinances, Local Laws, etc. *Revised Ordinances of the City of Worcester, Massachusetts 1974: General Ordinances.* 1974. xxx + 338pp.
A continuously updated book of the ordinances governing the city of Worcester. It also contains the city charter, special ordinances, special acts of the state applicable to the city, statutes accepted by the city, and an index. Although the salary ordinance, zoning ordinance, fire prevention code, and building code are listed appendixes, these are kept separately from the general ordinance.

MA34. Worcester. Social Services Corporation. *Human Services: A Directory.* (340 Main St., Worcester 01608). Irregular. $10.
This directory attempts to locate and describe all human service agencies in the city and the nine surrounding towns. Each agency is thoroughly described.

Collections

MA35. Worcester Public Library. Salem Sq., Worcester 01608 (617)752-3751.
The library attempts to collect all publicly available documents issued by the city and any other organization or governmental unit. Most material on local subjects cannot be loaned. The library participates in Greenwood Press's *Index to Current Urban Documents*. There is no newspaper index; there is an extensive clipping file dating back to the 1940s.

MICHIGAN

General Publications

MI1. Michigan Municipal League. *Directory of Michigan Municipal Officials.* Ann Arbor (1675 Green Rd., P.O. Box 1487, Ann Arbor 48106), 1928- . Semi-annual. $12.
This is a directory of executive, legislative, and administrative officials in every city and village of the state.

DETROIT

With few exceptions (i.e., the *Municipal Manual* and the *Directory of Officials*, the miscellaneous statistics section in the city's *Annual Financial Report* and earlier publications, the current leaflets issued by the public information department, or the *Charter* and the official codes), the city of Detroit has not produced many publications for the specific purpose of reference and information. However, some knowledge of city activities can be gained from documents exemplified in the following list, particularly from the annual reports issued by many city departments. Recently, awareness of the need for information on city services has led to the publication of some new tools (the *Neighborhood Problem-Solving and City Services* is an example). Also of value is the greatly expanded and improved listing of city agencies in the local telephone directory (Michigan Bell Telephone Company). Incidentally, while the majority of Detroit documents are distributed free of charge, the supply is often limited. **Local Newspaper Indexing:** The general information department of the Detroit Public Library (see **MI24**) holds the *Detroit News* index, which has been issued by Bell and Howell since January 1976. The staff of the Burton Historical Collection indexes both the *Detroit News* and the *Detroit Free Press* for local history. The Municipal Reference Library maintains extensive newspaper clipping files arranged by subject, from 1945 to date, oriented toward its primary function. The sociology and economics department's clipping files contain current and selective retrospective material.

There are back files on the *Detroit Legal News* in the sociology and economics department, but no index. The paper publishes weekly; currently in each Friday issue are the complete proceedings of the regular session of the Detroit city council held on the preceding Wednesday, including the complete text of ordinances. Since the official notices of the city government must be published "in one or more daily newspapers of general circulation in the city," they may and do appear, variously, not only in the *Legal News* but also in other newspapers.

Publications

MI2. Detroit. Auditor General. *Annual Financial Report of the City. . . .* (1312 City-County Bldg., Detroit 48226) 1937/38– . Annual. Free.
This report includes the financial statements of the city. The material is presented by type of fund, with detailed breakdowns and informative annotations.

MI3. Detroit. Budget Department. *City of Detroit Budget.* (1100 City-County Bldg., Detroit 48226) 1898/99– . Annual. Free.
The tables on revenue sources and appropriations for the whole and each unit of city government during the current year are followed by a section on salaries of elected and appointed officials and classified employees. Retrospective summary tables show tax levies and tax rates. Data on staffing of city departments are published in a separate volume titled *Personnel Services.*

MI4. Detroit. Board of Education. *Directory, Detroit Public Schools.* (5057 Woodward Ave., Detroit 48202) 1895– . Annual. Free.
Lists the offices and members of the central and regional school boards, the offices of special programs, all Detroit public schools and school-related organizations. In addition, the directory has a name index, map, statistics of total school population, and other information of interest to the school practitioner.

MI5. Detroit. City Clerk. *Directory of Officials, City of Detroit.* (1304 City-County Bldg., Detroit 48226) 1969– . Annual. Free.
Lists all Detroit city government departments and the Wayne County departments. It gives addresses and telephone numbers for agencies, agency heads and their principal assistants.

MI6. Detroit. City Clerk. *Municipal Manual of the City of Detroit.* (1304 City-County Bldg., Detroit 48226) 1861– . Irregular.
The latest issue is dated 1972. The 1978 edition will reflect the changes in governmental structure and department names which resulted. It will also update the "Incidental Information on Many Subjects of General Interest." The manual is the single, most inclusive, though brief, general reference source on Detroit city government. The largest part of the manual consists of sections on the various departments of city government, citing charter or ordinance authority for their establishment, significant historical facts, a description of their current functions, and related information.

MI7. Detroit. City Council. *Journal of the City Council, from January 2, 1975–December 17, 1975.* City Clerk (1304 City-County Bldg., Detroit 48226), 1977. 399, 2,564pp. Weekly with annual bound vols. $10 per year ($15 for bound volumes).
Includes the texts of proposed ordinances, introductory statements to ordinances, letters, petitions, votes taken, and occasional brief reports. Speeches are not included. A detailed index is included in the bound volumes. Current issues have neither index nor table of contents; however, the order of proceedings usually follows a standard pattern.

MI8. Detroit. City Council. Division of Research and Analysis. *Neighborhood Problem-Solving and City Services.* (1340 City-County Bldg., Detroit 48226) 1975. 67pp. Free.
This is a guide to the city agencies which assist people in everyday problems.

Helpful hints on steps to follow are given in an easy-to-read narrative form. A new edition is currently in preparation.

MI9. Detroit. Department of Health. Statistical Analysis Division. *Data Book.* (Herman Kiefer Complex, 1151 Taylor, Detroit 48202) 1967- . Annual. Free.
Vital statistics and other demographic data, population estimates and disease statistics make up this volume. While most figures are for the current year, there are also retrospective tables; population back to 1701, and birth and death statistics to 1966 or earlier.

MI10. Detroit. League of Women Voters. *They Represent You! A Citizen's Guide to Elected Officials.* (2230 Witherell, Detroit 48201) n.d. Biennial. Free.
The small folder lists the names, locations, telephone numbers, terms of office, and salaries of the elected Detroit and Wayne County officials and those representing Detroit in the state and federal governments. Selected city government offices, maps of legislative districts, and other useful information are added features.

MI11. Detroit. Mayor. *Moving Detroit Forward: A Plan for Urban Economic Revitalization.* (1126 City-County Bldg., Detroit 48226) 1977. 162 leaves. Free.
Background data on existing conditions or previous work introduce each of the chapters of Detroit's comprehensive five-year development plan.

MI12. Detroit. Mayor. *Proposed Capital Agenda, 1977-78 to 1981-82.* (1126 City-County Bldg., Detroit 48226) 1975- . Annual. Free.
An introductory section describes the major sources of revenue available to the city of Detroit for capital projects. The proposed capital improvement projects are listed in summary form under categories such as "Civic Center," "Data Processing," and "Transit Projects." Sources of funding, including private funds, are projects for each year of the five-year period.

MI13. Detroit. Neighborhood Services Department. *Service Directory.* (5031 Grandy Ave., Detroit 48211) 1975- . Annual. Free.
The department is the successor to the antipoverty agencies of the 1960s. The programs offered through its Neighborhood Service Centers and other cooperating organizations include family services, employment training, medical and dental services, child development, youth and senior citizens programs, food and transportation assistance, substance abuse treatment, etc. Information is given for each program, along with the names of contact persons, telephone numbers, addresses, and eligibility criteria.

MI14. Detroit. Ordinances, Local Laws, etc. *The Code of the City of Detroit.* Charlottesville, VA: Michie City Pub. Co., 1825- . Supplements issued semi-annually. $40 (plus $10 for supplements). (Available from: City Clerk, 1304 City-County Bldg., Detroit 48226.)
The code consists of the charter and the codified city ordinances currently in force. The names of major city officials are included, but not an organization chart. It should be noted that several important ordinances—such as the official building code—are not set out in the city code but are published separately. The various codes comprising the building code are published and sold, for the most part, by the Detroit Building and Safety Engineering Department (401 City-County Bldg., Detroit 48226); prices vary.

MI15. Detroit. Personnel Department. *Departmental Organization Charts.* (316 City-County Bldg., Detroit 48226) 1976- . Biennial. Free.
The charts from 1948 to 1974 were issued by the Civil Service Commission. The chart book contains one organization chart for Detroit city government as a whole and one or more charts for each of the 45 departments. The following information is provided for each department and its subdivisions: the legal authority for its creation, its functions, the name and title of the department head, addresses, functions, and staffing of department units.

MI16. Detroit. Planning Department. *A Profile of Detroit, 1970.* (801 City-County Bldg., Detroit 48226) 1974. 4 vols. $1 per vol. (except $2 for the volume on UCS subcommunities).
Selected data derived from the 1970 U.S. Census of Population and Housing are compiled in these volumes for four kinds of small areas within the city of Detroit. These four are police precincts, health department areas, UCS (United Community Services of Metropolitan Detroit) subcommunities, and school regions.

MI17. Detroit. Police Department. *Annual Report.* (1300 Beaubien, Detroit 48226) 1865/66- . Annual. Free.
The parts of the report that are frequently consulted for general information purposes are its fairly extensive section on Detroit crime statistics, its maps of police precincts, and its summary of the major events of the year.

MI18. Detroit. Public Library. *MRL Bulletin.* (Municipal Reference Library, 1004 City-County Bldg., Detroit 48226) 1945- . Irregular. Free.
The publication, which was planned as a current awareness source for city and county officials and employees, is a selected subject list of recent books, pamphlets, and periodical articles in the Municipal Reference Library. City and county publications are also included. The publication has not been issued since May/June 1976. However, it should be resumed in the near future.

MI19. Federal Reserve Bank of Chicago. Detroit Branch. *The Detroit Area Economic Fact Book.* Detroit: Detroit Area Economic Forum, 1960- . Annual. Free. (Available from: *Detroit Free Press*, 321 W. Lafayette, Detroit 48226.)
Comparative statistical data on the Detroit metropolitan area, the state of Michigan, and the United States are presented in sections dealing with population, manufacturing, employment, construction, trade, and finance.

MI20. Southeast Michigan Council of Governments. *Annual Report.* (800 Book Bldg., Detroit 48226) 1968- . Annual. Free.
The Southeast Michigan Council of Governments is the Detroit area regional planning and development agency. In this annual report, there is a record of the following activities: overall planning and information gathering for the region; water quality, transportation and land use planning; housing and public safety (crime prevention) programs; coordinating development, and functioning as the regional federal grant review (A-95) clearinghouse.

MI21. Southeast Michigan Council of Governments. *Population and Occupied Dwelling Units in Southeastern Michigan.* (800 Book Bldg., Detroit 48226). Annual. Free.
The estimates presented in these tables are as of July 1 of the year and are shown alongside the 1970 census figures.

MI22. United Community Services of Metropolitan Detroit. *Community Services Directory.* (51 W. Warren, Detroit 48201) 1976. 288pp. $12.

This is a comprehensive guide to nearly 1,500 community resources serving the populations of Macomb, Oakland, and Wayne counties. Included are voluntary and government agencies. Among these are the major city of Detroit departments which render direct service to people.

MI23. Wayne County. County Clerk. ***Wayne County Directory.*** (201 City-County Bldg., Detroit 48226) 1918/19– . Biennial. Free.
Includes county agencies and officials, and the major officials of the cities, villages, and townships within the county. The directory also has a section on the courts having jurisdiction in the county, selected state and federal officials, foreign consulates in Detroit, some statistical data, and excerpts from the state laws governing county government.

Collections

MI24. Detroit Public Library. 5201 Woodward Ave., Detroit 48202 (313) 833-1400.
Major municipal collections within the library are: Municipal Reference Library, 1004 City-County Bldg., Detroit 48226 (313)224-3885; Sociology and Economics Department, 5201 Woodward Ave., Detroit 48202 (313)833-1440; and Burton Historical Collection, 5201 Woodward Ave., Detroit 48202 (313)833-1480. Scattered Detroit municipal publications are found in other subject departments of the library.

The Municipal Reference Library has been a depository for "all official public reports and documents" of the city since 1952. It contributes a substantial amount of the city's output to Greenwood Press for inclusion in the *Index to Current Urban Documents.*

The Burton Historical Collection is noted for its holdings of early Detroit documents from the beginning of the nineteenth century, as well as of prior territorial materials. The Sociology and Economics Department maintains an extensive collection of early as well as current Detroit municipal documents.

All Detroit Public Library collections are available to anyone for use on the premises. Interlibrary loan requests will be honored within the limits prescribed by the needs of the respective departments' primary users. Special rules apply to the Burton Historical Collection. Out-of-town queries calling for simple searches may be accepted; under certain circumstances more extensive work may be arranged for a service charge related to the difficulty and time involved.

(See also entry **US4.**)

FLINT

Local Newspaper Indexing: See entry **MI30.**

Publications

MI25. Flint. Board of Education. ***Directory of Public Schools.*** 1917–

MI26. Flint. Board of Education. ***Organization Charts.*** 1974. 9pp.

MI27. Flint. City Commission. ***City Board and Commissions: Official Source.*** City Clerk's Office, 1975.
This publication is prepared for use by the city agencies.

MI28. Flint. City Manager. ***Flint: A City in Change.*** 1977.

This report and calendar contains the city departments in condensed form, organization charts, descriptions of city services, summarized budget data, maps, statistical information, boards and commissions, historical information, and a calendar of meetings, sports, and cultural events for the coming year. Ephemeral but filled with information!

MI29. Flint. Division of Finance. *Annual Report.* 1916– . Annual.
Contains important statistical information not easily accessible elsewhere.

MI30. Mideastern Michigan Library Cooperative. *Index to the Flint Journal Newspaper.* 1963– . Monthly with annual cumulations. $90 (monthly), $60 (annual cumulation), $150 (both). (Available from: *Flint Journal* Index, 1026 E. Kearsley, Flint 48502.)
This index is compiled from the final home edition. It is intended as a guide to newspaper articles of interest and importance about Michigan people, places, and things; emphasis is on Flint, Genesee County, and the surrounding area.

Collections

MI31. Flint Public Library. 1026 E. Kearsley St., Flint 48502 (313)232-7111.
All documents acquired by the library are submitted to Greenwood Press for inclusion in the *Index to Current Urban Documents.* Most of the documents in the library's collection are noncirculating.

GRAND RAPIDS

Local Newspaper Indexing: The staff of the Michigan Room of the Grand Rapids Public Library (see entry **MI36**) maintains a card file index to the *Grand Rapids Press* from 1960 to the present. The index is to items concerning Grand Rapids. Inquiries will be accepted.

Publications

MI32. Grand Rapids. *Boards and Commissions.* n.p., n.d. Loose-leaf with annual revisions.

MI33. Grand Rapids. *Organization Directory of the City of Grand Rapids.* n.p., n.d. Loose-leaf with annual revisions.

MI34. Grand Rapids. Systems and Fiscal Management Department. *Final Fiscal Plan.* Annual.
This report contains planning information and program objectives for the city departments.

MI35. Kent Intermediate School District. *Directory.* (2650 E. Beltline, Grand Rapids 49506.)

Collections

MI36. Grand Rapids Public Library. Library Plaza N.E., Grand Rapids 49503 (616)456-4400, ext. 4361.
The municipal documents are housed in the Michigan Room (456-4424) and do not circulate. However, they can be copied for a small per page charge.

MINNESOTA

General Publications

MN1. *Directory of Minnesota Municipal Officials.* St. Paul: League of Minnesota Municipalities (300 Hanover Bldg., 480 Cedar St., St. Paul 55101). Annual.

MN2. Minnesota. Department of Manpower Services. *Employment Trends.* February 1946– .
Prepared by the Minnesota Department of Manpower Services, this publication includes monthly Duluth employment statistics.

Collections

MN3. Center for Urban and Regional Affairs. 311 Walter Library, 117 Pleasant St. S.E., University of Minnesota, Minneapolis 55455.
Deals with large regional topics and local matters.

BLOOMINGTON

According to the city manager, the city has no significant publication operation and has no listing of its publications. The Promotion and Development Committee of Bloomington has some free booklets on police, fire, health, parks and recreation, general city government, and cultural activities. Some information on the city can be found in the publications of the Metropolitan Councils.

Publications

MN4. Bloomington. League of Women Voters. *Bloomington in Brief: A League of Women Voters Handbook.* (4409 W. 84 St., Bloomington 55437) 1973. 19pp. 50¢.

DULUTH

Local Newspaper Indexing: The Duluth Public Library (see entry **MN21**) indexes information on the local history of Duluth and surrounding area industries. Clippings from newspapers and periodicals have been collected and placed in 16 loose-leaf notebooks since the late 1930s. "Duluth History and Biography Index" is an index covering both newspapers and periodicals and was started in the late 1930s.

Publications

MN5. Arrowhead Regional Development Commission. *The Arrowhead Regional Report*, Vol. 1, June 1971– .
This monthly newsletter highlights activities of this seven-county commission and has information on the publications of the commission.

MN6. Duluth. *Organizational Chart of the City of Duluth, Minnesota.* 1971. Supplement 1976.

MN7. Duluth. Board of Education. *Duluth Public Schools Directory.* 1923/24–1944/45, 1946/47, 1959/60, 1962/63–1965/66, 1967/68, 1972/73–
Lists teachers and schools where they teach. It also gives school enrollments.

MN8. Duluth. Chamber of Commerce. *Duluth Profile of Manufacturers: Wholesalers.* 1976.
This directory lists addresses, types of products, heads of firms, number of employees, and telephone numbers of wholesaling firms. It is updated regularly.

MN9. Duluth. Chamber of Commerce. *Duluth Profile of Retail Establishments.* 1976.
This directory lists addresses, heads of firms, number of employees, and telephone numbers. It is updated regularly.

MN10. Duluth. Department of Research and Planning. *Demographic Statistical Handbook.* 1971.
This is a series of tables which contain selected demographic and socioeconomic data, comparable for the city of Duluth as a whole and its component planning areas and neighborhoods.

MN11. Duluth. Department of Research and Planning. *Here's Duluth: General Information about Duluth, Minnesota.* 1975.
A brief pamphlet which gives basic facts about the city.

MN12. Duluth. Senior Citizen's Community Center. *A Senior Citizen's Guide to Community Resources in the Duluth Area.* 1976.

MN13. Human Resources Planning Coalition. *The Duluth Directory of Human Service Agencies.* Duluth, 1972.
This organization has disbanded. Later editions have not been published.

MN14. Human Resources Planning Coalition. *Duluth Indian Human Service Directory.* Duluth, 1973.
Prepared on request of the Duluth City Council and with the cooperation of the participating Indian human service programs to assist in better referral and understanding of what services are available to Indians in the Duluth area. This has not been updated.

MN15. Krossner, William J. *A City Examines Itself: The 1974 Duluth Attitude Survey.* Report No. 1 and Report No. 2—Detailed Statistical Analysis. Duluth: Center for Urban and Regional Affairs, University of Minnesota, 1975.

MN16. Lydecker, Ryck, and Lawrence Sommer, editors. *Duluth—Sketches of the Past: A Bicentennial Collection*, 1976.

This collection of essays, prepared by Duluthians, covers many important facets of Duluth's history.

MN17. Minnesota. Department of Economic Development. *Duluth, Minnesota: Community Profile.* n.d.
This pamphlet is regularly updated.

MN18. Minnesota. University of Minnesota at Duluth. Department of Business and Economic Research. *Duluth Business Indicators.* 1951- . Monthly.
This monthly publication includes such information as the Duluth Business Index, information on the labor market, a retail sales index, a report on Duluth financial activity, as well as a discussion of current economic conditions.

MN19. Scott, James Allen, editor. *Duluth's Legacy. City of 1974.* Vol. 1, Architecture. Duluth: Department of Research and Planning.
This is the first volume of a series of books on Duluth being prepared by the Department of Research and Planning. It deals with the architectural history of selected homes and buildings.

MN20. Western Lake Superior Sanitary District. *Tempo.* Vol. 1, no. 1. (May 24, 1972- .)
A newsletter detailing the activities that encompass the management of water and solid waste in Duluth and the surrounding communities.

Collections

MN21. Duluth Public Library. 101 W. Second St., Duluth 55802 (218) 722-5803.
The library has over 20,000 Minnesota state documents and more than 10,000 city and county documents. The library has not been designated by the city government as a depository for all municipal documents but attempts to collect as many current ones as possible. Some items are routinely sent to the library, such as annual reports of city departments and council proceedings. The Duluth City Clerk's Office serves as a depository for those municipal documents that have a public document number, but the documents are not cataloged.
The Duluth Collection is a wide range of city documents and materials fully cataloged in the main card catalog of the library. A member of the staff is indexing the Duluth City Council proceedings. The city of Duluth does not put out a checklist of city publications; hence, it is not always easy to acquire city documents. For local items, the library staff relies heavily on their vertical file of newspaper clippings that detail government and other activities in the city.
A great strength of the library collection is the archival material that goes back to the early days of Duluth and touches on many facets of Duluth life and its institutions. The Duluth Collection materials do not circulate unless there is a duplicate copy. Those who use the collection can, of course, photocopy materials for a fee.

MINNEAPOLIS

No centralized document service or publication list exists. City ordinance requires distribution of departmental documents to the local public library but is subject to cooperation and goodwill of individual departments. The Municipal Information Library (see entry **MN41**) is the closest collection to a depository; the staff engages in intensive solicitation activities. It has contributed citations of Minneapolis documents to Greenwood Press's *Index to Current Urban Documents* since January 1976. The library has compiled a bibliography to publications of the largest producer of municipal documents in the city, *Publications of the Department of Planning and Development* (August 1976).

Severe strains placed on the city government's finances have caused a reevaluation of publishing and distribution programs. A number of annual reports for smaller agencies are no longer being produced and those that remain are being produced in smaller numbers.

The production of the *State of the City* report (see entry **MN36**) provides users with an up-to-date compendium of statistical information about the city complete with source notes and bibliographic references. This outstanding resource fills what had previously been a substantial gap in information between censuses.

Bibliographic control for the publications of semiindependent agencies like the park board and the Housing and Redevelopment Authority still remains a problem. The depository role filled by the Municipal Information Library has greatly increased bibliographic control over city publications. As closer ties are established with semi-independent agencies, the library's knowledge of their publications will undoubtedly increase. **Local Newspaper Indexing:** The *Minneapolis Tribune and Minneapolis Star Index* has been prepared and published by the staff of the Minneapolis Public Library since 1970 (see entry **MN38**).

Publications

MN22. *Directory '76: Hennepin County and City of Minneapolis.* Minneapolis: Hennepin County, Department of Central Services (Government Center, Minneapolis 55487), 1976. 66pp. $1.
This biannual publication is a directory listing location and phone numbers for city and county employees and offices. The three parts are an alphabetical listing of city and county employees, a listing of county offices, and a listing of city offices.

MN23. Minneapolis. Board of Estimate and Taxation. *City of Minneapolis 1976 Financial Program.* (208 City Hall, Minneapolis 55415). Annual. Free.
The booklet is prepared by the Board of Estimate and Taxation to explain the budget and the budgetary process to citizens. It is not an official city financial document, and the figures have been derived primarily from a companion publication, *Budget and Financial Statistics.* The publication contains a brief description of the budgetary process, the tax supported funds budget, the municipal enterprises fund budget, the capital improvements bond program procedure and budget, and statistics for the federal programs fund budget.

MN24. Minneapolis. City Comptroller (Since January 1, 1976, Comptroller-Treasurer). *Annual Financial Report for the Fiscal Year Ended December 31, 1975.* (331 City Hall, Minneapolis 55415) 1976. 193pp. Annual. Free.
This document was prepared in accordance with generally accepted standards of the Municipal Finance Officers Association. The report is divided into sections on the basis of schedules. The combined financial section ("A" Series Schedules) contains financial statements applicable to all funds. The section is intended to give an overview of the financial condition of the city. Balance sheets for the general fund ("B" Series Schedules) show expenditures for general operations of the city including administration, public safety, highways and streets, health and welfare, sanitation, and culture and recreation. Special revenue funds ("C" Series Schedules) are used to account for funds earmarked for specific purposes including park rehabilitation, federal programs, lake pollution control, and the Municipal Building Commission. Other funds reported on include the special assessment fund ("D"

Series Schedules), and the enterprise fund ("E" Series Schedules). The document concludes with a statistical section showing revenue and expenditures and the legal debt margin for the last ten fiscal years.

MN25. Minneapolis. City Council. *Proceedings of the City Council of the City of Minneapolis, Minnesota from. . . .* Office of the City Clerk (311 City Hall, Minneapolis 55415). Irregular. Not for sale.
The proceedings contain the minutes of council meetings, reported in an abbreviated fashion. The volume also contains ordinances, resolutions passed by the council, election results for the city primary and general elections, and a list of municipal officers from 1881–1973. An extensive index is provided.

MN26. Minneapolis. Health Department. *Minneapolis Public Health Statistics, 1973.* (250 S. Fourth St., Minneapolis 55415). Annual. Free.
The report presents statistical information that would be of use to individuals and agencies planning health services and facilities in the city. The statistics also reflect the types of activities and services the health department provides.

MN27. Minneapolis. Industrial Development Commission. *1976 Annual Report.* (200 City Hall, Minneapolis 55415) 1971– . Annual. Free.
The publication details the activities of the commission, which provides information and assistance to industries interested in new or expanded plant locations and promotes the use of industrial areas in the city. Progress in new city-sponsored industrial parks and districts is presented. Maps and photographs graphically reveal the progress made through the commission's efforts. A table of revenue bonds issued to private firms through the department and the impact of such expenditures is included.

MN28. Minneapolis. League of Women Voters. *Citizen Participation in Minneapolis.* (1200 Second Ave. S., Minneapolis 55403) 1976. $1.65 (plus postage).
This publication discusses citizen participation within the framework of Minneapolis city government. The effectiveness of current participation mechanisms and the community council concept are discussed.

MN29. Minneapolis. League of Women Voters. *Housing Rehabilitation in Minneapolis.* (1200 Second Ave. S., Minneapolis 55403) April 1975. 26pp. $1 (plus postage).
A succinct description of the problems of a declining housing stock and the various government, nonprofit and private sector efforts working to upgrade the existing housing stock. The publication provides a starting point for research. There is a substantial bibliography of persons and printed materials.

MN30. Minneapolis. League of Women Voters. *Minneapolis: A Handbook on City Government.* (1200 Second Ave. S., Minneapolis 55403) 1972. 60pp. Free.
This publication is the most complete description of city government available in one source. Administrative reorganization and a charter change calling for a major reorientation of city government (effective January 1978) make the information dated. A new edition is currently being prepared. None of the descriptions of departments or functions is very detailed.

MN31. Minneapolis. Planning and Development Department. *Community Development Block Grant Program Grantee Performance Report.* (210 City Hall, Minneapolis 55415) 1977. Free.

This annual publication is a description of progress made on projects funded through the Housing and Community Development Act of 1974. This document is important because of the substantial amount of federal funds invested in these projects.

MN32. Minneapolis. Planning and Development Department. *Community Planning and Management (CPM) System (Data Bases).* (210 City Hall, Minneapolis 55415) n.d.
The CPM program seeks to maintain a current inventory of social, economic, and physical characteristics more up-to-date during noncensus years than decennial census data. The CPM is now completing its fourth year of expanding and coordinating a wide range of current data bases. These bases include the city's Property Management System (PMS) and the Housing Resource Management System (HRMS). The CPM program is supported from HUD 701 and local funds and has recently received community development revenue sharing funds.

MN33. Minneapolis. Planning and Development Department. *Minneapolis Housing Vacancy and Turnover.* (210 City Hall, Minneapolis 55415). Quarterly with the fourth issue an annual summary. Free.
This publication surveys residential vacancy and turnover in the city by monitoring public utility billing records. The survey includes approximately 85 percent of the city's housing stock.

MN34. Minneapolis. Planning and Development Department. *The 1970 Profile of Minneapolis Communities: An Inventory of 1970 Social Characteristics Relating to the City of Minneapolis and Its Communities and a Parallelism with Demographic Data.* (210 City Hall, Minneapolis 55415) Fall 1972. 214pp.
This publication primarily represents an attempt to make 1970 census data comprehensible and available by community. It covers a wide variety of social statistics such as race, community health, and income.

MN35. Minneapolis. Planning and Development Department. *Population and Housing Summary of Minneapolis, 1970.* (210 City Hall, Minneapolis 55415) 1970. Free.
This publication was prepared to facilitate the use of census data by city agencies and citizen groups working on the revision of the comprehensive municipal plan. The summary was compiled from the 1960 and 1970 census data.

MN36. Minneapolis. Planning and Development Department. *State of the City—1976.* (210 City Hall, Minneapolis 55415) 1976. 2 vols. Free.
The *State of the City* is an annual publication which attempts to make available data maintained in the Minneapolis Community Planning and Management (CPM) data bases. The CPM program maintains a current inventory of social, economic, and physical characteristics that postdate census data. The first volume is a collection of indices of conditions, problems and characteristics profiling the city's population, income distribution, employment, public assistance recipients, health, vital statistics, crime, housing, land uses and values, and transportation. The second volume focuses on current funded response to the conditions and problems cited in the other volume. A progress report on the first year Community Development Block Grant Programs and a catalog of available programs and services by city subarea are also included in volume two. The report is well illustrated with maps and tables.

MN37. Minneapolis. Police Department, Bureau of Records. *Minneapolis Police Department Annual Statistical Report.* (21 City Hall, Minneapolis 55415). Annual. Free.

The report provides data for the major divisions and bureaus of the police department. A salary schedule for the department and a list of personnel receiving awards in the past year are included. Statistics are presented in tabular form. Statistics for the past five years are often cited to facilitate comparison. A table of offense reports by precinct and a citywide table of adult arrests by formal charge are included.

MN38. Minneapolis. Public Library and Information Center. *Minneapolis Tribune and Minneapolis Star Index.* (300 Nicollet Mall, Minneapolis 55401). Monthly with annual cumulations. $120 per year.
This publication is an index to both Minneapolis daily newspapers. The index includes all local and regional news but does cite items covered by nationally published indexes. All public opinion polls and editorials are indexed. Daily columnists are generally omitted unless the material has local or regional importance. The subject entries are brief and unannotated. More than one reference often will be made for articles. Entries are made under the names of local political figures.

MN39. Minneapolis. Public Works Department. Traffic Engineering Division. *City of Minneapolis Central Business District 1975 Cordon Count.* (203 City Hall, Minneapolis 55415). Biannual in even-numbered years (the 1975 report was conducted with special funds from the Downtown Council). Free.
The data presented was gathered by public works department personnel in a twelve-hour period one weekday in September. The data presented is a summary of a count of all vehicles and persons entering and leaving the central business district during the period. Summary data extending back to 1958 is provided. Motor vehicle traffic is divided into categories of auto, bus, and light, medium, and heavy trucking. For the surveyed year, data is presented for fifteen-minute periods throughout the surveyed time.

MN40. Minneapolis. Public Works Department. Minneapolis Water Works. *Statistical and Financial Report of the Minneapolis Water Department (for the) Year Ending December 31, 1974.* 1975. 57pp. Free.
As the title implies, this annual report is concerned with providing statistics on the finances and the services provided by the water department. The mineral and chemical content of the water is described as well as filtration and softening plan data. The cost of providing services and the department's income, buildings, and equipment are shown in tabular form.

Collections

MN41. Municipal Information Library. 302 City Hall, Minneapolis 55415 (612) 348-8139.
The library has the largest collection of city of Minneapolis documents available. Circulation is available only to city of Minneapolis employees and officials; room use for all others. A reasonable amount of photocopying will be done free for requesting agencies outside Minneapolis city government. The Municipal Information Library is outstanding for its collection of city of Minneapolis documents. It is virtually the only agency which attempts to monitor and obtain all city documents. The library staff publishes a recent additions list (currently available on an in-house basis only) which lists new documents as they are produced.

ST. PAUL

Lists of city officials are irregularly issued by various departments and agencies. It is difficult to obtain current and complete information as personnel change so frequently. The St. Paul Public Library depends on mimeographed sheets from the departments, the League of Women Voters, the *City of St. Paul, County of Ramsey Yearbook* (biennial), and department telephone directories. Some names of municipal officers are available in the annual *Directory of Minnesota Municipal Officials* (see entry **MN1**); county officials are named in the annual *Minnesota Legislative Manual*.

Departmental annual reports and the public library's newspaper index are the best sources for information on what is happening in city government. The increasing role of the Metropolitan council (an umbrella organization created by the Minnesota legislature) in planning for Twin Cities area development is reflected in their fine publications. St. Paul has tried to maintain its own identity while recognizing that it is only one unit in the seven-county metropolitan area.

There is no centralized document service or publication list for the city. City ordinance requires distribution of departmental documents to the local public library. **Local Newspaper Indexing:** The St. Paul Public Library (see **MN50**) began indexing the *St. Paul Dispatch* and *Pioneer Press* (daily morning and evening papers) in 1967. Until 1971 coverage extends to all major state news. Subscription rates are $100 per year for public-supported institutions and $140 for commercial institutions. This price includes ten monthly supplements and two semiannual cumulations. The library staff are happy to answer inquiries regarding index citations and will send samples of subject headings used. A legislative index is prepared separately to cover the activities of the legislature while it is in session. The index, in general, is strong in biography, city, county, and Metropolitan-Council news. A search fee is charged to fulfill mail requests.

Publications

MN42. *The Catalog: Metropolitan Youth Resources.* Minneapolis: Minneapolis Enablers Inc. (140 W. Franklin Ave., Minneapolis 55404), 1973-   . $10. Looseleaf format with irregularly issued supplements.
Agencies and social service organizations specializing in services for youth are cited.

MN43. Empson, Donald. *The Street Where You Live: A Guide to the Street Names of St. Paul.* St. Paul: Witsend Press (1809 Stanford Ave., St. Paul 55105), 1975. $4.95.
A popular history of existing St. Paul streets and how they were named.

MN44. St. Paul Community Planning Organization Inc. *Information Directory.* (333 Sibley St., St. Paul 55101) 1976. 548pp. $10.
A compilation of all the social service agencies in a three-county umbrella organization, collected and compiled by the Information and Referral Service operated by the Community Planning Organization.

MN45. St. Paul. James J. Hill Reference Library. *Library and Informational Resources in the Twin City Area.* Edited by Marilyn Mauritz. (80 W. Fourth St., St. Paul 55102) 1972. 403pp. o.p.
Describes the collections of all local libraries and gives hours, personnel, and special features of the collections. A new edition is being compiled.

MN46. St. Paul. Metropolitan Library Service Agency. *MELSA Manual.* (Griggs-Midway Bldg., Rm. S-275, 1821 University Ave., St. Paul 55104) 1975-   . Loose-leaf format with supplements issued irregularly.
Directory of the Metropolitan Library Service Agency giving information on hours, loan policies, fine schedule, and personnel for the ten city and county library systems in the Twin Cities metropolitan area.

MN47. St. Paul Public Schools. Independent School District 625. *Directory 1976/1977.* (360 Colborne St., St. Paul 55102) 1976. 169pp. $5.

MN48. St. Paul. City of St. Paul Offices. *Telephone Directory.* City Hall-Courthouse (St. Paul 55101). Annual.

MN49. *Women's Network Directory 1976.* Minneapolis: Women's Network Inc. (210 Ramar Bldg., 111 E. Franklin, Minneapolis 55404), 1975. 262pp. $3.95.
List of resources, alternatives, and services available to Twin Cities women. Also offers articles and art work contributed by 75 Twin Cities women.

Collections

MN50. St. Paul Public Library. 90 W. Fourth St., St. Paul 55102 (612)224-3383. Teletype Service: (910)563-3709.
The library's St. Paul collection of municipal documents extends back to 1854 when the city was incorporated. City council proceedings date from then. The library has a strong collection of city department annual reports as well as departmental journals, newsletters, special reports, and studies. The collection of city newspapers is excellent. The library has an extensive collection of St. Paul public and private high school yearbooks for 24 schools extending as far back as 1897. There are several library indexes:

1. Index to microfilmed St. Paul newspaper clippings. Clippings date from the late 1920s until 1967 when the newspaper index was begun. Strong points are information about people, buildings, businesses, churches, theatres, cemetaries, neighborhoods, ethnic groups, and hotels.
2. Index to Minnesota and St. Paul clipping file. A subject index to the clippings on state and city history and news collected in the library from the 1920s to 1967.
3. St. Paul Street Directory. Compiled by Robert E. Hoag in 1976. Lists current and former street names with notes to location.
4. Bibliography of information pertaining to St. Paul neighborhoods (29pp.) and bibliography of information pertaining to St. Paul ethnic groups (14pp.). These two bibliographies were compiled by Carole Martinson, of the reference staff, and include city newspaper and periodical articles, pamphlets, and books in the library collection pertaining to the subjects.

MISSISSIPPI

General Publications

MS1. *Directory of Mississippi Elective Officials: State, State Districts, County and County Districts, 1972-1976.* Jackson: Secretary of State, 1972. 50pp.
Contains a listing by county of local elected officials at the county level.

MS2. *Directory of Mississippi Municipal Officials, 1973-1977.* Compiled by Heber Ladner. Jackson: Secretary of State, 1973. 35pp.
A listing of municipal officials by county.

MS3. *A Directory of Mississippi Municipalities, 1974.* Edited by Star W. Hy, and Donald S. Vaughan. University of Mississippi: Bureau of Governmental Research, 1974. 170pp. $5.

MS4. *Governmental Guide, 1976-1977 (Mississippi).* Edited by Georgia Robles Boone, Madison, TN: Governmental Guides (P.O. Drawer 299, Madison, TN 37115), 1976. 88pp. $5.50.
This guide contains current governmental information on both state and local levels. Local organizations and elected officials are identified and geographical boundaries noted. It is a useful and quick reference source.

MS5. *Mississippi Business.* University of Mississippi: Bureau of Business and Economic Research, School of Business Administration, 1942-   . Vol. 1, 1942- Bimonthly.

MS6. *Mississippi Business Review.* Mississippi State: Mississippi Business Review (P.O. Box 5288, Mississippi State 39762), 1940-   . Vol. 1, 1940-   . Monthly. $3.50 annually.

MS7. *Mississippi Government.* Austin, TX: Steck-Waughn Co., 1972. 32pp.
A general textbook divided equally between state and local government.

MS8. *Mississippi Municipalities.* Jackson: Mississippi Municipal Association (230 Barefield Complex, 455 N. Lamar St., Jackson 39202), 1953-   . Vol. 1, January 1953-   . Monthly. $5.
A current newsletter of Mississippi municipalities.

MS9. *Mississippi Official and Statistical Register, 1972-1976.* Compiled by Heber Ladner. Jackson: Secretary of State, 1972. 491pp.

MS10. Mississippi Research and Development Center. *Data Summary: Gulfport, Mississippi.* Jackson: Community Development Division (3825 Ridgewood Rd., Jackson 39211), 1976. 139pp.
A fact book on both natural and human resources; includes economic, industrial, commercial, public safety, and services.

MS11. *Mississippi State Government: The Constitution, Legislature and Administration.* Prepared by Leon A. Wilber. Hattiesburg: Department of Political Science, University of Southern Mississippi, 1972. 93pp.

MS12. *Mississippi Statistical Abstract, 1976.* Mississippi State: Division of Research, College of Business and Research, Mississippi State University (Drawer 5288, Mississippi State 39762), 1976. 532pp. $8.95.

MS13. *1977 Mississippi Manufacturers Directory.* Jackson: Mississippi Research and Development Center (P.O. Drawer 2470, Jackson 39205), 286pp. $15.

BILOXI AND GULFPORT

Publications

MS14. Biloxi. Ordinances, Local Laws, etc. *Code of Ordinances: City of Biloxi, Mississippi.* Tallahassee, FL: Municipal Code Corp., 1960. 285pp.

MS15. Gulfport. Ordinances, Local Laws, etc. *Code of Ordinances: City of Gulfport, Mississippi.* Tallahassee, FL: Municipal Code Corp. 1960. 1,224pp.

JACKSON

Publications

MS16. *Capital Improvements Plan, 1975–1976 through 1980–1980, for City of Jackson, Mississippi.* Jackson: Jackson City Planning Board (P.O. Box 22568, Jackson 39205), 1976.
An annual study of capital improvements needs within the city.

MS17. *Crossroads.* Jackson: City of Jackson Public Relations Department, 1976- . Bimonthly.
Contains articles on city employees and activities.

MS18. *Economic Analysis: Jackson Metropolitan Area.* Jackson: Jackson City Planning Board (P.O. Drawer 22568, Jackson 39205), 1972.
Covers rural and urban labor, industry, and resources available for growth.

MS19. Jackson. Ordinances, Local Laws, etc. *Code of Ordinances, City of Jackson, Mississippi.* Tallahassee, FL: Municipal Code Corp., 1971. 134pp.

Collections

MS20. Mississippi Department of Archives and History. P.O. Box 571, Jackson 39205 (601)354-6218.
This library is a retrospective depository for state and local documents. There are no interlibrary loans or circulation of materials.

MISSOURI

General Publications

MO1. Missouri. Department of Elementary and Secondary Education. *Missouri School Directory.* Jefferson City (P.O. Box 480, Jefferson City 65101), 1910?- . Annual. Free.
The directory provides classification of each school district, assessed valuation, tax levy, and statistics on number of teachers, enrollment, and number of pupils living outside the school district. Enrollment is also given for individual schools. Key school board officials and school officials are listed. Number of years experience in district is provided for school officials. Addresses and phone numbers of schools are given.

MO2. Missouri Municipal League. *Directory of Missouri Municipal Officials.* Jefferson City (1913 William St., Jefferson City 65101), 1951- . Annual. $15.
The directory gives names of officials and times of council meetings for all municipalities. Where available, a city government telephone number is given. The directory is published every year after the April elections. Updates appear in monthly *Missouri Municipal Review.*

KANSAS CITY

Weaknesses and gaps seem to dominate publishing for Kansas City, Missouri. There is no clearinghouse for information and no indexing or bibliographic control generated from a single point. In general, materials published are for a specific and rather confined area (e.g., strategy plans) and are neither widely circulated nor publicized. Publishing appears confined to what is expected (city plans) or mandated (financial information). Information, especially statistical information, seems to be accessible via computer more so than via hard copy publication. Local Newspaper Indexing: See entry MO9.

Publications

MO3. Kansas City. Board of Education. *Annual Report of the Secretary to Board of Education, the School District Kansas City, Missouri.* (Kansas City School District, Office of the Secretary, 1211 McGee St., Kansas City 64106) 1968- . Annual.
Annual publication designed to provide KCSD board with needed information on the operation of the Office of Board Services as well as to preserve some historical information about the school district. Data are presented in statistical, tabular, and narrative form.

MO4. Kansas City. Board of Education. Office of the Superintendent. *Handbook.* (1211 McGee St., Kansas City 64106) 1976/77. Annual.
The standard handbook for teachers within the KCSD, it includes salary schedules for all employees, a directory of schools with address and principal, a directory of the administrative office personnel and departments, and bibliography of approved textbooks.

MO5. Kansas City. Department of Finance. *Annual Financial Report of the City of Kansas City, Missouri.* (City Hall, Kansas City 64106). Annual.
A report in five parts that presents the most complete information on the finances of Kansas City.

MO6. Kansas City. Office of City Manager. *Budget for the Fiscal Year.* (Budget and Systems, 13 Floor, City Hall, Kansas City 64106). Annual.
Annual adopted budget of city of Kansas City presented in two parts: a section on the budget by department and one by program. Also included is an appendix consisting of one table relating to property valuations and tax rates and one table on the number of personnel authorized to each department.

MO7. Mid-America Regional Council. *Public Officials Directory.* Kansas City (20 W. Ninth St., Kansas City 64106). Annual.
Handy guide to elected and key appointed officials in the Kansas City metropolitan region (eight counties in Missouri and Kansas and approximately 110 communities). Additional listing of news media, A-95 clearinghouses and A-95 federal agency contact-compliance points.

MO8. Kansas City. Ordinances, Local Laws, etc. *The Charter, Administrative Code and Code of General Ordinances of Kansas City, Missouri.* Tallahassee, FL: Municipal Code Corp., n.d. Loose-leaf.
Four-volume loose-leaf service containing the charter, administrative code, and code of general ordinances. Updated on an irregular basis, the service excludes the building code, the fire prevention code, and zoning ordinances of Kansas City.

Collections

MO9. Kansas City Public Library. 311 E. 12 St., Kansas City 64106 (816) 221-2685.
Newspaper clippings concerning Kansas City deemed of any interest are maintained by the Missouri Valley Room. The collection is now in the process of being microfilmed. The collection is comprehensive, arranged by broad subject headings and quite searchable. Research queries are accepted. During legislative sessions, all articles (from Kansas City *Star and Times*) are clipped and arranged in looseleaf notebook. Indexing by subject notebooks presently maintained from 1974 to date. Notebook is comprehensive, indexing and clipping done by present documents librarian. Research queries are accepted.

ST. LOUIS

Local Newspaper Indexing: The St. Louis Public Library (see entry **MO12**) publishes the *Index to St. Louis Newspapers*, edited by James J. Michael. It has been published monthly since 1975 and is $125 per year. It provides a monthly index to the St. Louis *Globe-Democrat*, the St. Louis *Post-Dispatch*, St. Louis *Argus*, St. Louis *Jewish Light*, and the St. Louis *Sentinel.* This index includes new feature articles and editorials of St. Louis local, metropolitan, and regional interest which will provide a usable, durable file of local and regional history. The index generally excludes coverage included in nationally published newspaper indexes.

Publications

MO10. St. Louis. Public Library. Municipal Reference Library. *Who's Who in St. Louis Government: A List of Officials.* Compiled by Charles H. Cornwell. City Hall, St. Louis 63103) 1967- .
Contains the names, addresses, and telephone numbers of elective officials under city charter and state law, officials appointed by the mayor, and the directors of area boards.

MO11. *St. Louis Statistical Abstract.* St. Louis University (Pius XII Memorial Library, St. Louis), 1971- . Annual. Price varies.
The *St. Louis Statistical Abstract* contains 639 tables arranged in 14 subject categories. Data have been gathered from federal, state, and local sources with appropriate sources cited.

Collections

MO12. St. Louis Public Library. 1301 Olive, St. Louis 63103 (314)241-2288.
The St. Louis Municipal Reference Library has a large collection of St. Louis and St. Louis area government and history publications.

(See also entry **US4**.)

SPRINGFIELD

Local Newspaper Indexing: A member of the reference staff of the Central Library of the Springfield-Greene County Library (see entry **MO17**) does selective newspaper indexing. Queries are accepted.

Publications

MO13. Springfield. Office of the City Manager. *City of Springfield, Missouri Monthly Financial and Activity Report.* (City Hall, 830 Boonville, Springfield 65802) 1958- . Monthly.
Summarizes expenditures and activities of various units of city government in statistical and narrative form.

MO14. Springfield. Planning Department and Missouri State Highway Department. *Springfield Transportation Study.* 2 vols. (City Hall, 830 Boonville, Springfield 65802) n.d. 262pp.
Volume 1, covering transportation and travel facts, surveys current traffic conditions, gives an inventory of transportation facilities, and discusses travel characteristics and land use. Included are tables, graphs, statistics, and illustrations. Volume 2, covering future transportation needs, is oriented toward the future and covers population and land use, the projected plan, analysis and projection techniques, 1980 travel patterns, and thoroughfare development. Includes graphs, charts, statistics, and illustrations.

MO15. Springfield. Zoning and Planning Commission. *Capital Improvement Program.* (City Hall, 830 Boonville, Springfield 65802) 1966- . Annual.
This publication is issued annually and should cover a seven-year time span,

i.e., 1966-1972, 1967-1973, etc. Its format varies from year to year, but usually includes present project summaries, planned capital improvements, an analysis of financial resources, a glossary of terms, and detailed summaries, forms, maps, and charts relating to various city projects. This document focuses on areas such as city utilities, community buildings, recreation, arterials, sanitary sewer system, airport, the Land Clearance for Redevelopment Authority, schools, and county units and facilities.

MO16. Springfield. Zoning and Planning Commission, Long-Range Section. *Comparative Statistical Areas.* (City Hall, 830 Boonville, Springfield 65802) 1972. 93pp.
This is a statistical analysis of block numbers, population, and dwelling units for each decade, 1950, 1960, 1970; referenced by study zone, census tract, neighborhood number, and ward number.

Collections

MO17. **Springfield-Greene County Library.** Interlibrary loan. Box 737 MPO, Springfield 65801 (417)862-4621.
The Springfield-Greene County Library is not an official depository for city publications, but does receive most important documents relating to the city government. These are cataloged and housed in the Missouri Room, which also houses a vertical file of material relating to Springfield and a vertical file of material relating to Missouri and the Ozarks. Also included in this room is an extensive local history and area geneaology collection and complete microfilms of Springfield newspapers.

MONTANA

BILLINGS

Local Newspaper Indexing: See entry MT2.

Publications

MT1. Billings. *Official Directory.* n.p. Annual.
The directory lists all elected officials, appointed officials, department heads, and members of the various boards and commissions. Home and office phones are included.

MT2. Parmly Billings Library. *Billings Gazette Index.* Billings, 1974– .
Monthly with yearly cumulations. $400.
The Billings *Gazette* is the only daily newspaper in Billings and has been published since 1912. The *Gazette* index, covering 1974 to date, has assigned Library of Congress subject headings to all articles in the newspaper that deal with events throughout Montana and the city of Billings, from automobile accidents to government affairs. Personal names of major importance in articles and obituaries are included. Headlines and article locations follow the subject heading in the final computer print-out.

Collections

MT3. Parmly Billings Library. 510 N. Broadway, Billings 59101 (406)248-7391.
Teletype Service: TWX (910)975-1190.
The Parmly Billings Library is a depository for Billings documents, including annual reports, codes, special publications, and research reports of all city departments. City law requires such materials to be permanently on file and available to the public at the library. All reference and municipal special collection material must be used within the library. A photocopy service is available for a small per page charge.

GREAT FALLS

Local Newspaper Indexing: The Great Falls Public Library (see entry **MT8**) has indexed the *Great Falls Tribune* daily since 1963. The index is basically an information file with local and state information that is difficult to obtain in any other form. Queries from other cities are accepted for limited research.

The staff of the University of Montana Library (see entry **MT7**) has comprehensively indexed the *Great Falls Tribune*, as it relates to the state. They will accept queries and will do research as time permits.

Publications

MT4. *Everything You Always Wanted to Know about Other City Departments but Didn't Know How to Ask.* Compiled by Georgia Beaulieu, Pat Mahoney, and Nancy Skoog. Great Falls: n.p., 1977. 54pp.
This notebook was compiled after the city election, April 5, 1977. It has an organizational chart of the city departments with heads of departments listed. There is a further listing of the city commission and the time of meetings. Information is given as to the function of each department along with the positions of the employees.

MT5. Great Falls. Alcohol and Drug Dependence Bureau. *Directory of Alcohol and Drug Abuse Agencies.* n.d. 28pp.
This directory is designed for those who desire information or assistance relating to alcohol and drugs. This does not presume to be adequate for all needs but tries to offer services of which one may not be aware.

MT6. Great Falls Public Schools. *Directory of Great Falls Public Schools, Great Falls, Montana.* n.d.
This is a listing of the public schools in Great Falls, showing the roster of teachers for each school, along with the address and telephone number of each. The Board of Trustees is also listed.

MT7. University of Montana Library. *Great Falls Tribune—Subject Index.* 1972– . Catalog card index (to be microfilmed). Daily. Approx. $15 per reel.
The *Great Falls Tribune* Index consists of approximately 10,000 entries for each year covered. Entries are arranged alphabetically by subject. Each entry consists of the subject heading, the headline, and the date, page, and column numbers. All articles, letters, and editorials of local, state, and regional significance are indexed beginning January 1, 1976. The library is now preparing the card files for microfilming which it hopes to complete soon.

Collections

MT8. Great Falls Public Library. Second Ave. N. at Third St., Great Falls 59401 (406)453-0349. Teletype Service: TWX (910)975-1945.
Reference material, microfilm, and periodicals are not loaned. If genealogy books requested are in good condition, they may be loaned for use in the library only. Photocopies are available for a small per page charge.

HELENA

Publications

MT9. Helena. City Manager's Office. *Office Directory.* Compiled by Arlene Loble. 1975. 10pp. Irregular. Free.
A directory of Helena elected officials, appointed officials, and department heads. Address, and office and residence telephone numbers are listed for each official and employee.

MT10. Helena. Service and Information Office. *City of Helena Extension Numbers.* 1977. 7pp.
A list of telephone extension numbers of Helena city employees. There is also a section which lists city departments with telephone extension numbers.

MT11. Helena. School District No. 1. *Directory School District No. 1, Helena, Montana, 1976-1977.* 1923- . 51pp. Annual. Free.
This publication lists Board of Trustees, administration, and all employees by schools within the district, with addresses and telephone numbers.

MT12. Southwestern Areawide Planning Council. *Health Resources and Services Organization Manual (for Helena, Montana).* Helena, 197? 123pp.
This publication lists health and welfare agencies with services provided and eligibility requirements. While this directory primairly lists service organizations for Helena, other cities in Montana are represented.

MISSOULA

Local Newspaper Indexing: The staff of the City-County Library of Missoula (see entries **MT13** and **MT20**) has comprehensively indexed the *Missoulian* since 1973, as far as Montana news is concerned (see entry **MT13**). The staff will accept reference queries about information contained in the Index.

Publications

MT13. City-County Library of Missoula. *Missoulian—Subject Index.* 1973-
Catalog card index (to be microfilmed). Daily. Approximately $15 per reel.
The *Missoulian* subject index contains approximately 10,000 entries for each year covered. Entries are arranged alphabetically by subject. Each entry consists of the subject heading, the headline, and the data, page, and column number. All articles, letters, and editorials of local, state, and regional significance are indexed from each day's newspaper. Obituaries have been indexed beginning January 1, 1976. The library is now preparing the card files for microfilming which it hopes to complete soon.

MT14. Missoula. League of Women Voters. *Missoula City and County Government: 1974.* 8pp. Free to libraries.
The 1974 edition is an updating of the more complete 1968 booklet, *Your Missoula Government* (see entry **MT15**). It includes a chart of the form of government, brief geographical statistics, a breakdown of the tax dollar, an explanation of government bodies providing public services in the area, and a population map.

MT15. Missoula. League of Women Voters. *Your Missoula Government, 1968. . . .* (Variation of *Missoula City and County Government*). 39pp. Free to libraries.
This publication is updated by the 1974 edition of *Missoula City and County Government.* However, for basic and historic information on each branch of municipal government, this edition remains useful.

MT16. Missoula. School District One. *Missoula Public Schools District No. One, Missoula, Montana Directory, 1976-1977.* n.p. Annual. Free on request.
A listing by departments and schools, positions, and telephone numbers.

MT17. Missoula Area Chamber of Commerce. *1976-1977 Directory—Missoula Churches, Community Organizations, Local Officials.* $2.
Material listed includes name of church, address, pastor, telephone number, name of organization, present head of organization, address of head of organization, government officials, their titles, addresses, and telephone numbers.

MT18. Missoula County High Schools. *Missoula County High School Directory—1976-1977* (includes the city of Missoula). Missoula: n.p., 1976. Annual. Free.
Lists the Board of Trustees, administration, faculty and staff along with home addresses, school, and department.

MT19. Montana University. Department of Social Work. *Health and Welfare Resources Guide—Missoula, Montana, 1975.* Compiled by Morton L. Arkava et al. Missoula: 1975. 71 pp. Irregular. Copies no longer available.
The work is intended as a reference for customers of health and welfare services in western Montana, citing specifically agencies with services provided and eligibility requirements. A Missoula city map is included to aid individuals in locating desired agencies.

Collections

MT20. City-County Library of Missoula. 101 Adams, Missoula 59801 (406)728-5900, ext. 26. Teletype Service: TWX (910)963-2040.
Missoula municipal documents are housed with the Montana collection which does not circulate. The library collects Missoula municipal documents as the staff becomes aware of them. There is no all-inclusive program for depositing these documents with the library. There is a per page photocopy charge.

MT21. University of Montana Library. Missoula 59812 (406)243-6800. Teletype Service: TWX (910)963-2048.
See entry **MT7.**

NEBRASKA

General Publications

NE1. Mertens, Ronald J. *Understanding Nebraska Municipal Government.* n.p., n.d.
This publication is a state document which covers municipal government in the state of Nebraska, its operation, organizational forms, and laws by which it is governed.

LINCOLN
Collections

NE2. **The Bennet Martin Public Library.** 136 S. 14, Lincoln 68508 (402)435-2146. Teletype Service: (910)621-8121.
There is no municipally produced checklist or bibliography of city publications. The city clerk receives a depository copy of most city documents. The public library receives many of the city documents as deposit copies and participates in the *Index to Current Urban Documents.* Citations to and microfiche of many city documents are available through the publishers of this index, Greenwood Press. The public library keeps an index of city officials. There is also a county-city telephone directory which lists departments and principal officers. Information on city governmental structure may be obtained from the Office of the Mayor, County-City Building, 555 S. 10 St., Lincoln 68508. The public library maintains a clipping file of the *Lincoln Journal* and *Lincoln Star* newspaper articles related to city-county government.

OMAHA

The city of Omaha publishes a veritable plethora of documents obtainable at the City-County Building in downtown Omaha. A strong point is the publication of a number of detailed documents concerning urban renewal and the Riverfront Beautification Project. A noticeable weakness in the publication of Omaha's municipal documents is the lack of good bibliographies. Also the city's distribution of documents to libraries is almost nonexistent. The documents are available from individual government offices in the City-County Building rather than a central office or some type of city government library.

Publications

NE3. Douglas County. *Douglas County Offices PBX Directory.* Omaha. n.d.
This publication, which is updated periodically, contains the telephone numbers

of county offices, the hospital, human services agency, health department, and the social services. The Douglas County offices are located in the same building as the city municipal offices. Douglas County predominately comprises the city of Omaha.

NE4. League of Nebraska Municipalities. *Nebraska Directory of Municipal Officials.* n.p. 1977.
This publication is a detailed list of the cities in the state. Included is the size of the population, type of government, phone number of city hall and the mayor's home, business hours, names of officials, mill levy, bonded department, assessed valuation, and when meetings are held.

NE5. National College of the State Judiciary, The Court Studies Division. *System Analysis of Omaha, Nebraska, Fourth Judicial District.* n.p., n.d.
This publication is the final report of the study of the Fourth Judicial District Court of Nebraska conducted by the Court Studies Division. It presents in chronological order the results of an action-oriented system analysis of the Omaha-based court. The study consisted of four phases. It has summaries of all individual reports relating to the Omaha system.

NE6. Omaha. *City of Omaha 1976 Calendar Year Budget.* Annual.
This publication contains the mayor's budget message, city funds, grant funds, revenue estimates, recommended budget appropriations, budgetary account details, and council actions.

NE7. Omaha. *City of Omaha Offices Telephone Directory.* n.d.
Contains the names and telephone numbers of city officials, department heads, and agencies, county offices, and city boards. There is also an alphabetical listing of city employees.

NE8. Omaha. *Position Classificastion Plan.* n.d.
Continuously updated, this publication lists every type of job available in the municipality. It includes the nature of the work, examples of the work performed, and the required knowledge, ability, and skill.

Collections

NE9. **Omaha Public Library.** Fifteenth and Harney, Omaha 68102 (402)444-4800.
The library does not have an active program of collecting municipal documents. A number of its documents are outdated.

NE10. **University of Nebraska at Omaha.** Library, P.O. Box 688, Omaha 68101.
The library has some municipal documents. However, the collection is small and the staff does not actively acquire municipal publications.

NEVADA

The University of Nevada, Reno, Bureau of Business and Economic Research, provides a computer data base NEIRS (Nevada Economic Information Retrieval System), which includes over 300 socioeconomic indicators by county, state, and metropolitan area. The data base is available to local and state government in the state or to private consultants and researchers through Operations Manager, NEIRS, University of Nevada, Reno 89557. **Local Newspaper Indexing:** Selective indexing (chiefly historical and topics of local or state interest only) is done by the Nevada State Library (see entry **NV4**) for three newspapers: (1) *Nevada Appeal* (Carson City); (2) *Nevada State Journal* (Reno); and (3) *Reno Evening Gazette* (Reno) beginning 1976–1977. The library will accept inqueries.

General Publications

NV1. Nevada. Employment Security Department. *Annual Area Labor Review: An Evaluation of the Economic Situation, Reno Standard Metropolitan Statistical Area.* Carson City (Employment Security Research, Capitol Complex, Carson City 89710), 1976. Quarterly.
Includes descriptions of the Reno area, housing vacancy survey, consumer prices, Nevada's free port law, area labor force, establishment-based employment, area wage survey, public works employment, affirmative acton data, and supply and demand outlook.

NV2. Nevada. Employment Security Department. *Economic Update.* Carson City (Employment Security Research, Capitol Complex, Carson City 89710), 1976. Monthly.

NV3. Nevada. Office of the State Planning Coordinator and Department of Economic Development. *County Datafile: Washoe County, Nevada.* Carson City (Capitol Complex, Carson City 89710), 1976. 4pp.
Includes compilation of data from various state and federal sources on population, income, retail sales, wages, wholesale trade, service industries, employment, labor force, financial institutions, manufacturing, housing, agriculture, mining, gaming, transportation, community service, tourism, recreation, media, utilities, land ownership, education, and climate.

Collections

NV4. Nevada State Library. Capitol Complex, Carson City 89710. (702)885-5160. Teletype Service: (910)395-0139.
The State Library is a depository designated by state law for all city and county

documents produced for public distribution. This includes all 17 counties, all incorporated cities, and most towns in the state. The local documents collection consists of all texts identified and owned by the Nevada State Library since becoming a depository for all county and city publications in 1971. It also includes major reference documents such as auditor's and assessor's reports from the early 1900s.

LAS VEGAS

Although most parts of the governments are separate (police and fire service have been combined), Las Vegas and Clark County are probably synonymous in most researchers' minds. The Strip with its hotels and casinos is all in the county. The University is also outside the city limits as is the Convention Center.

Las Vegas publishes few documents of significance, and those are difficult to obtain on a regular basis. Out-of-staters might have an easier time obtaining information from the city or county than local libraries do. The Chamber of Commerce is geared mostly to the tourist trade and publishes no significant statistics or lists. These are no better updated in state or county publications. City directories are a very real problem. There were three years between the last two. Telephone directores are issued twice a year. **Local Newspaper Indexing:** Indexing of the Las Vegas *Review Journal* and the Las Vegas *Sun* is done by staff of the Downtown Branch of the Clark County Library District (see entry **NV21**). It was begun in November 1971 and was quite limited until 1974. It is a selective index which covers local news and very limited state news, except for the biennial legislative sessions, which are covered thoroughly. Prior to the start of the index a clipping file was maintained and is available; however, it has several gaps. Inquiries can be directed to the library.

Publications

NV5. *City of Las Vegas, Final Budget, Fiscal Year July 1, 1977–June 30, 1978.* City Manager (City of Las Vegas, 400 E. Stewart, Las Vegas 89101). Annual. Detailed budget of the 190 accounts for prior year, current year, and tentative and approved for next budget year. Includes bond and short-term financing schedules and intergovernmental activity.

NV6. *City of Las Vegas, New Directions in City Government: Summary Report.* March 1975. 138pp. Paging not continuous.
This is a summary of a management study of city government, which identifies weaknesses in government and makes recommendations for improving it. Several parts of the study relate to the relevant sections of the Housing and Community Act of 1974. The report includes criteria for development of a city plan and a discussion of basic management functions. It then describes in detail recommendations for Las Vegas government reorganization.

NV7. Clark County. *Budget, Statistical and Staffing Report.* Clark County Administrator (Clark County Courthouse, Las Vegas 89101), 1958-1970 (*Clark County Statistical Report*), 1971-1972 (*Budget, Statistical and Staffing Report*). 195pp. Annual.
After the detailed budget in the first section, a statistical report gives charts and diagrams, then goes into facts and figures including retrospective to 1930 or 1950 for employees, population (by city), birth, voting, marriage, divorce, transportation, and school statistics. It also lists all state, county, and city (Las Vegas,

North Las Vegas, Henderson, Boulder City) officials including boards. A map in the front shows all paved roads in the county, as well as area and population.

NV8. Clark County School District. *Clark County District (Year) Budget.* (2832 E. Flamingo Rd., Las Vegas 89121) 1964-75. Annual.
The extensive budget includes statistical data and maps showing schools.

NV9. Las Vegas. Board of City Commissioners. *Agenda, Annotated Agenda, Minutes.* City Clerk (400 E. Stewart, Las Vegas 89101), pages vary. First and third Wednesday or varies.
The agenda for the city commission meetings is published just prior to the meetings. The annotated agenda, showing commission action on all items on the agenda, is published just after the meetings. The publication of the minutes, which are transcripts of the meetings, varies.

NV10. Las Vegas Convention Bureau. Visitors Authority. *Financial Statements.* Essentially an audit report of the agency which runs the convention center, collects the room and gaming taxes from the hotels and motels, and apportions them to the county and cities in the area.

NV11. Las Vegas Convention Bureau. Visitors Authority. *Las Vegas Composite Visitor Profile, 1975.* Prepared by Lawrence Dandurand and Henry A. Sciullo. Annual. 161pp. (Available from: Las Vegas Convention Bureau, P.O. Box 14006, Las Vegas 89114.)
This publication is a composite of quarterly reports. Questionnaires and interviews of randomly selected visitors' reactions to Las Vegas were collected. Data include type of lodging, shows attended, whether the visitors liked the city, and whether they thought it was a good place to visit with children. Demographic and economic characteristics are given.

NV12. Las Vegas. Department of Community Development. *Five Year Capital Improvements Plan 1973-1978.* (City Hall, 400 E. Stewart, Las Vegas 89101) 1974? 236pp.
The improvements plan consists of projects needed to fulfill the general plan of the city, subject to change as needs change. The projects are listed by department, with summaries of projects, priority rating, and individual project descriptions. Also included are tables of costs and revenues, past and projected.

NV13. Las Vegas. Department of Community Development. *Let's Take a Look at Downtown Las Vegas.* (City Hall, 400 E. Stewart, Las Vegas 89101) 1975. Unpaged. Irregular.
The downtown area of Las Vegas is described in this report in terms of economic growth. It includes information on the increase of tourist facilities, office buildings, and pedestrian and vehicle traffic counts. It also discusses the loss of major retailers in the area. The major portion of the report consists of detailed tables of yearly construction values from 1960-1975, giving statistical evidence of the economic growth of the area.

NV14. Las Vegas. Department of Personnel and Employee Relations. *City of Las Vegas* (City Hall, 400 E. Stewart, Las Vegas 89101) January 1975. 74pp. Irregular.
This is a compilation of rules governing and protecting city employees, duties of the Civil Service Board and the Department of Personnel, grievance procedures, and the like.

NV15. *Las Vegas General Plan: A Statement of Policies and Guidelines.* Las Vegas, n.p., 1975. 81pp.
This plan defines areas of concern, desirable changes, and suggestions regarding implementation of policies. It also mentions guidelines for cooperative arrangements with areas (principally Clark County) outside the city limits. The report is divided into several sections which include growth policy, land use, housing, transportation, etc. It includes some statistics, tables, and a land use map.

NV16. Laventhol and Horwath. *City of Las Vegas Financial Report.* Las Vegas: City Hall (400 E. Stewart, Las Vegas 89101). Annual.
Audit report for accounts and funds of the city.

NV17. Nevada. Employment Security Department. *Economic Update: Las Vegas.* (135 S. Eighth St., Las Vegas 89101) 1961– . Monthly.
Gives a narrative summary of employment trends, tables of the work force, the totals by industry, and the economic indicators for Clark County. Tables also provide the labor turnover in mining and manufacturing and the average hours and earnings in selected industries.

NV18. Nevada. Employment Security Department. *Area Manpower Review: Las Vegas Standard Metropolitan Statistical Area.* Carson City (500 E. Third St., Carson City 89713), 1968– . Semiannual.
After an overall look at the employment situation in the area projections are given, followed by ten pages of the outlook for specific jobs.

NV19. Nevada. Employment Security Department. *Las Vegas Area Wage Survey.* Carson City (500 E. Third St., Carson City 89713). Annual.
Contains occupational descriptions, wage data, union wage information, and salary range for specific occupations of county workers.

NV20. Regional Street and Highway Commission. *Clark County Transportation Study: 1976 Annual Report.* Las Vegas: Clark County Transportation Study Policy Committee (P.O. Box 396, Las Vegas 89101). n.d. 48pp.
Details accomplishments and provides population and projections, school enrollments, employment, vehicle registration, and other planning factors.

Collections

NV21. Clark County Library District. 1401 E. Flamingo Rd., Las Vegas 89109 (702)733-7810. Teletype Service: (910)397-6890.
The Clark County Library District (CCLD) is a designated state documents depository, second in priority of distribution of limited copies in southern Nevada to the University of Nevada, Las Vegas Library. Prior to 1973, the Downtown Branch of CCLD (formerly City of Las Vegas Public Library) collected local materials on its own, but the effort was limited. After a contract merger in 1973, it began to receive second copies of CCLD's depository documents, which include city and county documents. These are few, however, and both district headquarters and the Downtown Branch cooperate in collecting local documents as they can, with emphasis on county documents at headquarters and municipal documents at the Downtown Branch. Most documents are from the past ten years. Neither collection is outstanding. Material from either one is available through interlibrary loan.

NV22. University of Nevada, Las Vegas. James R. Dickinson Library, 4505 Maryland Pkwy., Las Vegas 89154 (702)739-3280. Teletype Service: (910)397-6862.
The library collects local materials, but active collection attempts have been sporadic. The current collection is in no way outstanding. However, the Special Collections Department does house the manuscript collection from Oran Gragson, mayor of Las Vegas from 1959 to 1975; archives of the Las Vegas Valley League of Women Voters; records of the Clark County Economic Opportunity Board; and selected Las Vegas municipal documents (late 1930s to mid 1940s). The manuscript correspondence of Assemblymen Paul May, Jean Ford, Thomas Hickey, and Zel Lowman include correspondence related to municipal concerns. Southern Nevada Oral History Project includes some taped interviews with public employees and officials.

RENO

Most of the reference material published in Reno and Washoe County comes in the form of planning documents issued or sponsored by the various planning agencies, including the Area Council of Governments and the Regional Planning Commission.

Publications

NV23. Area Council of Governments. *Blue Ribbon Task Force on Growth and Development.* Reno: Regional Planning Commission (241 Ridge St., Reno 89502), 1974. 10 vols.
This report is one of ten Blue Ribbon Task Force committee reports. The Economics of Growth volume helps define the problems of growth in the Washoe County area and proposes amendments to plans, ordinances, and codes of the cities and county.

NV24. Criminal Justice Planning Committee. *Criminal Justice Plan of Washoe County.* Carson City (Nevada Commission on Crime, Delinquency and Corrections, Capitol Complex, Carson City 89710), 1975.
Includes an inventory of existing criminal justice systems and available resources, an evaluation of current systems, and a multiyear plan.

NV25. Criminal Justice Planning Committee. *Supportive Services Guide.* Reno (Commission on Crime, Delinquency and Corrections, P.O. Box 11130 Reno), 1976. Free.
This directory of community service and helping agencies includes a telephone list of public agencies which lend support in many areas as well as private and charitable organizations providing helping services in the areas of clothing and furniture, education and training, food and meals, health care, emergency housing, housing projects, transportation, counseling, and youth services.

NV26. Kafoury, Armstrong, Turner and Co., Certified Public Accountants. *Washoe County.* Reno: Washoe County Auditor, n.d. Annual.
Auditor's report and examination of complete financial transactions of the county.

NV27. Reno. City Council. *Final Budgets.* (Courthouse, Reno 89502). Annual.
Includes full documentation of the city budget as approved.

NV28. Regional Planning Commission of Reno, Sparks, and Washoe County. *Regional Planning 1975.* (P.O. Box 1286, 241 Ridge St., Reno 89504) 1976. 46 leaves.
This report is a resource document for information on the following: form and function work and work program of the planning commission, zoning of Truckee Meadows and adjacent valleys, and growth in Washoe County from 1870-1975.

NV29. Reno-Sparks Convention Authority. *Reno:* Reno Convention Bureau (P.O. Box 837, Reno 89504), 1976.
Includes information on visitor attractions, transportation, accommodations, convention services, and hotels.

NV30. University of Nevada, Reno. Bureau of Business and Economic Research. *Washoe County Data Book, 1950-75.* (University Station, Reno 89557) 1977. 311pp.
Economic trends in the growth and development of the county during the time period.

NV31. Walters Engineering, Civil Engineering Consultants. *Areawide Water Quality Management Plan: Phase 1 Washoe County.* Prepared in association with Metcalf and Eddy Engineers Inc. Reno: Washoe Council of Governments (350 S. Center St., Suite 480, P.O. Box 3516, Reno 89505), n.d. 250pp.
Concerned with wastewater facilities planning, this report outlines existing water quality standards and projected deficiencies. It also summarizes past and future related planning efforts. The final chapter outlines the historical development of the Truckee River water quality monitoring program and includes recommendations for future supplemental sampling and monitoring programs.

NV32. Washoe Council of Governments. *Areawide Housing Plan and Program: Phase 1, Housing Plan and Analysis.* Reno, 1975. 96pp.
This report inventories the existing housing stock, public and private, in the county. It outlines the condition of current housing stock, current construction trends, value range of housing with emphasis upon availability of housing for the low income, elderly, married students, and the handicapped. Preliminary recommendations are given for the preservation and rehabilitation of existing housing, as well as forecasting future population growth and related housing needs.

NV33. Washoe Council of Governments. *Open Space Plan and Open Space Program for the Washoe Council of Governments.* Reno, 1974. 237pp. o.p.
This is one of the elements of the Long-Range Comprehensive General Plan for the Washoe County area. The report may be borrowed on microfiche or hard copy from the State Library.

Collections

NV34. University of Nevada, Reno. Library. Reno 89557 (702)784-6500. Teletype Service: (910)395-7054.
The library is a depository for city, county, and state publications.

NV35. Washoe County Library. P.O. Box 2151, Reno 89505 (702)785-4190. Teletype Service: (910)395-7022.
The library is a depository for both city and county publications. The Nevada vertical file includes local history and newspaper clippings filed by subject.

NEW HAMPSHIRE

General Publications

NH1. *New Hampshire Register, State Year Book and Legislative Manual.*
Portland, ME: Tower Publishing Co. (355 Forest Ave., Portland 04101). Annual. $38.
This directory has comprehensive coverage of state and local governments. It
lists municipal officials for the state and overviews the structure of municipal governments. The communities are listed alphabetically and a contact for additional
information is shown.

NH2. *State of New Hampshire Manual for the General Court.* Concord:
Department of State (State House, Concord 03301), 1930– . Biennial. $4.

CONCORD
Collections

NH3. **Concord Public Library.** 45 Green St., Concord 03301 (603)225-2743.
The library makes no concerted effort to collect official Concord publications. The
city is an infrequent publisher of municipal information.

MANCHESTER

Data not available at this time.

NASHUA

Data not available at this time.

NEW JERSEY

CAMDEN

Publications

NJ1. *Camden City and Camden County Inter-Office Directory.* Camden: Camden County Court House, 1975 or 1976. 38pp.
The directory, intended for interoffice use, lists staff in each municipal and county office with phone numbers. There is no index by name of individual.

NJ2. Camden County. Planning Department. *Directory of Camden County, Federal, State, County and Municipal Officials.* Pennsauken (2276 N. 43 St., Pennsauken 08110), Summer 1976.
The directory lists officials for each municipality in the county. It includes each official's address and phone number as well as meeting dates for various governmental bodies.

NJ3. Camden County. Superintendent of Schools. *Camden County, New Jersey Public Schools Directory.* Pennsauken (Court House Annex Bldg., 2276 N. 43 St., Pennsauken 08110), 1974-75. Annual. Free.
For each municipality in the county the directory lists the superintendent of schools, school addresses and phone numbers, principals, school secretaries, nurses, and attendance officers. The officers of several local educational organizations are also included.

NJ4. Camden County. Superintendent of Schools. *Directory of the Boards of Education of Camden County, New Jersey.* Pennsauken (Court House Annex Bldg., 2276 N. 43 St., Pennsauken 08110), 1975. Annual. Free.
The directory lists the members of the boards of education of each municipality in the county with their addresses. Monthly meeting dates, municipal auditors, and solicitors are also included.

NJ5. South Jersey Chamber of Commerce. *Guide to Business and Industrial Firms in Burlington, Camden and Gloucester Counties.* Pennsauken: Chamber of Commerce (N. Park Dr., Pennsauken 08110), 1976. 48pp.
Firms in the three counties are listed by city. Entries include company name, address, phone numbers, products, and number of employees. No index.

Collections

NJ6. Camden County Library. 8 Echelon Mall, Voorhees 08043. (609)772-1636.
Emphasis is on Camden County publications.

ELIZABETH

Local Newspaper Indexing: The Free Public Library of Elizabeth (see entry **NJ10**) prepares a card index of the *Elizabeth Daily Journal*, from 1915 to the present. Concentration is on city, county, and state news. Mail queries will be accepted.

Publications

NJ7. Elizabeth. City Clerk. *Administrative Code Adopted January 24, 1961 Including Subsequent Supplements and Amendments as of December 1969 and Incorporated as Chapter 4 of the Code of the City of Elizabeth, NJ, Adopted October 22, 1968. (and) Rules of Procedure Governing the City Council Adopted March 28, 1961.* (City Hall, 50 W. Scott Place, Elizabeth 07201) 40pp. Free.
Outlines the organization of the city government and elaborates on operating procedures. Current as of July 1977.

NJ8. Elizabeth. City Clerk. *Roster of City Officials for the Year 1977.* (City Hall, 50 W. Scott Place, Elizabeth 07201) Annual. Free.
A directory of elected and appointed city officials indicating term of office, regularly scheduled meetings, and an explanation of how appointments are made. Brief financial data on city presented.

NJ9. *Elizabeth (Union County, NJ) City Directory.* New Haven, CT: Price & Lee Co. (270 Orange St., New Haven, CT 06509), 1869–1971.

Collections

NJ10. The Free Public Library of Elizabeth. 11 S. Broad St., Elizabeth 07202. (201)354-6060.
The library maintains a large Elizabeth Room which provides resource material of all kinds about the city of Elizabeth, Union County, and neighboring communities. The library also maintains a card file of local clubs and organizations.

JERSEY CITY

The city does not publish a complete directory of all employees. It occasionally issues a list of department, division, and agency heads but does not provide updates to this list. The public library, however, does attempt to maintain a list of principal city employees, which it obtains from the personnel office and revises on the basis of newspaper reports. The library's list is not circulated in order to prevent the dissemination of outdated information. Written and telephone inquiries to the New Jersey Room are welcome (see entry **NJ15**).

The library does not necessarily receive all city publications, but it probably has most of them. A list of the city publications received by the library between 1971 and June 1977 is available (see entry **NJ14**). The major producer of city material is the planning office, which does send the library its publications. Other agencies and departments send material when requested. The difficulty is in obtaining materials which are not published. For example, department and committee reports are usually typed, not printed, and narrowly distributed. A similar problem exists with regard to the city council minutes which have not been printed since 1970 and, therefore, are available only in the city clerk's office. For the years 1853 to 1970, the library has the published minutes of the council or its governing equivalent. **Local Newspaper Indexing:** The New Jersey Room of the Jersey City Free

Public Library (see entry **NJ15**) has an index to the *Jersey Journal* (originally the *Evening Journal*) for the years 1904–1954. This index was prepared by the staff of the newspaper and varies enormously in the depth of the indexing. Selective indexing of the *Jersey Journal* has been done by the staff of the library since 1968. Emphasis is on governmental news for the city, county, and the state. The index is maintained on typed cards. Inquiries will be accepted.

Publications

NJ11. Hudson County. Board of Chosen Freeholders. *Directory of County and Municipal Officials of the County of Hudson, New Jersey.* Jersey City (Administration Bldg., 595 Newark Ave., Jersey City 07306), 1975. 28pp.
Lists county officials and city managers, council members and directors for each city in Hudson County.

NJ12. Jersey City. *Budget.* Jersey City Offices (280 Grove St., Jersey City 07302), 1973–   . Annual.
In addition to listing revenues and appropriations, the publication provides a directory of officials, number of personnel in each division, and an indication of the administrative components of the agency, authority, office, and department.

NJ13. Jersey City. *Municipal Directory.* Jersey City Offices (280 Grove St., Jersey City 07302), 1976.
A listing of telephone numbers and addresses of administrative offices. There is also an alphabetical listing of employees of the Board of Education and the departments. Employees of most independent agencies are not included in the alphabetical list.

NJ14. Jersey City Free Public Library. *Jersey City, New Jersey, Municipal Publications Received by the New Jersey Room of the Jersey City Public Library During the Period 1971 to June 1977.* (472 Jersey Ave., Jersey City 07302) 1977. 4pp.
A partially annotated checklist of municipal publications received by the library.

Collections

NJ15. Jersey City Free Public Library. New Jersey Room. 472 Jersey Ave., Jersey City 07302 (201)547-4503.
Municipal publications held in the New Jersey Room are not made available on interlibrary loan. The library's collection of municipally related material for the years 1850 to 1925 is good. For those years the library has the minutes of the city council, the city charters, the commercially produced directories, and several major published histories. For the years after 1925, there are no city directories except the telephone directories which the library owns beginning with 1939 and the current real estate atlas for the county. The library has the city council minutes through 1970 when publication and distribution ceased. It continues to receive the printed minutes of the Board of Education. The histories published since 1925 are either brief, in comparison with the earlier histories, or else concentrate upon just one aspect of city life. The library has the laws of the city, which have been codified through 1975. For later years, copies of current ordinances are received periodically from the city clerk. In addition to municipal documents, the library has some Hudson County publications.

NEWARK

Newark, America's third oldest city, was founded in 1666. The original records of the township of Newark were reprinted by the New Jersey Historical Society in 1966 and reindexed by Charles Cummings. The entire records of the township are found in a single volume and cover the period 1666–1835. They can best be described as "quaint."

More modern documents which include printed publications of the city of Newark are acquired by the New Jersey Reference Division of the Newark Public Library (see entry NJ18). Annual reports from different Newark agencies often date back to the late nineteenth century and in the case of the Board of Education go back more than 100 years. In the past ten years the number of municipal reports has mushroomed partly because of the efforts of the mayor's Policy Development Office. In addition to government publications, there are any number of quasi-official agency reports that contain considerable information. Both official and quasi-official documents are entered by division staff in a typed card file. Although not in the scope of this project, considerable information can be obtained from the New Jersey state document collections.

Beginning in 1972, the public library began participating in Greenwood Press's *Index to Current Urban Documents*. The library will not lend materials outside the state to nonlibraries. **Local Newspaper Indexing:** The New Jersey Reference Division of the Newark Public Library (see entry NJ18) has 423 index volumes available for the Newark *Evening News* and *Sunday News* for the period 1912 to 1972. The indexing was done by newspaper staff. Charles Cummings (supervising librarian, N. J. Reference Division) has indexed the Newark *Star Ledger* since 1972. Work has begun on indexing the Newark *Sentinel of Freedom* and the *Daily Advertiser* for selected census years from the nineteenth century.

Publications

NJ16. Axel-Lute, Paul. *Selected Federal Documents on Newark, New Jersey.* Newark: Rutgers Newark Law Library (180 University Ave., Newark 07102), 1976. 8pp. 50¢.
The list is grouped by subject area and provides the Superintendent of Documents classification number.

NJ17. Newark Public Library. New Jersey Reference Division. *Facts about Newark.* (5 Washington St., Newark 07101) 1975. 1p. Free.
The fact sheet provides miscellaneous information such as number of schools, notable citizens, tall buildings, cultural institutions, top employers, and historical landmarks. It also provides brief statistical profiles and a list of city officials.

Collections

NJ18. **Newark Public Library. New Jersey Reference Division.** 5 Washington St., Newark 07101 (201)733-7775/6.
The document collection contains the publications of the city, Essex County, and the state. Some of the agencies in this collection are the Port of New York Authority, the New Jersey Turnpike Authority, the Delaware Valley Regional Planning Commission, and the Palisades Interstate Park Commission.

PATERSON

Paterson is indeed an adequate publisher of municipal sources of current information. Private sources are equally adequate in giving assistance to the researcher into the city's past. Paterson's planning board publications have been periodically issued since 1949 and each one of the titles demonstrates the importance of the planning board to the past three decades of the city's development.

The local Board of Education has provided the public library with annual reports through 1971, but since that time, apparently due to budgetary problems or for other reasons, has kept its reports at 33 Church St., Paterson.

The *Revised City Ordinances* have 1972 as the latest date. The *Directory of Services Rendered by Private and Public Agencies of the City of Paterson* also needs updating from 1972/1973 (see entry **NJ23**).

The city's various administrative departments are well represented in the reference collection with annual reports. For example, those of the police department range from 1919 to 1971, which is the latest published. **Local Newspaper Indexing:** The Reference Division of the Paterson Public Library (see entry **NJ30**) selectively indexes the Paterson *Evening News*.

Publications

NJ19. McManis Associates. *Functional Analysis of the Government of the City of Paterson.* Mayor's Office (City Hall, Market St., Paterson 07505), 1972.

NJ20. Passaic County. Board of Chosen Freeholders. *1976 Directory of Passaic County Government.* Paterson (317 Pennsylvania Ave., Paterson 07503) 1976. Annual. Free.
In addition to covering the county, a current list of city officials for Paterson is also given.

NJ21. Passaic County. Planning Board. *Passaic County Industrial Directory.* Paterson (County Administration Bldg., 317 Pennsylvania Ave., Paterson 07503), 1976. $5 (free to libraries).
All industries having ten or more workers within the 14-town Passaic area were invited to be included. Some firms were not included because they declined to verify information for listing or did not return the questionnaire on time.

NJ22. Paterson. Board of Finance. *City of Paterson Local Budget.* (City Hall, Market St., Paterson 07505) 1944–   . Annual.

NJ23. Paterson. Consumer Affairs Committee. *Directory of Services Rendered by Private and Public Agencies, City of Paterson.* (City Hall Annex, 137 Ellison St., Paterson 07505) 1972/73. 62pp. $3.

NJ24. Paterson. Department of Community Development. Division of Planning and Zoning. *School Capacities to 1980.* (52 Church St., Paterson 07505) 78pp.

NJ25. Paterson. League of Women Voters. *Paterson Community Resources Directory.* Edited by Mary B. Brett. Paterson (265 Graham Ave., Paterson 07501) 1971. 59pp.
Included are public and voluntary agencies offering services in the fields of health, social welfare, education, and recreation located in the city. Mental health agencies are not listed.

NJ26. Paterson. Mayor's Office. *Annual Report.* (City Hall) Annual.
A well-illustrated report of the mayor's accomplishments for the year. There is a listing of department heads and members of the city council with information on terms of services, accomplishments, and expectations.

NJ27. Paterson. Planning Board. *Community Renewal Program: Final Report.* (City Hall) 1972.

NJ28. Paterson. Planning Board. *Meet the People.* (City Hall) 1973. 107pp.
This is an especially valuable population analysis which is much in demand.

NJ29. United Way of Passaic Valley. Community Affairs Committee. Subcommittee on Data Collection. *Directory of Community Resources, Listing Health, Education, Recreation and Welfare Services.* Nutley: Hoffman-LaRoche Inc. (340 Kingsland Ave., Nutley), 1975. 103pp.
The greatest proportion of entries are for services in Paterson. The information has been either supplied by each agency or verified with them.

Collections

NJ30. Paterson Public Library. Danforth Memorial, 250 Broadway, Paterson 07501 (201)279-4200, ext. 30.
At present the municipal reference collection satisfies both functional and basic needs for research. There are several landmark items which should be noted: The papers of the Society for Useful Manufactures are now in the library's possession and are for the most part indexed. They include charters, deeds, leases, certificates, contracts, and correspondence over the 1791 to 1905 period. Another landmark item is the Reid Photo Collection consisting of 220 photos covering nineteenth- and early twentieth-century Paterson. The library's staff photographer has made excellent recent reproductions of the Reid collection, and makes photographic records of many current municipal activities. Among many historical sources of worth, the historical writings of William Nelson, Charles Shriner, and Levi Trumbull are outstanding and much in demand in any study of Paterson's rich heritage.
The Paterson planning board's publications are numerous and generally of high quality, as are the majority of city department reports. The *Paterson-Clifton-Passaic Census* edition, in brochure form, has periodic projections and is particularly useful. The *Passaic County Real Estate Atlases* are current and readily available.
The genealogical holdings are being steadily increased, as evidenced by a file of ancestral information for local residents which increases daily. An adult services project on the subject has brought good results.
The Great Falls Development Corporation of Paterson is active in the study of Paterson archaeology. Reports issued by the corporation are a considerable addition to the reference collection.
The Paterson Bicentennial Committee (Monsignor Joseph J. Gallo, Chairman) succeeded in publishing a fine *Bicentennial Journal, 1776-1976*. It has an excellent text and is illustrated with some interesting pictures.

TRENTON

The city of Trenton does not publish very much material. That material which is published does not appear to be widely recognized or distributed by either the libraries or the city agencies themselves. There is a striking lack of bibliographic control. Perhaps this stems from the fact that the agencies do not publish on any regular schedule, and the publications themselves are often quite ephemeral. In addition, many publications are either not printed or merely appear in the local newspapers. **Local Newspaper Indexing:** The New Jersey State Library (see entry **NJ37**) selectively clips and indexes the *Trentonian* and the *Trenton Times*.

But the emphasis is upon that information which is considered to be of interest to state government.

The Trenton Free Public Library (see entry **NJ38**) selectively indexes the *Trenton Times* and the *Trentonian* for the purposes of inclusion within the Trentoniana Collection. The *Trenton Times* has been selectively indexed since the 1930s, and the *Trentonian* has been indexed for the past ten years.

NJ31. Greater Mercer Comprehensive Planning Council and Princeton Area Council of Community Services. *Directory of Human Services, Mercer County.* Trenton (Box 2103, Trenton 08607), 1974. 371 pp. $6. (Also available from: Princeton Area Council of Community Services, Box 201, Princeton 08540.)
Covers all private and public nonprofit health, welfare, recreation, and educational agencies serving residents of the county.

NJ32. Jersey Central Power and Light Co. *This Is Mercer County.* Morristown (Public and Community Relations Department, Madison Ave. at Punchbowl Rd., Morristown 07960) Annual. Free.
An economic and informational study of the county to assist in the evaluation of the area for location of businesses.

NJ33. *Mercer County Almanac and Historical Guide.* Trenton: Mercer Research Group (Box 3555, Trenton 08629), 1976.
This gives a brief profile of Trenton (mayor, council members, and an overview of the city). Includes population for municipalities, vital statistics, and income. Lists day care centers, child care centers, election results, etc.

Publications

NJ34. Chamber of Commerce. *Trenton Magazine.* (88 E. State St., Trenton 08608) 1924– . Monthly. $9 per year.
The January issue has a roster of businesses in the county, many of which are located in Trenton.

NJ35. Mercer County. Office of Economic Development. *Industrial Directory.* (Administration Bldg., Trenton 08607) Irregular. $2.
Lists company names, addresses, telephone numbers, number of employees, the type of business, and the SIC number.

NJ36. Trenton. League of Women Voters. *Our Trenton Schools.* (212 W. State St., Trenton 08608), n.d. 50¢.
This lists schools in Trenton, the principals, and the addresses of the schools. It gives salaries, teacher ethnic distribution, pupil distribution, school curriculum, special education services, and current operating budget revenues.

Collections

NJ37. **New Jersey State Library.** 185 W. State St., Trenton 08625 (609)292-6294.
There are no major municipal collections, as the emphasis is more on the county and state.

NJ38. Trenton Free Public Library. 120 Academy St., Trenton 08608 (609) 392-7188.
In the Trentoniana Collection, emphasis is on historical material pertaining to the city of Trenton. Some current material is included.

NEW MEXICO

General Publications

NM1. New Mexico Municipal League. *Directory of New Mexico Municipal Officials.* Santa Fe (P.O. Box 846, Santa Fe 87501) n.d. $10.

NM2. *New Mexico Statistical Abstract.* Albuquerque: University of New Mexico (Bureau of Business and Economic Research, Albuquerque 87131), n.d. Much of the information relates to the county level. However, some of it pertains to municipalities.

ALBUQUERQUE

Local Newspaper Indexing: The *Albuquerque Tribune* and *Albuquerque Journal* have been indexed by a joint archives service. For details consult the staff of the Municipal Reference Library (see entry **NM16**).

Publications

NM3. Albuquerque-Bernalillo County. Manpower Planning Council. *Organization and Plan for Bernalillo County Overall Economic Development Program.* Albuquerque, 1972. 69pp.

NM4. Albuquerque-Bernalillo County. Planning Department. *Albuquerque Urban Information System.* Albuquerque, 1972. 73pp.

NM5. Albuquerque-Bernalillo County. Planning Department. *City of Albuquerque Development Regulations and Policies.* Albuquerque, 1974.

NM6. Albuquerque-Bernalillo County. Planning Department. *The Comprehensive Plan: A New View of Albuquerque.* Albuquerque, n.d. 10pp.

NM7. Albuquerque-Bernalillo County. *Costs and Revenues of a Typical Subdivision.* Albuquerque: n.p., 1972. 17pp.

NM8. Albuquerque. City Manager. *Advisory Boards and Committees.* n.d.

NM9. Albuquerque. City Manager. *Budget.* n.d.
The budget contains a brief description of departmental functions and responsibilities.

NM10. Albuquerque. Community Renewal Program. *Albuquerque Area Housing Analysis.* Albuquerque, 1972. 158pp.

NM11. Albuquerque. Finance Department. *City of Albuquerque: Revenue History and Forecast, 1959–1977.* Prepared by Robert E. Boyer. Albuquerque, 1972.

NM12. Albuquerque. Office of Manpower Programs. *Directory of Manpower for Area Comprehensive Advisory Council.* Albuquerque, 1971.

NM13. Albuquerque. Urban Renewal Agency. *Information Booklet.* 1972. 128pp.

NM14. Industrial Development Services Inc. *Albuquerque Model Cities Development Data Book.* Albuquerque, 1971. 22pp.

NM15. Middle Rio Grande Council of Governments. *1995 Development Patterns Reflecting Continuation of Past Trends and Current Socioeconomic Projections: A Summary Report.* Albuquerque, 1972. 20pp.
A summary of the full report, which is listed as *Special Report 50* (1972, 208pp.).

Collections

NM16. **Municipal Reference Library.** 400 Marquette Ave. N.W., City Hall, Rm. 702, P.O. Box 1293, Albuquerque 87103 (505)766-7414.
The library collects in the areas of urban affairs, planning, fiscal management, sociology, and personnel. The staff has issued *MIRA* (*Municipal Information-Reference-Accession*), a bimonthly checklist of municipal publications, and has sent municipal publications on interlibrary loan.

SANTA FE

Data not available at this time.

NEW YORK

General Publications

NY1. New York (State). Department of Commerce. *Current Business Statistics.* (99 Washington Ave., Albany 12210) Quarterly.
Economic, financial, and business activity are reviewed for the state in numerous charts and tables, compiled from public and private sources. An annual summary is included.

NY2. New York (State). Department of State. *Local Government Primer.* Albany, 1976. 6pp. Free.
This pamphlet provides a brief introduction to government structure, forms of municipalities and districts, and taxes.

NY3. New York (State). Department of Taxation and Finance. *The New York State and Local Tax System.* Albany, n.d. 74pp. Free.
This recurring, undated booklet presents the evolution of tax systems and how they work. Major forms of taxes in the state are listed with their responsible agencies, and tables are given.

NY4. New York (State). Division of the Budget. *New York State Statistical Yearbook.* Albany (Gift and Exchange Section, New York State Library, Albany 12234). Annual.
A variety of data are given, often on a county basis (including the five boroughs of New York City). Among the statistics that are presented are census figures, data on municipal government, and county and state spending.

NY5. *New York State Industrial Directory.* New York: New York State Industrial Directory (2 Penn Plaza, New York 10001). Annual.
The directory is divided into an alphabetical list of firms, an index to counties and municipalities, a classified buyer's guide, and a geographical listing of firms, addresses, square footage, employees, products, and SIC numbers. There are sections for the New York City metropolitan area, Manhattan, and upstate New York (by county).

NY6. New York (State). Legislature. *Manual for the Use of the Legislature of the State of New York.* Albany (Gift and Exchange Section, New York State Library, Albany 12234). Annual.
This legislative manual also includes a description of office-holders and their addresses, a description of legislative districts, some census figures, and election results. In recent years publication of the manual has been less frequent and delayed.

NY7. New York (State). Metropolitan Transportation Authority. *Annual Report.* Albany. Annual. (Available from: Gift and Exchange Section, New York State Library, Albany 12234.)

NY8. New York (State). Municipal Assistance Corporation for the City of New York. *New Issue, Official Statement (on Bond Offerings).* New York: Municipal Assistance Corporation (2 World Trade Center, New York 10047). Occasional.
The statement is prepared for the prospective buyer of forthcoming "big MAC" bonds. Each is intended to give a true picture of the city's financial condition, and is released prior to sale. A typical issue would cover present taxes, management litigation, financial outlook, credit, and debt service.

NY9. New York (State). Secretary of State. *Local Laws of the Cities, Counties, and Villages in the State of New York.* Albany, 1924– . Annual. (Available from: Gift and Exchange Section, New York State Library, Albany 12234.)
Contains all laws passed by local authorities and approved by the state. Bound volumes in this set are usually slow in appearing. For New York City all local laws are also published in the daily *City Record.*

NY10. *New York Tax Service.* Englewood Cliffs, NJ: Prentice-Hall Inc. Loose-leaf, 3 vols.

ALBANY

Coverage of Albany city and county documents remains poor, with relatively few being listed in the *Index to Current Urban Documents,* and little coverage in other bibliographies. Although several libraries in the Albany area do collect municipal publications, none appear to do so comprehensively. Libraries with an interest in area documents are listed in *Albany Municipal Documents: A Directory of Sources* (see entry **NY28**). The New York Public Library's *Catalog of Government Publications in the Research Library* (G. K. Hall, 1972, 40 vols.—see entry **NY159**) does list many of the older Albany documents that may have historical interest.

Publications

NY11. Albany (City). Common Council. *Proceedings of the Common Council of the City of Albany.* Annual.
The 1970 volume was in two parts, the first containing the proceedings and the second containing the message of the mayor and reports of city agencies.

NY12. Albany (City). Department of Finance, Comptroller's Office. *Annual Report to the Mayor and Common Council for the Fiscal Period Ending. . . .* Annual.

NY13. Albany (City). Department of Health. *Annual Report.* Annual.

NY14. Albany County. Legislature. *Journal.* 1969– .
Before 1969 this was issued as the *Journal of the Albany County Board of Supervisors.*

NY15. Albany County. Legislature and County Planning Department. *Implementing the Albany County Charter.* Albany, 1974. 99, 128pp. App., figures.
The report was prepared by Boeing Computer Services Inc., Consulting Division, New York; it was then submitted by the County Improvements Committee.

NY16. Albany County. Planning Board. *Albany County Comprehensive Plan, 1971–77: Study Design.* June 1971. 46pp. o.p.
The board has announced a forthcoming review of "the overall program design" for December 1977, that will replace this report.

NY17. Albany County. Planning Board. *Albany County Housing and Construction Study.* July 1971. 45pp. Charts, graphs, illus., tables.
This study is a basic inventory of housing and of present requirements.

NY18. Albany Port District Commission. *Annual Report.* Annual.

NY19. Albany Public Library, Pruyn Library of Albany History. *Source Materials for Black History of Albany, New York.* Albany: New York State Library, 1972. 1 reel microfilm.

NY20. Capital District Regional Planning Commission. *Allocation Model for Low- and Moderate-Income Housing in the Capital District.* Albany (Executive Park Tower, Stuyvesant Plaza, Albany 12203). 1974, 39pp.

NY21. Capital District Regional Planning Commission. *Annual Reports.* Albany (Executive Park Tower, Stuyvesant Plaza, Albany 12203). Annual.

NY22. Capital District Regional Planning Commission. *Apartments and Mobile Homes in the Capital District—Trends, Policies, and Impacts.* Albany (Executive Park Tower, Stuyvesant Plaza, Albany 12203), 1974. 150pp. $5.

NY23. Capital District Regional Planning Commission. *Inventory of Social Services in the Capital District.* Albany (Executive Park Tower, Stuyvesant Plaza, Albany 12203), June 1975. 114pp. $4.

NY24. Capital District Regional Planning Commission. *The Perceptual Environment: Quality Assessment in the Capital District.* (Technical Report 200-4). Albany (79 N. Pearl St., Albany 12207), 1975. 47pp. $6.50.
Bibliography, figures, maps, and tables.

NY25. Capital District Regional Planning Commission. *Regional Development Plan: A Consultation Document.* Albany (Executive Park Tower, Stuyvesant Plaza, Albany 12203), March 1975. 164pp. $10.

NY26. New York (State). Department of Commerce. *Business Fact Book, 1971–72; Part 1, Business and Manufacturing: Capital District.* Albany, 1972. 28pp. Tables, charts, maps. Free. (Available from: Gifts and Exchange Section, New York State Library, Albany 12234.)

NY27. New York State Library. *Information Resources of Selected New York State Agencies, Albany Area Directory, 1975.* Albany, 1975. 52pp. (Available from: Gifts and Exchange Section, New York State Library, Albany 12234.)

NY28. State University of New York at Albany. School of Library and Information Science. *Albany Municipal Documents: A Directory of Sources.* Albany, 1974. 48l.
This directory is the first attempt to list all major Albany municipal documents and was developed as part of a seminar team project under the direction of Prof. Joseph Morehead. The publication does not attempt to provide a full bibliographic listing

of all major Albany documents but rather is a guide to city agencies, their addresses, hours, officers to contact, facilities, publications, services, and holdings of documents. The appendixes review the state structure of government, state law in regard to public records, and local ordinances as well. This directory was out-of-print in 1977, but a new addition is being planned.

Collections

NY29. **Albany Public Library.** Main Branch. Pruyn Library of Albany History. 161 Washington Ave., Albany 12210 (518)449-3380.
The library has an archival-type collection, and holdings include Board of Education reports, child welfare reports, city directories, County Planning Board reports, Journal of the County Board of Supervisors, police commissioner reports, and proceedings of the Common Council.

NY30. **City Hall Library. Department for Historical Services.** 27 Western Ave., Albany 12206 (518)472-6144/5.
Holdings include enrollment of voters, Board of Education minutes and materials, city directories, proceedings of the Common Council, and of the Board of Estimate and Apportionment. The library has selected nineteenth- and twentieth-century documents, including property tax assessment rolls. The State University of New York at Albany will loan municipal publications. There is neither a directory of city officials nor a published index to local newspapers. Students engaged in research may use the newspaper files by appointment, but it is necessary to contact the *Knickerbocker News-Union Star*, 645 Albany-Shaker Rd., Colonie, NY.

NY31. **New York State Library.** History and Manuscripts Division. State Education Building, Washington Ave., Albany 12234 (518)474-5963.
This reference collection includes one of the most complete groupings of pre-1900 Albany area documents. It includes Albany maps, enrollments of voters, census data from the eighteenth century in manuscript and microform, charters (including the Dongan charter), city hall accounts, minutes of the Common Council, ordinances, school district reports, and police and court records.

NY32. **New York State Library.** Legislative Reference Library. State Education Building, Washington Ave., Albany 12234 (518)474-5943.
The library is chiefly concerned with state government and issues publications, studies, bibliographies, and legislative research papers. It also has a collection of documents from the Albany Citizen Advisory Commission, the Albany Community Improvement Program, Albany County Planning Board, Albany Port Commissioner, Board of Elections, departments of Public Welfare, Public Works, and Urban Redevelopment. It also houses various budgets, charters, directories, laws and ordinances, the Journal of the Board of Supervisors (1858–1968) and the Journal of the Albany County Legislature (1969–   ).

BUFFALO

The largest collection of local documents is probably located at the Buffalo and Erie County Public Library (see entry **NY60**), although some are also collected at the State University of New York at Buffalo (see entry **NY61**). Coverage by the *Index to Current Urban Documents* is inadequate and bibliographic reporting for the region needs to be improved, particularly for the special, nonrecurring type of study. County government is strong, with some municipal functions performed at that level. If bibliographic control is to be improved upon, it would be best undertaken at the public library, with county support. **Local Newspaper Indexing:** The *Buffalo Evening News* and the *Courier Express* are indexed at the Buffalo and Erie County Public Library (see entry **NY60**), and the local historical society also does some indexing. The *Buffalo Evening News* also has its own index.

Publications

NY33. Buffalo and Erie County Public Library. *Annual Report.* (Lafayette Sq., Buffalo 13202) Annual.
These are generally short reports with illustrations and tables.

NY34. Buffalo. Common Council. *Proceedings.* Semimonthly issues and annual cumulative volumes.

NY35. Buffalo. Comptroller. *Annual Report.* Department of Audit and Control. Annual.
The 1973 issue was the 141st annual report. Generally they chiefly contain financial tables, and may have an organization chart.

NY36. Buffalo. Department of Community Development. *City of Buffalo Study of Social Programs.* 1973. 143pp.

NY37. Buffalo. Executive Department, Division of the Budget. *Annual Budget . . . for the Fiscal Year.* Tables. Annual.

NY38. Buffalo. Fire Department, Bureau of Fire Prevention. *Annual Report.* Annual.

NY39. Buffalo. Office of the Mayor. *Insight Buffalo.* Department of Community Development, November 1976. 195pp. Maps.
This report on the state of the city provides a very detailed analysis of demographic and housing trends, the economy of the region, crime and law enforcement, fire protection, utilities, education, leisure, transportation, and land use. The data are divided into smaller communities and special districts, and local maps are included.

NY40. Buffalo. Office of the Mayor. *The Regional Center: A Comprehensive Plan for Downtown Buffalo.* 1971. 56pp. Maps, photos.
This plan for downtown renewal includes charts of sales, employment, and space. The report covers land use, investment opportunities, transportation, and projected development.

NY41. Buffalo. Sewer Authority. *Annual Report.* 1971. 99pp. Graphs, tables, illus.

NY42. Buffalo. Youth Board. *A Survey of 16- to 20-Year Old Offenders Arrested During the Year 1971.* October 1972. 32l. Charts, tables. Cover title: "Youth Crime Report."

NY43. "Buffalo's 1974 Housing Guide." *In Buffalo.* vol. 49: 25ff (March 1974). This issue of the periodical includes a directory of builders and developers, apartment houses, and realtors in the Buffalo metropolitan area.

NY44. Center for Governmental Research Inc. *City Finances in Perspective: Rochester, Buffalo and Syracuse, New York, 1975-76.* Rochester (37 S. Washington St., Rochester 14608), 1976. $2.

NY45. Erie and Niagara Counties Regional Planning Board. *Citizen Information and Participation Program.* Grand Island, 1971. 30pp.

NY46. Erie and Niagara Counties Regional Planning Board. *Federal Program Project Review Procedure.* Grand Island, 1971. 35pp.

NY47. Erie and Niagara Counties Regional Planning Board. *Niagara River Environmental Plan, Summary Report.* Buffalo, 1972. 54pp.

NY48. Erie and Niagara Counties Regional Planning Board. *The Review of Environmental Impact Statements, Notes from a Metropolitan Clearing House.* Grand Island, 1972. 18pp.

NY49. Erie County (New York). Department of Finance. *Annual Report, Tax Collections 1975.* Buffalo, 1976. 9pp.

NY50. Erie County (New York). Department of Finance, Division of Real Property Tax. *Annual Report of the 1975 Equalization Rates, 1976 Tax Rates.* Buffalo, 1975. 14pp.

NY51. Erie County (New York). Department of Health. *Annual Report 1974.* Buffalo, 1975. 29pp. fig.

NY52. Erie County (New York). Legislature. *Proceedings.* Buffalo. Annual.
The annual collection of proceedings are often over 1,500 pages and are indexed.

NY53. New York (State). Department of Commerce. *Business Fact Book, 1971–72: Part 1, Business and Manufacturing, Buffalo Area.* Albany, 1972. 28pp. Tables, charts, maps.

NY54. New York (State). Department of Commerce. *Business Fact Book, 1976: Part 1, Profile of Business and Industry, Buffalo Area.* Albany, 1976. 24pp. Tables, charts.

NY55. New York (State). Department of Labor. *Comparative Urban Indicators in the New York and Buffalo Area.* Albany, August 1973.
Both Buffalo and New York City are compared with and ranked among the other major cities of the United States. Among the matters considered are general conditions of the city (both improving and deteriorating), employment, housing, mortality, and crime.

NY56. Niagara Frontier Transportation Authority. *Port of Buffalo Handbook.* Buffalo, 1973. 26pp.

NY57. Niagara Frontier Transportation Authority. *Summary Report, Niagara Frontier Mass Transit Study.* Buffalo, September 1971. 30pp.

NY58. Paaswell, Robert E., and Wilfred W. Recker. *Problems of the Carless: Final Report.* Washington, DC: U.S. Department of Transportation, Office of University Research. June 1976. 52pp. Illus., tables, charts, maps. Free.
This report was prepared by members of the Department of Civil Engineering at the State University of New York, Buffalo. It contains data based on a survey of over 400 respondents in Buffalo, and includes information on car ownership, travel, local transit, and the elderly.

NY59. Smith, H. Perry. *History of the City of Buffalo and Erie County.* Syracuse, 1884 (reprinted 1976). 2 vols.

Collections

NY60. Buffalo and Erie County Public Library. Lafayette Sq., Buffalo 13202. The public library is the designated depository for both the city of Buffalo and Erie County, although not all documents are received.

NY61. State University of New York at Buffalo. Lockwood Memorial Library. Buffalo 14214 (716)831-4027.
The Documents and Microforms Department collects some local Buffalo documents, while others may be collected at the separate Law Library of the University at Buffalo.

NEW YORK CITY

(Separate data for the individual boroughs of Bronx, Brooklyn, Manhattan, Queens, and Staten Island are not available at this time.)
Extensive bibliographic coverage of New York City documents has been provided by the *Municipal Reference and Research Center Notes*, formerly the *Municipal Reference Library Notes* (see entry **NY146**). The center (see entry **NY196**) has long been a depository for local government publications and has operated an exchange program with other cities. Unfortunately, the *Notes* has ceased publication because of fiscal cutbacks. Replacing it for a while was an accessions list, but that too has now been suspended. Cooperation with Greenwood Press's *Index to Current Urban Documents* has been good, and most New York City documents are now listed in that index. A variety of other libraries in the New York City area also collect local documents, and some, such as the Tri-State Regional Planning Commission, publish acquisitions lists. The New York Chapter of the Special Libraries Association has issued a guide, *Special Libraries Directory of Greater New York*, now in its 14th edition (see entry **NY175**). The New York Public Library also has a good collection of city documents, and many are listed in its *Catalog of Government Publications*, issued by G. K. Hall in 40 volumes (see entry **NY159**). Recent documents are also listed in the book catalog of the research collections. Specialized, historical collections in the New York City area provide much additional depth, and some guides are available to them. The Municipal Reference and Research Center has recently been expanded to incorporate the library, the city archives, and the city's record management program, with a corresponding increase of documents coverage. It is also expected to move to new facilities.

Recently, wide cutbacks in the publication programs of city agencies have occured in New York due to budgetary restrictions. Some annuals now appear less frequently (only to reappear later without warning). Although many annuals are listed below, the term may now be a misnomer, and some will have ceased. Among those discontinued is the *Statistical Guide for New York City* (see entry **NY118**). The overall best-seller in New York City documents is still the *Official Directory of the City of New York* (see entry **NY86**). Harold Eiberson's guide, *Sources for the Study of the New York City Area* (see entry **NY70**), remains one of the most useful, if now dated, bibliographic guides to reference material for the area.

The New York Metropolitan Reference and Research Library Agency (METRO) appointed a Data Base Inventory Task Force to prepare a directory of on-line data bases in the New York City area. As of late 1977 the directory was being planned to include an alphabetical listing of 60 or 70 data bases, with descriptions and the names of libraries with terminals. **Local Newspaper Indexing:** The New York

Municipal Reference and Research Center (see entry **NY194**) clips and files the *New York Times*, and *Daily News*, and did clip the *Post* in vertical files by subject. No index file as such is maintained on newspapers. The *New York Times* has been published since 1851, and the *New York Times Index* since 1913 (see entry **NY162**).

Publications

NY62. American Institute of Architects, New York Chapter. *AIA Guide to New York City.* New York: Macmillan Co., 1968. 464pp. Maps, photos. $6.95.

NY63. Alpern, Robert. *Pratt Guide to Planning and Renewal for New Yorkers.* New York: Quadrangle, 1973. 463pp. $15.
The guide is intended for community action and assistance, and contains a directory of official agencies, both city and federal; the procedures before the agencies that are of local concern; the budget process; transportation; rent action; urban planning; and health.

NY64. Berenyi, John, editor. *The Quality of Life in Urban America; New York City: A Regional and National Comparative Analysis.* New York: New York City Office of Administration, 1971. 2 vols.
In this analysis New York is compared statistically with other major cities in matters of crime control, environmental quality, budget, taxation, and welfare.

NY65. Burstein, Abraham C. *A Demographic Profile of New York City.* New York: Human Resources Administration (250 Broadway, New York 10013), 1973. 229pp.

NY66. Carman, Harry J., and Arthur Thompson. *A Guide to the Principal Sources for American Civilization, 1800-1900, in the City of New York: Printed Materials.* New York: Columbia University Press, 1962. 630pp.
This bibliographic survey includes many local, official publications, records, and sources. A companion volume covering manuscripts has also been published. The volume serves as a continuation of the book by Evarts Greene and Richard Morris, *A Guide to the Principal Sources for Early American History (1600-1800) in the City of New York,* New York: Columbia University Press, 1953. 400pp.

NY67. Citizens Union. *Voters Directory.* New York (15 Park Row, New York 10038). Annual.
The pamphlet directory lists principal officers and candidates with their campaign statements on major issues. It is issued prior to the yearly general elections. District maps are included.

NY68. Community Council of Greater New York Inc. *Directory of Social and Health Agencies of New York, 1977-78.* Edited by Rowena McDade and William James Smith. New York: Columbia University Press, 1977. 642pp. Biennial.
1977 marked the 61st edition of this useful survey of both public and voluntary health and welfare agencies serving the New York City area. Government, education, and religious organizations are included if they offer such services, as are the local offices of national bodies operating in this field. Agencies listed have been carefully screened. The book is divided into 24 subject fields including addiction services, adult health services, community development programs, education, housing, hospitals, legal assistance agencies, etc. There is an agency index with officers and addresses, and a more detailed subject guide. Additional sections are a guide to "Selected Information and Referral Services in the United States and Canada," and a list of other directories of use in the 24 subject fields.

NY69. *Directory of Directors in the City of New York. Beginning 1898.* New York: Director of Directors Co., 1959. Occasional.
This is a directory to leading executives, personnel, and firms, of the larger concerns with offices in New York.

NY70. Eiberson, Harold. *Sources for the Study of the New York City Area.* New York: City College Press, 1960. 128pp. (Available from: Associated College Presses, 32 Washington Pl., New York City.) This bibliography and guide book provides coverage on all types of literature up to 1960, with chapters on bibliographies and indexes, library resources, local law, government administration, population, business, and the economy. This bibliography is intended for the student, so that much attention is given to evaluating the literature available. It provides a review on historical bibliography, and surveys the major municipal documents published.

NY71. Family Council of New York City. *Family Planning Fact Book of New York City.* New York: Family Planning Council, 1974. 101pp.
Various demographic statistics are arranged by health districts in this volume that covers ethnicity, age, births, fertility, abortions, infant mortality, welfare, etc.

NY72. Federal Writers Project, New York (City). *New York City Guide: A Comprehensive Guide to the Five Boroughs of the Metropolis—Manhattan, Brooklyn, the Bronx, Queens, and Richmond.* New York: Random House, 1939.
Somewhat older information and historical background is provided about the sections and neighborhoods of the city.

NY73. Furer, Howard B. *New York: A Chronological and Documentary History, 1524-1970.* Dobbs Ferry, Oceana, 1974. 153pp.

NY74. *Greater New York City and Surrounding Territories: Business Classified Directory.* Brooklyn: Directory Publishing Corporation, 1958.
This directory lists thousands of manufacturers, distributors, and services under type of business or product.

NY75. *Greater New York Industrial Directory, Plus the Greater New York Industrial Marketplace. 1959-60.* New York: Greater New York Industrial Directory Corp., 1959.
Business and manufacturing firms are identified, with address, product, personnel, and size. Arrangement is by county in the New York metropolitan region. There is a classified buyer's guide, and SIC numbers are given.

NY76. Greene, Evarts B., and Richard B. Morris. *A Guide to the Principal Sources for Early American History (1600-1800) in the City of New York.* 2d ed., rev. New York: Columbia University Press, 1953.

NY77. Hanrieder, Barbara. *Characteristics of the Population in New York City Health Areas: 1970.* New York: Community Council of Greater New York, 1973. 3 vols.
Arranged by health area, statistics are presented from the 1970 census of population, relating to income level, family composition, and characteristics. This permits the correlation of census data with birth, death, and disease rates for the entire city.

NY78. Kranich, Nancy. *Guide to Information Sources in Public Administration.* New York: New York University Graduate School in Public Administration, 1977. 65pp.

Intended for the student, this guide includes information on New York City library collections, major types of information available, and has a list of sources.

NY79. Kronman, Barbara. *NYPIRG's Guide to N.Y.C. Public Records.* New York: New York Public Interest Research Group Inc., 1975. 59pp.
Major collections and types of public records are described under headings such as business, courts, general reference, election, health, housing, personal, property, welfare, etc. Suggestions are made according to scope, addresses, and access. The pamphlet has a subject index.

NY80. G. W. Bromley and Co. Inc. *Manhattan Land Book of the City of New York.* New York, 1955.
This atlas presents in great detail plans of every building in the borough, and is regularly used in matters of land assessment, insurance, property valuation, construction, and fire prevention. A subscription service provides updated insertions.

NY81. *Municipal Telephone Service Directory.* New York, 1975. $6. (Available from: City Record Sales Office, Rm. 2213 Municipal Bldg., New York.)

NY82. New York (City). *Annual Report (of Various Departments).* Various city departments have issued annual reports, varying in value and content, and including those of the Departments of Air Pollution Control, Commerce, Community Mental Health, Corrections, Elections, Fire, Health, Hospitals, Housing, Labor, Police, Public Works, Water Supply, etc. More recently, the pattern of publishing these has become irregular, with some appearing at biannual intervals, and others ceasing altogether. All are listed in the *Notes* and lists of *Recent Acquisitions* published by the Municipal Reference and Research Center.

NY83. New York (City). *Building Code of the City of New York.* New York: Van Nostrand Reinhold, 1970. 472, 422pp.
The building code is frequently revised, but amendments are not reflected in this edition of the trade publisher. A current edition, from time to time is also prepared and sold by the City Record Sales Office. Amendments are published in the City Record.

NY84. New York (City). *The City Record, Official Journal of the City of New York.* New York: City Record (City Record Sales Office, 2213 Municipal Bldg., New York 10007). Daily except Saturday, Sunday, and holidays. $100 per year.
Issued as the official gazette of the city, this contains all public notices, local laws and executive orders having legal effect, results of examinations, civil service requirements, etc. The various budgets of the city are issued as supplements, and in previous years the minutes of the city council were included in the City Record, although they are now printed separately.

NY85. New York (City). *The Civil List.* New York: City Record. Annual. Not available for purchase.
The Civil List contains the names and addresses of all city employees, and often extends to ten volumes or more. Only a few copies are made available, but it is open to the public at the Municipal Reference and Research Center.

NY86. New York (City). *Official Directory of the City of New York.* New York. City Record (City Record Sales Office, 2213 Municipal Bldg., New York 10007). $4.
Known as the "Little Green Book" this serves as a directory of federal, state, and city officials and offices within New York City. There is a detailed table of contents

arranged by department, and a personal name index. Also included is a list of local licenses and permits and a small amount of historical and statistical information.

NY87. New York (City). Agency for Child Development. *Directory of Programs.* (240 Church St., New York 10013).

NY88. New York (City). Board of Education. *New York City Public Schools: Facts and Figures.* (110 Livingston St., Brooklyn 11201) Biennial.
This brief pamphlet contains data on the operation of the school system as a whole; information is not given on individual schools.

NY89. New York (City). Board of Education. *School Profiles.* Vol. 1, 1972. (110 Livingston St., Brooklyn 11201) Biennial.
This extensive volume provides statistics on pupil education, characteristics and achievements, staffing patterns of the schools, and funds allocated. Intended for use by community groups the book is arranged by school district, and then individual school. Figures are given on ethnic composition, and reading and math scores.

NY90. New York (City). Board of Elections. *Annual Report.* (Board of Elections, 80 Varick St., New York 10013) Annual.
This annual report presents a statistical analysis of primary and general election returns arranged by assembly district.

NY91. New York (City). Board of Elections. *List of Enrolled Voters.* New York, annual bound volume, or separate parts. City Record (City Record Sales Office, 2213 Municipal Bldg., New York 10007). Varies.
Arranged by borough, assembly, and election district, this lists all current members of political parties, their addresses and affiliations, for those having enrolled in the primaries.

NY92. New York (City). Board of Elections. *List of Registered Voters.* Annual.
With volumes for each of the boroughs this lists voters and addresses, arranged by election district.

NY93. New York (City). Board of Elections. *Official Canvass of the Votes Cast in the Counties of New York, Bronx, Kings, Queens and Richmond in the General Election.* (City Record Sales Office, 2213 Municipal Bldg., New York 10007). Varies.
This contains a statistical tally of the votes cast for each party, and is arranged by borough, assembly district, and election district.

NY94. New York (City). Board of Estimate. *Journal of Proceedings of Meetings.* Annual subscription. (City Record Sales Office, 2213 Municipal Bldg., New York 10007) $100.
The Board of Estimate occupies a crucial position in the preparation and passage of the city budget. Its minutes provide a great deal of information on administration and legislative actions taken during a given year. The minutes were formerly included in the City Record; more recently they have been made available as separately printed pamphlets. Annual, bound volumes have been printed with indexes.

NY95. New York (City). Board of Water Supply. *Annual Report.* (1250 Broadway, New York 10001). Annual.
The annual report generally includes the report of the chief engineer.

New York (City). *Charter.* See **NY154.**

NY96. New York (City). City Council. *Journal of Proceedings of Meetings.*
(City Record Sales Office, 2213 Municipal Bldg., New York 10007).
Minutes of the city council meetings were formerly included in the City Record.
Now, however, they may appear as pamphlet supplements to the Record. They include lists of bills, proposed laws as reported, and the text of laws after passage.
Reports of investigative committees of the city council are from time to time included.

NY97. New York (City). City Planning Commission. *Community Planning
District Profiles.* (2213 Municipal Bldg., New York 10007) 1973. 2 vols. Free.
Brief statistical profiles are given on each community planning district. Volume 1
covers population and housing; volume 2 is on socioeconomic characteristics.

NY98. New York (City). City Planning Commission. *Community Planning
Handbook General Information Guides.* (2 Lafayette St., New York 10007)
1974– . Free.
Intended to assist community workers and groups who are using the commission's
Community Planning Handbooks this series of brief guides in pamphlet form contain
directories and descriptions of city offices, officials, programs, charts, glossaries
of planning terms, etc.

NY99. New York (City). City Planning Commission. *Community Planning
Handbook Series.* (2 Lafayette St., New York 10007) 1973. 62 vols. Loose-leaf.
A separate, loose-leaf volume is kept current for each district, with a wide range of
statistical data, political maps, and directories to both public and private agencies
and officials. Information is given on neighborhood population, education, housing,
economy, health, social services, and the capital budget. These volumes may be
used to update the information in *Plan for New York City, a Proposal* (1969). (see
entry **NY102**).

NY100. New York (City). City Planning Commission. *Infill Zoning.* (2 Lafayette
St., New York 10007) 1972. $1.
A discussion is given of present zoning for residential structures, with proposed
changes. Diagrams are given of permitted residential buildings and land use.

NY101. New York (City). City Planning Commission. *Minutes of Meetings.* (2
Lafayette St., New York 10007).
The City Planning Commission, in addition to the usual planning and zoning functions, is responsible for the initial preparation of the city budget. The minutes therefore include matters of budget, planning, and zoning. Pamphlet copies appear
after each meeting of the commission. An annual, bound volume has also been
published.

NY102. New York (City). City Planning Commission. *Plan for New York City,
a Proposal.* New York, 1969. 6 vols. (Available from: M.I.T. Press, 28 Carleton St.,
Cambridge, MA 02142.) $90.
This major undertaking contains a survey of all community and municipal facilities
and improvements, including those that have been proposed. A basic volume on
critical issues gives a citywide perspective to the social and economic situation in
the city. Some attention is given to governmental reform and innovations in urban
development, but the volumes are largely neighborhood oriented, with chapters on
each community district. Land use and site maps are included for all of the 62
community planning districts, along with some brief historical and social commen-

tary on each area. Tables are also given on population, conditions, and services for each.

NY103. New York (City). City Planning Commission. *Planning for Jobs.* (2 Lafayette St., New York 10007) March 1971. $5.
A survey of the city's industrial space and the potentials for an increase in manufacturing, this volume contains many proposals, with charts, tables, and statistical projections.

NY104. New York (City). City Planning Commission. *Publications and Information Guide.* (Department of City Planning, 2 Lafayette St., New York 10007). Occasional.
This brief guide (the 1972 issue was five pages) is a bibliography, sales list, and directory of sources. It lists available publications of the commission, various maps (census, base, zoning, land use, and health areas), and the addresses of other, related city agencies.

NY105. New York (City). City Planning Commission. *The Waterfront.* (2 Lafayette St., New York 10007) January 1971. 106pp.
This was issued as a supplement to the *Plan for New York City* and contains a review of waterfront facilities, housing, recreation, industry, transportation, etc. Numerous maps are included.

NY106. New York (City). Commission on the Delivery of Personal Health Services. *Community Health Services for New York City, Report and Staff Studies.* New York: Praeger, 1969. 675pp.

NY107. New York (City). Commission on the Status of Women. *First Year of the Commission on the Status of Women, 1975-76: A Report by the Chairperson.* (250 Broadway, New York 10007) 1976. 161pp.

NY108. New York (City). Committee on Housing Statistics. *Housing Statistics Handbook.* 1974- . Occasional.

NY109. New York (City). Common Council. *Manual of the Corporation of the City of New York, 1841-70.* New York, 1841-70.
Known as Valentine's Manuals, each served as a directory and guidebook to the city's institutions, both public and private, during the nineteenth century. An index to the series was published by Harper in 1900. In the early part of the twentieth century a second series of Valentine's Manuals was begun, but it contained more of a miscellany of historical and social information. Many illustrations were included in the annual volumes of both series.

NY110. New York (City). Common Council. *Minutes of the Common Council of the City of New York, 1784-1831.* New York: City of New York, 1917. 19 vols.
Detailed, day-to-day accounts on municipal operations as reflected in city council records for the period.

NY111. New York (City). Community Development Agency. *Program Directory.* (349 Broadway, New York 10013) Annual.
This is issued jointly with the Council Against Poverty.

NY112. New York (City). Community Renewal Program. *Between Promise and Performance: A Proposed Ten-Year Program of Community Renewal for New York City.:* December 1968. 161pp. Maps, tables, photos.

Using frequent examples of actual developments and sites, this report discusses the philosophy and approaches of renewal and future alternatives. Frequent use is made of maps and photographs showing housing, education, recreation, and the strategy of renewal.

NY113. New York City Council on Economic Education. *Fact Book, Tables and Charts on the New York Metropolitan Region.* 1974. 166pp.
This recurring, unofficial publication presents handy, citywide statistics of considerable range on the economy and outlook of New York City, its boroughs, and suburbs. Data and maps are presented covering geography, population, business, labor, income, poverty, welfare, budget, prices, health, education, housing, transportation, crime, etc. The material is largely compiled from other sources.

NY114. New York (City). Criminal Justice Coordinating Council. *City of New York Criminal Justice Plan.* (111 John St., Rm. 100, New York 10038) 1971-   . Annual.

NY115. New York City Cultural Council. *New York City Resources for the Arts and Artists.* New York, 1973. 95pp.

NY116. *New York Daily Tribune Index 1906-1975.* New York: New York Tribune Assn., 1906-1975. Annual.

NY117. New York (City). Department of City Planning. *Zoning Resolution, the City of New York, Including All Amendments through May 24, 1973.* (City Planning Commission, 2 Lafayette St., New York 10007) 1973-   . 2 vols. Loose-leaf.

NY118. New York (City). Department of Commerce and Public Events. *Statistical Guide for New York City.* New York, 1958-66. Publication suspended.
This very useful summary of data gathered information from both public and private sectors and covered a great variety of topics. It unfortunately is no longer issued. Volume 1, for 1957, appeared in 1958, and the last volume was apparently number 9 for 1966.

NY119. New York (City). Department of Consumer Affairs. Consumers' Advisory Council. *How to Sue in Small Claims Court in New York City.* (80 Lafayette St., New York 10013) 1970. 27pp. Free.

NY120. New York (City). Department of Finance. *New York City Tax Guide.* (Office of Legal Affairs, 225 Broadway, New York 10007) 1976. 38pp. Free.
The pamphlet explains the major taxes and charges imposed by the city.

NY121. New York (City). Department of Health. *Vital Statistics, by Health Areas and Health Center Districts.* New York: Bureau of Health Statistics and Analysis (125 Worth St., New York 10013). Annual.
Annual statistics are given of births and deaths by cause and location. Figures are divided by age, race, and location.

NY122. New York (City). Department of Personnel. *Rules and Regulations of the Department of Personnel—City Civil Service Commission.* City Record (City Record Sales Office, 2213 Municipal Bldg., New York 10007), n.d. $8.50.

NY123. New York (City). Department of Social Services. *Directory of Services 1975: A Borough-by-Borough Listing of the Services Operated or*

Funded by the Human Resources Administration. (Department of Social Services, 250 Church St., New York 10007) 1975. 57pp.

NY124. New York (City). Department of Traffic, Bureau of Plans and Surveys. *Bridge Traffic Volumes 1975.* 1976. 252pp. (Available from: Department of Traffic, 28-11 Bridge Plaza N., Long Island City 11101.)

NY125. New York (City). Housing and Development Administration. *Analysis of Housing Supply.* (100 Gold St., New York 10038). 1969? 61L.

NY126. New York (City). Housing and Development Administration. *Annual Report.* (100 Gold St., New York 10038) 1968-   . Annual.

NY127. New York (City). Housing and Development Administration. *Neighborhood Conservation in New York City.* (100 Gold St., New York 10038) 1966. 183pp.

NY128. New York (City). Housing Authority. *Annual Fiscal Report.* (250 Broadway, New York 10007).

NY129. New York (City). Housing Authority. *Project Statistics.* (250 Broadway, New York 10007) Annual.
Title sometimes given as *Project Data.* This occasional publication presents a statistical review on city, state, and federally financed housing projects, apartments, population, value, etc. With a decline of public housing finance and construction recent issues of *Project Statistics* have not appeared.

NY130. New York (City). Human Resources Administration. *Annual Report.* (250 Church St., New York 10013) Annual.

NY131. New York (City). Human Resources Administration. *Human Resources Newsletter.* (250 Church St., New York 10013).

NY132. New York (City). Human Resources Administration. *Monthly Statistical Report.* Beginning with vol. 34, 1973-   . Previously issued as *Department of Social Services Monthly Statistical Report.* (250 Broadway, New York 10013) Free. Figures are presented on welfare and the various public assistance programs on a monthly basis. Each issue also has a quarterly summary. Data are arranged by community areas.

NY133. New York (City). Human Resources Administration. *Public Assistance Directory.* (250 Broadway, New York 10013).
Beginning in 1973 issued in five parts.

NY134. New York (City). Human Resources Administration, Office of Policy Research. *Welfare and Nonwelfare Poor in New York City.* New York: Rand Institute, 1974. 243pp.

NY135. New York (City). Law Department. *Cumulative Compilation of the Rules and Regulations of New York City Agencies, Including All Rules and Regulations Filed by Heads of Agencies in the Office of City Clerk from January 1, 1938 through February 28, 1946.* Supplement: March 1, 1946 through December 31, 1952; rev. ed. June 1967. 2 vols. New York: 1946, 1952, 1967. o.p.

The rules and regulations include administrative acts not found in the *New York City Charter and Administrative Code*. Revisions and additions are reported in *The City Record, Official Journal of the City of New York,* issued daily. This compilation has long been out of date, but is kept current by the files of the Municipal Reference and Research Center, which clips and arranges new regulations into loose-leaf volumes, the only such current record available to the public.

NY136. New York (City). League of Women Voters. *They Represent You.* Annual.
This pamphlet listing office holders contains maps showing the outlines of the city's various political districts.

NY137. New York (City). Mayor. *City of New York Federal Legislative Program 1977.* New York, January 1977. 124pp.

NY138. New York (City). Mayor. *Executive Capital Budget.* (City Record Sales Office, 2213 Municipal Bldg., New York 10007). Annual. $6.
Issued yearly, this contains the initial proposal for expenditures on capital improvements, as requested by the mayor. The volume includes tables showing prospective improvements, arranged by community. Later, after approval and amendment by the city council and Board of Estimate, the budget is reissued as the *Capital Budget,* also printed annually. Both volumes are available for sale on an individual basis, or as supplements to the annual subscription to the *City Record.*

NY139. New York (City). Mayor. *Expense Budget.* City Record (City Record Sales Office, 2213 Municipal Bldg., New York 10007). Annual. $5.50.
The *Expense Budget* shows the yearly projected expenditure for personnel, supplies, and other noncapital expenses. There are some data for individual institutions, such as hospitals, colleges, museums, etc., and a brief description of city departments is given.

NY140. New York (City). Mayor. *Expense, Revenue, and Capital Budget.* City Record (City Record Sales Office, 2213 Municipal Bldg., New York 10007), 1977- . Annual. $6.
The *Expense, Revenue, and Capital Budget,* to be issued annually, records the projected expenditures for the following year, and incorporates financial data that was formerly reported in separate volumes. It purports to contain a complete and accurate review of the city's financial condition, and contains some financial analysis of individual community districts. From time to time the City Planning Commission issues an updated version of its pamphlets, *Guide to the Capital Budget Process,* available from the commission, free.

NY141. New York (City). Mayor. *Management Plan and Report Manual.* May 1976. 100l. Charts, tables.

NY142. New York (City). Mayor. *Mayor's Management Report, Feb. 18, 1977.* (City Record Sales Office, 2213 Municipal Bldg., New York 10007) 1977. 151pp. Tables. $3.

NY143. New York (City). Mayor's Task Force on the New York City Health and Hospitals Corporation Fiscal Operations. *Report.* December 13, 1976. 153pp. Tables.

NY144. *New York Metropolitan Region Survey.* Cambridge, MA: Harvard University Press, 1959–60. 9 vols.
This series is the result of a project financed by the Ford Foundation and the Rockefeller Brothers Fund. Each volume is a monograph on a particular topic, with individual editors and authors. A volume in the series by Robert Wood, *1400 Governments*, is a leading study of governmental patterns in the New York metropolitan area.

NY145. New York (City). Model Cities Administration. *Quarterly Report.* (2 Lafayette St., New York 10007) Quarterly.

NY146. New York (City). Municipal Reference and Research Center. *Municipal Reference and Research Center Notes.* Vol. 1, 1974–1975. Monthly. Publication suspended.
This invaluable publication began in 1914 as the *Municipal Reference Library Notes*, with a modification of the title, when the library was reorganized in 1974. Each issue contained a full bibliography of recent city documents and of other publications about the city. Many special, topical bibliographies also appeared, as well as occasional short articles on the city's history. When this monthly was suspended in 1975 for budgetary reasons, it was partially replaced by an accessions list, which unfortunately was also later suspended.

NY147. New York (City). Office of Administration. *New York Urban Research Inventory.* 1969– . Loose-leaf.
This guide to research in progress on New York City urban affairs covers that undertaken both by the city, and by area universities. Unfortunately, it has been updated only infrequently.

NY148. New York (City). Office of Administration. *Organization: Executive, Staff, and Operating Agencies.* 1971. 1 vol., loose-leaf.

NY149. New York (City). Office of Collective Bargaining. *Directory of New York City Public Employee Organizations.* (250 Broadway, New York 10007), 1968/69– . Occasional.

NY150. New York (City). Office of Lower Manhattan Development. *Lower Manhattan Waterfront.* New York: City Planning Commission (2 Lafayette St., New York 10007), June 1975. 115pp. Maps, charts.
The Lower Manhattan Waterfront Development includes several major projects, including Manhattan Landing, South Street Seaport, and Battery Park City. All are discussed, as are the concepts of special zoning districts, legal and administrative frameworks, urban design controls, and zoning.

NY151. New York (City). Office of the Aging. *Directory of Services for Older New Yorkers.* (Bureau of Research, Planning and Evaluation, 250 Broadway, New York 10007) 1976. 5 parts.
This was issued as part of the series, "Facts for Action," and appeared in five parts, one for each borough.

NY152. New York (City). Office of the Comptroller. *Annual Report.* (Rm. 530, Municipal Bldg., New York 10007) Annual. Free.
The comptroller's report contains a complete review of city expenditures during the preceding year, for both capital improvements and ongoing expenses. The 1975–1976 report was issued in 1976 with 161 pages.

NY153. New York (City). Office of the Comptroller. *Comptroller's Report.* (Rm. 530, Municipal Bldg., New York 10007) 1976–   . Monthly.
This brief newsletter reviews the ongoing changes in the comptroller's office, current investigations, new accounting procedures, the city's financial condition, etc.

NY154. New York (City). Ordinances, Local Laws, etc. *New York City Charter and Administrative Code, Annotated. A Complete Text of the New York City Charter and the New York City Administrative Code with Court Decisions from the Time of the Enactment of the Code and Charter.* Albany: Williams Press, 1976. 7 numbered vols. plus index vol.
Volume 1 contains the charter of the city, and volumes 2 through 7 the administrative code, with "all the laws which have been adopted in accordance with the power of the City to enact local laws." This set does not contain the rules and regulations promulgated by individual departments of the city. At times the city charter has also been sold as a separate pamphlet by the City Record Sales Office. The charter and administrative code has been issued since 1938; the Williams Press edition offers the convenience of annotations to court decisions and a useful index. Portions of the code on specific topics have also been issued separately, i.e., the health code, and the noise control code, air pollution control code, building code, collective bargaining law, electrical code, code of ethics, etc. These separate pamphlets of individual codes are priced separately and frequently revised. They may be purchased from the City Record Sales Office, 2213 Municipal Building, New York 10007.

NY155. New York (City). Parking Violations Bureau. *Manual of Adjudication.* (475 Park Ave. S., New York 10016) 1973–   . Loose-leaf.

NY156. New York (City). Police Department. *Police Department Manual.* (1 Police Plaza, New York 10038) 1972. Loose-leaf.
The manual governs daily operating procedures and indicates proper forms, dispositions, summonses, etc., for various violations.

NY157. New York (City). Police Department. *Spring 3100.* (1 Police Plaza, New York 10038) n.d.
This newsletter is intended for staff and personnel of the police department and covers the operations and activities of the department.

NY158. *New York Port Handbook.* New York: Port Resources Information Committee, 1959.

NY159. New York Public Library. Research Libraries. *Catalog of Government Publications in the Research Libraries.* Boston, MA: G. K. Hall, 1972. 40 vols., plus supplementary vols.

NY160. New York (State). Department of Labor. *Comparative Urban Indicators of New York and Buffalo Areas.* (Labor Research Report 1973-75). Albany, August 1973.
This report compares and ranks both New York and Buffalo among the other leading cities of the United States. It includes information on general conditions (both improving and deteriorating), employment, housing, mortality, and crime.

NY161. *New York Times.* New York, 1851-   . (229 W. 43 St., New York 10036)
Daily.
The *New York Times* has from time-to-time compiled and published invaluable
statistical analyses of the city, among which are the following: racial patterns by
borough (Mar. 6, 1972); growth of poverty and welfare areas (Apr. 10, 1972); Puerto
Rican and Spanish language areas (Oct. 2, 1972); Italian areas (Feb. 4, 1973); public
school enrollment by race and district (May 29, 1973); school districts by race
(Oct. 23, 1973); racial patterns of Congressional districts (Jan. 7, 1974); crime by
precinct (Feb. 15, 1972); crime by precinct, race, income, age and welfare (July 30,
1973); city spending by district and governmental function (Nov. 13, 1972); New York
crime compared to other cities (Apr. 15, 1974); public opinions of New Yorkers
(Jan. 14-21, 1974, and later years). A considerable amount of information is also
available through the *New York Times* data bank. The newspaper is also available on microfilm. Reprints of biographical stories are available on a subscription basis.

NY162. *New York Times Index.* New York: The New York Times Co., 1913-   .
Frequency varies from 1913-1947; from 1948 to date, issued semimonthly with
annual cumulations. (Available from: Microfilming Corp. of America, 21 Harristown
Rd., Glen Rock, NJ 07452.) $125 for 24 semimonthly issues, $125 for the annual
cumulation; or for a combined subscription price of $225.

NY163. Paperno, Lloyd I., and Arthur Goldstein. *Criminal Procedure in New
York.* Amityville: Acme Law Book Co. Inc., 1971. Annual supplements.
The authors have also published in a separate volume the Penal Code of the State of
New York. Both volumes are annotated and contain a discussion of current prac-
tice, under convenient headings. Both volumes are indexed, and while covering
state law, they of course pertain to New York City.

NY164. Port Authority of New York and New Jersey. *Airport Rules and Regulations.* New York (1 World Trade Center, New York 10048).

NY165. Port Authority of New York and New Jersey. *The New York—New
Jersey Metropolitan Area Industrial Development Guide.* New York (1 World
Trade Center, New York 10048) 1971. 278pp. $10.
This volume provides an overall view of the region's economy with numerous charts
and graphs. Information is provided on markets, labor supply, education and
colleges, industries, space, land use, transportation, utilities and taxes. A directory
of municipal agencies in the three-state region that serve industry is included.

NY166. Port Authority of New York and New Jersey. *Oceanborne Foreign
Trade at the Port of New York.* New York (1 World Trade Center, New York 10048).
Annual.

NY167. Port Authority of New York and New Jersey. *A Selected Bibliography, 1921-1960.* New York (1 World Trade Center, New York 10048), September
1960.

NY168. Rasch, Joseph. *New York Landlord and Tenant Rent Control.*
Rochester: Lawyer's Cooperative Publ. Co., 1973 (with annual supplements).

NY169. *Regional Plan of New York and Its Environs.* New York, Regional
Plan of New York and Its Environs, 1929-31.

Issued in 2 volumes: vol. 1, the graphic regional plan, atlas and description (1929); vol. 2, the building of the city (1931). This is a comprehensive survey of the state of urban planning at that time, with many illustrations and maps of projects planned for and applied in New York City. Charts and statistical information are included. These volumes present many city developments in the context of their surroundings at the time of construction.

NY170. *Regional Survey of New York and Its Environs.* New York: Regional Plan of New York and Its Environs, 1927–31. 8 vols. in 10.
This major study presented an overview of the city's financial and economic condition, its industries, population, traffic and transit, recreation, public services, neighborhoods, and community planning. It is still used by researchers and analysts, though long out of date.

NY171. *Sanborn Manhattan Land Book of the City of New York.* Pelham: Sanborn Map Co., 1975. 188 plates of plans and maps.

NY172. Sayre, Wallace S., and Herbert Kaufman. *Governing New York City: Politics in the Metroplis.* New York: Russell Sage Foundation, 1960. 815pp. (W. W. Norton & Co., publishers). $2.95.
This is a classic study of New York City politics and government, with considerable historical and statistical data, compiled from a three-year investigative effort. Functions of major city departments are analyzed, as are the political parties, courts, administrative structure, and public authorities. An extensive bibliography is included. This work is now somewhat dated but has not been superceded. Tables provide older, useful statistics for comparative purposes.

NY173. Simpson, Antony E. *Guide to Library Research in Public Administration.* New York: John Jay College of Criminal Justice, Center for Productive Public Management (445 W. 59 St., New York 10019), 1976.

NY174. Smith, Thelma E. *Guide to the Municipal Government of the City of New York.* New York: Meilen Press, n.d.
This is the most useful of guidebooks to city government structure and functions. Brief history is given on the development of city agencies, with arrangement by department. Chapters are also devoted to the budget process and city legislation.

NY175. *Special Libraries Directory of Greater New York, Thirteenth Edition.* New York: Special Libraries Association, New York Chapter, 1974. 189pp. (Dorothy Kasman, Coopers & Lybrand Library, 1251 Ave. of the Americas, New York 10020). The 14th ed. (1977) has been announced at $18.
In the 1974 edition, 1,100 libraries were surveyed. The directory is arranged by broad subject, i.e., law, public administration, social science, transportation, etc. Under the name of each organization will be found the address, major subjects of the collection, size, staff, hours, interlibrary loan, and photocopying facilities and user policies. It is indexed by librarian, by name of library, and by subject.

NY176. Sternlieb, George, and James W. Hughes. *Housing and People in New York City.* New York: Department of Rent and Housing Maintenance (Housing and Development Administration, 100 Gold St., New York 10038), 1973. 290pp.

NY177. Stokes, I. N. Phelps. *The Iconography of Manhattan Island, 1498–1909: Compiled from Original Sources and Illustrated by Photo-Intaglio Reproductions of Important Maps, Plans, Views and Documents in Public and Private Collections.* New York: Robert H. Dodd, 1916–1928. 6 vols.
This is the most complete collection of factual information on the history, development, and government of Manhattan. Volumes 5 through 6 have a thorough chronology of the city, and volume 6 also contains a very detailed index with dates and a bibliography listing city archives, documents, and official records. This set is particularly useful in establishing the dates of governmental acts and decisions.

NY178. Tauber, Gilbert, and Samuel Kaplan. *The New York City Handbook.* Garden City: Doubleday & Co., 1968. 622pp. $3.95.
This extensive guidebook has a number of chapters relating to city services and provides hints for the consumer and resident on the ways for obtaining information and assistance. There are chapters on housing, property, rent, utilities, zoning, education, employment, transportation, health, city government, the courts, political parties, civic associations, ethnic groups, and community profiles.

NY179. Tri-State Transportation Commission. *Tri-State Transportation 1985: An Interim Plan.* New York (New York State Tri-State Regional Planning Commission, 1 World Trade Center, New York 10048), May 1966. Charts, maps.
The three-state area of New York, New Jersey and Connecticut is discussed in terms of projected development, land use, population, and transportation. Maps of the region are included.

NY180. U.S. Bureau of Labor Statistics, Middle Atlantic Regional office. *Poverty Area Profile.* New York, 1970. 42pp.

NY181. U.S. Bureau of Labor Statistics, Middle Atlantic Regional Office. *Professional, Administrative, Technical and Clerical Pay in New York.* (Regional report 43). New York, 1974. 98pp.

NY182. U.S. Bureau of Labor Statistics, Middle Atlantic Regional office. *A Regional Profile of Labor Force, Employment and Unemployment in 1973.* (Regional report 40). New York, September 1974. 38pp.

NY183. U.S. Bureau of Labor Statistics, Middle Atlantic Regional Office. *Socio-Economic Profile of Puerto Rican New Yorkers.* (Regional report 46). New York, July 1975. 138pp.

NY184. U.S. Bureau of Labor Statistics, Middle Atlantic Regional Office. *Wages in New York.* (Regional report 44). New York, June 1975. 52pp.

NY185. U.S. Department of Commerce, Bureau of the Census. *Employment Profiles of Selected Low-Income Areas.* Washington, DC: Government Printing Office, n.d.
Within this statistical series for metropolitan areas, New York City is covered in 11 volumes. Based on the 1970 census of population and housing, further information is given on wages, labor experience, desire for employment, population characteristics, etc. Each volume covers a different area. Issued as Census Bureau series PHC(3), the volumes pertaining to New York City are as follows:

2 New York, NY—All Survey Areas

3 New York, NY—Puerto Rican Population of Survey Areas

4 Manhattan Borough, New York City—Summary

5 Manhattan Borough, New York City—Area I

6 Manhattan Borough, New York City—Area II

7 Brooklyn Borough, New York City—Summary

8 Brooklyn Borough, New York City—Area I

9 Brooklyn Borough, New York City—Area II

10 Brooklyn Borough, New York City—Area III

11 Bronx Borough, New York City

12 Queens Borough, New York City

NY186. *Who's Who in New York (City and State): Biography in Dictionary Form of the Leaders of All Phases of Life in the Metropolis and the Commonwealth.* 13th ed. New York: Lewis Historical Publishing Co., 1960.

NY187. Williams, Sam P. *Guide to Research Collections of the New York Public Library.* Chicago, IL, 1975. 336pp.

Collections

NY188. Association of the Bar of the City of New York. 42 W. 44 St. New York 10036 (212)682-0606.
Primarily for members, this extensive law library will provide some reference service to the wider community if time permits. Founded in 1870 the law collection now numbers more than 400,000 volumes, on every aspect of law. It has a good collection of local laws, rules, regulations, and decisions.

NY189. Citizens Budget Commission. 51 E. 42 St., New York 10017.
This independent, nonprofit organization undertakes studies of municipal organization, management effectiveness, the budget process, and expenditures. It publishes a number of bulletins and research reports.

NY190. Citizens Housing and Planning Council of N.Y. 120 E. 81 St., New York 10028 (212)391-9030.
The council is a nonpartisan group for the study of housing problems and neighborhood conditions. The collection is strong on housing, social aspects of city and regional planning, discrimination, and renewal.

NY191. Citizens Union. 15 Park Row, New York 10038.
The Citizens Union is an independent study group concerned with municipal operations and administration. It publishes the newsletter, "Across from City Hall," and an annual voters' directory.

NY192. Community Council of Greater New York. 345 E. 45 St., New York 10017.
A voluntary organization of representatives from various organizations concerned with matters of social, health, and welfare service. It publishes short statements of statistical analysis on a continuing basis, and a directory of services in the New York area.

NY193. Institute of Public Administration Library. 55 W. 44 St., New York 10036 (212)661-2540.
The collection covers all areas of public administration and policy, management, metropolitan area problems, public health, civil service, municipal finance and

taxation, housing, local government, transportation, and economics. Although the New York region is emphasized, publications from and relating to other cities around the world are collected for comparative purposes.

NY194. National Municipal League. Murray Seasongood Library, 47 E. 68 St., Second Floor. New York 10021. (212)535-5700.
Government documents and trade publications on municipal and state government, and public administration.

NY195. New York (City). Department of City Planning. 2 Lafayette St., New York 10007 (212)566-7600.
At one time the department shared with other agencies a Housing and Planning Library, but that collection has been disbanded. The department publishes and disseminates many municipal reports, and occasionally issues a publications list and information guide that includes maps and plans as well as documents.

NY196. New York Municipal Reference and Research Center. Department of Records & Information Services. 2230 Municipal Bldg., New York 10007 (212) 566-4285.
Most extensive collection of New York City documents. Current and retrospective limited state documents referring to New York City. Unofficial documents by other than city mayoral agencies. Some documents from other cities. The library has been in existence since the turn of the century, and for many years operated as a branch of the New York Public Library under the name of Municipal Reference Library. Its newer name reflects reorganization as an independent city agency that now also includes the city archives as well as the city's record management services. It is the mandatory depository for all city documents, and is particularly strong in the fields of politics, history, government, and law. It regularly sorts and files all city regulations and may have the most complete such file open to the public. It formerly issued a monthly, the *Municipal Reference Library Notes*, which included an accessions list of current documents received. That unfortunately has been suspended, but the *Index to Current Urban Documents* (Greenwood Press) now includes most of the new documents published. Other strong areas of the collection include the following: extensive collection of clippings and other materials on New York City officials (biographical notebooks); file of current year New York State bills and legislation; proceedings, New York City Council and Board of Estimates; limited file of casebooks for New York City courts; New York City Community Planning Board minutes; limited collection of official reports from Old City of Brooklyn; civil lists; file on New York City committees; extensive vertical file on politics; extensive vertical file on city neighborhoods; file on city rules and regulations; extensive civil service collection including lists, civil service examinations, and announcements; large collection of Arco Civil Service books; New York City street name file (origins, history, legislation); New York City map collection (political, street, historical, etc.), New York City photograph collection; and past directories for the city (in microform and hardcopy).

NY197. New York Historical Society Library. 170 Central Park W., New York 10024 (212)873-3400.
Local documents are included in the very extensive collection of historical material. The library also has a fine collection of prints, illustrations, maps, and atlases relating to New York. The library has published a *Guide to the Manuscript Collections*, by Arthur Breton (1972). Printed and published documents held by the library are referred to in Carman and Thompson's *Guide to the Principal Sources for American Civilization, 1800-1900, in the City of New York: Printed Materials* (New York:

Columbia University Press, 1972, 630pp.) They are also referred to in Greene and Morris, *Guide to the Principal Sources for Early American History (1600–1800) in the City of New York* (New York: Columbia University Press, 1953, 400pp).

NY198. New York Public Library. The Research Libraries. Fifth Ave. and 42 St., New York 10018 (212)790-6161.
The New York Public Library has a particularly strong collection of state and municipal documents. It is a depository for the states of New York, Washington, and California, and receives most of the documents of New Jersey. Holdings for individual localities varies; the library attempts to acquire the municipal publications of all cities in the United States with a 1970 population of 400,000 or more. A statement of the collection policy is given (see entry **NY187**) in Sam Williams's *Guide to the Research Collections of the New York Public Library* (Chicago: American Library Association, 1975). The New York Public Library (see entry **NY159**) has also published the *Catalog of Government Publications in the Research Library* (Boston: G. K. Hall, 1972, 40 vols.). A dictionary catalog for the entire collection is published on a continuing, subscription basis. The Economics Division of the library houses many of the government documents, at one time a responsibility shared with the Municipal Reference Library. Today, within the New York Public Library the Economics Division has the largest group of current local documents. Since much of the compilation of Public Affairs Information Service is also done at the library, that service also reflects to some extent the holdings of the library.

NY199. New York University. Elmer Bobst Library. Documents Center. 70 Washington Sq. S., New York 10012 (212)598-7515.
Holds New York City and state documents. The Documents Center forms one of the best such collections in the state, with U.S. and international documents predominating. Local documents form a lesser part of the collection. Service is handled by specialists trained in government documents.

NY200. Regional Plan Association Library. 235 E. 45 St., New York 10017 (212)682-7750.
Holds regional planning reports, urban development, housing, transportation studies. This independent, nonprofit research organization has published a number of studies on the New York metropolitan area's growth and development. To member-subscribers it issues the *Regional Plan News*, a series of pamphlets on various planning topics. A price list of its publications is available; included are Map Series of the New York Metropolitan Region and Environs; Zoning Bulletin (quarterly); the Race for Open Space (1960); Spread City (1962); Research Bulletins (series); Man in Metropolis, the New York Metropolitan Region Study (nine volumes available through Harvard University Press); the Second Regional Plan (1964); Building Communities; High-Speed Railroads and Transportation Action; Planning the Hudson (1966); and the Transportation and Manhattan Business District (1966). The library of the association collects municipal documents, studies and trade publications from throughout the metropolitan area.

NY201. Tri-State Regional Planning Commission Library. 100 Church St., 18th Floor, New York, 10007 (212)433-4230.
Collection includes material on regional and local planning, transportation, ecology, housing, population, and land use for the New York metropolitan region. The commission issues a number of research publications, including the following series: *Technical Information Reports, Transportation and Land-use Planning Reports,* and *Grant Project Reports.* The commission is the local agency designated for the review of federal grant proposals. The library collects many studies and reports issued by municipalities in the three-state region. It issues a monthly list of library acquisitions.

NY202. **U.S. Department of Labor.** Bureau of Labor Statistics. Middle Atlantic Regional Office. 1515 Broadway, Rm. 3400, New York 10036.
The regional office collects and disseminates local data on manpower, wages, employment (including civil service), prices, housing conditions, and economic growth. It publishes occasional regional reports on economic topics. At the same address the bureau also maintains an Office of Information, Publications, and Reports.

NY203. **World Trade Information Center.** 1 World Trade Center, Suite 3311, New York 10048 (212)466-3063.
Data on ports and trade world-wide, and development plans for the New York region.

(See also entry **US4**.)

ROCHESTER

The collecting of local documents in Rochester is shared by three libraries with good contact and interchange of information between them. The University of Rochester Library (see entry **NY274**) has a documents collection that actively collects local documents. Good coverage is provided by the Local History Division of the Rochester Public Library (see entry **NY273**), which also clips local newspapers, and the private Center for Governmental Research Inc. provides excellent reference service in local government, planning, social and economic activity. As of mid-1977 the Rochester Regional Research Library Council had published its third issue of a checklist, *Local Agency Publications.* The checklist indicates issuing body, title, date, frequency, pages, source, copies, cost, and library with holdings. Presently the *Index to Current Urban Documents* provides only moderate coverage, with some omissions of special studies and monographs. For the Rochester area, the Monroe County government publications are important.

Publications

NY204. Center for Governmental Research Inc. *Assessment of Real Property in Monroe County, Summary.* Rochester (37 S. Washington St., Rochester 14608), 1975. $5.
This study has been updated by a supplement, titled "A study of assessment inequities" (1976).

NY205. Center for Governmental Research Inc. *Cable Television in Monroe County.* Rochester (37 S. Washington St., Rochester 14608), 1971. $2.

NY206. Center for Governmental Research Inc. *Central Library Services in Monroe County.* Rochester (37 S. Washington St., Rochester 14608), 1968. $4.

NY207. Center for Governmental Research Inc. *City Budget Task Force (Report).* Rochester (37 S. Washington St., Rochester 14608), 1970. Free.

NY208. Center for Governmental Research Inc. *City Finances in Perspective: Rochester, Buffalo and Syracuse, New York, 1975-76.* Rochester (37 S. Washington St., Rochester 14608), 1976. $2.

NY209. Center for Governmental Research Inc. *A Cooperative Framework for the Arts.* Rochester (37 S. Washington St., Rochester 14608), 1970. Free.

NY210. Center for Governmental Research Inc. *Criminal Offenses in Downtown Rochester.* Rochester (37 S. Washington St., Rochester 14608), 1973.

NY211. Center for Governmental Research Inc. *A Critical Review of the Property Tax System.* Rochester (37 S. Washington St., Rochester 14608), 1971. $1.

NY212. Center for Governmental Research Inc. *Demographic and Housing Characteristics Maps, City of Rochester.* Rochester (37 S. Washington St., Rochester 14608), 1973.

NY213. Center for Governmental Research Inc. *The Governance of Rochester.* Rochester (37 S. Washington St., Rochester 14608), 1973. 334pp. 28 maps. This study prepared for the Rochester Charter Commission covers governmental decision-making and managerial processes, representation, citizen participation, newer concerns of government, and charter revision. The current status and weakness of the present power structure is discussed along with alternatives for the future. The formation of community councils is advised. The report provides an effective, independent review of the municipal government structure, with emphasis on charter reform, council roles, representation, and agency housekeeping tasks.

NY214. Center for Governmental Research Inc. *Guidelines to Effective Management in Town Government.* Rochester (37 S. Washington St., Rochester 14608), 1971. $5.

NY215. Center for Governmental Research Inc. *The Monroe County Housing Market, 1970-1980.* Rochester (37 S. Washington St., Rochester 14608), 1974.

NY216. Center for Governmental Research Inc. *A Plan for Better Government in Monroe County: A Report to the Monroe County Legislature.* Rochester (37 S. Washington St., Rochester 14608), 1974.

NY217. Center for Governmental Research Inc. *A Plan for Court and Probation Services.* Rochester (37 S. Washington St., Rochester 14608), 1968. $4.

NY218. Center for Governmental Research Inc. *Regional Viability in the Southern Tier East Area.* Rochester (37 S. Washington St., Rochester 14608), 1973.

NY219. Center for Governmental Research Inc. *The State-Local Tax Structure: A Comparative Perspective.* Rochester (37 S. Washington St., Rochester 14608). 1975. $1.

NY220. Center for Governmental Research Inc. *A Study of Drug Abuse in Rochester and Monroe County.* Rochester (37 S. Washington St., Rochester 14608), 1974.

NY221. Center for Governmental Research Inc. *Planning for Comprehensive Youth Services in Monroe County.* Rochester (37 S. Washington St., Rochester 14608), 1976. 2 vols. and summary. Vol. 1 and 2, $8 each, summary, $1.

NY222. Center for Governmental Research Inc. *Tax Reform—Issues—Impacts—Alternatives.* Rochester (37 S. Washington St., Rochester 14608), 1975. $7.

NY223. Center for Governmental Research Inc. *Town Zoning and Housing Shortage.* Rochester (37 S. Washington St., Rochester 14608), 1967. $1.

NY224. Center for Governmental Research Inc. *Two-tiered Government in Monroe County, New York.* Rochester (37 S. Washington St., Rochester 14608), 1975. Free.

NY225. Center for Environmental Research. *Directory of Environmental Organization.* Albany (33 S. Washington St., Rochester 14608), 1977.

NY226. Clark, Maryanne. *Rochester Regional Research Council Union List of Serials.* Rochester, 1970. 554pp.

NY227. Economic Consultants Organization Inc. *Housing Subsidies and Municipal Finances.* Rochester: City Planning Commission, June 1974. 113pp.

NY228. Federal Writers Project, New York. *Rochester and Monroe County* [American Guide Series] New York: AMS Press, 1937 (reprinted). $25.

NY229. Genesee-Finger Lakes Regional Planning Board. *Economic Prospects of Manufacturing: A Regional Survey.* Rochester (Suite 500, Ebenezer Watts Bldg., 47 S. Fitzhugh St., Rochester 14614), 1971.

NY230. Genesee-Finger Lakes Regional Planning Board. *Housing in the Genesee-Finger Lakes Region: An Interim Report.* Rochester (Suite 500, Ebenezer Watts Bldg., 47 S. Fitzhugh St., Rochester 14614), 1971.

NY231. Genesee-Finger Lakes Regional Planning Board. *Housing Market Analysis.* Rochester (Suite 500, Ebenezer Watts Bldg., 47 S. Fitzhugh St., Rochester 14614), 1972.

NY232. Genesee-Finger Lakes Regional Planning Board. *Industrial Development: A Regional Survey.* Rochester (Suite 500, Ebenezer Watts Bldg., 47 S. Fitzhugh St., Rochester 14614), 1971.

NY233. Genesee-Finger Lakes Regional Planning Board. *Regional Economic and Demographic Analysis.* Rochester (Suite 500, Ebenezer Watts Bldg., 47 S. Fitzhugh St., Rochester 14614), 1970.

NY234. Genesee-Finger Lakes Regional Planning Board. *Senior Citizens Housing Survey, Preliminary Report.* Rochester (Suite 500, Ebenezer Watts Bldg., 47 S. Fitzhugh St., Rochester 14614), 1971.

NY235. Genesee-Finger Lakes Regional Planning Board. *Social Services: A Regional Survey.* Rochester (Suite 500, Ebenezer Watts Bldg., 47 S. Fitzhugh St., Rochester 14614), 1970.

NY236. Harland Bartholomew and Assoc. *A Major Street Plan for Rochester New York.* St. Louis, MO, 1929.

NY237. McGuire, Marion. *Index to Newspapers Published in Rochester, New York, 1818-1897.* Rochester: Rochester Public Library.
This is the result of a project of the U.S. National Youth Administration. Copies are held by the University of Rochester and the Rochester Public Library.

NY238. McKelvey, Blake. *Rochester on the Genesee.* (New York State Studies) Syracuse: Syracuse University Press, 1973. 292pp. $7.50.

NY239. Malo, Paul. *Landmarks of Rochester and Monroe County.* Syracuse: Syracuse University Press, 1974. 276pp. $15.

NY240. Monroe County Metropolitan Arts Resource Committee. *The Role of Arts Organizations in Monroe County.* Rochester, 1976. 20pp.

NY241. Monroe County. Board of Elections. *Official Canvass of Monroe County.* Rochester, 1969- .

NY242. Monroe County. County Manager and County Budget Director. *Monroe County Budget Plan.* Rochester. Annual.

NY243. Monroe County. County Manager. *Proposed Budget for the County of Monroe.* Rochester: County Manager's Office. Annual.

NY244. Monroe County. Human Relations Committee. *Report.* Rochester. Annual.

NY245. Monroe County. Legislature. *Directory of County, Towns, and City Officials.* Rochester, 1977. 40pp.
The University of Rochester Library holds issues for 1967-1977.

NY246. Monroe County. Legislature. *Proceedings of the Legislature of the county of Monroe.* Rochester. Annual.

NY247. Monroe County. Office for the Aging. *Annual Report.* Rochester. Annual.

NY248. Monroe County. Planning Council. *Housing Population.* Rochester, 1969- .

NY249. New York (State). Department of Commerce. *Business Fact Book, 1971-72; Part 1, Business and Manufacturing; Rochester Area.* Albany, 1972. 27pp.

NY250. New York (State). Department of Commerce. *Business Fact Book, 1974: Part 2, Profile of People, Jobs and Housing: Rochester Area.* Albany, 1974.

NY251. New York (State). Department of Commerce. *Business Fact Book, 1976: Part 1, Profile of Business and Industry, Rochester Area.* Albany, 1976.

NY252. Osborne, Florence. *Rochester, New York: A Check List of Official Publications.* Rochester: Rochester Public Library, 1935.

NY253. Rochester. *Code of the City of Rochester.* Spenceport: General Code Publishers Corporation, 1966. 2 vols. with amendments and supplements.

NY254. Rochester. Board of Education. *Official Proceedings of the Board of Education of the City of Rochester.* Tables, index. Annual.

NY255. Rochester. City Council. *Proceedings of the Council of the City of Rochester.* Annual.

NY256. *Rochester City Directory.* Boston, MA: R. L. Polk & Co. $80.

NY257. Rochester. City Manager. *Budget.* Annual (for fiscal year).
The budget of the city manager (previously of the city administrator) covers fiscal year, and includes organization charts with descriptions of departmental functions.

NY258. Rochester. City School District. *Budget of the Public Schools of Rochester.* Annual (for fiscal year).

NY259. Rochester. Community Services Coordination. *Directory of Advisory-Review Boards and Commissions. Updates.* 1976. 40pp.

NY260. Rochester. Community Services Coordination. *Rochester Neighborhood Association List.* February 1977.

NY261. Rochester, Comptroller. *Budget of the City of Rochester.* Annual (for fiscal year).

NY262. Rochester. Department of Community Development, Planning Bureau. *An Analysis of the Housing Assistance Needs of Lower Income Households and Characteristics of Selected Other Household Groups.* February 1976. 90pp.

NY263. Rochester. Department of Community Development. *Preliminary Capital Improvement Program: 1976-1982.* March 1976. 88pp. and appendixes.

NY264. Rochester. Department of Community Development. *Rochester Facts and Facets.* June 1976. $1.80.

NY265. Rochester Metropolitan Area League of Women Voters. *Local Governments, Rochester—Monroe County.* Washington, DC: League of Women Voters Education Fund, 1971.

NY266. Rochester Metropolitan Area League of Women Voters. *Productivity, Local Government and You.* Rochester, 1976. 20pp.

NY267. Rochester. Personnel Department. *1974 Monroe County Employment Directory.* 1974. 50pp.

NY268. *Rochester Suburban Directory.* Boston, MA: R. L. Polk. $80.

NY269. Rochester Times-Union. *Fifty Years of Growth.* Rochester, 1968.
This forms part of the "Collection of newspapers relating to centennial celebrations and histories of United States localities," reel 22 no. 4, held by the New York Public Library.

NY270. United Community Chest of Greater Rochester Inc. *Coordination and Centralization of Day Care Services in the Greater Rochester Area, March 1975-April 1976. Final Report, Vol. 1.* Rochester, 1976. 118pp.

NY271. United Community Chest of Greater Rochester Inc. *Directory of Community Service.* Rochester, 1974. $3.

Collections

NY272. Center for Governmental Research Inc. 33 S. Washington St., Rochester 14608.
The Center is an independent, nonpartisan group, originally founded in 1915 by

George Eastman as the Rochester Bureau of Municipal Research. The Center conducts urban research in the area, often under contract by city government as well as the private sector. The Center has issued a number of studies on matters of current community concern in the Rochester area. Its library has a good collection of local documents for the region that are of ongoing reference value or interest, particularly in regard to present-day problems. Local documents are also gathered from other areas on an occasional basis for comparative purposes. The Center has a professional staff trained in various fields of planning, economics, etc. The Center is a good source for census and other statistical data.

NY273. Rochester Public Library. Local History Division. 115 South Ave., Rochester 14604.
The Rochester Public Library maintains a wide range of important local documents and publications available for reference in the Local History Division. The division also has a clipping file from 1937 to date. In 1935 the library issued a checklist of official publications. It has also compiled an index to newspapers in Rochester (1818–1897).

NY274. University of Rochester Library. Documents Section. River Campus. Rochester 14627.
Current documents on Rochester area government and politics are collected, including those of the Board of Education, the city budget, codes, laws, etc. The official canvass of votes are held from 1969, the county budget from 1964, a directory of county, town, and city officials for Monroe County from 1967, etc.

SCHENECTADY

Schenectady does not participate in the *Index to Current Urban Documents*, or any other comprehensive listing of local documents. Nonetheless, its documents (largely of serial nature) are actively collected by several libraries within the city. A guide to the municipal records of Schenectady has been published by the State University of New York at Albany (see entry **NY275**), and it locates holdings of documents in more than 60 official bodies.

Publications

NY275. State University of New York at Albany. School of Library and Information Science. *Schenectady County: A Guide to the Municipal Records.* Albany (School of Library and Information Science, State University of New York, 1400 Washington Ave., Albany, 12222), 1977. 136pp $2.
This guide was prepared by students in a graduate seminar on municipal documents. It lists agencies and departments of the county of Schenectady, the city of Schenectady, the various towns and villages, school districts, churches and other nonmunicipal organizations of the area. For each agency there is given the address and a detailed list of holdings. Unpublished records are not distinguished from printed documents. A glossary and charts of government structure are appended.

Collections

NY276. City Hall History Library. City Hall. Jay St., Schenectady 12305 (518)382-5088.
Some documents may circulate. The library houses a collection of tape recordings, and an extensive collection of city directories from 1855. The city archives collection also includes 160 volumes of photographs. Holdings include annual

reports and budgets of the city from 1906, *Proceedings of the Board of Estimate and Apportionment* (1918-1964), city charters (*Rules of Order of the Common Council and Municipal Statistics*, 1905-1955), minutes of the city court, various reports of the City Planning Commission, the *Annual Directory of Officers and Teachers* (of the City School District, 1915-1957), the various building, housing, and plumbing codes, *Minutes of the Common Council* (1798 to present), *Proceedings of the Common Council* (1854-1959), various maps, and directories of officials. Annual reports are filed from the City Planning Commission, and the Departments of Health, Water, and Police.

NY277. Schenectady County Historical Society. 32 Washington Ave., Schenectady 12305. (518)374-0263.
The library maintains a collection of city and county municipal documents, records of various churches, city directories (from 1857) and a collection of manuscripts and legal papers. Among the city documents are city charters, *Proceedings of the Common Council*, various account books and financial records, tax records, and records of the school districts.

NY278. Schenectady County Public Library. Main Branch. Liberty and Clinton St., Schenectady 12305. (518)382-3511.
Schenectady documents are collected as part of the reference collection. Single copies do not circulate, although they may be duplicated. Holdings include the annual reports of the city from 1937, the *Proceedings of the Board of Representatives* (1860-1974), county and city budgets,city charters, *Common Council Proceedings* (1908 to present), ordinances and directories. Annual reports are received and filed from the Boards of Health and Education, fire commissioners, and the Departments of Engineering and Public Works, Finance, Health, Water, etc.

NY279. Union College Library. Union St., Schenectady 12305. (518)370-6281.
The library has a collection of laws and ordinances, city directories (from 1841), enrollments of voters, *Proceedings of the Board of Estimate and Apportionment* (1904-35), *Proceedings of the Board of Representatives*, *Proceedings of the Board of Supervisors* (1860-1965), *Common Council Proceedings* (1854-1937), building and fire codes, miscellaneous reports of the City Planning Commission, *Bulletins* of the Bureau of Municipal Research, and various annual reports of city departments.

SYRACUSE

The Onondaga County Public Library (see entry **NY308**) maintains one of the few collections of Syracuse documents, and also collects state publications that relate to the local Syracuse area, including *Manpower Trends, Employment Trends,* and *Syracuse Labor Area Summary*. For additional economic information the library also collects "local job-flow fiches," on a daily and monthly basis, as well as reports from local analysts. The *Index to Current Urban Documents* is relied on for coverage of official publications although the number of entries has not been great. No bibliography of local documents has been published.

Publications

NY280. Center for Governmental Research Inc. *City Finances in Perspective: Rochester, Buffalo and Syracuse, New York, 1975-76.* Rochester (37 S. Washington St., Rochester 14608), 1976. $2.

NY281. Central New York Regional Planning and Development Board. *Annual Report.* Syracuse. Annual.

NY282. Central New York Regional Planning and Development Board. *Environmental Resources Management Handbook.* Syracuse, 1973. 41pp.
With charts, maps and tables, this provides a useful guide to those interested in the protection of environmental resources.

NY283. Citizen's Advisory Committee to Study Libraries in Onondaga County. *Library Services in Onondaga County: A Report.* Syracuse, 1973. 22l. Map, organization charts, tables.

NY284. Frederickson, H. George. *Power, Public Opinion and Policy in a Metropolitan Community.* New York, 1973. 184pp.

NY285. Freeman, Linton G. *Patterns of Local Community Leadership.* Indianapolis, IN: Bobbs-Merrill, 1968. 138pp. $4.

NY286. Governmental Research Bureau. *Robbery Cases in the City of Syracuse: A Report to the Greater Syracuse Chamber of Commerce.* Syracuse, 1970. 41pp. Bibliography.

NY287. New York (State). Department of Commerce. *Business Fact Book, 1972: Part 1, Business and Manufacturing, 1971-72, Syracuse Area.* Albany (Gift and Exchange Section, New York State Library, Albany. 12234), 1972. 24pp. Tables, charts. Free.

NY288. New York (State). Department of Commerce. *Business Fact Book, 1974: Part 2, Profile of People, Jobs, and Housing, Syracuse Area.* Albany (Gift and Exchange Section, New York State Library, Albany 12234), 1974. Free.

NY289. New York (State). Department of Commerce. *Business Fact Book, 1976: Part 1, Profile of Business and Industry, Syracuse Area.* Albany (Gift and Exchange Section, New York State Library, Albany 12234). 1976. Free.

NY290. Onondaga County. Clerk. *Annual Report.* Syracuse. Annual. Tables.

NY291. Onondaga County. Comptroller. *Annual Report for the Fiscal Year....* Syracuse. Annual. Tables.

NY292. Onondaga County. Health Department, Bureau of Vital Statistics. *Annual Report.* Syracuse. Annual. Tables.

NY293. Onondaga County. Legislature. *Journal.* Syracuse. Annual.

NY294. Onondaga County. Library System. *Annual Report.* Syracuse. Annual.

NY295. Onondaga County. Probation Department. *Annual Report.* Syracuse. Annual. Tables, organization charts.

NY296. Syracuse. Budget Administration. *Annual Budget of the City of Syracuse for the year. . . .* Syracuse. Annual. Tables.

NY297. Syracuse. Common Council. *Proceedings for the Fiscal Year.* Syracuse. Annual. Index, photographs, tables.
Includes the annual budget of the city of Syracuse.

NY298. Syracuse. Department of Engineering. *Annual Report of the City Engineer.* Syracuse. Annual. Charts, tables.

NY299. Syracuse. Department of Finance. *Annual Report of the Commissioner of Finance.* Syracuse. Annual. Tables.

NY300. Syracuse. Department of Transportation. *Annual Report.* Syracuse. Annual. Figures, tables.

NY301. Syracuse. Fire Department. *Annual Report.* Syracuse. Annual. Tables.

NY302. Syracuse. Human Rights Commission of Syracuse and Onondaga County. *Annual Report.* Syracuse. Annual. Tables.

NY303. Syracuse. Mayor. *Annual Report.* Syracuse. Annual. Tables.
Issues may include a brief description of departmental organization and functions.

NY304. Syracuse. Mayor's Long-range Capital Improvement Committee. *City of Syracuse Capital Improvement Program, 1975-1980.* Syracuse, 1974. Tables.

NY305. Syracuse Metropolitan Area. League of Women Voters. *Patterns of Government in Onondaga County, New York.* Syracuse (Midtown Plaza, 700 E. Water St., Syracuse). Free.

NY306. Syracuse. Public Library. *Annual Report.* Syracuse. Annual.

NY307. Syracuse-Onondaga County Planning Agency. *Job Accessibility.* Syracuse, 1969. 31pp.

Collections

NY308. **Onondaga County Public Library.** 335 Montgomery St., Syracuse 13202.
Within the library economic, employment, and budgetary data are collected by the Business and Industrial Department, while annual reports of city departments, council proceedings, and studies on metropolitan area government are collected by the Local History and Genealogy Department.

NY309. **Onondaga Historical Association.** 311 Montgomery St., Syracuse 13202.

UTICA

Data not available at this time.

YONKERS

There are no locally produced checklists or bibliographies of Yonkers documents. Some are collected by the Yonkers Public Library (see entry **NY339**), which also compiles an unpublished directory to city government. Some of the local publications are listed in the *Index to Current Urban Documents.*

Publications

NY310. International Association of Chiefs of Police, Field Operations Division. *A Survey of the Police Department, Yonkers, NY.* Gaithersburg, MD (11 First Field Rd., Gaithersburg 20760), 1971.

NY311. New York Study Team. *Occupational Education for Youth in the City of Yonkers.* New York: New York University School of Education, 1968.

NY312. Steigman, Arnold L. *Mayor-Council Government: Yonkers, New York, 1908-39: A Study of Failure and Abandonment.* New York: New York University Graduate School of Public Administration, 1967.

NY313. Yonkers. *Application to the Department of Housing and Urban Development for a Grant to Plan a Comprehensive Model Cities Program.* Yonkers, 1968.

NY314. Yonkers. *$83,660,000 General Obligation Serial Bonds, 1976.* New York: Hawkins, Delafield and Wood, 1977.
Contains a review of the city's financial condition.

NY315. Yonkers. *Records of the Town of Yonkers, New York; Minutes of Town Meetings, 1820-1852. Transcribed by Fred C. Haacker.* 1955. 43pp. Typescript at New York Public Library.

NY316. Yonkers. Board of Education. *Yonkers Public Schools Superintendent's Recommended 1974/75 Education Plan and Budget and 1974/75-1978/79 Capital Improvement Program.* Yonkers, 1974.

NY317. Yonkers. City Manager. *Operating and Capital Budget.* Yonkers. Annual.
There are separate issues for the proposed and operating budgets, both being issued annually for the fiscal year, with charts and tables. Organization charts and a description of departmental functions are also included. The city manager also publishes the Capital Improvement Plan.

NY318. Yonkers. City Planning Board. *City of Yonkers Neighborhood Analysis, Report 4.* Yonkers, 1975.

NY319. Yonkers. City Planning Board. *Yonkers Major Thoroughfare Plan, Report 6.* Yonkers, 1970.

NY320. Yonkers. City Planning Board. *Yonkers Master Plan: Report Number 2 and 3, Land Use and Community Facilities Plan.* Yonkers, 1970.

NY321. Yonkers. Common Council. *Code of the City of Yonkers, New York.* Spencersport: General Code Publishers Corporation, 1967. 2 vols.

NY322. Yonkers. Department of Assessment and Taxation. *Assessment Department, Horizons on Display, 1776-1976, Land and Building Information System.* Yonkers: Department of Development, 1976.

NY323. Yonkers. Department of Development. *Economic Study of the City of Yonkers.* (53 S. Broadway, Yonkers 10701) 1973.

NY324. Yonkers. Department of Development. *Getty Square Development Program.* (53 S. Broadway, Yonkers 10701) 1973.

NY325. Yonkers. Department of Development. *Hudson Riverfront Program, Report Number 9.* (53 S. Broadway, Yonkers 10701) November, 1973. 31pp. illus., figures, maps.

NY326. Yonkers. Department of Development. *Land Use and Waterfront Development.* (53 S. Broadway, Yonkers 10701) n.d.

NY327. Yonkers. Department of Development. *Policies for Future Land Development.* (53 S. Broadway, Yonkers 10701) 1977.

NY328. Yonkers. Department of Development. *Policies for Housing, Development and Preservation.* (53 S. Broadway, Yonkers 10701) 1977.

NY329. Yonkers. Department of Development. *Population and Housing Trends.* (53 S. Broadway, 10701) 1972.

NY330. Yonkers. Department of Development. *Statistical Information by Census Tract, Department of Development Report 8.* Yonkers (53 S. Broadway, Yonkers 10701), August 1973. Stapled. 55pp. maps.
Data are arranged by census tract for population and housing characteristics and such social indices as overcrowding, crime rates, welfare cases, drug and youth arrests, and health statistics.

NY331. Yonkers. Department of Development. *Yonkers City Center, Summary Report and Addendum Report.* (53 S. Broadway, Yonkers 10701) 1973.

NY332. Yonkers. Department of Health. *Annual Statistical Report, 1970.* Yonkers, 1971.

NY333. Yonkers. Department of Public Safety. *Annual Report.* Yonkers. Annual. Tables.

NY334. Yonkers. Office of the Comptroller. *Annual Financial Report for the Year Ended. . . .* Yonkers. Annual. Tables.

NY335. Yonkers Public Schools. *Policies, Regulations, By-Laws, Yonkers Public Schools.* New London, CT: Croft Publications (current).

NY336. Yonkers. Task Force for Quality Education. *Profile of the Yonkers Public Schools District.* Yonkers, 1976. 38l. Tables.

NY337. Yonkers. Youth Services Agency. *Annual Report.* Yonkers. Annual.

NY338. Yonkers. Youth Services Agency, Research Bureau. *Youth Crime: A Survey of Youth Arrests in Yonkers During 1974.* Yonkers, 1976. 84l., maps, tables.

Collections

NY339. Yonkers Public Library. Reference Department. 70 S. Broadway, Yonkers 10701.
The Yonkers Public Library collects city documents. It also maintains a nonpublished file that serves as a directory of agencies, functions, and officials (the *Yonkers Government Manual*). The Reference Department of the library keeps a clipping file of Yonkers information from local newspapers.

NORTH CAROLINA

Collections

NC1. **University of North Carolina at Chapel Hill.** Wilson Library, Chapel Hill 27514 (919)933-1326. Teletype Service: (510)920-0760.
Publications from all cities in the state are collected. The library staff clips local and state-wide newspapers daily for a clipping file relating to North Carolina and North Carolinians.

CHARLOTTE
Publications

NC2. Charlotte. *Annual Budget, 1975–76.* n.p.

NC3. Charlotte. Public Service and Information Office. *Around City Hall.* Monthly.

NC4. Charlotte-Mecklenburg County. Board of Education. *Charlotte-Mecklenburg School's Directory 1975/76.*

Collections

NC5. **Public Library of Charlotte and Mecklenburg County.** 310 N. Tryon St., Charlotte 28202 (704)374-2725.
A limited number of municipal documents are collected by the Carolina Room (a reference area for both local history and genealogy), but municipal publications are not automatically distributed to libraries; they are difficult to acquire. The staff of the Carolina Room selectively clips from the newspaper and files the clippings by subject. Usually annual budgets, financial reports, school directories, and minutes of the County Board of Commissioners are the basic items collected. The public library issues *Local Government Documents Received by the Public Library* of Charlotte and Mecklenburg County, which is an annual sheet of acquisitions.

DURHAM

Local Newspaper Indexing: The Perkins Library of Duke University, Durham 27706 (Newspaper and Microforms Department) indexes the *Durham Morning Herald-Sun.* The index, which was begun in 1930, is limited in scope to Duke and the Durham area.

Publications

NC6. Durham. *Annual Financial Report.* n.p. Annual.
Shows municipal expenditures for the fiscal year.

NC7. Durham. Inter-Agency Forum. *Directory of Community Services.*
1973. 65pp. Irregular.
This helpful, but dated, directory lists services available to residents of and visitors
to Durham County.

NC8. *Durham North Carolina.* Woodland Hills, CA: Windsor Publications
1977. 64pp. Free to libraries. (Available from: Greater Durham Chamber of Commerce, P.O. Box 610, Durham 27702.)
This colorful booklet gives an up-to-date picture of life in Durham through the
eyes of the business community. It is meant to encourage commercial development but also gives a good picture of social and economic life in the city. There is
a brief sketch on the mechanics of local government.

GREENSBORO

Local Newspaper Indexing: The local history librarian of the Greensboro Public
Library (see entry **NC12**) indexes the *Greensboro Daily News* and the *Greensboro
Record.* Done in index card format, the indexing is selective and focuses on
Greensboro, Guilford County, and North Carolina, in that order. Queries will be
accepted.

Publications

NC9. *Cross-Reference Directory, Greater Greensboro, High Point, Gib-
sonville, Guilford College, Julian, Liberty, Monticello, Summerfield, Randle-
man, Thomasville.* Independence, KS: City Pub. Co., 1974.
This includes a street section with listings of resident by street and numbers, a
rural route list with maps and descriptors for each city, and a numerical listing by
telephone number.

NC10. Greensboro. Chamber of Commerce. *Greensboro Atlas.* 3rd ed. 1974.
$2.50.
The atlas has maps of the city and covers schools, parks, community facilities,
etc.

NC11. Greensboro. Chamber of Commerce. Council on Research. *Directory
of Firms in Greensboro, North Carolina, Employing 100 or More Persons.*
1976. 28pp.
Name, address, telephone number, and number of employees for each firm are
given.

Collections

NC12. Greensboro Public Library. P.O. Drawer X-4, Greensboro 27402
(919)373-2471.
The library collects the city code; code of technical ordinances; annual reports of
some city departments, boards, and commissions; the budget; city council minutes; special reports prepared by or for departments and agencies of the city;
and city maps.

RALEIGH

Data not available at this time.

WINSTON-SALEM

Publications

NC13. *Cross-Reference Directory, Greater Winston-Salem.* Independence, KS: City Pub. Co., 1971.
See abstract for entry **NC9**.

NC14. Greater Winston-Salem Chamber of Commerce. *Winston-Salem and Forsyth County Pocket Library.* 3rd ed. 1972. 54pp.

NC15. Hill's Winston-Salem (North Carolina) City Directory. *Winston-Salem (Forsyth County, North Carolina) City Directory.* Richmond, VA. Annual. $80. A buyer's guide and classified business directory, alphabetical directory, street directory, and numerical telephone directory are included.

NC16. *Winston-Salem, North Carolina.* Woodland Hills, CA: Windsor Publications, c.1975. 104pp. (Available from: Winston-Salem Chamber of Commerce.) This booklet gives a recent picture of life in the city through the eyes of the business community. It is meant to encourage commercial development but also gives a good picture of social and economic life in Winston-Salem.

NORTH DAKOTA

General Publications

ND1. North Dakota League of Cities. *Directory of North Dakota City Officials, 1976-78.* Bismarck (P.O. Box 2235, Bismarck 58501) 64pp. Biennial. $5.
Contains population figures from the 1970 Census, indicates 1975 taxable valuation, and identifies major municipal officials for each of North Dakota's incorporated cities.

ND2. University of North Dakota. Bureau of Governmental Affairs. *Officials in North Dakota, 1977-78.* Edited by Denise Laugtug. Grand Forks. (Grand Forks 58202). 166pp. Biennial.
In the area pertaining directly to municipalities, the publication names each city's mayor and auditor, providing telephone numbers. For the larger cities, additional officials are listed. The directory also includes sections on local school administrators, municipal park districts, fire districts, and librarians.

BISMARCK

The single most significant weakness with city documents is accessibility; between the community development office, city hall, and the public library there has been no coordinated effort to insure public access to documents through a local depository. The city lacks a government handbook, a detailed guide to city services, and a checklist of its publications.

Publications

ND3. Bismarck. City Commission. *Citizens Report 1977.* City Hall (609 E. Thayer, Bismarck 58505), 1977. Annual. 23pp.
This supplement to the daily newspaper reviews city operations, personnel, services, problems, trends, and plans.

ND4. Bismarck. City Commission. *City of Bismarck, North Dakota Annual Report.* City Hall (609 E. Thayer, Bismarck 58505). Annual.
First the report summarizes the city's financial condition with particular reference to current and projected programs. Then it develops in detail the proposed budget, tax levy, and estimated expenditure for the coming year.

ND5. Bismarck. City Commission. *City of Bismarck, North Dakota Park District Annual Report.* Compiled by the clerk of the park board. City Hall (609 E. Thayer, Bismarck 58505). Annual.

The report provides a review of the budget for the city parks and details expenditure estimates for the upcoming year.

ND6. Bismarck. Ordinances, Local Laws, etc. *Code of Ordinances, Bismarck, North Dakota.* City Hall (609 E. Thayer, Bismarck 58505), 1973- . $35.
The municipal code lists present city officials and has a subject index and code comparative table used for locating revised ordinances.

ND7. Veterans Memorial Public Library. *Area Information Directory for the Citizens of Bismarck and the Surrounding Area.* Bismarck (520 Ave. A East, Bismarck 58501), 1976. 51pp. Free.
A subject index identifies general problem areas and then references the local, county, state, or federal agency that offers services correspondent to the need. The second part of the directory furnishes a list of civic groups and their contacts in Bismarck.

Collections

ND8. Bismarck City Hall. 609 E. Thayer Ave., Bismarck 58501 (701)223-4170.
Because each city department has its own internal library, locating city publications is a matter of personal contact and really cannot be done conveniently without some knowledge of government operations. The most centralized library is fairly new and as of now only somewhat organized. The public library maintains no municipal reference besides the municipal code.

FARGO

Data not available at this time.

OHIO

General Publications

OH1. Crowley, Joseph H. *Ohio Municipal Law: Procedure and Forms.* Revised by John E. Gotherman. Cleveland: Banks-Baldwin Pub Co., 1975. 3 vols.
Describes the law regulating Ohio municipal corporations. It includes the differences between charter and noncharter cities and references to constitutional provisions, statutes, administrative regulations, and law cases.

OH2. Gotherman, John E. *Gotherman's Guide: A Handbook for Municipal Councilmen.* Cincinnati: W. H. Anderson Co., 1962; Supplement, 1966.
Describes the powers, duties, and authority of members of legislative bodies in municipalities. The handbook is intended to supplement the Ohio Revised Code with explanations intended for individuals in towns and cities which operate under the statutory plan of government.

OH3. Gotherman, John E. *Gotherman's Ohio Municipal Service.* Cleveland: Banks-Baldwin Pub. Co., 1976- . Loose-leaf. Quarterly.
Updates Crowley's *Ohio Municipal Law* (1975 revision by Gotherman) including laws enacted and revised, administrative rules, court decisions, ethics commission opinions, attorney general's opinions, federal laws and regulations, model ordinances and suggested ordinances, legal forms, and status of current legislation.

OH4. Ohio. Attorney General's Office. *Charitable Foundations Directory of Ohio.* 2nd ed. Columbus: Department of Attorney General (30 E. Broad St., Columbus 43215), 1975. 135pp.
Contains an alphabetical list of those charitable foundations that reported to the Ohio attorney general.

OH5. Ohio. Auditor of State. *Compatible and Incompatible Offices in State and Local Government.* Columbus (State House, Columbus 43215), 1973. 40pp.
A list of references to cases of compatibility and incompatibility of offices that have been ruled by the attorney general with citations to the relevant volumes of the opinions of the attorney general. Intended to be used as a reference for cases in which individuals hold more than one position.

OH6. Ohio. Auditor of State. *Financial Report: Ohio Cities.* Columbus (State House, Columbus 43215). Annual.
This report consists of fiscal data for each of Ohio's cities. Receipts for taxes and other revenue and expenditures by program are listed as well as nongovernmental and other expenditures.

OH7. Ohio. Auditor of State. *Financial Report: Ohio Villages.* Columbus (State House, Columbus 43215). Annual.
This report consists of fiscal data for those Ohio municipalities that operate under the village form of government. Receipts for taxes and other revenue and expenditures by program are listed as well as nongovernmental and other expenditures.

OH8. Ohio. Chamber of Commerce. *Chambers of Commerce in Ohio, 1976.* Columbus (17 S. High St., Eighth Floor, Columbus 43215), 25pp. $5.20.
An alphabetically arranged directory of Chambers of Commerce, with address, telephone number, and the name of a contact person.

OH9. Ohio. Department of Development. *Model Subdivision Regulations.* Columbus, 1971. 71pp.
Includes subdivision regulations which will guide municipal, county, and regional planning commissions in the state. The regulations must be modified to meet local needs.

OH10. Ohio. Department of Development. Planning Division. *Model Zoning Regulations.* Columbus, 1971. 123pp.
Consists of recommended zoning regulations applicable to municipal, county, and regional planning commissions, which may be modified to suit local needs.

OH11. Ohio. Department of Education. *Ohio Educational Directory.* Columbus (65 S. Front St., Columbus 43215), 1908– . Annual.
Covers departmental personnel, related organizations, and institutions in the state approved for teacher education. It lists schools and their officials by school district.

OH12. Ohio. League of Women Voters. *Know Your Ohio Government.* 2nd ed. Columbus, 1973. 115pp.
A guide to state and local government organization and operation.

OH13. Ohio Municipal Advisory Council. *Maps of 88 Ohio Counties Showing Public School Districts as of July 1, 1973.* Cleveland, 1973.
This publication, a revision of the 1968 edition, includes changes in school district boundaries.

OH14. Ohio. Secretary of State. *Ohio Election Statistics, the General Election. . . .* Columbus (State Office Tower, 30 E. Broad St., Columbus 43215). Biennial.
Registration, primary and general election statistics by county or district, township and city or village.

OH15. Ohio. Secretary of State. *Ohio Roster of Municipal and Township Officers and Members of Boards of Education.* Columbus: F. J. Heer Print Co. (Available from: Secretary of State, State Office Tower, 30 E. Broad St., Columbus 43215.)
Lists officers of municipal, township, and county governments. Also includes county court and municipal judges and boards of education.

OH16. Yon, Paul D. *Guide to County and Municipal Records for Urban Research.* Columbus: Ohio Historical Society, 1973. 216pp.
The purpose of the guide is to assist researchers in locating specific records. In 1970 the Ohio Historical Society formed a network of American History Research Centers, dividing the state into eight geographic areas for the purpose of records preservation. Records are listed by county and the location is given for each record series.

Collections

OH17. **Kent State University Libraries.** Kent 44242 (216)672-2670. Teletype Service: (810)431-2335.
The library's planning report collecton consists primarily of materials for northeastern Ohio. There are reports for other cities and for regional planning agencies in Ohio and other selected cities and agencies in the nation. There is a complete set of reports of the Tri-County Regional Planning Agency and its successor, the Northeast Four-County Regional Planning Organization. There is also a collection of Cleveland reports ranging from those of the old Cleveland Metropolitan Planning Commission to the Cleveland Seven-County Planning Organization and the present Northeastern Ohio Areawide Coordinating Agency.

AKRON

Publications

OH18. Akron Regional Development Board. *Akron Area Business Patterns.* (One Cascade Plaza, Eighth Floor, Akron 44308). Monthly.
This newsletter focuses each issue on a particular local or regional economic or business problem. Topics covered include unemployment, inflation, and annual economic reviews. The presentations include both text and statistics and are drawn from a wide variety of sources.

OH19. Health Systems Agency of Summit-Portage County. *Summit County Health Services Directory.* 1976. 54pp.
Provides information on services of health-related agencies, institutions, and organizations.

OH20. United Community Council. *Services and Referral Manual.* Akron, 1971. 174pp.
Lists service agencies, both governmental and private, in the health and welfare field for Akron and Summit County.

CANTON

Publications

OH21. Canton. City Planning Commission. Community Renewal Program, and City Planning Associates Inc. *Background for Community Renewal.* Mishawaka, IN: City Planning Associates, 1970. 109pp.
Covers the administrative organization of the city of Canton; a review of the legislative enactments, codes and ordinances concerning the renewal process; and an appraisal of the financial structure and capabilities of the city.

OH22. Canton. City Planning Department. Community Renewal Program, and City Planning Associates Inc. *Broadening Minority Opportunities.* Mishawaka, IN: City Planning Associates, 1971. 134pp. (Available from: City Planning Department, City Hall, Canton 44702).
Identifies minority problems in the areas of employment, education, economics, and housing; and compares these problems to local solutions.

OH23. Canton. City Planning Department. Community Renewal Program, and City Planning Associates Inc. *Canton, Ohio Community Renewal Program*

Urban Renewal Plan: Final Report. Mishawaka, IN: City Planning Associates, 1972. 46pp.
Summarizes the findings and recommendations of 14 preliminary reports.

OH24. Canton. City Planning Commission. Community Renewal Program, and City Planning Associates Inc. *A Physical Inventory.* Mishawaka, IN: City Planning Associates, 1971. 75pp. (Available from: City Planning Department, City Hall, Canton 44702.)
Presents an inventory and analysis of the physical conditions which exist in the city of Canton. There is also a review of the physical facilities provided by various units of local government and semipublic agencies in the city. The report includes an analysis and evaluation of a broad range of physical factors such as land use, structural conditions, environmental conditions, community facilities, and utilities.

OH25. Canton. City Planning Department. Community Renewal Program, and City Planning Associates Inc. *Social Characteristics.* Mishawaka, IN: City Planning Associates, 1970. 93pp. (Available from: City Planning Department, City Hall, Canton 44702.)
Concerns the social aspects of the community and presents data concerning the socioeconomic characteristics of the population, their housing, and characteristics of social disorganization in the community. The purpose of the report is to identify areas of the city in which critical socioeconomic and physical problems are apparent, as well as to indicate potential problem areas.

OH26. Greater Canton Chamber of Commerce. *Directory of Manufacturers of Greater Canton, Ohio Area.* Canton (229 Wells Ave. N.W., Canton 44703), 1957.

OH27. Canton. Stark County Area Transportation Study. *Annual Report.* (630 County Office Bldg., Canton 44702). 1963–
The report is a compilation of projects, special studies, and activities during the year.

OH28. Canton. Stark County Area Transportation Study. *Transportation Systems Statistics Report.* Canton, 1975. 76pp.
The report presents the characteristics of the various modes of transportation available in the county. The purpose of the report is to make the data collected by SCATS on transportation characteristics available to other agencies and the general public. In the past, this type of report has included only information on the highway system in the county. Now the report presents characteristics of mass transit, taxicabs, special purpose transit, AMTRAK, and airports, in addition to highways.

OH29. Canton. Stark County Regional Planning Commission. *A-95 Review Guidelines—Stark County, Ohio.* 1974.
This report provides a comprehensive set of guidelines for the administration of Office of Management and Budget Circular A-95. It also outlines the policies and criteria used by the Regional Planning Commission as the areawide clearinghouse for Stark County in evaluating Federal grant applications.

Collections

OH30. **Stark County District Library.** 236 Third St., S.W., Canton 44702 (216)452-0665. Teletype Service: (810)432-9072.
Local newspaper articles on Canton, Stark County, and the state of Ohio are clipped by library staff and retained in a comprehensive vertical file.

CINCINNATI

Local Newspaper Indexing: The Municipal Reference Library (see entry **OH31**) maintains a collection of local newspaper items arranged by the Glidden System. The Public Library of Cincinnati and Hamilton County (see entry **OH32**) has indexed the Cincinnati *Enquirer* and *Post* from the early years of publication.

Collections

OH31. Municipal Reference Library. City Hall, Rm. 224, 801 Plum St., Cincinnati 45202.
The Municipal Reference Library handles primarily intergovernmental requests and refers most other requests to the public library. The library maintains a current collection of departmental annual reports and specific transportation reports, as well as copies of the *City Bulletin* issued by the clerk of the council.

OH32. Public Library of Cincinnati and Hamilton County. 800 Vine St., Cincinnati 45202 (513)369-6000.
The library receives most city publications through the Municipal Reference Library, City Hall. The collection includes most current annual reports and many series of departmental reports from 1850 to date. Most items are to be found in the Business and Government Documents Section.

CLEVELAND

Local Newspaper Indexing: An index to the Cleveland *Plain Dealer* and the *Cleveland Press*, compiled by the Cleveland Public Library (325 Superior Ave., Cleveland 44114), began publication in 1976.

Publications

OH33. Governmental Research Institute. ***Governmental Facts.*** Cleveland (502 Euclid Bldg., Cleveland 44115). Irregular.
This newsletter contains factual information relating to the city of Cleveland and Cuyahoga County. Recent topics include a summary of changes in the tax base over a 30-year period, voting statistics and variation in voting on different issues, property tax rates, and variations in tax assessments.

OH34. Governmental Research Institute. *How [They] Voted: November 2, 1976 Election Results in Cuyahoga County* (Cover title: *Election Results Databook for Cuyahoga County*). Cleveland (502 Euclid Bldg., Cleveland 44115), 1977. 24pp. $3.
Comprises description of the election results with text, tables, maps, and charts. Includes an analysis of local splits on national officials, registration and actual vote, and local and county issues.

OH35. Governmental Research Institute. *The Inconspicuous Governments: An Inventory of Special Governmental Agencies in Cuyahoga County.* Cleveland (502 Euclid Bldg., Cleveland 44115), 1976. 108pp. $5.
Directory of 59 special local governmental agencies operating within the county. Each agency is described according to its legal basis, organization and staffing, financial base, and interagency relationships and services.

COLUMBUS

Local Newspaper Indexing: The Columbus and Ohio Division of the Public Library of Columbus and Franklin County (see entry **OH38**) has maintained a selective newspaper index of the two major area newspapers since 1974. Inquiries are invited. Generally, obituaries and sports events are not indexed unless they have major importance.

Publications

OH36. Columbus. City Clerk. *Annual Report: The City Bulletin.* (90 W. Broad, Columbus 43215) 1858– . Annual. (A limited issue item.)
Contains financial reports of city departments, listings of city officials (and their salaries in early years), and listing of major expense items.

OH37. Columbus. Health Department. *Columbus Health Bulletin.* (181 S. Washington Blvd., Columbus 43215) Monthly. Free.
A report of cases of communicable diseases, birth and death rates, departmental services, and publicity of in-house activities.

Collections

OH38. Public Library of Columbus and Franklin County. 28 S. Hamilton Rd., Columbus 43213 (614)461-6573. Teletype Service: (810)482-1161.
With the transfer of the entire collection of Columbus and Franklin County government documents to the Columbus and Ohio Division from the State Historical Society, the library began developing a substantial series of departmental, divisional, board, and commission annual reports. Prior to 1971 the Columbus Public Library was the only area library to retain these records, other than the issuing agencies themselves. The library has a complete set of Columbus city ordinances passed since 1913 and a complete set of city annual reports since 1916. Early holdings date back to 1838 but are incomplete. The city directory collection is complete from the publication's beginning in 1843. The library collects county and regional planning commission reports. It also is a state document depository; municipal projects are reported in various state documents. The audiovisual collection has copies of videotapes of library-produced local history shows and local television programs on local history.

The *City Bulletin of the City of Columbus* reports on a weekly basis the proceedings of city council and all ordinances and resolutions passed by the council. The Columbus and Ohio Division has a complete set of this publication from its beginning in 1913. The most significant gaps in the divisional collections are all Franklin County Regional Planning Commission studies and reports prior to 1964 and all *Abstracts of Votes Cast at the General Election* published by the Franklin County Board of Elections prior to 1976. Most departmental reports are scattered before 1971 with complete sets dating from that time. It must be noted that many of the issuing agencies also do not have publications that the library lacks. Neither the city nor the county have libraries in their buildings to which all city publications are deposited.

DAYTON

Local Newspaper Indexing: The Reference Department of the University of Dayton has been selectively indexing the *Dayton News* since January 1973. Requests for newspaper citations should be addressed to the University of Dayton Library, Reference Department, 300 College Park, Dayton 45469.

Publications

OH39. Dayton. City Plan Board. *Downtown Dayton in '74: A Space Use Survey.* (101 W. Third St., Dayton 45402) 1974. 102pp.
Identifies the amount and geographic location of growth and change in specific activities in the downtown area.

OH40. Dayton. Department of Planning. *An Estimation of Dayton's Current and Future Black and White Population from School Enrollment Data.* (Municipal Bldg., Third and Ludlow Sts., Dayton 45402) 1976. 12pp.

OH41. Greater Dayton Area. League of Women Voters. *Directory of Public Officials.* (120 W. Second St., Rm. 638, Dayton 45402) Annual.
This roster of elected officials in Montgomery County includes county officials as well as the local officials of cities, villages, and townships. In addition, there is a list of court officials and the school boards.

Collections

OH42. Dayton and Montgomery County Public Library. 215 E. Third, Dayton 45402 (513)224-1651.
The library attempts to acquire current local documents and does not participate in Greenwood Press's *Index to Current Urban Documents.*

PARMA

Collections

OH43. Parma Regional Library. 5850 Ridge Rd., Parma 44129 (216)885-5362.
The *Codified Ordinances of the City of Parma* is the only publication of the city, and the library includes it in its holdings.

OH44. Toledo. Lucas County. Mental Health and Mental Retardation Board. *Directory of Services: Mental Health.* (One Stranahan Sq., Toledo 43604) 1976? 30pp.
An alphabetical listing of agencies including the mailing address, telephone number, and services provided.

TOLEDO

Publications

OH45. McFarland, Margaret. *Whither Greater Toledo? An Analysis of Population Trends.* Toledo: Toledo-Lucas County Planning Commission (415 St. Clair St., Toledo 43604), 1976. 110pp. $1.50.
A statistical analysis of metropolitan Toledo population covering 1880 to 1974.

OH46. Toledo Area Council of Churches. . . . *Church Directory of the Toledo Area Council of Churches.* 1968–   . Annual.

OH47. Toledo. Toledo Area Governmental Research Association. *Bulletin.* (Rm. 241, Community Services Bldg., One Stranahan Sq., Toledo 43604) n.d.
The association issues short bulletins concerning various areas of interest that

involve the Toledo area. Examples of these bulletins are: "Comparison of Administrative Salaries and Fringe Benefits," "Area Public Schools," and "An Unrecognized Asset" (which discussed sludge). These reports are not indexed.

OH48. Toledo. Toledo Area Governmental Research Association. *Report.* n.d.
The association issues short reports concerning various areas of interest that involve the Toledo area. Three recent examples of these reports are: "Report 177, School Cost and Enrollment: A Comparison of Trends, 1969/70 through 1974/75"; "Report 178, Toledo City Government Organization"; and "Report 179, Salaries and Fringe Benefits Public and Private Employment in Toledo." These reports are not indexed.

OH49. *The Toledo Black Business Who's Who Directory.* Profile Magazine (P.O. Box 3164 Sta. C., Toledo 43607), 1970- .
Black businesses are arranged by subject.

OH50. *Toledo Blade. Profiles of Toledo's Mayors.* n.d. 44pp.

OH51. Toledo. Chamber of Commerce. *Directory of Toledo Area Manufacturers.* (218 Huron St., Toledo 43604) 1921- . Irregular. $6 (plus postage).
Provides information on Toledo area companies.

OH52. Toledo. Commission of Publicity and Efficiency. *Annual Report. Toledo Blade*, 1953- . Annual. 45¢.
Issued as a paid advertisement in the *Toledo Blade*, Sunday edition, it lists names and provides photographs of city council members and the mayor. There is a brief summarization of select city departments for the past year. Most issues show an organizational chart of city government and city finances.

OH53. Toledo Community Planning Council of Northwest Ohio. *Community Resources: Serving the Greater Toledo Area, Ottawa, and Wood County.* (246 Community Services Bldg., One Stranahan Sq., Toledo 43604) 1921?- .
Biennial. $3.
Provides information about the social services available to the citizens of Lucas, Wood, and Ottawa counties from health and welfare agencies and organizations.

OH54. Toledo. Health Planning Association of Northwest Ohio. *An Emergency Environmental Health Resource Guide for Northwest Ohio.* 1974? 54pp.
A listing of services that are available from various governmental and volunteer agencies in northwest Ohio in the event of a disaster.

OH55. Toledo-Lucas County Public Library. Business Department. *Information about Toledo Businesses at Your Toledo-Lucas County Public Library Business Department.* Toledo. (325 Michigan Ave., Toledo 43624), 1977. Folder.
Brief guide to major sources for the area business person, which emphasizes unique sources and files in the library.

OH56. Toledo Metropolitan Area Council of Governments. *Toledo Metropolitan Area Directory.* (Rm. 725, 420 Madison Ave., Toledo 43604) Annual.
A directory of officials and judges in Lucas, Wood, Ottawa, Erie, and Sandusky counties in Ohio and Whiteford, Beford, and Erie townships in Michigan.

OH57. Toledo. Municipal Court. *Official Bar Directory of Lucas County.* Toledo Bar Association, 1950- .

YOUNGSTOWN

Local Newspaper Indexing: There is no index to the *Youngstown Vindicator*, but the reference staff of the Public Library of Youngstown and Mahoning County (see entry **OH64**) does maintain a clipping file of articles about local government activities and an index to articles about prominent local people. Photocopies of this information are available at a small per page charge.

Publications

OH58. The Burch Directory Company. *Youngstown Official City Directory.* Akron: Burch Directory Co. (1735 S. Hawkins Ave., Akron 44320), 1880- . $85. The directory embraces a list of all citizens over 16 years of age; a classified business directory; a record of city and county officials, churches, schools, societies, and organizations.

OH59. Health and Welfare Council of Greater Youngstown. *Directory of Community Services.* Youngstown: n.p., 1974. $1.
Social agencies, community groups, and services within the local area are briefly described.

OH60. Mahoning County Welfare Department. *MCWD Public Assistance Summary.* Youngstown (932 Belmont Ave., Youngstown 44504), 1970- . Monthly. Free.
From 1970 through 1973 the monthly report contained a considerable amount of text discussing various aspects of the public welfare system and its applications in the county; in 1974 the format changed and the report is now almost wholly statistical.

OH61. Youngstown. Chamber of Commerce. *Youngstown Area: Directory of Manufacturers.* (200 Wick Bldg., Youngstown 44503) n.d. 31pp. $10.
This directory identifies manufacturers in Youngstown, the number of employees they have, address, telephone number, major officer, and products. Firms engaged in export are also noted.

OH62. Youngstown. Eastgate Development and Transportation Agency. *Eastgate Development and Transportation Agency.* Youngstown, 1976.
This revised edition is an inventory of community facilities and services in the counties of Ashtabula, Columbiana, Mahoning, and Trumbull.

OH63. Youngstown. Public Library of Youngstown and Mahoning County. *Youngstown Area Program Resources Directory.* Compiled by Louisa Lipari Berger. (305 Wick Ave., Youngstown 44503) 1971. 257pp.
The directory provides information for program planning in the Youngstown area. Indication is given as to possible speakers and if there is a fee for their services. The speakers range from a variety of governmental, social service, business, educational, and cultural agencies and organizations.

Collections

OH64. Public Library of Youngstown and Mahoning County. 305 Wick Ave., Youngstown 44503 (216)744-8636, ext. 51/52. Teletype Service; (810)435-2840.
The library has begun a local archives program and has tried to acquire publica-

tions of local governmental agencies. Since there is no comprehensive listing of what is published by these agencies, this collection is not complete. All titles listed in the Youngstown section are part of the reference collection and may be consulted at the library. While interlibrary loan is not possible, the library staff will photocopy material from the collection.

OH65. Youngstown State University Library. Special Collections. Oral History Project. 410 Wick Ave., Youngstown 44555.
Several Youngstown mayors have been interviewed for this oral history project; none of them has placed any restrictions on the interviews. As the tapes are processed and typed they are deposited in the Youngstown State University Library. Information about exactly what is available may be obtained from the Oral History Project.

OKLAHOMA

General Publications

OK1. Oklahoma. Department of Education. *Oklahoma Educational Directory.* Oklahoma City (Oliver Hodge Memorial Education Bldg., Oklahoma City), 1909/10- . Annual. Free.
A listing of departmental employees, colleges and universities, and schools.

OK2. Oklahoma. Department of Industrial Development. *Directory of Services for the Benefit of Oklahoma Business and Industry.* Oklahoma City (508 Will Rogers Memorial Office Bldg., Oklahoma City 73105), 1972. 192pp. $3.
A directory of local, state, and federal service agencies which provide aid and information to businesses and industries. Includes a brief description of the various services available and where to write or call for further information. In addition, Oklahoma's tax and pollution laws are discussed.

OK3. Oklahoma. Department of Libraries. *Annual Report and Directory of Libraries in Oklahoma.* Oklahoma City (200 N.E. 18 St., Oklahoma City 73105), 1968- . Annual. Free.
A listing of libraries, librarians, and public library trustees.

OK4. Oklahoma. Employment Security Commission. Research and Planning Division. *County Employment and Wage Data.* Oklahoma City (Will Rogers Memorial Office Bldg., Oklahoma City 73105), 1949/50- . Annual. $1.
This handbook contains county employment, payroll totals, and weekly earnings for each county in the state.

OK5. Oklahoma. Employment Security Commission. Research and Planning Division. *Handbook of Labor Force Data for Selected Areas of Oklahoma, 1970-73.* Vol. 4. Oklahoma City (Will Rogers Memorial Office Bldg., Oklahoma City 73105), 1976. 154pp. $2.
This publication contains historical data concerning labor force, unemployment, and employment for selected areas of Oklahoma for the period from 1970 to 1973. Labor force data for years prior to 1970 are published in other volumes of the handbook.

OK6. Oklahoma Municipal League. *Handbook for Oklahoma Municipal Officials.* Edited by David Fudge. Oklahoma City (201 N.E. 23 St., Oklahoma City 73105), 1973. $6.
Outlines the power and functions of municipal government in the state.

OK7. University of Oklahoma. Bureau of Business and Economic Research. *Statistical Abstract of Oklahoma.* Norman: Bureau of Business and Economic Research (307 W. Brooks, Norman 73019), 1972- . Irregular. $7.50.
A compilation of important information on many sectors of Oklahoma's social, political, educational, and economic activities.

OKLAHOMA CITY

Local Newspaper Indexing: Local newspaper indexing is conducted by the Oklahoma Department of Libraries, 200 N.E. 18 St., Oklahoma City 73105.

Publications

OK8. Oklahoma City. Board of Education. *Personnel Directory, Oklahoma City Public Schools.* (Oliver Hodge Memorial Education Bldg., Oklahoma City) 1945- . Annual. $2.
A listing of the Board of Education, administrative personnel, cooperating organizations, schools and their personnel, and the annual school calendar.

OK9. Oklahoma City. Chamber of Commerce. *Oklahoma City: The Myriad City.* (1 Santa Fe Plaza, Oklahoma City 73102) 1975. $2.50.
Picture story of the Oklahoma City metropolitan area, with emphasis on its growth and development.

OK10. Oklahoma City. Chamber of Commerce. Economic Development Division. *Manufacturers in Oklahoma City.* (1 Santa Fe Plaza, Oklahoma City 73102) 1971- . Irregular. $5.
Provides an alphabetical listing of firms.

OK11. Oklahoma City. Department of Planning. *Oklahoma City Comprehensive Plan.* (200 N. Walker, Oklahoma City 73102) 1974-76. 16 vols. $32.
An unprecedented collection of information on several important aspects of life in Oklahoma City. It covers the environment, sociodemographics, economics, land use, housing, public utilities, data management, goals, and policies.

OK12. Oklahoma City. Office of Management and Budget. *Annual Budget for the Fiscal Year.* (200 N. Walker, Oklahoma City 73102) 1971- . Annual. $5.
Proposed budget as submitted to the mayor and the city council. Mostly graphs and charts.

OK13. Oklahoma City. Office of Management and Budget. *Statement of Financial Condition.* (200 N. Walker, Oklahoma City 73102) 1973- . Annual. $1.
Statement of management of the various funds of Oklahoma, Canadian, Cleveland, McClain, and Pottawatomie counties for the fiscal year.

OK14. University of Oklahoma. Health Sciences Center. Faculty Women's Club. *Experience Oklahoma City: A Handbook for Newcomers.* (N.E. 13 St. and Phillips, Oklahoma City) 1974. $3.09.
Designed to acquaint newcomers and prospective residents with various aspects of life in the city. For example, it covers civic, cultural, social, and religious life.

Collections

OK15. Oklahoma County Libraries System. 131 N.W. Third, Oklahoma City 73102 (405)235-0571.
Almost all documents are classified reference. Although they do not circulate outside of the library. photocopy can be provided for a small per page charge. The County Libraries System's collection of municipal documents is in the developmental stage. The most outstanding documents in the collection are those concerned with city planning, urban renewal, and labor statistics.

TULSA

Publications

OK16. Indian Nations Council of Governments. *The Indian Nations Council of Governments.* Tulsa (630 W. Seventh, Tulsa 74119), 1976. 7pp. plus appendix. Free.
Introduces the council to its new board members and alternates, new committee members, and the general public.

OK17. Tulsa. *A Citizens Handbook for Neighborhood Planning.* Prepared by Community Planning Associates. n.p., 1973. 70pp. o.p. Paper and microfiche copies. (Available from: Tulsa City-County Library, 400 Civic Center, Tulsa 74103.)
This is a planning report written for the citizens to help them understand and improve their community.

OK18. Tulsa Area Health and Hospital Planning Council. *Annotated Bibliography of TAHHPC Publications.* Tulsa (420 S. Main, Tulsa 74103), 1975. 6pp. Free.
This bibliography lists 23 publications relating to Indian health care, ambulance service, nursing home resources and needs, health education, etc., in the Tulsa area. The TAHHPC became operative in April 1968 but federal funding terminated June 1976. A limited supply of the publication is still available.

OK19. Tulsa Area Health and Hospital Planning Council. *Data Management Manual.* Tulsa (420 S. Main, Tulsa 74103), 1974. 61pp. Free.
Identifies data maintained by the council and available through other sources. It has a directory and description of Oklahoma health data collected.

OK20. Tulsa County. *Telephone Directory.* Tulsa: Central Services (Tulsa County Court House, 320 W. Fifth, Tulsa 74103), 1977. 37pp. Free (limited supply available).
Includes city and county offices and personnel.

OK21. Tulsa. League of Women Voters. *Political Directory—Tulsa, 1977-79.* (808 S. Peoria, Tulsa 74120) 1977. 32pp. Approximately triennial. Free. (Send stamped, self-addressed envelope.)
Provides city officials, city boards, county commission district map, county officials, county boards, schools in Tulsa, other local boards, state officials, Senate district map, House district map, national officials, voter information, and most used telephone numbers.

OK22. Tulsa Urban Renewal Authority. *Urban Renewal Handbook.* Prepared by Community Planning Associates. Tulsa (200 Civic Center, Tulsa 74103), 1974. 62pp. $5.

This handbook, which was written so citizens would know more about urban renewal and the stability of neighborhoods, is divided into six chapters covering the economic and social problems of the city, urban renewal, performance evaluation, and the future.

Collections

OK23. Tulsa City-County Library. 400 Civic Center, Tulsa 74103 (918) 581-5320.

The Library has a local government documents collection, Tulsa historical files, microform copies of local newspapers, and Tulsa flood plain information collection. The library collects publications from city, county, and regional agencies. It also participates in Greenwood Press's *Index to Current Urban Documents.* Tulsa City-County Library has a special collection which includes books about the city and those written by Tulsans. The Tulsa Historical Society has its own separate book collection which is also housed in the Tulsa City-County Library.

OREGON

Local Newspaper Indexing: The Library Association of Portland (see entry **OR5**) maintains an index to the *Oregonian*, *Oregon Journal*, and *Willamette Weekly*. The index covers Oregon and Oregon territory events and people from 1905 to the present.

General Publications

OR1. Oregon. Board of Education. *Government in Oregon.* Salem (942 Lancaster Dr. N.E., Salem 97310), 1971. 302pp.
A teaching aid containing information about state and local governments. The information is dated but emphasizes intergovernmental relationships.

OR2. Oregon. Secretary of State. *Oregon Blue Book.* Salem (State Capitol, Salem 97310), 1911– . Biennial. $1.50.
A compendium of information on the state, much of which is statistical in nature. Some of the information pertains to local government. The *Blue Book* profiles each county in the state and lists officials of incorporated cities and towns.

EUGENE

Local Newspaper Indexing: The Eugene Public Library (see entry **OR4**) and Lane Community College (4000 E. 30 Ave., Eugene 97405) selectively index the *Register Guard*.

Publications

OR3. *Eugene, Springfield . . . City Directory.* Eugene: Johnson Pub. Co. (3048 Whitbeck Blvd., Eugene 97401), 1910– . Annual. $85.

Collections

OR4. Eugene Public Library. 100 W. 13 Ave., Eugene 97401 (503)687-5450.
The library retains selected city, county, state, and Lane Council of Governments publications.

PORTLAND

Collections

OR5. Library Association of Portland. 801 S.W. Tenth, Portland 97205 (503) 223-7201, ext. 40. Teletype Service: (910)464-2380.
The library's Oregon collection contains material on the state as well as the city of Portland. A municipal collection is in the developmental stage. No central collection now exists, but each city office does maintain a separate file.

PENNSYLVANIA

ALLENTOWN

Allentown municipal documents published on a regular basis are: the city of Allentown budget, the school district budget, the police department annual report, the quarterly reports and annual cumulation of the Police Juvenile Bureau, the acquisition list of the City Planning Library, and the minutes and committee minutes of city council (kept one year only). The Allentown Public Library (see entry **PA18**) is supposed to receive all municipal documents as published. Many departments do not publish on a regular basis, however, and revise as they feel necessary. **Local Newspaper Indexing:** The two Allentown newspapers, the *Morning Call* and the *Chronicle*, maintain a central index from 1957-1977 at the *Call-Chronicle* office building, 101 N. Sixth St., Allentown 18101. It is comprehensive for local issues and selective for national and international news.

Publications

PA1. Allentown. Bureau of Police. *Annual Report of the Bureau of Police.* (435 Hamilton St., Allentown 18101) 1973-1976. Annual.
This report contains statistics on cases handled by the police, including a comparison report for 1969 through 1976 of offenses reported to the FBI, causes of arrest, offenses by reporting area, division summaries, and police-sponsored programs. .

PA2. Allentown. Bureau of Police. Juvenile Division. *Police Work with Children.* (435 Hamilton St., Allentown 18101) 1970-   . Quarterly with annual cumulations.
These reports list complaints against juveniles by class of complaint, disposition of each complaint, and number of complaints per census tract.

PA3. Allentown. Bureau of Recreation. *Recreation Opportunities: Allentown, Pennsylvania.* (3003 Parkway Blvd., Allentown 18104) 1971. 15pp.
This booklet describes the city park system and summarizes the facilities available at each park. It lists programs offered by the Recreation Commission throughout the year and facilities for different sports. There is also a list of both city and school playgrounds describing facilities and programs. A map is included.

PA4. Allentown. Charter Commission. *Findings and Recommendations by the Allentown Charter Commission.* 1967.
This is the final report of a commission formed to study different forms of municipal government available to Pennsylvania third-class cities and to make recommendations. The recommendation was to drop the commission type of government and

adopt a mayor-council form with a mayor and seven councilmen elected at large. The report includes a detailed explanation of this type of government, date set for a referendum, and the form of the question on the ballot. The proposed charter is given in full in the appendix.

PA5. Allentown. City Council. *Zoning Ordinance.* City Planning Commission (435 Hamilton St., Allentown 18101), 1970. 98pp.
This ordinance divides the city into zones and regulates the location, bulk, and use of buildings and other structures, and the use of land. It lists 13 types of zones with detailed requirements for each type, general regulations, exceptions, penalties, etc. A map is included.

PA6. Allentown. Department of Administration. Bureau of Administrative Services. *City of Allentown Telephone Directory.* (435 Hamilton St., Allentown 18101) 1975.
The directory of the Allentown Centrex telephone system lists numbers, first by the name of the official and then by the function of the departments of the city government.

PA7. Allentown. Department of Community Development. Planning Library. *Planning Library Accessions.* (435 Hamilton St., Allentown 18101) January 1976-Spring 1977.
Each issue of this publication lists additions to the library collection, including materials published by or concerning the city of Allentown and useful publications in the field of urban studies.

PA8. Allentown. Fire Department. *Annual Report.* (435 Hamilton St., Allentown 18101) 1972-1976. Annual.
This report includes a personnel directory, a map of fire station locations, a list of vehicles at each station, training schools and man training hours per month, statistics on fire alarms answered with a detailed breakdown of types and causes of fires, public information and fire prevention programs, and civil defense activities for the year.

PA9. Allentown-Lehigh County Chamber of Commerce. *Chamber News.* Allentown (462 Walnut St., Allentown 18102), 1976- . Monthly.
This publication reports events concerning the area, projects endorsed by the chamber, new members, and important chamber dates.

PA10. Allentown. Office of the Mayor. *Budget.* (435 Hamilton St., Allentown 18101) Annual.
The budget lists general funds for each department, tax revenues, and receipts and expenditures for departments where the information is applicable.

PA11. Allentown. Redevelopment Authority. *Redevelopment Authority of the City of Allentown, Progress Report 1956-76.* (723 Chew St., Allentown 18102) 1976.
This report describes work done or planned for specific areas of the city such as urban renewal and the Hamilton Mall. A financial statement concludes the report.

PA12. Allentown. School District. *Budget: School District of the City of Allentown.* (31 S. Penn St., Allentown 18105) 1976.
The budget is divided into four sections: (1) general budget, (2) athletic council, (3) food services, and (4) public library. The legal basis for budgeting from state

law is quoted, and figures are given for the adopted 1975-76 budget and the proposed 1976-77 budget.

PA13. Allentown. Urban Observatory. *Citizen Participation in the 1970s: The Case of Allentown, Pennsylvania.* Planning Commission (435 Hamilton St., Allentown 18101) n.d.
This study gives an overview of citizen participation in the political life of Allentown. It details the results of citywide questionnaires and offers conclusions and recommendations. Bibliography.

PA14. Allentown. Urban Observatory. *A Productivity Improvement Project on Inspections and Housing Rehabilitations in the City of Allentown, Pennsylvania.* By Mikell P. Groover and John J. Fagan. (435 Hamilton St., Allentown 18101), 1976. 145pp.
The report summarizes the operations of the Housing Rehabilitation Department and the Bureau of Inspections and recommends approaches and procedures for their improvement and possible consolidation.

PA15. David M. Walker Associates. *Allentown Central City Study: Technical Report.* Philadelphia, 1968. 241pp. Maps, tables, photographs.
The study contains a plan for center city renewal. The studies which support it include parking, traffic flow, economic base, access highways, land use, and pedestrian circulation. A full set of recommendations necessary to carry out the plan is included.

PA16. Pennsylvania General Assembly. *City Charter: An Act to Incorporate the City of Allentown.* n.p. General Assembly, n.d. 11pp.
The act tells what departments the city must have, what officials the city needs to run these departments, and the powers and duties of these officials.

PA17. United States Department of the Army. Philadelphia District Corps of Engineers. *Flood Plain Information: Lehigh River—Jordan Creek—Trout Creek-City of Allentown, Pennsylvania.* Philadelphia: United States Army Corps of Engineers, 1971. 25pp.
This report surveys flood damage and presents ways to prevent future damage through management of the flood plain and the construction of dams.

Collections

PA18. Allentown Public Library. 914 Hamilton Mall, Allentown, PA 18101 (215) 434-4894.
The Allentown Public Library acquires annual reports and budgets by requesting them from departments which publish them. Minutes and committee minutes of city council are sent to the Allentown Library and kept one year only. The city planning commission sends their documents as issued but because of budgetary cutbacks have produced very little since 1971. The collection includes city and school district budgets, city council and council committee minutes, and annual reports of various city departments. It also includes documents produced by studies made by groups such as the Allentown City Planning Commission and the Urban Observatory. Most of the material produced by the Lehigh-Northampton Counties Joint Planning Commission is held by the Allentown Public Library and much of it applies to the city.

ERIE

Data not available at this time.

PHILADELPHIA

The Philadelphia municipal government produces from the city council, bills, calendars of bills, journal (slip and annual bound volumes) and ordinances (slip and annual volumes); the *Philadelphia Code* (loose-leaf); proposed operating budget; financial reports; and reports of departments. The quantity published is very small.

Publications

PA19. Philadelphia. Board of Education. *Directory.* (21 Parkway, Philadelphia 19103) 1898/99-   . Annual. Free.

PA20. Philadelphia. City Planning Commission. *Capital Program.* (13 Floor, City Hall Annex, Philadelphia 19107) 1945/50-   . Annual. Free.
Proposed program as adopted for a six-year period subject to enabling ordinance annually.

PA21. Philadelphia. Division of Communication Services. *Municipal Telephone Directory.* (Rm. 630, City Hall, Philadelphia 19107) 1947-   . Annual. Free.
Departmental directory; alphabetical personal index; departmental directory index.

PA22. Philadelphia. Office of City Economist. *Philadelphia Statistical Data.* (Rm. 1680, Municipal Services Bldg., Philadelphia 19107) 1974-   . Annual. Free.
Statistics concerning the economy of Philadelphia, i.e., population, income, labor force, industry profile, wages, hire and quit rates, work stoppages, building costs, land and construction costs, rental fees, current and planned center city construction, financing, taxes (state and local), transportation, budget costs, and housing.

PA23. Philadelphia. Office of the City Representative. *Manual of the City of Philadelphia.* 1859/60-   . Annual. (Available from: Procurement Department, 13 Floor, Municipal Services Bldg., Philadelphia 19107.)
Directory of key personnel of the city with a number of quasi-governmental and allied agencies. Voting information. Ward boundaries.

PA24. Philadelphia. Office of the Managing Director. *Update.* (Rm. 1660, Municipal Services Bldg., Philadelphia 19107) Irregular. Free.
News of city administration plans.

Collections

PA25. Free Library of Philadelphia. Government Publications Department. Logan Sq., Philadelphia 19103 (215)686-5329.
The library has maintained a federal depository collection since 1897, and has a good collection of publications of all 50 states (most current); a collection of current publications of 35 large cities, plus a selection of Greenwood Press's *Index to Current Urban Documents;* a small collection of foreign government publications; and a good collection of international organization publications.

(See also entry **US4.**)

PITTSBURGH

Carnegie Library of Pittsburgh has an extensive archival collection of municipal documents from the mid-1800s through the mid-1900s. After this period the library's holdings are incomplete. A small number of city agencies are continuing to supply their publications regularly. However, having no checklist of municipal publications, it is difficult to discern the number of publications issued by the city which are not being received by the library. This material is available for use in the library only, but library staff will answer most inquiries and will photocopy material if requested.
Local Newspaper Indexing: The Pennsylvania Division of the Carnegie Library, 4400 Forbes Ave., Pittsburgh 15213 (412)622-3131, maintains a selective index of items pertinent to events and persons in Pittsburgh and its environs. Holdings include clippings from about 1900 to date; a newspaper index, February 1953 to date; death notices, 1786-1913; an index of all death notices from the *Pittsburgh Gazette*, 1911-September 1968; obituaries selectively indexed, October 1968-74, and death notices from Pittsburgh *Post-Gazette* and from *Pittsburgh Press* since 1975.

Publications

PA26. Pittsburgh. City Council. *Municipal Record, Minutes of the Proceedings of the Council.* 1868- . Annual.
Includes addresses and remarks of the council members, communications to the council, and ordinances and resolutions passed by the council within the year.

PA27. Pittsburgh. City Planning Commission. *Six-Year Development Program of the City of Pittsburgh.* 1972- . Biennial.
Includes recommended capital programs as guides to capital investments by the city. Maps of geographic areas of projects are included.

PA28. Pittsburgh. Department of the City Comptroller. *Annual Report.* 1870/71- . Annual.
Includes detailed statements of cash receipts and expenditures for each fiscal year and other financial data; valuations of city property by wards, and a table of territorial growth of the city.

PA29. Pittsburgh. Department of the City Comptroller. *Monthly and Quarterly Statements of Appropriations, Bonds, Trusts and Sinking Fund Accounts.* 1932- .
Includes detailed information on appropriations, expenditures and revenues of the governmental departments of the city.

PA30. Pittsburgh. Government Study Commission. *Records of the Commission Relating to a Proposed Home Rule Charter for the City of Pittsburgh, 1973-1974.* Pittsburgh.
Includes correspondence, legal opinions, minutes of the commission, committees and public meetings, personnel records, background information, and preliminary and final drafts of the city charter.

PA31. Pittsburgh. Mayor. *Budget of the City of Pittsburgh.* Pittsburgh, 1946- . Annual.
Includes the mayor's state of the city address, estimated revenues and expenditures for the succeeding year, summary of operating costs and revenues, salaries of city employees, and organization charts for city departments.

PA32. Pittsburgh. Mayor. *Capital Budget.* Pittsburgh, 1958-   . Annual.
The mayor's proposed capital budget for the succeeding year, allocating funds for permanent physical improvements such as public buildings, playgrounds, and sewage systems. The budgets are based on the Six-Year Development Program drafts of the City Planning Commission.

PA33. Pittsburgh. School District, Board of Education. *Pittsburgh Public Schools Personnel Directory.* (Board of Education Bldg., Bellefield St., Pittsburgh 15213) 1912-   . Annual.
Lists members of the Board of Education and administrative officers, faculties, and staff of individual schools in the district; organization charts; school calendar.

PA34. Pittsburgh. School District, Board of Education. *Preliminary and Final Budgets.* (Board of Education Bldg., Bellefield St., Pittsburgh 15213), 1975- Annual.
Includes statistical tables of appropriations, revenues, expenditures and budgets by departments, enrollment by schools, organization chart of school district, and descriptions of functions of departments.

SCRANTON

The city of Scranton is most definitely lacking in its publication of bibliographies or checklists of city materials. Virtually none exist. Many needed publications are "in progress." A personnel manual is being written, and a new zoning regulations handbook is under review.

Publications

PA35. Scranton. Greater Scranton Area Chamber of Commerce. *The Greater Scranton Area Chamber of Commerce Membership Directory and Buyer's Guide.* (426 Mulberry St., Scranton 18503) 1977. Annual. 74pp.

PA36. Scranton. Greater Scranton Area Chamber of Commerce. *Scranton-Lackawanna County, Pennsylvania, 1975-76: Directory of Clubs and Associations.* (426 Mulberry St., Scranton 18503). 1975. 29pp.

PA37. Scranton. City Clerk. *Budget and Salaries, 1977.* (Office of City Clerk, 340 N. Washington Ave., Scranton 18503) 1977. Annual.
Contains the adopted budget of the city of Scranton for the fiscal year.

PA38. Scranton. City Comptroller. *Financial Report of City Comptroller for the Year Ended December 31, 1976.* (340 N. Washington Ave., Scranton 18503) 1976. Annual.
Contains the report of the city comptroller for the year ending December 31, 1976.

PA39. Scranton. City Planning Commission. *Master Plan for the City of Scranton.* 1973.
Contains population and housing information, land use plan, transportation, recreation, community, public buildings, parks, and thoroughfares. There is also available through the city planner's office, a 1975 revision of this master plan.

PA40. Scranton. Home Rule Study Commission. *Scranton Home Rule Charter.* (Office of City Clerk, 340 N. Washington Ave., Scranton 18503) 1974. 6pp.
Gives the recommended administrative chart, preamble and nine articles of the home rule charter of the city of Scranton. This is the ruling body of laws for the city.

PA41. Scranton. Office of City Clerk. *Action Sheet.* (340 N. Washington Ave., Scranton 18503) 1977. Weekly.
A summary of important happenings at weekly city council meetings, published before the official minutes. They are distributed to all city departments for a quick glance of what has transpired at the meetings.

PA42. Scranton. Office of City Comptroller. *City Comptroller Report for Month Ending . . . .* 1977. Monthly. (Available from: City Clerk's Office, 340 N. Washington Ave., Scranton 18503.)
Includes financial data in the following accounts: report of general fund budget, report of special city account, report of liquid fuel account, report of CETA fund account, report of community development fund account, and report of city treasurer. There is a monthly listing of receipts in computer print-out form, plus a narrative by the city comptroller of the happenings with the budget for that particular month.

PA43. Scranton. Ordinances, Local Laws, etc. *Codified Ordinance of the City of Scranton.* Scranton: Walter Drake and Co., 1967. (Available from: City Clerk's Office, 340 N. Washington Ave., Scranton 18503.)
Contains the administrative code, business and taxation code, traffic code, general offenses code, streets, utilities, and public service code, public health code, zoning code, fire prevention code, building code, housing code, and general index.

PA44. Scranton. Police Department. *Manual of the Bureau of Police Rules and Regulations.* Police Planning Division (City Clerk's Office, 340 N. Washington Ave., Scranton 18503), 1973. 147pp.
Part 1 explains the organization of the Bureau of Police and includes an organizational chart. Part 2 lists general regulations for all members. Part 3 includes regulations relating to procedures. A glossary is also included.

PA45. Scranton. School District. *Register and Directory of Scranton Public Schools.* (425 N. Washington Ave., Scranton 18503) 1976. Annual.

PA46. Touche Ross and Co. *Report on Examination of Financial Statements, Year Ended December 31, 1976.* Scranton: Touche Ross, 1977. 135pp. (Available from: City Clerk's Office, 340 N. Washington Ave., Scranton 18503.)
Contains accountant's report, balance sheet, description of funds and combined summary of significant accounting policies, general funds, special revenue funds, CETA funds, community development funds, federal revenue sharing funds, etc. Also included is the interim management letter dated April 21, 1977 and the letter of comment dated December 31, 1976.

Collections

PA47. Scranton Public Library. Vine St. and N. Washington Ave., Scranton 18503 (717)961-2451.
The Scranton Public Library, through the Special Information Services Department, works closely with the city clerk's office of Scranton. Through weekly attendance at city council meetings, the library is kept abreast of happenings within the city government, and an effort is made to collect pertinent materials to be kept on reserve in the library. Codified ordinances, the city budget, master plans, minutes of city council meetings, comptroller's reports, etc., are all contained in the library. The library makes an effort to collect any and all information that the city publishes, no matter how incidental. The library also works closely with local business organizations, and has all of the material which the Greater Scranton Area Chamber of Commerce publishes.

RHODE ISLAND

Very few reference documents are published at the municipal level. For example, the vital statistics from the *Providence Registrar* are forwarded to the Rhode Island Department of Health where the data is eventually compiled into the state document. Providence, the capital, last published a data book in approximately 1963.

General Publications

RI1. Council for Community Services Inc. *1975–1977 Directory: Rhode Island Health, Recreation, Welfare Agencies.* Providence (229 Waterman St., Providence 02906), 231pp. Biennial. $4.50.
Listing of agencies by official title and listing by subject such as alcoholism.

RI2. Rhode Island. Department of Community Affairs. *Annual State Report on Local Government Finances and Tax Equalization.* Providence (150 Washington St., Providence, 02903), 1976. 133pp. Annual. Free.
Contains fiscal facts such as revenue and expenditures for Providence and Warwick.

RI3. Rhode Island. Department of Community Affairs. *Directory of City and Town Officials, 1977.* Providence (150 Washington St., Providence 02903), 1977. Annual. Free.

RI4. Rhode Island. Department of Economic Development. *Rhode Island Basic Economic Statistics, 1975.* Providence (1 Weybosset Hill, Providence 02903), 1975. 196pp. Biennial. Free.
Includes population, family incomes, and retail sales by county, city, and town. It is the major reference work relative to economic statistics in the state.

RI5. Rhode Island. Department of Economic Development. *Rhode Island Directory of Manufacturers.* Providence (1 Weybosset Hill, Providence 02903), 1977. 250pp. Irregular. $3.
Arrangement by SIC group, then by city and town alphabetically. Includes a listing of commercial establishments by city and town. It is the only reference guide of its sort in the state.

RI6. Rhode Island. Department of Health. Division of Vital Statistics. *Vital Statistics 1975.* Providence (Davis St., Providence), 1977. 141pp. Annual. Free.
There are 44 tables based chiefly on birth, death, marriage, divorce, and fetal death certificates, which are required by state law. There are 32 pages of text which include graphs, charts, etc. This is a major reference work.

RI7. Rhode Island. Department of Health. Planning and Resource Development. *Rhode Island Health Agency Guide.* Providence: Health Library (Davis St., Providence), 1976. Free.
Guide to the health agencies in the state, both governmental and private. Fairly good listing. This source is presently out of print. A new issue is being compiled.

RI8. Rhode Island. Health Service Research Inc. *Rhode Island Community Health Profiles, 1976.* Vol. 1: *Cities and Towns.* Providence (56 Pine St., Providence 02903), 1976. Irregular. Free.
For all the towns and cities there are statistical tables on, among others, population by age and sex, natality, communicable diseases, mortality—deaths by cause. Excellent reference work on health statistics.

RI9. Rhode Island. John Hope Settlement House. *Community Information and Referral Guide of John Hope Settlement House.* Providence (7 Burgess Ave., Providence 02914), 1977. 21pp. Free.
Handy reference tool for Providence. Approximately nine major subject areas such as "Need a Job" and "Where to Go."

RI10. Rhode Island. State Police. *Crime in Rhode Island, 1975.* Providence, 1976. 118pp. Annual. Free.

RI11. Sheehan, Dennis D., and Joseph E. Coduri. *Rhode Island Assessor's Handbook.* Research series number 17. Kingston: Bureau of Government Research (University of Rhode Island, Kingston 02881), 1975. $5.
Reference tool relative to the assessing function of Rhode Island towns and cities. Includes laws, exemptions, assessment administration, and methodology of assessment.

RI12. University of Rhode Island. Bureau of Government Research. *Handbook for Rhode Island Town and City Clerks.* Compiled by Joseph E. Coduri. Kingston (University of Rhode Island, Kingston 02881), 1973. 135pp. $2.
This handbook provides a good look at the provisions of the state law which relate to the office, duties, and responsibilities of the town and city clerks in the state. Though a bit old there have been very few changes in the law.

RI13. University of Rhode Island. Bureau of Government Research. *Rhode Island Local Government Past, Present, Future.* Edited by Robert W. Sutton, Jr., Kingston (University of Rhode Island, Kingston 02881), 1974. 166pp. $3.
Series of good articles relative to Rhode Island local government. Includes an annotated bibliography of works relating to the development of local government in Rhode Island, 1636-1972.

PROVIDENCE

Local Newspaper Indexing: The Providence Public Library, 150 Empire St., Providence, (401)521-7722, ext. 229, Teletype, instate: 76-TT0034; TWX: (701) 381-1599, indexes the *Providence Journal* and *Providence Bulletin.*

Publications

RI14. Providence. League of Women Voters. *Providence: Know Your City.* Providence (Old Stone Bank, Providence), 1974. 58pp. Free.
The two major divisions of the book are the city and its government (legislative,

executive, and judicial) and city departments, boards and commissions. Although it was done in 1974, this is a major recent book relative to Providence government.

RI15. Rhode Island. Department of Economic Development. *City of Providence Monograph.* Rhode Island City and Town Monographs. Providence (1 Weybosset Hill, Providence 02903), 1976. 24pp. Irregular. Free.
The volume includes population characteristics, labor force, general economy, municipal government, education, and recreation facilities.

WARWICK

Publications

RI16. Rhode Island. Department of Economic Development. *City of Warwick Monograph.* Rhode Island City and Town Monographs. Providence (1 Weybosset Hill, Providence 02903), 1976. 23pp. Irregular. Free.
Volume includes population characteristics, labor force, general economy, municipal government, education, and recreation facilities.

Collections

RI17. **Warwick Public Library.** 600 Sandy Lane, Warwick 02886 (401)739-1919. Teletype Service: (76)TT034.
The library maintains a card file listing state historical documents but has very few of these documents in its collection.

SOUTH CAROLINA

CHARLESTON

The city of Charleston does not have a checklist of publications. Materials such as council journal, audits, and budget are made available on a continuing basis to the Charleston County Library in mimeographed form and are not actually published for distribution. Publications available for sale include the Code of the City of Charleston, a study guide for the licensing of tourist's guides, and various building codes and restrictions. From 1880 through 1951, all city officials and departments submitted annual reports which were printed in the *City of Charleston Yearbook* and thereby made available for sale. This is no longer compiled, but all back issues are retained in the County Library for examination. Publication of a directory and a handbook by the city is anticipated in the near future. **Local Newspaper Indexing:** The reference staff of the Charleston County Library (see entry **SC3**) has indexed the *News and Courier* since 1931 on a selective basis. Emphasis is on local and state history and events. National news is not indexed. The index, which is not available for purchase, is housed at the library. Queries will be accepted, but extensive research will not be undertaken.

Publications

SC1. Charleston County. League of Women Voters. *Directory of Public Officials.* Charleston (24 Vendue Range, Charleston 29401), 1950- . Biennial. $1. This publication identifies all public officials whether federal, state, county, or city with offices in Charleston County. Arrangement is by governmental body, subdivided by office, board, and commission. Each citation contains individual members' names, positions, addresses, telephone numbers, terms of office, and in some cases, salary. There is no individual name index.

SC2. Charleston Trident Chamber of Commerce. Market Research Department. *Charleston—At a Glance.* (P.O. Box 975, Charleston 29402) Unpaged. Monthly. Free.
Charleston—At a Glance is a statistical compilation which analyzes the present and projected economy of the metropolitan area using data accumulated from various sources and market research department estimates. Organization is by broad topic in tabular form, in many cases showing breakdown of figures by municipal area.

Collections

SC3. Charleston County Library. 404 King St., Charleston 29403 (803) 723-1645. Teletype Service: TWX (810)881-1864.
The Charleston County Library is the only public library in the metropolitan area and

collects all current municipal publications from the city of Charleston as well as other municipalities in the county. The collection includes archival materials dating from the incorporation of Charleston in 1783. Major series include the city of Charleston death records, 1821-1926; city of Charleston birth records, Nov. 1877-1926; city of Charleston yearbooks, 1880-1951; microfilm collection of all city newspapers, the earliest dating from 1732; ordinances of the city council, 1783 to present; journal of the city council, 1967 to present; and all editions of the city code.

COLUMBIA

The city of Columbia itself does not have an extensive publications program nor a checklist of its publications. Its brief annual reports of recent years appear regularly in calendar format, and its employee newsletter, *Inside Columbia*, is published regularly. The city's annual budget would be available at its City Hall offices.

Richland County, for which Columbia is the county seat, last year issued its first annual report. Its annual budgets are available from the county offices. The county does not publish a list of its documents. The most comprehensive documents on Columbia city planning and research are now compiled by or under the auspices of the Central Midlands Regional Planning Council. A bibliography of their publications is available from their office at 800 Dutch Square Blvd., Columbia 29201. **Local Newspaper Indexing:** The reference department of the Richland County Public Library (see entry **SC31**) indexes the two daily Columbia newspapers, the *Record* and *State*. This is done on a comprehensive basis, beginning with November 1973. The November 1973 to December 31, 1975 portion of the index is on microfilm and available for sale. The 1976 index on microfilm became available in September 1977. The reference department will accept queries from other cities for index citations. (Obituaries are not being indexed except for civic leaders or other prominent people. Birth and marriage notices are not included.)

Publications

SC4. Central Midlands Regional Planning Council. *Columbia, South Carolina 1973 Census Tract* [data by] *Street.* Columbia (800 Dutch Square Blvd., Columbia 29201), 1973. 186pp.

SC5. Columbia Area. League of Women Voters. *Directory of Public Officials: Richland-Lexington Counties and Greater Columbia.* Columbia (2838 Devine St., Columbia 29205). Annual. $1.

SC6. Columbia. City Council. *Annual Report and Calendar.* (City Hall, 1737 Main St., Columbia 29201) Annual. Free.

SC7. Columbia. Ordinances, Local Laws, etc. *Code of Ordinances, City of Columbia, South Carolina.* Tallahassee, FL: Municipal Code Corp., n.d. $45. (Available from: City Council, City Hall, 1737 Main St., Columbia 29201.)

SC8. Columbia. City Council. *Zoning Ordinance.* (City Hall, 1737 Main St., Columbia 29201) n.d. Loose-leaf format.

SC9. Greater Columbia Chamber of Commerce. *Columbia: Facts and Figures.* Columbia (P.O. Box 1360, Columbia 29202), 1970? 22pp.

SC10. Greater Columbia Chamber of Commerce. *Membership Directory and Buyer's Guide.* Columbia (P.O. Box 1360, Columbia 29202), 1976. 60pp. Free to members.

SC11. Greater Columbia Chamber of Commerce. *Update: Official Publication of the Greater Columbia Chamber of Commerce.* Columbia (P.O. Box 1360, Columbia 29202). Monthly. $2.60 annually.
Includes information on the chamber's programs, a listing of new members, and facts on selected government activities and economic statistics of the area.

SC12. Greater Columbia Chamber of Commerce. Columbia Area Manufacturer's Council. *Manufacturers' Handbook and Directory.* Columbia (P.O. Box 1360, Columbia 29202), 1973? 51pp.

SC13. Industrial Development Commission of Greater Columbia. *Greater Columbia Data Book.* Columbia, 1973. 105pp. (Available from: Chamber of Commerce, P.O. Box 1360, Columbia 29202.)
Provides a comprehensive account of the economic, cultural, and political climate of the area.

SC14. *Inside Columbia.* (City Hall, 1737 Main St., Columbia 29201) Biweekly. Free.

SC15. Municipal Association of South Carolina. *Directory of South Carolina Municipal Officials.* Columbia (P.O. Box 11558, Columbia 29211). Annual. $15.

SC16. Pilot Club of Columbia. *Access Columbia: A Guide to Metropolitan Columbia for Persons with Mobility Difficulties.* 1977. 50pp. Free. (Available from: Chamber of Commerce, P.O. Box 1360, Columbia 29202.)

SC17. Richland County and City of Columbia Study Commission. *Report and Recommendation of the Richland County-City of Columbia Study Commission.* Columbia, 1972. 51pp. Free.
This is a summary report on local government structure, policy making, administration, and finances in Richland County to determine the capability of the local governments within the county to resolve their public problems and to set patterns of intergovernmental cooperation. The commission also studies the goals, needs, and trends of the county and sets forth recommendations for reorganization of local and county government structures to lead toward home rule.

SC18. Richland County Council. *Annual Financial Report . . . for the Fiscal Year.* Columbia (2020 Hampton St., Columbia 29204). Annual. Free.

SC19. Richland County Council. *County Capsule.* Columbia (2020 Hampton St., Columbia 29204), 1976- . Bimonthly. Free.
This bulletin summarizes the actions of the county council.

SC20. Richland County Council. *Richland County Annual Budget.* Columbia (2020 Hampton St., Columbia 29204), 1967-68; 1973/74- . Annual. Free.

SC21. Richland County Council. *Richland County Annual Report.* Columbia (2020 Hampton St., Columbia 29204), 1975/76- . Annual. Free.

SC22. Richland County. Ordinances, Local Laws, etc. *The Code of Richland County: The General Ordinances of the County.* Atlanta, GA: PRM Law Publishers, 1976- . $40 (supplements, $20 per year). (Available from: Richland County Council, 2020 Hampton St., Columbia 29204.)

SC23. Richland County Recreation Commission. *Fun Finder: Enjoy Your County Parks.* Columbia (5819 Shakespeare Rd., Columbia 29204). Annual. Free.
This is a directory of parks, community centers, recreation programs, and classes.

SC24. Richland County School District One. *District One Has a Lot to Offer.* Columbia (1616 Richland St., Columbia 29201), 1976. 32pp. Free.
This booklet provides basic information regarding the various kinds of services and programs offered by the school district, as well as names and telephone numbers of persons to contact for additional information.

SC25. Richland County School District One. *Program Catalog.* Columbia (1616 Richland St., Columbia 29201), 1976. 82pp. Free.

SC26. Richland County School District One. *Richland County School District One News Clippings.* Columbia (1616 Richland St., Columbia 29201). Semi-annual.

SC27. Richland County School District One. *The School Book.* Columbia (1616 Richland St., Columbia 29201), 1977. 76pp. Free.
This is a directory of all the schools in the county.

SC28. Richland County School District One. *Year-Round Schools: A Chronological Selected Bibliography from 1907 to 1972.* Columbia (1616 Richland St., Columbia 29201), 1972. 43pp. Free.

SC29. South Carolina Land Resources Conservation Commission. *The South Carolina County and Municipal Public Land Ownership Inventory.* Columbia (Division of Land Resource Data Acquisition and Analysis, 1400 Lady St., Columbia 29211), n.d. 302pp. Free (in limited supply).
This report is an initial inventory and includes maps showing land owned by the city of Columbia, with accompanying lists indicating number of acres in each parcel of city-owned property.

SC30. United Way of the Midlands. *Directory of Human Services.* Columbia, 1976. 120pp. Free. (Available from: Information and Referral Center, 1813 Main St., P.O. Box 152, Columbia 29202.)

Collections

SC31. Richland County Public Library. 1400 Sumter St., Columbia 29201 (803)799-9084.
The Richland Public Library is the only public library in the Columbia metropolitan area, and it is collecting all current municipal, county, and regional publications. The major series held are the Columbia *Annual Reports*, Columbia *City Code*, Columbia *Zoning Ordinance*, Columbia city directories, publications of the county school districts, annual reports and budgets of the county, Central Midlands Regional Planning Council planning and research reports, and specific reports of the city (also the county and various joint councils) on programs and planning for Columbia.

SOUTH DAKOTA

General Publications

SD1. South Dakota. State Planning Bureau. *South Dakota Facts: An Abstract of Statistics and Graphics Concerning the People and Resources of South Dakota.* Pierre (State Capitol, Pierre 57501).
A computer-based publication of statistical data needed for planning both on statewide and local levels.

SD2. South Dakota Municipal League. *Directory of South Dakota Municipal Officials.* Pierre (214 E. Capitol, Pierre 57501), 1976. 67pp. Annual. $6.

RAPID CITY

Local Newspaper Indexing: The newspaper staff librarian of the Rapid City Public Library (see entry **SD6**) does some indexing of the Rapid City *Journal.* At present, queries about the information will not be accepted.

Publications

SD3. Rapid City. Ordinances, Local Laws, etc. *Revised Ordinances of the City of Rapid City, South Dakota.* Tallahassee, FL: Municipal Code Corp., 1969. 1441pp. $125 hardbound ($120 paperbound, $25 for annual supplement.) (Available from: City Finance Officer, 22 Main St., Rapid City 57701.)
A complete codification of all ordinances of a general and permanent nature enacted by the common council.

SD4. Sixth District Council of Local Government. *Directory of Human Resource Organizations and Agencies.* 3rd ed. Rapid City (306 E. St. Joseph St., Rapid City 55701), 1976. 95pp. Irregular. $2.50 (plus postage and handling).
A directory which includes federal, state, and municipal agencies as well as local clubs and organizations which are human resource agencies in the 11 western counties of South Dakota.

SD5. Sixth District Council of Local Governments. *A Survey and Analysis of Municipal Finances.* Rapid City (306 E. St. Joseph St., Rapid City 55701), 1977. $6.
The study, which gives data on municipal finances for selected municipalities within the Sixth District, describes the financial structure and accounting system of the municipal governments. It enumerates the services and programs provided by these governments and analyzes their expenditure patterns.

Collections

SD6. Rapid City Public Library. P.O. Box 3090, Rapid City 57709 (605) 394-4171. Teletype Service: (510)366-8020.
The library maintains a local and state historical collection.

SIOUX FALLS

Local Newspaper Indexing: Although there is no indexing, the Sioux Falls Public Library (see entry **SD10**) maintains a clipping file of regional articles taken from the *Argus Leader;* the material dates from 1946. The *Argus Leader* library has a file from 1951.

Publications

SD7. Sioux Falls. *Annual Reports of All City Departments.* n.p.

SD8. Sioux Falls. Ordinances, Local Laws, etc. *Revised Ordinances of Sioux Falls.* Tallahassee, FL: Municipal Code Corp., 1977. Loose-leaf.

SD9. South Dakota State Historical Society. *Checklist of South Dakota Newspapers in the South Dakota State Historical Society.* Pierre (Memorial Bldg., Capital Ave., Pierre 57501), 1976.
Lists 29 Sioux Falls newspaper holdings on microfilm.

Collections

SD10. Sioux Falls Public Library. 201 N. Main Ave., Sioux Falls 57101 (605) 339-7082. Teletype Service: (910)660-0013.
The Sioux Falls Public Library maintains a clipping file of regional articles taken from the *Argus Leader;* the material dates from 1946.

TENNESSEE

General Publications

TN1. Tennessee. Department of Economic and Community Development. *1975 Tennessee Manufacturers Directory.* Nashville (1012 Andrew Jackson State Office Bldg., Nashville 37219).
Although intended to be used with the SIC Major Group number, industries are also listed in the City Guide section. The name, address, major executives, and number of employees are cited.

TN2. Tennessee. State Planning Commission. *Directory of State Statistics for Local Areas in Tennessee.* Nashville (State Office, C2-208, Central Services Bldg., Nashville 37219), 1970. 130pp.
This directory covers statistical resources of state agencies for governmental and socioeconomic units which fall below the state level. The units comprise the SMSA, counties, and cities. There is also a bibliography of official state publications.

CHATTANOOGA

Data not available at this time.

KNOXVILLE

Data not available at this time.

MEMPHIS

Data not available at this time.

NASHVILLE

Publications

TN3. Coomer, James C., and Charlie B. Tyler. *Nashville Metropolitan Government: The First Decade.* Knoxville: Bureau of Public Administration, University of Tennessee, 1974. 106pp.
This monograph presents a descriptive overview of metropolitan efforts in the first decade. Divided into three sections, the report covers the historical background, a ten-year analysis of some of the changes, and several innovative programs. Tables, figures, charts, and a 16-item bibliography are included.

TN4. Nashville. *Nashville and Davidson County Libraries Directory.* Nashville Library Club, 1970-   . Irregular.
This publication is an alphabetical membership list. The directory of libraries for 1976/77 is only those represented by membership. A list of Nashville Library Club officers since 1926 is appended.

TN5. Nashville and Davidson County. *Charter of the Metropolitan Government of Nashville and Davidson County Tennessee.* Charlottesville, VA: Michie City Publications, 1967-   . 279pp. Loose-leaf.

TN6. Nashville and Davidson County. Historical Commission. *Metropolitan Historical Markers.* Nashville, 1973. 24pp.
The text of 50 markers and a map of their location is reproduced for interested travelers.

TN7. Nashville and Davidson County. Historical Commission. *Nashville: A Short History and Selected Buildings.* Edited by Eleanor Graham. Nashville, 1974. 284pp. $12.95 hardbound ($5.95 paperbound).
For this illustrated study of Nashville's architecture, the city is divided into eight sections. Following a 45-page historical introduction, Nashville's buildings are discussed and given informative annotations of varying length. A list of national register sites, architectural awards, and organizations for historic preservation is appended. There is a 62-item bibliography and an index.

TN8. Nashville and Davidson County. Metro. *Directory of Personnel and Services.* Nashville: Metro, n.d.

TN9. Nashville and Davidson County. Planning Commission. *1970 Census Tract Informational Profiles for Nashville-Davidson County Standard Metropolitan Statistical Area.* Nashville: Central Printing Office, 1973. 123pp.
Based on the 1970 U.S. Census of Population and Housing. These profiles are in a more convenient form than the U.S. census tracts. Twenty-four different pieces of information are given in tabular or chart form. Three maps and a 1960 to 1970 tract comparison guide are included.

TN10. Nashville and Davidson County Planning Commission. *Published Reports and Staff Memorandums of the Planning Commission.* Nashville (301 Metro Office Bldg., Nashville 37201), 1977. 6pp.

TN11. Nashville and Davidson County. Planning Commission. *Social Types in Nashville-Davidson County, Tennessee: A Geographic Distribution, 1950-1970.* Nashville, 1976. 80l.
Basically, this publication is a planning document based on the characteristics of Nashville's population by geographic area. The association between social types and selected variables and changes in types of population between 1950 and 1970 are covered. This study includes 12 tables and three full-color maps.

TN12. Nashville and Davidson County. Public Library of Nashville and Davidson County. Nashville Room. *Index to Classified Obituaries, The Tennessean.* Compiled by Janita Rose. Nashville (Eighth Ave. North and Union, Nashville 37203), 1974-   . Annual.
Arranged alphabetically by deceased's last name, this index carries the date of the first appearance of the obituary in the *Tennessean.* The compiler attempts to verify the name in the event of typographic errors and cites full name whenever possible.

†N13. *1977 Nashville (Davidson County, TN) City Directory.* Taylor, MI: R. L. Polk and Co. (6400 Monroe Blvd., P.O. Box 500 Taylor, MI 48180), 1977. $105. This is the familiar criss-cross directory. The four major sections are the buyer's guide (busir ss advertisements), alphabetical list of names of residents, directory of housel   ars including street and avenue guide, and numerical telephone directory. The 31-page introduction covers basic statistics of bank clearings, postal receipts, building permits, etc. In addition, social and cultural information is given. Metropolitan government offices appear on pages 504–506.

TN14. Nashville. League of Women Voters. *Your Metropolitan Government: A Handbook about Nashville and Davidson County, Tennessee.* 1973. 52pp.
An instructive introduction to the structure and functions of metropolitan government. The legislative, executive, and judicial branches are covered. In addition, there are two chapters on taxation and finance, and the popular control of government. Four charts and one map are included. Indexed.

TN15. Nashville Area Chamber of Commerce. Education Committee. *Nashville Education.* (161 Fourth Ave. N., Nashville 37219) 1974. 28pp.
This directory catalogs all educational opportunities available in the area. These opportunities are classified into five fields: higher education, elementary-secondary education, vocational-technical education, special-interest schools and training, and schools for the physically and mentally handicapped. A list of libraries and of educational radio and television is included. Indexed.

TN16. Nashville Area Chamber of Commerce. *Nashville SMSA Directory of Manufacturers, 1973.* 1973. 109pp. $5.
The Nashville SMSA includes Davidson, Dickson, Robertson, Rutherford, Sumner, and Wilson counties. The directory is divided into four major categories: alphabetical, city-county, product, and corporate affiliation guides. The industrial portrait includes name, address, corporate affiliation, major executive, total employees (also breakdown by male and female), SIC code, and product.

Collections

TN17. **Public Library of Nashville and Davidson County.** Eighth Ave. North and Union, Nashville 37203 (615)244-4700. TWX (810)371-1541.
On April 1, 1963 Nashville and Davidson County merged. The library has a special collection, the Nashville Room, pertaining to local history. The mayor requested a municipal reference service under the auspices of the reference department and issued an executive order requiring all agencies to file their publications in the library. The department maintains an agency file with a list of contact persons. It also maintains an on-line computer based newspaper index. A daily print-out of the index is sent to the agencies; an annual cumulation is being considered. The reference staff maintains a loose-leaf binder entitled "Local Resources," which is a compendium of useful information on services within the city.

TN18. **Tennessee State Library and Archives.** 403 Seventh Ave. N., Nashville 37219 (615)741-2764. TWX (810)371-1164.
The library has a limited collection of local documents, except for a special collection of county records.

TEXAS

The state of Texas publishes extensive statistical material, much of which pertains to municipalities. Beginning in 1967 Texas committed itself to the regional planning concept. As a result, much municipal information, including statistics and directories, is available at the regional council of government level. Texas is perhaps unique in offering a 1,400-item computer print-out of information over 500 municipalities. While the service was designed to attract industry to the state, the compilation of information on the given municipality is invaluable to librarians and researchers. The Legislative Reference Library (Capitol Bldg., P.O. Box 12488, Capitol Station, Austin 78711) may be able to furnish additional information about the service. In addition, the Legislative Reference Library maintains a toll-free Texas legislative information telephone service which operates only during Texas legislative sessions (biennial in odd-numbered years). The information covers bills introduced on a particular subject, author, bill number, bill status, companion bills, and committee hearings scheduled on the bill.

General Publications

TX1. Huffman, Jack W. *Survey of Statistical and Planning Data Collected by Texas State Agencies.* Austin: Governor's Office, Division of Planning Coordination, 1970. 35pp. Available on interlibrary loan from any Texas document depository. For each state agency there is an annotated list of publications, unpublished printed materials, and data files on magnetic tape.

TX2. Mendiola, Tacho. *Demographic Profile of Texas and Selected Cities: Some Recent Trends, 1950-1970.* Houston: University of Houston, Center for Human Resources, 1974. 59pp. Available as ERIC report: ED 097047.

TX3. North Central Texas Council of Governments. *Legislative Directory for the North Central Texas Region.* Arlington (P.O. Drawer COG, Arlington 76011), 1977. 63pp. $1.
North central Texas is a 16-county metropolitan region centered around Dallas and Fort Worth. This directory, compiled after the November 2 general election of 1976 by the North Central Texas Council of Governments, includes a listing and maps of the Council of Governments, state, and federal officials.

TX4. North Texas State University. Center for Community Services. *Texas Municipal Election Law.* Denton (P.O. Box 5344, NTSU Sta., Denton 76203), c. 1971- . Annual.
This loose-leaf handbook is written for county elections and is of value to judges and clerks. The election calendar is updated on a regular basis.

TX5. Texas. Department of Community Affairs. County and Rural Services Division. *Community Development Catalog: A Guide to State and Federal Programs.* Austin (P.O. Box 13166, Capitol Station, Austin 78711), 1975– . Loose-leaf with annual update. Free.
Designed for total community assistance information, this loose-leaf describes each program and provides the name of a contact person.

TX6. Texas. Employment Commission. *Texas Labor Directory.* Austin, 1977. 300pp. (Available from: AFL-CIO, 1106 Lavaca, Suite 200, Austin.)
This gives the names and telephone numbers of union officers for 73 towns and cities in Texas.

TX7. Texas. Governor's Office. Division of Budget and Planning. *Directory [of] Regional Councils in Texas.* Austin (411 W. 13, Austin 78701), 1968– . Annual. Free.
Discusses the relationship between local governments and their regional councils of government. The regional councils are described; for each council there is a section which includes all the publications issued for the past year.

TX8. Texas. Industrial Commission. *General Community Profile.* Austin (P.O. Box 12728, Austin 78711) n.d. $15 each.
These profiles, which cover over 500 Texas cities and towns, are available from the Industrial Commission in a computer print-out format.

TX9. Texas Municipal League. *Directory of Texas City Officials.* Austin (1020 Southwest Tower), 1954– . Annual.

TX10. Texas. State Library. State Publications Clearinghouse. *Texas State Documents: Documents Received by Texas State Library During the Month.* Austin (Box 12927, Capitol Staton, Austin 78711), 1922– . Monthly. Free.
Beginning in July 1975, this checklist began to cover Texas Regional Council of Governments publications. These publications contain important municipal information.

TX11. University of Texas at Arlington. Institute of Urban Studies. *Handbook for Interlocal Contracting in Texas.* Arlington (Arlington 76019), 1972. 239pp.
The Texas Legislature has passed general enabling legislation for local governmental units to allow for cooperation in any venture that each alone could legally perform. This handbook is designed to assist municipal planners in achieving cooperation.

Collections

TX12. Texas Municipal League. 1020 Southwest Tower. Austin (512)478-6601.
The league has a collection of Texas municipal codes and public administration. More important than the collection is the information compiled by the league, which is the major source in the state for comparative data on services, rates, and the activities of municipalities in Texas. The league, which will answer queries, is responsible for numerous articles and publications such as the bimonthly *Municipal Law Bulletin* and the *Handbook for Mayors and Councilmen.* Write for a publications list.

AMARILLO

Local Newspaper Indexing: The reference staff of the Amarillo Public Library, P.O. Box 2171, Amarillo 79105 (806)372-4211, Teletype: (910)898-4158, selectively indexes the Amarillo *Daily News* and the Amarillo *Globe-Times*. The staff will answer queries regarding index citations; no fee involved.

Publications

TX13. Amarillo. Board of City Development. *Amarillo, Texas: Bright Star on the Industrial Horizon.* 1976. 88pp.
Presents a profile of the city for the purpose of attracting new industry.

TX14. Amarillo. Finance Division. *General Budget City of Amarillo, Texas.* 1976. 148pp.

TX15. Amarillo. Police Department. *1976 Annual Report of the Amarillo Police Department.* 1976. 22pp.
Presents an overall view of the operations of the department. There are charts and graphs for different areas of activity.

AUSTIN

Local Newspaper Indexing: The staff of the Austin-Travis Collection of the Austin Public Library (see entry **TX38**) indexes the Austin *American-Statesman* for items about Austin and Travis County. They will accept research questions.

Publications

TX16. Austin. Chamber of Commerce. *Associations Maintaining Headquarters in Austin.* (P.O. Box 1967, Austin 78767) Annual. $2.
These associations are international, national, regional, and district.

TX17. Austin. Chamber of Commerce. *Austin, the Good Life in Texas.* (Industrial Dept., P.O. Box 1967, Austin 78767) n.d.
Statistical data describing Austin's opportunities are presented in sections covering living conditions, education, government, research, market, taxes, transportation, labor, utilities, and industrial sites.

TX18. Austin. Chamber of Commerce. *1975 Directory of Austin Area Publications.* (P.O. Box 1967, Austin 78767) 1975. 29pp. $4.
Lists house organs, association newsletters, etc., published in the city.

TX19. Austin. City Manager. *Municipal Organization: City of Austin.* (P.O. Box 1088, Austin 78767) 1975. 64pp.
Organization charts show the structure of the city departments.

TX20. Austin. Department of Planning. *Austin Tomorrow: Technical Reports.* (P.O. Box 1088, Austin 78767) 1973–75.
These eight reports cover the major areas of investigation of the city planning department's research phase of the Austin Tomorrow program: economic base, population, transportation, housing, core area, neighborhoods, environment, and land use. The reports seek to identify the changes which have occurred since the Aus-

tin Development Plan was approved in 1961 and to project the city's major trends for the next 20 years.

TX21. Austin. Department of Planning. *Basic Data about Austin and Travis County.* (P.O. Box 1088, Austin 78767) 1955?- . Annual.
Statistics about the city and county are grouped under physical characteristics, population, education, tax structure, housing, economics, streets and utilities, services, and airports.

TX22. Austin. Human Relations Commission. *Your Austin 1976-1977: Where to Call Guide.* (P.O. Box 1088, Austin 78767) 1976. 30pp.
This is a directory of important community services available in Austin.

TX23. Austin. Independent School District. Early Childhood Special Education Program. *Directory of Services in Austin and Travis County for Handicapped Children.* (Carruth Administration Bldg., 6100 Guadalupe, Austin 78752) n.d.
A comprehensive and detailed source of information on the wide spectrum of services available in Austin and Travis County for handicapped children. It also provides information on services available for families of children with special needs.

TX24. Austin. League of Women Voters. *Citizen's Guide to Austin and Travis County: A Handbook of Local Government.* (P.O. Box 5365, Austin 78763) c.1975. 92pp.
Provides basic information on the structure, function, and financing of the local government.

TX25. Austin. League of Women Voters. *Directory: Appointed Boards, Commissions, and Committees, Austin and Travis County.* 1976. 62pp.

TX26. Austin. Office of Environmental Resource Management. *Environmental Handbook.* (P.O. Box 1088, Austin 78767) n.d. c.1,000pp.
The handbook was designed to help city departments in designing environmental projects and programs. It includes a checklist of local, state, and federal environmental laws, the city's environmental implementation policy, and a bibliography of sources in the city's public library and the Office of Environmental Resource Management.

TX27. Austin. Urban Transportation Department. *Proposed Transportation Plan for Austin, Texas.* (P.O. Box 1088, Austin 78767) 1976. 60l.
Austin's transit plan is flexible and compatible with the city's larger transportation plan. The transit's design of area and local terminals all feed into the central business district.

TX28. Austin-Travis County Mental Health. Mental Retardation Center. *Client Tracking System Handbook.* Austin (1430 Collier St., Austin 78704), 1974. 100pp.
Lists all categorical services provided in Travis County and informs interested persons of the availability and gaps in service delivery systems in the county.

TX29. Capital Area Planning Council. *Housing Conditions and Occupant Characteristics.* Austin (610 S. Congress, Suite 400, Austin 78704), 1975. 171pp.
Housing conditions in Austin and the surrounding counties are described with a view toward developing an areawide housing planning program.

TX30. Capital Area Planning Council. *Regional Directory.* Austin (610 S. Congress, Suite 400, Austin 78704), 1972– . Annual.
Includes city and county officials in the region, services, state officials, and miscellaneous items.

TX31. Church Women United. *Help for Hunger.* Austin, 1975. 22pp.
This is a directory of agencies and organizations in Austin that have programs to alleviate hunger.

TX32. *Cole's Directory: Cross-Reference Directory, Austin, Texas.* San Antonio: Cole Publications Inc. (4519 Rimrock, San Antonio 78228), 1957– . Annual. $52.
This directory covers buying power, zip code market, street addresses, government, office buildings, and telephone numbers.

TX33. Community Council of Austin and Travis County. *Directory of Community Services in Austin and Travis County.* Austin (1005 W. Sixth St., Austin 78703), 1968– . Annual.
Alphabetical listing of welfare, recreational, health, and educational agencies and organizations. Information is given on services, eligibility, means of application, fees, source of funds, and hours.

TX34. Monti, Lorna A. *Social Indicators for Austin, Texas: A Cluster Analysis of Census Tracts.* Austin: University of Texas, Bureau of Business Research, c.1975. 49pp. $3.
Existing status measures of demography, income, housing, education, safety, health, and patterns of change were clustered in Austin to demonstrate the potential of city social-indicator studies using existing data.

TX35. National Organization for Women. *The NOW Guide for Austin Women.* Austin (Austin Chapter, 1208 Baylor St., Austin 78703), 1974? 49pp. $1.
General information on health, rape, rape prevention, and self-defense is given. Particular information for women in Austin is given concerning day care, housing, employment, the law, credit, and organizations dealing with women's interests.

TX36. Southwest Information Associates. *Austin: Information.* Compiled by Jane Ulrich. Austin (2813 Rio Grande, Austin 78705), 1976. $2.50.
This guide lists alphabetically by source name extensive sources of information in Austin. It includes, among other sources, private and public libraries, newspapers, and organizations.

TX37. Travis County Program Building Committee. *Long-Range County Program.* Austin: Texas Agricultural Extension Service (100 San Antonio, Austin 78701), n.d. 171pp.
This reference source comprises statistical tables, explanations of county governmental structure, and descriptions of county services.

Collections

TX38. Austin Public Library. P.O. Box 2287, Austin 78767 (512)472-0299. Teletype Service: (910)874-2025.
The Austin-Travis Collection is the local history collection and includes maps, oral histories, municipal documents, and items published about the city and the county. The library staff encourages all city departments to send municipal documents for deposit in the Austin-Travis Collection; items in the collection are noncirculating.

TX39. Texas State Library. Public Services Department. P.O. Box 12927, Capitol Station, Austin 78711 (512)475-4355.
The State Library does not collect municipal publications on a systematic basis. The only municipal publications in the collection are those received through the regional planning councils. The library will send on interlibrary loan any state or regional document appearing in the Texas checklist of documents (see entry **TX10**).

TX40. University of Texas. Bureau of Business Research. Library. P.O. Box 7459, University Station, Austin 78712 (512)471-1616.
The library has county files which contain miscellaneous publications issued by Texas municipalities; none of these publications circulate. Newspapers from all over the state are read for articles about new industries which are locating in Texas, or about expansions, or about plants already located in the state. The information is published monthly in the *Texas Industrial Expansion.*

BEAUMONT

Local Newspaper Indexing: The periodicals librarian of the Beaumont Public Library, P.O. Box 3827, Beaumont 77704 (713)838-0812, indexes the Beaumont *Enterprise and Journal.* Coverage centers on city, county, and state activities.

Publications

TX41. Beaumont. City Clerk. *Annual Budget, City of Beaumont: Program Summary.* (Beaumont 77704) Annual.
Brief descriptions of the activities of the various city agencies and total funds allocated for the year.

TX42. Beaumont. City Clerk. *Annual Financial Report for the Year Ended September 30.* (Beaumont 77704) Annual.
Contains fiscal information for the city.

TX43. Texas Community Council of Beaumont. *Community Services Directory of Health, Welfare and Recreation for Beaumont, Texas.* 1972. 101pp. Irregular. $4.50.

CORPUS CHRISTI

Publications

TX44. Corpus Christi. City Clerk. *Annual Budget.* (302 S. Shoreline, Corpus Christi 78401) 1942-   . Annual.
Presents the proposed budget for the next fiscal year.

TX45. Corpus Christi. City Clerk. *Annual Financial Report.* (302 S. Shoreline, Corpus Christi 78401) 1956-   . Annual.

TX46. Coastal Bend Association for Mental Health. *1-2-3 Handbook.* Corpus Christi (334 Wilson Bldg., Corpus Christi 78401), 1970-   . Annual.
A handbook of social service organizations for the city and the ten-county area.

TX47. Nueces County. *Nueces County Auditor's Annual Financial Report.* Corpus Christi (Court House), 1964-   .. Annual. Unavailable.

The financial report for the county gives appropriations, expenditures, encumbrances, and other financial data.

Collections

TX48. La Retama Public Library. 505 N. Mesquite, Corpus Christi 78401 (512)882-1937. Teletype Service (910)876-1468.
The library has the city budget and the financial report. The library staff selectively clips local and regional newspaper articles.

DALLAS

Local Newspaper Indexing: The Texas Collection at the Dallas Public Library (see entry **TX60**) houses the clipping files of the Dallas *Morning News* and the Dallas *Times Herald.* They are arranged by subject and cover the period from early 1940 to date. The *Morning News* index is prepared by the library of the originating newspaper. Microfilm copies of the index from 1917 to date have been given to the Dallas Public Library. Only brief queries will be answered.

Publications

TX49. Dallas. City Manager. *City of Dallas Directory.* Director of Purchasing (City Hall, Dallas 75201), 1976. $4.67.
Covers the mayor, city council, department heads, employees, and services.

TX50. Dallas. City Manager. *City of Dallas, Texas, Operating Budget.* (Rm. 304, City Hall) Annual. $40.
Has a budget summary, the annual budget, the shared revenue budget, and the capital budget.

TX51. Dallas. Director of Personnel. *Administrative Directories.* (2018 Main St., Dallas 75201) Irregular.
Administrative directories are issued to improve service to the public through efficient management and to provide guidance for the uniform administration and coordination of functions of the city. The director of personnel will have administrative responsibility for publication and distribution of manuals, administrative directories, change notices, and current page check list. Departments will be responsible for the preparation and timeliness of material contained within their assigned section of the administrative manual. Manuals containing administrative directives will be issued serially upon request of the director of personnel. Directives remain in effect until officially revised, superseded, or canceled in writing.

TX52. Dallas. Independent School District. *School and Staff Directory.* (3700 Ross Ave., Dallas 75204) Annual. $6.50 (plus tax).

TX53. Dallas. Public Library. *Open Dallas: A Guide to Services and Special Resources.* 2nd ed. Edited by Margaret Warren. (1954 Commerce, Dallas 75201) 1976. 284pp. $2.90 (plus 50¢ postage).
A compilation of community resources in the city selected from the library's computerized community information file. Updated information on any resource is available at the library through the automated community information data base.

TX54. Dallas. Public Library. Business and Technology Division. *Business Information for Dallas.* Edited by Milton G. Ternberg. (1954 Commerce, Dallas 75201) 1976– . Bimonthly. Free.

This newsletter features a specific business problem and presents library resources useful in finding a solution.

TX55. Dallas. Public Library. History and Social Sciences Division. *Local Documents Received January 1973-December 1974.* (1954 Commerce, Dallas 75201) 1968– . Irregular. Free.
This checklist includes documents received from the city and county.

TX56. Dallas. Public Library. History and Social Sciences Division. *Municipal Services Reference Library Select Publications.* (1954 Commerce, Dallas 75201) 1974– . Bimonthly. Free.
This bulletin consists of books, catalogued documents for the city and county, and pertinent journal articles.

TX57. *Dallas County Telephone Directory and Guide to County Personnel.* Dallas (Records Bldg.), 1976. Irregular.

TX58. Executive Services Directory. *Executive Services Directory: The Dallas County Business Guide.* Dallas (5744 L.B.J. Freeway, Suite 205, Dallas 75240), 1973– . Annual. $1.
A list of businesses operating in Dallas County.

TX59. Southern Methodist University. Center for Urban and Environmental Studies. *Appointed Officials Handbook.* Dallas (Dallas 75222), 1975. 149pp. Irregular. $4.
A complete guide to Dallas city government which has organization charts, information on finances and administration, directory of city services, and a list of boards and services.

Collections

TX60. Dallas Public Library. 1954 Commerce, Dallas 75201 (214)748-9071, ext. 378. Teletype Service: (910)861-4057.
The Municipal Services Reference Collection is maintained primarily to serve the needs of municipal administrators and city employees in Dallas. Materials may be made available to the public on a selective basis.
APL/CAT (A Programmed Language/Community Access Tool) is a community information data base managed and maintained jointly by the Dallas Public Library and the North Central Texas Council of Governments. The data base includes information on groups, agencies, and services in the sixteen-county area.

EL PASO

The Department of Planning, Research and Development, city of El Paso, has been an active publisher since 1955. The Bureau of Business and Economic Research, University of Texas at El Paso, also publishes statistical material on the city, as well as the monthly *El Paso Economic Review.* **Local Newspaper Indexing:** The El Paso Public Library (see entry **TX64**) selectively indexes the El Paso *Times, Herald-Post,* and *Journal* for local news. Mail or interlibrary loan queries will be answered.

Publications

TX61. El Paso. Chamber of Commerce. *El Paso Area Fact Book.* (10 Civic Center Plaza, El Paso 79944) 1968– . Biennial. $5.

Intended primarily as an aid to industrial location analysis, the publication includes extensive information on population, labor, utilities, transportation, taxes, industrial facilities, natural resources, and community living.

TX62. El Paso. League of Women Voters. *Handbook of Government: El Paso County.* 1973. 44pp. Irregular.
Contains descriptive information on positions held by government officials, city departments, and the budgets of both city and county governments.

TX63. Texas University at El Paso. Bureau of Business and Economic Research. *Statistical Abstract of El Paso.* (El Paso 79999) 1973. 194pp.
Contains statistical tables on all aspects of El Paso, from population to agriculture and law enforcement.

Collections

TX64. **El Paso Public Library.** 501 N. Oregon, El Paso 79901 (915)533-3556. Teletype Service: (910)964-1381.
The library attempts to acquire all municipal publications and maintains extensive historical files (including photographs and maps) on all aspects of the city. City council *Minutes* from 1873–1908 are also in the collection.

FORT WORTH

Local Newspaper Indexing: The staff of the local history department of the Fort Worth Public Library (see entry **TX88**) have indexed local newspapers for Fort Worth and Tarrant County events since 1966. In 1974 the indexing was cut back to the *Morning Star-Telegram.* The department will answer queries involving one or two citations.

Publications

TX65. Fort Worth. Chamber of Commerce. *Fort Worth Area Census Tract and Market Fact Book.* 1972. 177pp.
This report, based on the U.S. Bureau of the Census count as of April 1970, provides population and housing data by census tracts for the Fort Worth Standard Metropolitan Statistical Area.

TX66. Fort Worth. Chamber of Commerce. *Fort Worth Buyer's Guide and Membership Directory.* 1977. 136pp.
A listing of member firms in the Chamber of Commerce.

TX67. Fort Worth. Chamber of Commerce. *Insight: Fort Worth in Perspective.* 1973. 48pp. $5.
An update of the demographic data of the decennial census.

TX68. Fort Worth. Chamber of Commerce. *Major Employers in Tarrant County.* 1976. 7pp.
Listing of companies arranged according to numbers of employees.

TX69. Fort Worth. City Manager's Office. *Capital Improvement Program, 1976-78.* 1976.
Includes the specific construction projects approved by the city council on December 29, 1975, and those tentatively scheduled for 1977 and 1978.

TX70. Fort Worth. City Manager's Office. *Services to Business and Industry by the City of Fort Worth.* 1966. 52pp.
Discussion of city services which are, or can be, advantageous to businesses and industries currently in the city and which can attract new businesses and industries to locate there.

TX71. Fort Worth. City Planning Department. *Sector-District Plans: A Compilation.* 1976. 126pp.
Provides a quick and easy reference to the sector and district plans adopted as a guide for the development and redevelopment of the city. Also included are the transportation maps to indicate significant changes that have occurred since adoption of some of the sector and district plans.

TX72. Fort Worth. Finance Department. *Annual Financial Report on the City of Fort Worth.* Annual.

TX73. Fort Worth. Municipal Reference Library. *Catalog of the City of Fort Worth Publications in the Municipal Reference Library.* 1970. 62pp.
Arrangement is by department and subject.

TX74. Fort Worth. Personnel Department. *City of Fort Worth Organizational Chart.* (1000 Throckmorton St., Fort Worth 76102) 1977. Unpaged. $16.
Gives organizational structure for each department and division, names of first-line supervisors and department heads, number of city and grant-funded positions, and assignments of all city employees and their classifications.

TX75. Fort Worth. Personnel Department. *Salary Schedules.* (1000 Throckmorton St., Fort Worth 76102) 1968-   . Annual.

TX76. Fort Worth. Research and Budget Department. *Facts and Figures, Fort Worth, 1971.* 1971. 136pp.
Contains performance data, work load comparisons, and information on personnel requirements, expenditures, and revenue over a three-year period; all of the data pertain to the city government.

TX77. Fort Worth. Research and Budget Department. *Budget Instruction Manual.* 1961-   . Annual.

TX78. Fort Worth. Research and Budget Department. *The Fort Worth Budgetary Process.* 1970.

TX79. Fort Worth. Research and Budget Department. *Guide to Governmental Services in Forth Worth.* n.d. 21pp.
A guide to federal, state, and city government services arranged by service categories and giving agency locations and telephone numbers.

TX80. Fort Worth. Research and Budget Department. *Your City Government.* 1976. 19pp.
Includes a list of elected representatives, a description of city council activities, a city organization chart, profiles of city officials, a discussion of board and commission responsibilities, and a listing of board and commission members.

TX81. Overman, William J. *A Guide to Historic Sites in Fort Worth and Tarrant County.* Fort Worth: Tarrant County Historical Society, 1975. 69pp.

Brief notes concerning historic sites in Fort Worth and Tarrant County. There is also information on some of the most influential early citizens in the area.

TX82. Penny, Linda Farrar. *Senior Citizens Services Guide*, *Tarrant County*. Fort Worth: n.p., 1974. 167pp.
This study lists services available to senior citizens and covers discounts, transportation, social centers, education and training, senior citizen's organizations and publications, and health services.

TX83. Southern Methodist University. Institute of Urban and Environmental Studies. *Dallas-Fort Worth Metroplex: Economic Potentials Handbook*. (Dallas 75222) 1973. Unpaged.
An economic report containing historical and projected indicators of the performance of the Dallas and Fort Worth economies based on a five-year study begun in 1968.

TX84. Tarrant County. Community Council. *Directory of Community Resources in Fort Worth and Tarrant County*. Fort Worth, 1973. 179pp.
A guide for the referral of persons to appropriate community resources. Generally the agencies listed are nonprofit, voluntary or tax supported, and offer health, welfare, education, recreation, and related services to residents of the county.

TX85. Tarrant County. League of Women Voters. *Your Local Elected Officials, 1976–77*. Fort Worth, 1976. 11pp.
A list of city officials in the cities of Tarrant County.

TX86. Texas Employment Commission. *Annual Planning Report: Dallas-Fort Worth SMSA*. Fort Worth, 1977.
Statistical and analytical data on the employment prospects of the area.

TX87. United Way of Metropolitan Tarrant County. *Agency Data Directory*. Fort Worth: United Way, 1974. 45pp.
Alphabetical listing of agencies receiving contributions from United Way. The program of the agency is given as well as the amount contributed by United Way. Also includes other financial sources of the agencies, total budget, address, telephone number, name of director and president.

Collections

TX88. Fort Worth Public Library. Ninth and Throckmorton Sts., Fort Worth 76102 (817)335-4781. Teletype Service: (910)893-5069.
The Municipal Reference Collection, formerly maintained at city hall, has been dispersed to city departments and to the public library. The Tarrant Collection of the library, a local history collection for use only in the library, includes some Chamber of Commerce publications, city publications, and urban studies done by area educational institutions.

HOUSTON

The city of Houston publishes annual reports of most city departments, many grant proposals for suggested municipal projects, and numerous reports relating to the city planning department's surveys of projected population growth and economic development of Houston. Several agencies not officially city departments (i.e., the Houston-Galveston Area Council, the Houston Chamber of Commerce, the Houston-Galveston Regional Transportation Study, or the Southwest Center for Urban Research) also publish materials important in describing Houston's present and future. In some cases, private architectural firms have been requested by the city of Houston to conduct feasibility studies of proposed city building or renovation projects.

Emphasis in the following section has been given to documents which may be borrowed through interlibrary loan for in-library use only from the Houston Public Library's research collection in the Texas and Local History Library. **Local Newspaper Indexing:** Bell and Howell Micro Photo Division (Old Mansfield Rd., Wooster OH 44691) has indexed the *Houston Post* since January 1976. The Houston Public Library (see entry **TX139**) has compiled clipping files from the *Houston Post, Houston Chronicle*, and *Houston Press* by subject for earlier articles. It also has microfiche copies of clippings on Houston from the files of the *Houston Chronicle* library. Newspaper research is limited to checking these files by subject.

Publications

TX89. Alan M. Voorhees and Associates. *Basic Characteristics of the Transit System in Houston.* Houston, 1971. 54pp. o.p.
Discusses route locations, service, equipment, and terminals. In addition, there is a brief history of Houston's bus service and a discussion of the Rapid Transit Lines' organization, management, operating costs, and fees. Many statistics as well as some charts and maps are included.

TX90. Alan M. Voorhees and Associates. *Profile in the City of Houston: A Survey of Bus Riders Using Rapid Transit Lines Inc.* Houston, 1971. 67pp. o.p.
Many statistical tables, charts, and maps cover the origins and destinations of passengers, their waiting time, income, their purpose of trip, their sex and ages, etc. A final chart shows by census tract the number of passengers originating from or destined for that tract, those going to the central business district, and those who have other means of transportation available.

TX91. American Institute of Architects. Houston Chapter. *Houston: An Architectural Guide.* Houston, 1972. 168pp. o.p.
Guidebook to representative architecture in the urban and suburban areas of greater Houston.

TX92. Bank of the Southwest, National Association. Industrial and Development Department. *Houston's Office Space Requirements and Projections, 1950-1990.* Houston, 1972. o.p.
This statistical survey examines the amount of available office space, level of occupancy, and trends in locations of office buildings for Houston's central business district and other areas of the city.

TX93. Business Extension Bureau of Texas Inc. *Executive Services Directory: The Harris County Business Guide.* Houston (4802 Travis, Houston 77002), 1973/74- . Biennial.
A listing by type of business of companies in Houston and in other areas of Harris County.

TX94. Harris County. Tax Assessor and Collector. *Voting Precinct Street Guide: Harris County, Texas.* Houston (301 San Jacinto, Houston 77002), 1953?- . Annual. $10.
This computer-produced directory lists by street name and number the city, pre-

cinct number, and zip code for that address as of March 31, 1977. This directory is often used with the League of Women Voters of Houston's *Voter's Key*, which includes a list of precinct numbers and gives the corresponding federal, state, and local officials.

TX95. Houston. *City of Houston Telephone Directory, June 1976.* Houston: n.p., 1940?- . Annual. Not available for distribution.
Arranged by city department and division, this directory lists city officials, their office addresses and telephone numbers.

TX96. Houston Business Journal. *Houston's Public Companies.* Edited by Mike Weingart. Houston: Cordovan Corp., 1972- . Biennial. $9.95. (Available from: Houston Business Journal, 5314 Bingle, Houston 77092.)
Information included in each entry of this directory of Houston-based public companies is the company name, address, phone, their designation symbol used by the New York or American Stock Exchange, which stock exchange lists the company, the officers' names and titles includinc the designation of the director and chief officers, the person in charge of securities information, the number of stockholders and roundlot holders, the date and place of the last annual meeting, stock price ranges, the date the company became public, the offering price, the name, headquarters, and stock exchange of the parent company, the date and place incorporated, the registrar and transfer agent, the investment banker, the certified public accountant firm, the legal counsel firm, the advertising agency, number of companywide and Houston-based employees, earnings, dividends, capitalization, background, and recent developments. The appendix includes those companies for which only limited information was available.

TX97. Houston. Chamber of Commerce. *Houston.* (25th Floor, 1100 Milam Bldg., Houston 77002) 1930- . Monthly. $10 annually (or $1 per copy).
This magazine highlights current trends and events in Houston's businesses, economy, cultural and recreational facilities, medicine, and government.

TX98. Houston. Chamber of Commerce. *Houston Organizations Directory: Business, Professional, Trade.* (25th Floor 1100 Milam Bldg., Houston, 77002) 1959- . Annual. $4 (plus tax and postage).
Includes the address and telephone numbers of the organizations and their major officials.

TX99. Houston. Chamber of Commerce. Census Tract Division. *1970 Census Data for the Houston Area.* (1100 Milam Bldg., Houston 77002) 1971. $18.90 (plus tax and postage).
This is a compilation of statistics based on the Houston Standard Metropolitan Statistical Area and nearby counties.

TX100. Houston. Chamber of Commerce. Communications Division. *Houston Area Media Guide.* (1100 Milan Bldg., Houston 77002) 1974- . Annual. Free.
A listing of newspapers, magazines, television stations, radio stations, and news bureaus in the greater Houston-Galveston area.

TX101. Houston. Chamber of Commerce. Economic Development Division. *Houston Corporate Directory.* (1100 Milam Bldg., Houston 77002) 1973/74- . Biennial. $20 (plus tax and postage).
Covers companies having major corporate management activities in the city.

TX102. Houston. Chamber of Commerce. Economic Development Division. *Houston International Business Directory.* (1100 Milam Bldg., Houston 77002) 1976. 184pp. $10 (plus tax and postage).
This is the first edition of a biennial directory of U.S. companies which have offices in foreign countries as well as in Houston, and foreign companies or foreign governments which maintain offices in Houston.

TX103. Houston. Chamber of Commerce. Research Committee. *Houston-Gulf Coast Area Manufacturer's Directory.* (1100 Milam Bldg., Houston 77002) 1958- . Irregular (but usually biennial). $25 (plus tax).
This directory contains information on manufacturing plants in Brazoria, Chambers, Fort Bend, Galveston, Harris, Liberty, Montgomery, and Waller counties.

TX104. Houston. Chamber of Commerce. Research Division. *Monthly Statistical Summary.* (1100 Milam Bldg., Houston 77002) 1948- . Monthly. Free to libraries.
This publication presents current statistics on Houston and Harris County automobile and truck registration, banking, building industry permits, business indexes, nonresidential construction contracts awarded, department store sales, electrical utilities, employment, natural gas consumption, Port of Houston tonnage handled, postage used, railroad tonnage, residential units completed, number of telephones, unemployment, utility connections, water meter connections, weather data, and a digest of the monthly statistical summary.

TX105. Houston. Chamber of Commerce. Research Division. *Population, Households, and Dwelling Units in Harris County Census Tracts, January 1, 1976.* (1100 Milam Bldg., Houston 77002) 1976. $20.
These statistical tables are estimates to update the 1970 census data.

TX106. Houston. City Planning Department. *Annual Report.* (P.O. Box 1562, Houston 77001) 1940?- . Annual. Free (limited supply).
Summarizes the activities of the department for the completed year. A list of the staff positions and corresponding names of personnel is included.

TX107. Houston. City Planning Department. *Citizen Participation: A Community Relations Handbook.* (P.O. Box 1562, Houston 77001) 1973. 32pp. o.p.
This handbook was written as part of Houston's Neighborhood Improvement Planning Program. It serves as a guideline for contacting, interviewing, and gathering information about neighborhood problems from community residents and local groups.

TX108. Houston. City Planning Department. *Data Book . . . Community Development Area.* (P.O. Box 1562, Houston 77001) 1976- . . Irregular. Not available for distribution.
This is a series of books with information on the present conditions of the 23 Houston areas designated to receive federal funds for neighborhood improvement under the Housing and Community Development Act of 1974. In each case, statistical information from the 1970 census and other sources is combined with descriptive text.

TX109. Houston. City Planning Department. *Houston CBD Data Book.* (P.O. Box 1562, Houston 77001) 1973. o.p.
Part of the Central Business District Study Program, this is a compilation of descriptive text, maps, and statistics compiled by the city departments and other

sources on the Central Business District's growth and development through 1972. A bibliography of reports and surveys, a list of definitions, and maps and other graphics are followed by descriptions, maps showing blocks, and statistics of Houston's Central Business District and the Central Traffic District: of land use for commercial buildings, cultural areas, open spaces, and parking areas; of tax assessment; of circulation and other traffic patterns; and of public utility locations in the area. There is also a chronology of major buldings constructed since 1910. Small maps compare the Dallas, Kansas City, and Houston Central Business Districts by blocks for their structural density; small maps for Dallas, Denver, Kansas City, and Houston compare their 20 blocks of highest tax assessment.

TX110. Houston. City Planning Department. *Houston's Environmental Concerns.* (P.O. Box 1562, Houston 77001) 1973. 36pp. o.p.
This report gives a brief survey of Houston's environment and environmental protection during the rapid development and expansion of the city, especially during the Neighborhood Improvement Planning Program. A brief history of Houston's environmental concerns is followed by a description of current efforts to protect the environment, and a summary of federal requirements in preparing environmental impact statements to accompany proposed federally funded projects which may significantly affect the environment.

TX111. Houston. City Planning Department. *Houston's Neighborhood Improvement Planning Program: Resources Manual.* (P.O. Box 1562, Houston 77001) 1973. 59pp. o.p.
This manual identifies and describes the neighborhood improvement publications and programs, both governmental and nongovernmental, at the federal and local levels. A "Home Improvement Checklist" designed to help residents evaluate their own homes is followed by a directory of various local organizations which can help residents improve their areas, a list of pamphlets on city services, and a directory of community service agencies and organizations.

TX112. Houston. City Planning Department. *Neighborhood Improvement Handbook.* (P.O. Box 1562, Houston 77001) 1976. 27pp. o.p.
This handbook informs residents of every Houston neighborhood about the individual participation method of planning and completing projects, the city's responsibilities toward improvement and the appropriate city ordinances, other neighborhood resources including governmental and nongovernmental organizations and agencies, and suggestions for conducting planning meetings and accomplishing projects. The appendixes include inventory sheets for evaluating neighborhood conditions, an outline of the city's *Code of Ordinances* showing the main topics covered by the sections, useful agency phone numbers, a release for work on private property, and maps showing neighborhood improvement planning areas.

TX113. Houston. City Planning Department. *Overall Program Design.* (P.O. Box 1562, Houston 77001) 1973. 106pp. o.p.
This document describes the planning activities and projects (including the department's related publications) of the department from 1964 through 1976.

TX114. Houston. City Secretary's Office. *Annual Report for the Year.* (City Hall, Houston 77002) 1958?- . Annual.
This brief report covers the duties, number, and positions of department personnel, accomplishments of the department, elections held, amount of correspondence handled, number of permits issued, and amount of revenue handled by the department.

TX115. Houston. Civil Service Department. Wage and Salary Division. *City of Houston Alphabetical Listing and Classification Codes of Class Titles, November 1976.* 1968?- . Not available for distribution.
This loose-leaf listing of job classifications of full-time employees in the city indicates the class code, the classification title of the position, the physical grade, the pay grade, and actual salary range on a biweekly basis. Supplementary pages are issued at irregular intervals to replace obsolete information.

TX116. Houston. Comptroller. *Comparative Revenues.* January 1963?- November 1976. Monthly (except no December issues from 1969 through 1976). o.p.
This statement of revenues collected by city departments is arranged by department and then by specific source within that department. For each source of funds, figures were given for the previous year's total collection, for the current year's collection as of the current month, and for the previous year's collection as of the corresponding month. Totals were also given for the revenues collected by the department as a whole.

TX117. Houston. Department of Public Works. *Metropolitan Water Systems: City of Houston, Resume.* (P.O. Box 1562, Houston 77001) 1975. 12pp. Free (supply limited).
A general description of the city's water system is followed by a more detailed discussion of the history of its usage, sources of groundwater, subsidence and groundwater control legislation, surface water supply, water conveyance system, current and proposed projects, and annexed water districts.

TX118. Houston. Fire Department. *History of the Houston Fire Department.* 1914. o.p.

TX119. Houston. Fire Department. *Houston Fire Department, 1838-1971.* 1971. 304pp. o.p.

TX120. Houston-Galveston Area Council. *Regional Atlas.* 2nd ed. (3701 W. Alabama, P.O. Box 22777, Houston 77027) 1972. 60pp. Free (supply limited).
Has over 80 maps covering the 13 Houston-area counties. These maps show locations of water and other natural resources, marine life and wildlife, population, housing, school districts, livestock and agricultural production, industry, transportation facilities, utilities, manufacturing and business establishments, employment, flood control projects, and recreation areas.

TX121. Houston-Galveston Area Council. *Regional Data Book.* (3701 W. Alabama, P.O. Box 22777, Houston 77027) 1972. 94pp. Free.
This sourcebook combines statistical information gathered from various federal, state, and local governmental agencies, and private organizations. Figures pertain to population and housing; income; education; health; welfare; local government financing and water usage; agriculture; transportation; selected community facilities including newspapers, post offices, libraries, radio stations, telephone companies, television stations, electrical and gas services, and hospitals; and business economic data. Although most of the tables cover a single year (usually 1970 to 1971), other tables are retrospective through the late 1950s and 1960s.

TX122. Houston. Health Department. Air Pollution Control Program. Technical Services Program. *Quarterly Report.* (1115 N. MacGregor, Houston 77030) 1975- . Quarterly. Free (limited supply).

Presents the statistics of this department's enforcement activities and of the air quality results from samples taken at each of its test sites.

TX123. Houston. Health Department. Statistical Section. *Houston Vital Statistics.* 1965-   . Annual. Free (limited supply).
These computer-produced charts include numbers of births and deaths, causes of death, and selected statistics by census tract.

TX124. Houston. Independent School District. *HISD Telephone Directory.* (Information Services Department, 3830 Richmond Ave., Houston 77027) 1974?-   . Biennial. Free (limited supply).
Includes a list of central office staff, of schools, of administrative personnel, and of Board of Education members.

TX125. Houston. League of Women Voters. *H.I.S.D. School Facts.* (614 Harold, Houston 77006) 1975. 108pp. $1.
This booklet presents nonevaluative, general information to the layman on the politics, administration, and instruction in the Houston Independent School District.

TX126. Houston. League of Women Voters. *Know Your City Government: A Guide for Houston's Citizens.* 3rd ed. (614 Harold, Houston 77006) 1977. $1.
Following a brief history of Houston's growth, this handbook describes the functions and organization of the various city departments involved in the administration, financing, public protection, public health, cultural and recreational facilities, and municipal services of Houston.

TX127. Houston. League of Women Voters. *Spring Branch School Facts.* (614 Harold, Houston 77006) 1973. 76pp. 50¢.
This is a handbook for teachers, administrators, and laymen on the schools in the Spring Branch Independent School District. It covers their administration, curricula, boundaries, financing, boards of trustees, and state regulation.

TX128. Houston. Mayor's Office. *Annual Budget.* 1943?-   . Annual. Not available for distribution.
The summary of the general budget is followed by a detailed description and budget breakdown for each city department. The mayor's letter transmitting the budget to city council is included. The 1977 budget was accompanied by the *Revenue Sharing Budget.*

TX129. Houston. Mayor's Office. *Capital Improvement Program.* (Policy Planning Division, P.O. Box 1562, Houston 77001) 1975/76-   . Irregular. Distribution limited to libraries and other institutions. Free (supply limited).
Provides the recommended Capital Improvement Program. The summary of funds, both available and required for the proposed improvements program, is followed by statistical charts for each proposed program and specific projects within that program.

TX130. Houston. Model City Department. *Model Cities Program Directory.* n.d. 38pp. o.p.
This directory lists agencies and projects under the Houston Model Cities Program as of January 1972. A list of Model Neighborhood Residents Commissioners and their alternates is included, as well as a map showing the districts of the program they represent.

TX131. Houston. Model City Department. *The Neighborhood: The Model Cities Monthly Newspaper.* November 1969–November 1971? o.p.
Included biographical sketches of staff, new projects approved for the urban renewal program, and descriptions of selected model cities projects.

TX132. *Houston Oil Directory.* Houston: Eaton Pub. Co. (5400 Memorial Dr., Suite 702, Houston 77007), 1977. $13 (plus postage, handling, and tax).
A directory of individuals and companies offering a variety of services to the oil industry in Houston.

TX133. Houston. Police Department. *Houston Police: Justice with Mercy, 1974-75.* 1975. 296pp. o.p.
This is a compilation of photographs with captions identifying division heads and other police personnel, municipal judges, city attorneys and their staff members, and the department's activities in earlier years. Descriptive text explains the function of each division in the department, and the history of law enforcement in what is now the city of Houston is traced chronologically from 1832 through 1967.

TX134. Houston Regional Minority Purchasing Council. *Houston Minority Vendors Directory for the Greater Houston Area.* (4101 San Jacinto, Suite 204, Houston 77004) 1977. Irregular. $25 (plus $15 per year for service update).
Arranged by type of service, this directory lists mainly Houston-area minority vendors who supply goods and services in the fields of construction, manufacturing, and special services.

TX135. Port of Houston Authority of Harris County. *Port of Houston Foreign Trade Statistics.* Houston (County Courthouse, 300 San Jacinto, Houston 77002), 1958?– . Annual. Free.
This computerized list indicates the number of tons and dollar value of imports and exports transported through the Port of Houston.

TX136. Tax Research Association of Houston and Harris County Inc. *Newsletter.* Houston (639 Capital National Bank Bldg., 1300 Main St., Houston 77002), 1947?– . Irregular. Free to members ($100 membership).
This publication contains information on Houston and Harris County's current tax structure: city bonds, public school financing, water districts, the debt structure, and other related topics.

TX137. United Fund of Houston and Harris County. *Directory of Community Resources and Services.* Houston (1010 Waugh Drive, P.O. Box 13668, Houston 77019), 1977. Irregular. $12.95.
This computerized list covers over 400 agencies (nonprofit, voluntary, and tax supported) offering social services to persons in the greater Houston area.

TX138. University of Texas. Bureau of Economic Geology. *Land and Water Resources in the Houston-Galveston Area Council.* Austin, 1975. 25pp. $5. (Available from: Houston-Galveston Area Council, Library, P.O. Box 22777, Houston 77027.)
Describes the natural resources including vegetation, mineral resources, energy resources, and natural hazards such as hurricanes, flooding, erosion, subsidence, and faulting. A selected bibliography and a glossary are included.

Collections

TX139. Houston Public Library. 500 McKinney Ave., Houston 77002 (713) 224-8575.
The public library is now the home of materials collected by the Houston Metropolitan Archives and Research Center which began in 1974 as a two-year federally funded project to locate, organize, and preserve historical records important in describing the history, growth, and development of what is now the Houston metropolitan area. Since May 1976, the printed documents including mansucripts, oral history, tapes, films, and microfilms that were collected by the project have been housed in the library's Houston Metropolitan Research Center. Continuing efforts are being made to discover and collect sources of information that will be valuable to future researchers examining Houston's history and growth. The Texas and Local History Library, one of the divisions within the Houston Metropolitan Research Center, contains material related to the history, geography, education, government, folklore and other literature, and arts of Texas and the Houston area.
    The Archives and Manuscripts Division houses films; records of local nongovernmental institutions including the Houston Chamber of Commerce, banks, transportation companies, and churches; local governmental records of Brazoria, Galveston, Matagorda, Fort Bend, Wharton, Jackson, and Harris counties; and manuscripts of persons prominent in Houston's past and present.
    The Houston Metropolitan Research Center's ongoing oral history program, its participation in the Regional Historical Resource Depository System, its development of a master index to the historical records of area churches, and its use of an Automated Data Retrieval System to index by subject and indicate institutional location of Houston-related documents, have made it a growing depository of research materials on Houston. The public library attempts to forward copies of all related municipal publications to Greenwood Press for inclusion in *Index to Current Urban Documents.*

(See also entry **US4.**)

LUBBOCK

Publications

TX140. Lubbock. City Council. *Annual Program of Services* (title page: *City of Lubbock Annual Report*). (City Hall, 916 Texas Ave., Lubbock 79401) 1955/56– . Annual.
Includes an organizational chart for the city, budget summaries, and details for every city department including a complete statement of capital outlay for the city.

TX141. Lubbock. Dept. of Finance. *Annual Financial Report of the City of Lubbock.* (City Hall, 916 Texas Ave., Lubbock 79401), 1956/57– . Annual.
Includes the accountants' report on financial statements, the general fund, capital projects funds, electric and water revenue funds, revenue sharing funds, and a statistical section.

TX142. Lubbock. Ordinances, Local Laws, etc. *The Code of the City of Lubbock.* Tallahassee, FL: Municipal Code Corp. (1700 Capital Circle S.W., Tallahassee, FL 32304), 1959– .
Contains the city charter and the code of ordinances, exclusive of the building codes. It is kept current with loose-leaf supplements.

TX143. Lubbock. Public Information Office. *City of Lubbock Telephones.* City Hall, 1977. $2.
A directory of city offices, administrative and department head personnel.

SAN ANTONIO

Local Newspaper Indexing: The history department of the San Antonio Public Library (see entry **TX147**) maintains a clipping and index file of the San Antonio *Light*, the *Express*, and the *Evening News* on matters of local and statewide interest, mainly people, places, and events.

Publications

TX144. Community Welfare Council of San Antonio. *Directory of Community Services, San Antonio and Bexar County, Texas.* United Way (Community Resources Department, 406 W. Market St., Rm. 401, San Antonio 78205), 1952– . Biennial. $5 (revisions, $3).
This directory of the welfare, recreational, health, and educational resources of San Antonio and Bexar County serves as a reference to local resources and services available to the public.

TX145. San Antonio. City Council. *Minutes of the City Council. . . .* 1965– .
A mimeographed copy of the regular meeting minutes is deposited with the public library (see entry **TX147**) after each session. The minutes are not cataloged but are collected separately as documents. The minutes are also being microfilmed as an ongoing project; the years 1965 to 1974 are currently available on microfilm. The minutes contain the discussion of proposals as well as the text of citations and ordinances.

TX146. San Antonio. League of Women Voters. *Local Government Handbook.* (1017 N. Main Ave., Rm. 223, San Antonio 78212) 1972. $3.
Though mostly concerned with Bexar County and San Antonio, it includes some material on suburban municipalities and local governments. It discusses the governmental and financial structure of the county and city; election procedures; public protection services; public utilities; urban planning and development entities; traffic control, transportation, and public works agencies; as well as housing, public health, and welfare services, community recreational and cultural facilities, and public education agencies. The handbook provides a directory of local offices and agencies.

Collections

TX147. San Antonio Public Library. 203 S. St. Mary's St., San Antonio 78205 (512)223-5538. Teletype Service: (910)871-1122.
The library's collection of city documents is newly acquired. The staff is just beginning to describe and index the collection.

UTAH

The Utah State Library Commission in cooperation with the Division of Archives and the Utah State University Library has collected, indexed, and microfiched all state publications in Utah. The State Library, as the hub of the depository system, collects all publications published by state agencies which are then sent to archives for microfiching. The archives sends a complete copy of fiche to both the Utah State Library and the Utah State University. The latter inputs all publications received into the computer and extracts an index by title, author, agency, key word, geographical location, plus the original entry. The computer tape is then sent back to archives and put on fiche. The index is known as the Utah Publication Retrieval System (UPRS).

OGDEN

Publications

UT1. North Ogden Planning Commission. *Comprehensive Land Use Master Plan North Ogden, Utah.* Ogden (505 E. 2600 N., Ogden 84404), 1972. 99pp. Irregular.
Found in the UPRS, this is a plan for the development and renewal of the urban area.

UT2. Ogden. City Park and Recreation Commission. *A Park and Recreation Master Plan Designed for the City of Ogden.* Prepared by Schiupp-Ferguson and Associates. 1969. 164pp. Irregular. (Available from: Ogden City Planning Commission, 714 Municipal Bldg., Ogden 84401.)
The master plan for the recreational needs of the community is found in the UPRS.

UT3. Ogden. City Planning Commission. *Comprehensive Land Use Master Plan.* (714 Municipal Bldg., Ogden 84401) June 1971. 188pp. Irregular.
This book, which is in the UPRS, gives a brief history of Ogden and discusses its existing land use. It proposes a plan of development for the next 20 years, 1970-1990.

UT4. Ogden. City Planning and Commission. *Housing Inventory and Needs Study Ogden, Utah 1973.* (714 Municipal Bldg., Ogden 84401) 1973. 66pp. Irregular.
Found in the UPRS, this document inventories residential quality and public services within the municipality.

UT5. Ogden. City Planning Commission. *Recommended Development Guidelines for the East Bench: An Environmental Study.* (714 Municipal Bldg., Ogden 84401) 1973. 12pp. Irregular.
This study, which is found in the UPRS, was undertaken in an effort to set up regulatory measures to minimize structural damage and personal injury caused by earthquakes.

UT6. Ogden. City Planning Commission. *Southeast Section Plan Ogden, Utah.* (714 Municipal Bldg., Ogden 84401) 1973. 33pp. Irregular.
This report, which is found in the UPRS, suggests priority for the development of a precise plan for the Southeast Section, because it represents significant potential for residential growth.

UT7. Ogden. City Planning Commission. *Southwest Section Plan Ogden, Utah.* (714 Municipal Bldg., Ogden 84401) 1974. 34pp. Irregular.
This report, which is also found in UPRS, is part of the city's comprehensive master land use plan.

UT8. Ogden. Ordinances, Local Laws, etc. *Revised Ordinances of Ogden City 1964: The Charter and the General Ordinances of the City.* Ogden: Star Printing Co., 1964– . Irregular. Loose-leaf. Free. (Available from: Recorder's Office, Municipal Bldg., Washington Blvd., Ogden 84401.)
This publication contains the charter, laws, and ordinances and their revisions.

UT9. Pleasant View Planning Commission. *Comprehensive Land Use Master Plan Pleasant View, Utah.* (Pleasant View 84404) 1973. 112pp.
Found in the UPRS, the report comprises the 1990 comprehensive plan for Pleasant View.

UT10. Riverdale City Planning Commission. *Riverdale Master Development Plan Riverdale, Utah.* Ogden (4459 S. 700 W., Ogden 84403), 1972. 105pp.
Found in the UPRS, this plan covers the time period from 1972 to 1990. As Riverdale is located between Salt Lake City and Ogden, it is in a growth-oriented area.

UT11. Weber Area Council of Governments. *Identification of Overlaps, Duplications and Inefficiencies.* Ogden: Weber State College, c. 1970. 48pp. Irregular. (Available from: Weber Area Council of Governments, 714 Municipal Bldg., Ogden 84401.)
This report is also found in UPRS.

UT12. Weber Area Council of Governments. *Weber Area Local Government Improvement Plan Summary.* Ogden (714 Municipal Bldg, Ogden 84401), 1971. 33pp. Irregular.
This is a study of 50 local government functions and organizations in Weber County with a view toward promoting economy and efficiency in operations and eliminating disparities, fragmentations, and duplications of services. If desired the complete report, *Weber Area Local Government Improvement Plan*, is available and totals 190 pages. It is also a 1971 publication.

UT13. Weber County Planning Commission. *Ogden Valley Human Resources Report.* (714 Municipal Bldg., Ogden 84401), 1974. 63pp. Irregular.
Found in the UPRS, this report overviews the history, geography, geology, climate, land status and uses, and agricultural production of the county.

UT14. Weber County Planning Commission. *Ogden Valley Natural Resources Evaluation.* Ogden (714 Municipal Bldg., Ogden 84401), 1975, 154pp. Irregular. Found in the UPRS, this report examines the natural resource constraints of the Ogden Valley.

UT15. Weber County Planning Commission. *Weber River Parkway Concept.* Prepared for Weber Area Council of Governments. Ogden (714 Municipal Bldg., Ogden 84401), 1973. Irregular.
Found in the UPRS, this report gives the history of the Weber River; purposes of the parkway; opportunities, objectives, financial aspects, and maps of the parkway.

Collections

UT16. Weber State College. Ogden 84408 (801)399-5941, ext. 689. Teletype Service: (910)971-5913.
The library retains one year of the *Ogden Standard Examiner* in hardbound.

SALT LAKE CITY

Local Newspaper Indexing: The *Salt Lake City Tribune* is indexed by Omniwest Microfilm. The index is comprehensive and the Salt Lake City Public Library (see entry **UT22**) will accept queries about the information contained in it.

Publications

UT17. Salt Lake City Corp. *International Airport Master Plan* (condensed version). Prepared by Richardson Associates, Boeing Aerospace Co., and Battelle. Seattle, WA: Richardson Associates, 1975. 127pp.

UT18. Salt Lake City Corp. *Salt Lake City Fire Department.* n.p. Annual.

UT19. Salt Lake City Corp. *Salt Lake City Police Department.* n.p. Annual.

UT20. Salt Lake City Corp. Planning Commission. *Central Community Development Plan.* n.d. 62pp.

UT21. Salt Lake City Corp. Planning Commission. *Salt Lake City Community Improvement Program.* 1972. 140pp.

Collections

UT22. Salt Lake City Public Library. 209 E. Fifth St., Salt Lake City 84111 (801)363-5733, ext. 56.
Material of a historical nature can be found in Special Collections or the clipping collection. The Information Center handles community information and the Business, Science and Technology Department oversees current local government. The library has a complete run of local newspapers on microfilm. Municipal publications are noncirculating but can be copied or microfilmed for a small per page charge. The Salt Lake City Public Library is in the process of developing a collection of local documents and at this point the collection is not truly comprehensive. The principal documents are indexed in Greenwood Press's *Index to Current Urban Documents.*

UT23. Utah State Library Commission. 2150 S. 300 W., Suite 16, Salt Lake City 84115 (801)533-5875 Teletype Service: (910)925-5170.
The library is a complete depository for state publications. The staff is hopeful that with the Utah Publications Retrieval System (UPRS) they can add to the collection of municipal publications. Photocopy service is available.

VERMONT

BURLINGTON

The city of Burlington publishes very little aside from the usual municipal yearly report. The majority of the publishing has been sponsored by the Planning Commission of the city. **Local Newspaper Indexing:** The Bailey Library of the University of Vermont has indexed the *Burlington Free Press* since 1959. The index covers state and local news only. Queries should be addressed to Special Collections Department.

Publications

VT1. Barton-Aschmen Associates. *Transit Technical Study, Chittenden County, Vermont.* Prepared for the Chittenden County Regional Planning Commission and the U.S. Department of Transportation. Washington, DC, 1973. 144pp. Irregular. (Photocopy available at cost from: Fletcher Free Library, 246 Main St., Burlington 05401.
This study covers past trends in local transit within Chittenden County, current transit service and alternative transit service concepts. It includes characteristics of present bus riders, travel characteristics of major employment centers, and household travel characteristics. Also included are fixed route system analysis, demand responsive system analysis, discussion of marketing, ownership and management alternatives, recommendations, and steps for program implementation.

VT2. Burlington. *Annual Report: City of Burlington, Vermont.* Queen City Printers. Annual. 206pp. (Available on interlibrary loan from: Fletcher Free Library, 246 Main St., Burlington 05401.)
Contains a chronological listing of the mayors of Burlington, city statistics, assessed valuation, bonded debt, list of alderman by ward, list of aldermanic committees, city officers, commissioners and board members, schedule of regular meetings of city commissioners, city budget, and annual reports of each department, plus a listing of salaries for each city employee.

VT3. Burlington. *Zoning Regulations.* n.p., 1973. 56pp. Irregular. (Photocopy available at cost from: Fletcher Free Library, 246 Main St., Burlington 05401.)
Covers establishment of districts, use requirements for specific districts, planned residential development, performance standards, minimum lot requirements, off-street parking and loading, site plan approval, Board of Adjustment, interpretation and administration, enforcement and penalties, remedies, and amendments.

VT4. Burlington. Ordinances, Local Laws, etc. *Code of Ordinances: City of Burlington, Vermont: The Charter, Related Laws and General Ordinances of the City.* Tallahassee, FL: Municipal Code Corp., 1973. 2752pp. Irregular. (Partial photocopy available at cost from: Fletcher Free Library, 246 Main St., Burlington 05401.)

Includes a list of officials of city at the time of codification, ordinance-adopting code, city charter and related laws, code of ordinances, zoning regulations, rules and regulations of the Board of Alderman, and rules and regulations of the Traffic Commission.

VT5. Burlington. Welfare Department. *Report of the Burlington Social Survey.* Burlington: Vermont Welfare Dept., 1967. 134pp. Irregular. (Photocopy available at cost from: Fletcher Free Library, 246 Main St., Burlington 05401.)

The report of this survey can be divided into four main sections. The introduction gives a statement of purpose, scope and method, as well as a timetable. The second section deals with social characteristics of Burlington households as discovered through the use of a household survey and an agency survey. The third section assesses social problems in Burlington households as related to poverty level. The last main section is a summary of findings and recommendations. Also included are ecological correlates of low income in the Burlington urban area.

VT6. Burlington-Lake Champlain Chamber of Commerce. *Chittenden County, Vermont.* n.p. 1973? 14pp. Irregular. (Photocopy available from: Fletcher Free Library, 246 Main St., Burlington 05401.)

This small promotional booklet gives pertinent information on the towns comprising Chittenden County. Types of information include climate, hospitals, schools, employment, banks, transportation, newspapers, electric power companies,automobile information, and taxes. Each town is analyzed separately and population, altitude, area, distance from Burlington, type of government, police protection, fire protection, taxes, zoning board, city water supply, electric, natural gas and telephone service, sewerage, schools, library, park and recreational facilities offered to city residents are given.

VT7. Chittenden County Regional Planning Commission. *We Are Not the Last Generation.* Richmond, 1975. 128pp. Irregular. (Photocopy at cost from: Fletcher Free Library, 246 Main St., Burlington 05401.)

This is a comprehensive plan for 14 municipalities within Chittenden County, including Burlington, providing guidelines for future development of the region. The study is comprised of nine sections divided as follows: introduction, history, population, housing, recreation and open space, economics, transportation, land use, and implementation. Each chapter gives an in-depth discussion of the topic, statistics relevant to the topic, and a delineation of goals in each area.

VT8. Greater Burlington Industrial Corporation. *Industries in Greater Burlington and Chittenden County, Vermont.* Burlington (191 College St., Burlington), 1972. 5pp. Irregular. (Also available from: Fletcher Free Library, 246 Main St., Burlington 05401.)

Information given in this list includes name of industry, address, brief description of product, president or owner(s), approximate employment, and telephone number. Industries listed lie within county lines unless indicated otherwise.

VT9. Hammer, Siler, George Associates. *The Burlington Civic Center: Economic Study.* Prepared for the Burlington City Planning Commission. Washington, DC (1140 Connecticut Ave. N.W., Washington, DC 20036), 1975 103pp. Irregular. The report, which consists of six sections and an appendix, focuses on the economic aspects of developing a civic center facility to serve Burlington and surrounding areas. Factors analyzed include the economy and economic change in Burlington and its markets, and existing audience support activities compared to an inventory of existing facilities. Prospects for new audience activities are analyzed, a recommendation for a civic center facility made, and a cost estimate given. Facility utilization, income and expenses are projected for a typical operating year. Location and financing are also discussed.

VT10. Hatch, Diane. *A Summary of Transportation Studies for Burlington, Vermont.* Prepared for the Burlington Planning Commission. Burlington: Burlington Planning Commission, 1973. 20pp. (Photocopy available at cost from: Fletcher Free Library, 246 Main St., Burlington 05401.)
This report capsulizes the important recommendations of ten previous studies on the transportation dilemma within the city of Burlington. It contains a list of the ten studies under comparison, a comparison of the recommendations and a one-page summary of each study. Each capsule report contains two series of overlays and two base maps, depicting each recommendation visually.

VT11. *Manning's Burlington and South Burlington, Winooski and Essex Junction Directory.* Greenfield, MA: H. A. Manning (278 Main St., Greenfield MA 01301). Annual. Available on subscription. (Also available on interlibrary loan, excepting the current edition, from: Fletcher Free Library, 246 Main St., Burlington 05401.)
Contains alphabetical directories of citizens, classified business directories, street directories, and a record of city, town, and state governments, societies, churches, etc.

Collections

VT12. Fletcher Free Library. 246 Main St., Burlington 05401 (802)863-3403.
The collection centers on annual reports, city directories, and planning commission reports. Reference materials do not circulate for interlibrary loan. Photocopy service is available for a small per page charge. The Fletcher Free Library attempts to acquire all current municipal publications from the city. It also has an extensive historical collection of Vermontiana and Burlingtoniana, some of which dates back to the 1700s. Reproductions of 15 early city documents are also housed in the library. A Vermontiana checklist of all library holdings on Vermont is available free of charge from the library. The annual report and the code of ordinances are sent on a regular basis to the Greenwood Press for inclusion in *Index to Current Urban Documents.*

RUTLAND

Publications

VT13. Rutland. City Clerk's Office. *84th Annual Report: July 1, 1975 to June 30, 1976.* 1893– . Annual. 116pp. Free.
Includes list of aldermanic committees, municipal directory, list of administrative personnel, list of ward officers, last tax levy, list of polling places, State Senators and State Representative from Rutland, bonded debts of the city for 24 years, significant dates in the city's year, list of retired and deceased city employees of the past year, where to get information on various services, reports of the mayor and of the various city departments, a list of former city mayors, listing of city and school department employees and their salaries, and general information about the city for visitors.

VT14. City Treasurer's Office. *Annual Report of the Treasurer of Rutland, Vermont for the Fiscal Year Ended June 30, 1976.* 1961– . Annual. 102pp. Free. Contains city treasurer's letter of transmittal, financial statements for individual funds including general fund, school fund, bond fund, trust agency funds, water utility fund, parking meter fund, sewage disposal fund, general fixed assets, general bonded debt, revenue sharing trust fund, combined balance sheet and statements, and statistical tables and data.

Collections

VT15. Rutland Free Library. Court St., Rutland 05701. (802)773-6880. The two Rutland municipal publications which the library has are the *City Reports* and *Financial Report*, both annual. The library does not circulate reference works. The library has a Vermont Historical Collection which is noncirculating and includes genealogical and more general historical works, and noncirculating microfilm of the *Rutland Daily Herald* (1792–). The *Rutland Daily Herald* is not indexed.

VIRGINIA

HAMPTON

Hampton has done a considerable amount of publishing. Unfortunately, there is no checklist of city publications. Publications can be requested from the various departments and also from the public library (see entry **VA8**) on an interlibrary loan basis, if available.

Publications

VA1. Hampton. City Council. *Inter-Office Telephone Directory, City of Hampton.* (City Hall, Hampton 23669) n.d. 15pp.
Offices are listed alphabetically. The departments with respective addresses are in alphabetical order with personnel, titles, and telephone numbers. Emergency and general information dialing is given at the end.

VA2. Hampton. City Manager. *City of Hampton, Virginia, Fiscal Year 1976–77 Budget.* (City Hall) 1976.
This operating budget includes legislative, law, constitutional, executive, community development, administrative services, community services, contributions, debt service, and school categories. The next four chapters are devoted to revenue sharing, revenue estimates, capital budget, and programs funded from sources other than general funds. There is a commentary on each office or category.

VA3. Hampton. City Planning Commission. *City of Hampton Proposed Comprehensive Plan.* (City Hall) 1977. 183pp.
A description of the long-range intentions of the city regarding physical development.

VA4. Hampton. Department of City Planning. *DATAB 75.* (City Hall) 1976. 117pp.
An original source document of statistical data on the city. Included is information on housing, population, transportation, land use, and the social characteristics of the populace, as well as an economic profile of the city. Data sources are the U.S. Bureau of the Census, 1974 Hampton School Census, and the Hampton city planning department. Charts and graphs containing retrospective data and projections to 2020 accompany the text.

VA5. Hampton. City Planning Commission. *Survey of Community Development Needs.* 1975. 187pp.
This publication should be considered a valuable information resource for updating the comprehensive plan and creating community development strategies for future programs.

VA6. Hampton. City Planning Commission. *Triennial School Census Analysis.* 1975. 71pp.
The purpose of the census is to determine the number of persons 1–19 years of age and to provide current information on population, economic, and housing characteristics. The data are presented on the basis of traffic zones and census tract divisions. Specific information includes type of residence, military households, number of automobiles, racial distribution, previous residence, year moved to residence, and place of work. A few maps supplement the tables.

VA7. Hampton. Department of Finance. *Capital Improvements Program, 1976-77 to 1980-81.* (City Hall) 1976.
A five-year plan developed and revised annually for the purpose of scheduling these major public improvements within the fiscal capabilities of the city. Each program has a project description as well as justification, a capital improvement program history, land requirements, and its relationship to the comprehensive plan. The programs fall under one of the six bond issue categories: schools, streets and roads, buildings, parks, fire equipment, and beach development.

Collections

VA8. Charles H. Taylor Memorial Library. 4205 Victoria Blvd., Hampton 23669 (804)727-6234.
The public library is fortunate in having as much early historical sources as it does in the Virginiana collection as so little exists for that geographic area until early 1900. The staff is now concentrating on building a current municipal collection.

NEWPORT NEWS

Newport News publishes ready reference handouts that are available in city hall and distributed elsewhere. There is no checklist of city publications, but the coverage appears broad in scope. Most publications can be obtained from the public library on interlibrary loan, if they are no longer available from the city (see entry **VA18**).

Publications

VA9. The Jacobs Company Inc. *A Management Improvement and Personnel Utilization Study for the City of Newport News.* Chicago, IL (55 W. Jackson Blvd. Chicago, IL), 1971. 173pp.
This analytical report studies each divisional unit and makes pertinent recommendations according to the findings. Present and proposed organizational charts are included.

VA10. Newport News. City Council. *Directory of City Officials.* (City Hall, 2400 Washington Ave., Newport News 23607) n.d. 8pp.
This mimeographed listing includes city council members, judicial officers, department heads, and members of boards and commissions.

VA11. Newport News. City Council. *Telephone Directory.* n.d. 40pp.
A listing of departments and employees which includes an organizational chart on the inside front cover.

VA12. Newport News. City Manager. *Annual Report.* Annual.
Consolidates the reports of all city departments submitted during the fiscal year. It contains an organizational chart.

VA13. Newport News. Department of City Planning and Community Development. *The Community Development Program.* 1973. 64pp.
Develops a short-range program planning capability in the city government and produces an initial program of public actions to deal effectively with the problems of the community. It summarizes the community conditions studies, the resource analyses, and the adopted set of community goals. It also presents the community development program which includes specific needs, program objectives, and recommended activities to be undertaken by the city government.

VA14. Newport News. Department of City Planning and Community Development. *Five-Year Program: 1975/76–1979/80.* 1974. 71pp.
This document describes major new city activities which are not regular extensions of the current operating budget or normal expansions of existing services.

VA15. Peninsula Chamber of Commerce. *Directory of Community Organizations.* Hampton (Coliseum Mall A-12, 1800 W. Mercury Blvd., Hampton 23666), 1977. 56pp.
A partial listing of the many civic, social, and private associations on the Virginia Peninsula.

VA16. *Profiles of Change: Newport News, 1975–1976.* 4 vols. Detroit, MI: R. L. Polk and Co. (Urban Statistical Division, 431 Howard St., Detroit, MI 48226), 1977.
This title comprises four volumes: *Management Digest*, a condensed and comprehensive overview of the city; *Map Series*, which includes over 300 computer-printed maps showing small-area (usually census tract) counts and rates; *Statistical Tables*, 26 reports displaying over 600 counts and percentages for each small area; *Small-Area Profiles and Rank Order Reports*, each on a one-page format, brings together 55 key counts and rates for each small area. The statistical data afford up-to-date inventory counts that describe current conditions and characteristics, and give components of year-to-year change. Twelve key indicators of status are used: persons per household; one-person households; households with children; female heads with children; retired heads; jobless heads; renters; current year vacancies; two-canvass vacancies; income index; commercial structures; and commercial vacancies. An accompanying user's guide has been published to maximize use.

VA17. *The Virginia Peninsula.* Newport News: Virginia Peninsula Industrial Committee (P.O. Box 338, Newport News 23607), 1972. 153pp. $6.
Provides a factual survey of the area for the benefit of persons seeking new locations for manufacturing, research, or distributive industries. Secondarily, the survey is intended for documentary and reference use. The contents include the physical, environmental, economic, governmental, and industrial aspects. There is even a section on future development.

Collections

VA18. Newport News Public Library. 110 Main St., Newport News 23601 (804)596-5723.
The library's administrative center, which is located in City Hall, has close contact with the city departments and receives copies of the publications for each branch. One branch has a special reading room for an early historical collection on the city; this is a good research source for the shipbuilding center.

NORFOLK

Norfolk has a substantial publishing program that creates an awareness of local government activity. Most municipal publications are available at the Norfolk Public Library (see entry **VA29**), if the respective agencies have no copies of their publications available.

Publications

VA19. Norfolk. Chamber of Commerce. *Blue Book of Business and Who's Who in Tidewater, Virginia.* (475 St. Paul's Blvd., P.O. Box 327, Norfolk 23501) Annual.
Includes the Board of Directors, an alphabetical listing of companies, businesses, and services with their addresses and name(s) of top executive(s), and an alphabetical classified listing of companies.

VA20. Norfolk. Chamber of Commerce. *Organization Directory.* 475 St. Paul's Blvd., P.O. Box 327, Norfolk 23501) n.d. 23pp. $2.
Includes business and professional, civic and service, cultural and historical, educational, political, religious, and other organizations.

VA21. Norfolk. City Council. *City of Norfolk, Virginia: Roster and Directory, 1976-77.* (City Hall, Norfolk 23501) 1976. xxxiv, 49pp.
Covers individuals, departments, bureaus, divisions, boards, commissions, and authorities.

VA22. Norfolk. City Hall. *Norfolk City Government.* Norfolk, n.d. 12pp.
This mimeographed handbook discusses the procedure of council meetings, the constituency and powers of the city government along with the listing of the organization and functions of the administrative departments. The last page is devoted to the judicial branch and is followed by two organizational charts.

VA23. Norfolk. City Manager. *Approved Operating Budget, July 1, 1977- June 30, 1978.* 1977. 177pp.
In addition to the budget message, the introduction covers comments on the significant impact of budget reductions, significant changes in format of organization, and graphs. The report also surveys each department.

VA24. Norfolk. City Planning Commission. *The General Plan of Norfolk.* 1967. 134pp. o.p.
This council-adopted plan has been updated each year since 1970 with pocket part amendments; it is the official statement of the city council on major city policies concerning physical developments of the community. It is comprehensive in that it involves both the short and the long range in terms of time, gives appropriate weight to social and economic factors along with guidance of physical change, and lastly, carefully considers regional implication. Concise histories of various factors are included.

VA25. Norfolk. Department of Community Improvement. *City of Norfolk Information Directory.* (123 City Hall Bldg., Norfolk 23501) n.d. 25pp.
This booklet gives a brief profile of Norfolk, its city council and manager, its court systems, and the various departments.

VA26. Norfolk. Department of Finance. *Annual Financial Report of the City of Norfolk. . . .* Annual.

This report covers the various funds, the newly purchased transit company, general and tax revenues, value of property, debt service, and reports on the employees retirement system and the Norfolk Port and Industrial Authority.

VA27. Norfolk. Office of the City Clerk. *City of Norfolk, Virginia, City Council Calendar, 1977.* (City Hall, Norfolk 23501) 1976.
Includes meetings, public hearings, deadlines, festivals, pertinent conferences, and holidays.

VA28. *Profiles of Change: Norfolk, Virginia.* Detroit, MI: R. L. Polk and Co. (Urban Statistical Division, 431 Howard St., Detroit, MI 48226) Annual.
This volume consists of a map series by planning districts. The statistical data afford up-to-date inventory counts that describe current conditions and character-istics, and give components of annual change. Twelve key indicators of status are used: persons per household; one-person households; households with children; female heads with children; retired heads; jobless heads; renters; current year vacancies; two-canvass vacancies; income index; commercial structures; and commercial vacancies.

Collections

VA29. Norfolk Public Library. 301 E. City Hall Ave., Norfolk 23510 (804) 441-2579.
The library is making strong, consistent efforts to collect local municipal publica-tions and has a fairly good collection. The Sargeant Memorial Room has many early newspapers from the area on microfilm along with a picture file, maps, mayors' messages, scrapbooks, manuscript files including business ledgers, and all the books on the city. The staff forwards all Norfolk publications to Greenwood Press to be entered into the *Index to Current Urban Documents.*

PORTSMOUTH

Portsmouth is an extensive publisher of documents. The City Planning Commission does exceptional quality work. Many city publications are available from the Portsmouth Public Library (see entry **VA41**) if they are no longer available from the city.

Publications

VA30. Hammer, Greene, Siler Associates. *Portsmouth: Problems, Prospects, and Potentials.* Washington, DC: Hammer, Siler, George Associates (1140 Connecticut Ave. N.W., Washington, DC 20036), 1970. 100pp.
This policy paper seeks to identify the major problems and issues of the city, its development potentials, and the "leverage points" for public and private policies. The overview is cast within an economic framework.

VA31. Portsmouth. Chamber of Commerce. *Community Guide.* (524 Middle St., Portsmouth 23705) 1976. 64pp.
This directory includes general information about the chamber, agency names and telephone numbers, and short comments regarding voting, hospitals, newspapers, automobiles, health care, recreation, transportation, utilities, etc. The remaining sections are Portsmouth, the city, elected officials in government, churches and synagogues, public schools, services of the public health department, recreation facilities, and clubs. The last half of the publication is devoted to advertising.

VA32. Portsmouth. Chamber of Commerce. *Who's Who in Portsmouth, Virginia: Membership Directory and Buyer's Guide.* (524 Middle St., Portsmouth 23705) 1974. 2nd ed. 29pp. $1.
This publication is divided into two sections: an alphabetical member list (corporate body name, address, and telephone number) and a classified subject list.

VA33. Portsmouth. City Council. *Citizens Information Directory.* (City Hall, 1 High St., Portsmouth 23704) n.d. 54pp. 46¢.
This directory, which is an educational tool for teaching students about their city government, acquaints the reader with the functions, responsibilities, and services of the various city agencies. A two-page description of the type of government is followed by alphabetized annotations of the departments.

VA34. Portsmouth. City Manager. *Annual Budget.* (City Hall, 1 High St., Portsmouth 23704) Annual. $8.04.
The budget contains statistical information including graphics on estimated revenue and expenditures, tax rate, and school budget for the last ten years.

VA35. Portsmouth. City Planning Commission. *Toward '88: General Plan Guidelines.* (City Hall) 1968.
This plan contains overall problems, analyses, and guidelines, along with functional plans for economic development, neighborhood analysis, land use, transportation, recreation, community facilities, public safety, health, utilities, and renewal plans. There are many graphs, charts, and maps.

VA36. Portsmouth. Community Planning and Management Office. *The State of the City, 1973: City of Portsmouth.* (City Hall) 1973. 243pp. $4.85.
This comprehensive report contains the following sections: community profile, community public safety, community human services, and community development.

VA37. Portsmouth. Office of City Planning. *Municipal Plant Inventory.* (City Hall) Annual. The use of this inventory aids in programming municipal investments. The report provides background information on real property owned within and outside the corporate limits.

VA38. Portsmouth. Office of Economic Analysis and Information. *Capital Improvement Program, 1976-77.* (City Hall) 1976. 171pp.
This plan begins with the project summary. Each program is accompanied by a graphic presentation and is divided into the following sections: program category, project title and number, description, justification, cost to city, schedule, funding distribution, recommended funding sources, impact on operating budget, site requirement, and responsible department and person.

VA39. Portsmouth. Office of Economic Analysis and Information. *The City of Portsmouth: Boards and Commissions.* (City Hall) 1975. 40pp.
This publication includes a commentary on Portsmouth's council-manager form of government along with the authorization, function, and description of each corporate body. The listing of members includes length of terms in years and expiration dates.

VA40. Portsmouth. Public Schools. *Personnel Directory.* (1 High St., Portsmouth 23704) Annual.
There is a name listing of city council members. In addition, the directory covers board members, administrative officers, faculty in all schools, and personnel in the center and service groups. The last section is devoted to associations and contact personnel followed by a list of retired personnel.

Collections

VA41. Portsmouth Public Library. 601 Court St., Portsmouth 23704 (804) 393-8501.
The library has a strong collection of Portsmouth publications. Two local historians have left their entire collections to the library. The library participates in the Greenwood Press program and forwards approximately 80 percent of its materials.

RICHMOND

Data not available at this time.

VIRGINIA BEACH

Although Virginia Beach is not a prolific publisher, the material published covers many different subjects. The number of copies for distribution is limited, but publications are available through the Municipal Reference Library on interlibrary loan.
Local Newspaper Indexing: Two staff members of the Municipal Reference Library (see entry **VA49**) are in charge of the indexing of five local newspapers, which are comprehensively clipped and indexed. Information for each item includes name of newspaper, date, and page number. Cross-references are made to as many as five or six subject headings. The project was begun in 1967. The library will accept queries from other cities.

Publications

VA42. Russell, Joseph D., Jr. *Citizen Information Handbook.* Virginia Beach: Public Information Office (Municipal Center, Virginia Beach 23456), 1973. 97pp.
Includes descriptions of each department and an organization chart. It also has an alphabetical listing of all services and a summary of historical points of interest.

VA43. Virginia Beach. City Council. *Calendar of Events.* (Municipal Center, Virginia Beach 23456) Annual.
This seventeen-month calendar lists meeting dates of committees, commissions, councils, boards, authorities, tournaments, festivals, holidays, and a short commentary of a city department for each month. There is a one-page alphabetized telephone directory for the city departments and a few other local groups.

VA44. Virginia Beach. City Manager. *City of Virginia Beach Operating Budget.* (Municipal Center, Virginia Beach 23456) Annual.
Covers all city departments in addition to the council and clerk, city manager, city attorney, and judiciary.

VA45. Virginia Beach. Department of Finance. *Capital Improvement Program, Five Years.* (Municipal Center, Virginia Beach 23456) Annual.
Includes the alphabetical listing of all projects with detail sheets, a listing of deleted projects previously considered, a summary of project estimates, and the means of financing with an annual summary.

VA46. Virginia Beach. Department of Planning. *Development Information Package.* (Municipal Center, Virginia Beach 23456) 1977. 20pp.
This mimeographed publication, updated approximately twice a year, includes the latest population data for all the cities in the Southeast Virginia Planning District

Commission (i.e., population history, population estimates and projections, and housing market analysis).

VA47. Virginia Beach. Public Information Office. *Municipal Government: An Outline.* (Municipal Center, Virginia Beach 23456) 1977. 2pp.
This brochure has a description of city government, an organization chart, a commentary on the responsibility of the city agencies, and an alphabetical listing of officials and offices.

VA48. Virginia Beach. School Board. *School Board Policies and Administrative Regulations.* (Municipal Center, Virginia Beach 23456) n.d.
This two-volume loose-leaf work is continuously updated. It covers policies and administrative regulations.

Collections

VA49. Municipal Reference Library. Department of Public Libraries, Municipal Center, Virginia Beach 23456 (804)427-4644.
There is a good working relationship between the library and the city departments, thereby making acquisition of publications much easier. The library participates in Greenwood Press's program and forwards about 75 percent of the publications. The library staff is currently working on a proposed ordinance that would enable the library to be the recipient of each publication.

WASHINGTON

Local Newspaper Indexing: The staff of the Pacific Northwest Collection of the University of Washington Libraries (see entry **WA14**) selectively indexes 20 daily regional newspapers and approximately 150 journal titles. They will accept reference queries.

General Publications

WA1. Municipal Research and Services Center of Washington (in cooperation with the Association of Washington Cities). *Court Decisions and Legal Opinions.* Information Bulletin Series. Seattle (4719 Brooklyn Ave. N.E., Seattle 98105), 1963- . Annual. $3.
This bulletin contains summaries of selected decisions of the State Supreme Court of Washington, the Washington Court of Appeals, and the United States Supreme Court; and the opinions of the attorney general, city attorney, and the Municipal Research and Services Center of Washington. The publication also includes the decisions of the Department of Labor and Industries and the Public Employment Relations Commission.

WA2. Municipal Research and Services Center of Washington (in cooperation with the Association of Washington Cities). *Digest of City Laws.* Information Bulletin Series. Seattle (4719 Brooklyn Ave. N.E., Seattle 98105), 1955- . Annual. $3.
Contains summaries of legislation enacted by the state legislature which affect the cities and towns in the state.

WA3. Municipal Research and Services Center of Washington (in cooperation with the Association of Washington Cities). *Legal Notes: Proceedings of the Attorneys' Conference.* Information Bulletin Series. Seattle (4719 Brooklyn Ave. N.E., Seattle 98105), 1959- . Semiannual.
Proceedings of the Washington State Association of Municipal Attorneys' meeting held in June and November of each year. Contains presentations on various subjects of interest to municipal attorneys in Washington State.

WA4. Municipal Research and Services Center of Washington (in cooperation with the Association of Washington Cities). *Officials of Washington Cities.* Seattle (4719 Brooklyn Ave. N.E., Seattle 98105), Annual. $7.50 (plus 25¢ postage; probably to be $10 with the next annual).
Primary directory for names and positions of city officials.

WA5. Municipal Research and Services Center of Washington (in cooperation with the Association of Washington Cities). *Subject Index to Selected Publica-*

tions of the Municipal Research and Services Center of Washington in Coop-eration with the Association of Washington Cities. Research Memorandum No. 95. Seattle (4719 Brooklyn Ave. N.E., Seattle 98105), 1977. 11pp. $2.

WA6. Municipal Research and Services Center of Washington (in cooperation with the Association of Washington Cities). *Washington City and County Employee Salary and Benefit Survey.* Seattle (4719 Brooklyn Ave. N.E., Seattle 98105), 1957– . Annual. $10.

SEATTLE

Publications

WA7. Seattle. Citizens Service Bureau. *To Whom It Does Concern* (a pro-cedural handbook). Dorothy Young Sale, researcher and author. (600 Fourth Ave. Seattle 98104) 1977. 127pp. $1 (plus 25¢ postage).
Recent factual and information guide to the city government for the citizen. It answers questions ranging from doing business with the city to the form of govern-ment, to aiding the handicapped, or to what to do about a barking dog (noise control). It is the only general guide to the city of Seattle.

WA8. Seattle. Department of Community Development. Office of Economic De-velopment. *Seattle: The Quick Facts.* (Rm. 210, Arctic Bldg., Third and Cherry, Seattle 98104) 1974. Folder. Free.
This handout is directed at the business community and contains basic demo-graphic and socioeconomic data.

WA9. Seattle. Department of General Services. *Telephone Directory (City of Seattle).* 1976. 38pp. $1.

WA10. Seattle. Department of Human Resources. *Human Services Inventory.* Periodically updated.
A directory for planning Seattle human services programs in conjunction with other government and nongovernment services to people. Four hundred programs are covered which relate to the people of Seattle but which may not be located in the city nor service the city as a whole. This comprehensive guide for Seattle is available at the Seattle Public Library (Education Department, 1000 Fourth Ave., Seattle 98104).

WA11. Seattle. Personnel Office. *City of Seattle, Organization Manual.* (Personnel-Civil Service Department, 600 Fourth Ave., Seattle 98104) 1973. 30pp. Free.
This publication has organizational charts for the city.

WA12. Seattle School District No. 1. *Demographic and Socioeconomic Pro-files of the Seattle School District and Its Twelve Constituent High School Attendance Areas.* (815 Fourth Ave. N., Seattle 98109) 1977. 70pp. Free.
An excellent source of data for Seattle and to a lesser extent King County and the state. Data pertains to demographic and socioeconomic characteristics, popula-tion distribution, vital statistics, and school enrollments. The U.S. Census, local, and state school statistics form the basis for most of the information.

Collections

WA13. Municipal Research and Services Center of Washington. 4719 Brooklyn Ave. N.E., Seattle 98105 (206)543-9050.
The center has a research collection for city officials and staff members; others may use it on a limited basis. The collection pertains to municipal administration and includes, among other materials, codes, ordinances, and technical reports.

WA14. University of Washington Libraries. Pacific Northwest Collection. Seattle 98195 (206)543-1929.
The Northwest Collection combines local documents, local history, and a newspaper index into one research service. Its coverage is best for Seattle but also includes surrounding King County as well as Washington State history. Local regional governments such as the Municipality of Metropolitan Seattle (METRO) and Puget Sound Council of Governments are collected. The Municipal Reference Library has the most complete municipal publications and information source in Seattle.

SPOKANE

Local Newspaper Indexing: The Spokane Public Library (see entry **WA15**) has a partial index to the *Spokesman Review* and *Chronicle*, but its vertical files on Spokane are more comprehensive.

Collections

WA15. Spokane Public Library. W. 906 Main Ave., Spokane 99201 (509)838-3361.
The library, which participates in Greenwood Press's *Index to Current Urban Documents*, receives almost all documents published by the Spokane city departments.

TACOMA

Publications

WA16. Tacoma. City Clerk. **Tacoma Data.** (Tacoma 98402) 1971– . Annual.
This publication lists pertinent statistics on Tacoma and the heads of city departments. It also outlines the structure of the city government.

WA17. Tacoma. City Council. **Council Agenda.** (Tacoma 98402) 1958– . Weekly.
This is the agenda of resolutions, ordinances, and other matters of concern which the city council considers each week. It includes the minutes of the previous week's meeting as well as the week's schedule of meetings.

WA18. Tacoma. City Manager. **Budget.** (Tacoma 98402) 1954– . Annual.
The city's annual budget outlines how city funds will be spent. The title varies somewhat between "budget," "city budget," and "annual budget." Also printed are preliminary, program, and administrative budgets.

WA19. Tacoma. Police Department. **Tacoma Police Department Monthly Report.** (Tacoma 98402) 1970– . Monthly.
This is a statistical record of criminal activity in Tacoma.

Collections

WA20. Tacoma Public Library. 1102 Tacoma Ave. S., Tacoma 98402 (206) 572-2000.

The Tacc   and Pierce County documents collection consists of many statistical reports of the various departments. The collection has virtually all city and county budgets issued. Since 1970, numerous environmental impact statements have been incorporated. The comprehensiveness of the collection has been handicapped over the years by the fact that city and county agencies have not automatically sent every publication issued to the library. The library has been participating in Greenwood Press's *Index to Current Urban Documents* for several years. Documents are restricted to library use only. The library maintains a clipping file of newspaper articles which have appeared in the *Tacoma News Tribune*, concerning Tacoma, Pierce County, Washington State, and the Pacific Northwest region.

WEST VIRGINIA

CHARLESTON

Data not available at this time.

HUNTINGTON

Most of the Huntington city departments, boards, and commissions produce annual reports, or studies and reports. However, these publications, which are the best sources of information on the city, receive only in-house distribution. Consequently the library of Marshall University (see entry **WV10**) has to keep in constant communication with municipal agencies in order to produce new publications. Most of the agencies have been willing to deposit their publications at Marshall University. The library of Marshall University has hired a field representative who keeps in touch not only with city agencies but also businesses, industries, community service organizations, and similar groups, to insure the continued growth of the library's local history collection.

Publications

WV1. Huntington Board of Park Commissioners. *A Survey of Public Recreation in Huntington, West Virginia and Other Leading Cities in the South.* Huntington: Wilkinson Foundation, 1960. 21pp. o.p.
A survey of public recreation facilities in the city and proposals for upgrading existing parks and recreation sites.

WV2. Huntington. City Council. *Annual Budget.* (City Hall, Huntington 25701) Annual. Free.
Shows the operating expenses of the city and gives a detailed report of revenues, resources and expenditures.

WV3. Huntington Civic Center Board. *Municipal Auditorium and Convention Center: A Feasibility Study.* Huntington: Downtown Improvement Group, 1968. 31pp. o.p.
A study showing the need for a civic center in the city. It covers topics such as existing facilities, hotel and motel accommodations, and potential for programs and events.

WV4. Huntington Fire Department. *Fire Services in Huntington, West Virginia, 1973.* Kent, OH: Eastman Association, 1973. 89pp. o.p.
A study of the fire department carried out on contract through the city manager. It analyzes personnel, organization, equipment, training, facilities, etc.

WV5. Huntington Flood Wall Board. *Flood Wall Board, Local Protection Project.* 1972. 30pp. o.p.
A report on the activities of the board and includes statistics, flood problems and damage, flood wall construction, costs, operations, and project status.

WV6. Huntington Planning Commission. *Annual Report.* (City Hall, Huntington 25701) Annual. Free.
Reports the activities, programs, and projects of the Planning Commission for the year.

WV7. Huntington Planning Commission. *Basic Studies, Huntington Study Area, West Virginia.* Huntington: Planit Ltd., 1973. 2 vols. o.p.
An exhaustive study of the city which includes population and economic profiles, community services, land use, environmental impact, recreation, schools, city governmental authority and control, and recommendations for a unified community developmental plan.

WV8. Huntington. Police Department. *Annual Report.* (City Hall, Huntington 25701) Annual. Free.
Reports the operations of the department and gives a summary of crimes and investigations, personnel training, selection and distribution, community services projects, and special programs.

WV9. Huntington. Urban Renewal Authority. *Final Project Reports.* n.p., 1963. 5 vols. o.p.
These reports give the final plans for the urban renewal of downtown Huntington. Information includes studies on minority groups, land conservation and reconditioning, land acquisition, labor standards, community requirements, and area impact studies. The library of Marshall University has approximately 1.5 linear feet of shelf space on documents from the Huntington Urban Renewal Authority.

Collections

WV10. Marshall University. James E. Morrow Library, Huntington 25701 (304) 696-2320. Teletype Service: (710)931-8013.
Huntington municipal documents are housed in the West Virginia Collection, Special Collections Department, at the James E. Morrow Library. Within the past two or three years the library staff has made a concerted effort to obtain municipal documents. Most of the materials in the library collection date from the mid-1960s. The Huntington municipal documents collection takes up nine linear feet of shelf space. Charleston, West Virginia, documents are also collected.

WISCONSIN

General Publications

WI1. Wisconsin. Department of Business Development. *Community Profile.* 1974– . Madison (123 W. Washington Ave., Madison 53702) 1976. 97 pieces. Free.
A collection of pieces about communities of Wisconsin cities, towns, and villages. The format is subject to change because continual updating is intended in order that the information about each community be current. Includes statistics on population, employment, industries, wages, transportation, taxes, education, etc. Address of each locality development organization and its contact person is given. Each piece is five pages in length. The only state-produced publication giving such useful information on the smaller communities as well as the larger cities. It is intended for industrial promotion, but can be used as background for study of the community.

WI2. Wisconsin. Department of Business Development. *Economic Profile.* Madison (123 W. Washington Ave., Madison 53702), 1976. 72 pieces.
A collection of pieces about the counties of Wisconsin intended to be continually revised and updated. This is actually its third edition. Previously it was published in 1962 and 1966. Its information has been taken from periodic censuses and indicates population, income, housing, and labor force. Information related to community economics, geography, and history is also developed. Information pertinent to understanding the social climate of each county is in the Wisconsin county social profile. Includes map for each county.

WI3. Wisconsin. Department of Local Affairs and Development. Bureau of Research and Policy Analysis. *Services for Wisconsin Communities: A Manual of Financial Aid and Technical Assistance Available to Wisconsin Communities: "The Orange Book."* Madison (123 W. Washington Ave., Madison 53702), 1977. 544pp.

WI4. Wisconsin. Division for Library Service. *Wisconsin Library Service Record.* Continues: *Wisconsin Public Libraries: Service Record, 1954–71.* Madison (126 Langdon St., Madison), 1965. Annual.
Continues a title which began in 1954 and since 1972 includes, besides public library statistics, the statistics for special academic libraries. From 1954 to 1965 this was issued by the Free Library Commission of Wisconsin.

WI5. Wisconsin. Division of Family Services. *Social Profile of Wisconsin Counties.* 1st ed. Madison (1 W. Wilson St., Madison 53702), 1969. 72 pieces.
A collection of pieces about the counties of Wisconsin. Its format is like the county Economic Profile but the information contained is that pertinent to the identification of problems of children and youth and their families. Statistical tables indicate such

values as pertain to housing and income; population and percentages as pertain to education; family status, institutionalizations, and employment. Information related to community economics, geography, and history is available in county economic profile. Intended to be updated every five years.

WI6. Wisconsin. Legislative Reference Bureau. *The Wisconsin Blue Book.* Title varies: 1853, *Manual for Use of the Assembly;* 1859-61, *A Manual of Customs, Precedents and Forms in Use in the Assembly of Wisconsin;* 1862-78, *The Legislative Manual of the State of Wisconsin;* 1879-1911, *The Blue Book of the State of Wisconsin.* Madison (Document Sales, Dept. of Administration, 202 S. Thornton Ave., Madison 53703) $1 paperbound ($2 hardbound). Biennial.
Although the Blue Book is generally considered useful only for overall state statistics it does contain some information on cities. Contains such matters as a list of the post offices of Wisconsin since 1853, election statistics since 1860, and population statistics since 1862. Rosters of city and village offices including act by which incorporated are given from 1921 to present. Indexed by two additional works: A Guide to Wisconsin Blue Book, 1853-1862, and Biography Index to the Wisconsin Blue Book, 1870-1973.

WI7. Wisconsin. Section of Statistical Services. Bureau of Health Statistics. *Vital Statistics for Selected Cities.* Madison: Wisconsin Division of Health (P.O. Box 309, Madison 53701), Free.
Supplement to the annual public health statistics report. Includes data on the 21 incorporated places in Wisconsin with over 30,000 population in the 1970 U.S. Census. Data are by place of residence, except marriage and divorce data which are by place of occurrence. The mortality data are tabulated according to the eighth revision of the International Statistical Classification of Diseases (ISCD).

Collections

WI8. State Historical Society of Wisconsin Library. 816 State St., Madison 53706 (608)262-3421.
Some of the collection does not circulate: rare books, ephemera, directories, bound newspapers, genealogy, pamphlets, fragile materials, etc. The municipal collection includes publications of Milwaukee and Madison, a good representation of all government publications of other municipalities and of counties of Wisconsin in a separate archivally arranged collection, which is in addition to the other holdings of the society of and about municipalities in its library, archives and area research centers. Its library also has a collection of city directories (not limited to Wisconsin cities) and a collection of Wisconsin local telephone directories.

MADISON

The Municipal Reference Service (see entry **WI16**; see also entry **WI18**) is attempting to provide bibliographic control of Dane County, city of Madison, and other political jurisdictions in Dane County government documents. The city has passed a depository ordinance and the county is in the process of writing one. In spite of this effort, it is difficult to identify everything as it is published.

Publications

WI9. Madison. City Clerk. *City Roster—Madison, Wisconsin.* (Rm. 103, 210 Monona Ave., Madison 53709) 1976-1977. Annual. Free.
The roster lists department-division heads, Board of Education members, city coun-

cil aldermen and Dane County supervisors that represent Madison. In all cases it gives their home address and phone number as well as their business phone number.

WI10. Madison. City Planning Department. *City Development.* (Rm. 414, 210 Monona Ave., Madison 53709) Annual. Free.
City Development gives statistics and a verbal description of such things as population, University of Wisconsin enrollment, annexations, subdivisions, and construction for the previous year. It also describes projects that the city planning department has been or is currently involved in.

WI11. Madison. City Planning Department. *Community Profile.* (Rm. 414, 210 Monona Ave., Madison 53709) Annual. Free.
The *Community Profile* is intended to answer general questions and provide information about Madison for business and industry wanting to locate in Madison. It includes such information as climate, taxes, gas and electric rates, water chemistry and costs, wages, housing costs, and industrial park maps.

WI12. Dane County. County Clerk's Office. *Official Directory: Dane County, Wisconsin.* Madison (Rm. 112, 210 Monona Ave., Madison 53709), 1976–1977. 66pp. Free.
In addition to listing Dane County officials, department heads and supervisors, it lists the local officials of all the cities, villages, and towns in Dane County.

WI13. Greater Madison Chamber of Commerce. *Membership Directory and Buyer's Guide.* Madison (615 E. Washington Ave., P.O. Box 71, Madison 53701). Annual.
Besides listing area businesses that are members of the chamber, the directory includes four pages of general information about Madison.

WI14. Madison. Mayor's Office. *City (of Madison, Wisconsin) Handbook 1977.* Compiled by Susan Bennett, Institute of Governmental Affairs, University of Wisconsin Extension. (Rm. 403, 210 Monona Ave., Madison 53709) 1977. 260pp. Annual. Free.
The *City Handbook* describes what each department or division is supposed to do and lists employees and their responsibilities. It also describes the budget process and summarizes the 1977 budget, describes the grants-in-aids the city receives, and explains the flow of business through the common council.

WI15. Madison. Ordinances, Local Laws, etc. *Madison (Wisconsin) General Ordinances.* City Attorney's Office (Rm. 401, 210 Monona Ave., Madison 53709), n.d. 2 vols. $90 set ($50 year for monthly updates).
Besides listing all the ordinances in force in the city, it includes a picture of the city flag and a list of city officers since 1955.

WI16. Madison Public Library. Municipal Reference Service. *A Bibliography of Government Publications by and about Madison, Dane County and Other Cities and Towns in Dane County, Wisconsin.* Edited by Ann Waidelich. (Rm. 103B City-County Bldg., 210 Monona Ave., Madison 53709) 1st ed. 1973; 1st supplement 1975; 2nd ed. in process. 185pp (plus 50pp supplement).
The bibliography lists "everything ever written about" Madison and Dane County. It is arranged into broad categories with a detailed subject, author, and title index.

WI17. Wisconsin State Historical Society. Office of Local History. *A Bibliography on the History of Dane County Based on the Collections of the (Wisconsin) State Historical Society.* Compiled by William J. Schereck and Lois C. Blaesing. (816 State St., Madison 53706), September 1959. 2,588 items listed. $5.

The bibliography is divided into four sections: Section 1 is devoted to books, manuscripts, archival records, and government publications; Section 2 is devoted to published and unpublished biographical and genealogical works; Section 3 is devoted to newspapers and periodicals published in Dane County; and Section 4 is devoted to maps and charts.

Collections

WI18. Madison Public Library. Municipal Reference Service. Rm. 103B City-County Building, 210 Monona Ave., Madison 53709 (608)266-6316.
Major municipal documents collected include Madison, Dane County, other cities, villages, towns in Dane County, Wisconsin. The Madison Public Library clips the two local newspapers and files by subject. The newspapers also maintain clipping files. The Madison Public Library is divided into three subject divisions. Local government documents are cataloged according to Dewey and shelved in the appropriate division (literature and social science, business and science and art and music). The Municipal Reference Service is a branch of the Madison Public Library and maintains a separate collection of local government documents.

MILWAUKEE

Publications

WI19. Milwaukee. Board of Election Commissioners. *Biennial Report.* (City Hall, Milwaukee 53202) 1915-16; 1920-1974-1975. 262pp. Biennial. Free.
The report consists entirely of statistics giving the results of all elections held in the biennium and statistical tables in regard to registration and voting.

WI20. Milwaukee. Bureau of Budget and Management. *Line Budget.* (City Hall, Rm. 307, 200 E. Wells St., Milwaukee 53202) 1977. 845pp. Annual.
Departments and purposes under control of common council are summarized giving appropriations and expenditures. Figures in the 1977 edition are given for 1974 and 1975 actual, 1975, 1976 and 1977 budgets. Borrowing authorizations, 1977 salary and wage rates, and boards and commissions not under control of common council also given. Same formats are also used for the budget giving in detail line-by-line including in addition pay range number, positions or units, and account numbers. Department of Public Works and special purpose accounts are further broken down for clarity. Budget is adopted annually by the common council by law, and printed in accordance with Chapter 65.05 (7) Wisconsin Statutes.

WI21. Milwaukee. Common Council. *Milwaukee Report.* City Clerk (Office of the City Clerk, City Hall, Rm. 205, Milwaukee 53202), 1921-1968; 1970-1975/76. Annual. Free.
The annual report contains summaries of the year's work of the various departments and commissions of the city government. Several statistical charts are included as well as basic facts about the city. Includes many illustrations and short biographies of members of the city council.

WI22. Milwaukee. Common Council. *Proceedings.* (City Clerk) 1872-
Bound annual ed. $15 (annual ed.).
Annual bound volume includes material for council year—April to April. Proceedings set forth each three-week council meeting accomplishments. Format follows council business giving reports of six standing committees and action taken, plus presentation of ordinances, communications from city officers, resolutions, and petitions,

remonstrances, etc. A file number is assigned each item and more detailed information could be obtained from a file, but proceedings include wording of ordinances and resolutions, and results of council votes. Includes indexes of matters introduced by each alderman, subject index, and numerical index. Paper copies of each three-week council meeting are printed during each succeeding year. This bound volume puts them all together annually.

WI23. Milwaukee. Comptroller. *Financial Summary.* (City Hall, Rm. 401, 200 E. Wells St., Milwaukee 53202) 1867-   . 244pp. Annual.
Report covers a calendar year. A brief organizational chart is given. Financial section gives combined statements and schedules, with a supplemental section. The statistical section presents 19 tables of a variety of statistics. Blue pages in volume set off various parts, and descriptions of different funds are given on the reverse of the blue sheets.

WI24. Milwaukee. Department of Public Works. *City of Milwaukee Department of Public Works Annual Report, 1975.* (841 N. Broadway, Milwaukee 53202) 1909-1920; 1965-1975. 16pp. Annual. Free.
Short descriptions of work of such agencies as bridges and public buildings, engineers, forestry, traffic engineering and sanitation. Contains statistics and many photographs.

WI25. Milwaukee. Fire Department. *Report.* (711 W. Wells St., Milwaukee 53233) 1872-   . Annual.
Organizational chart of the department, annual highlights given as well as alarm and loss statistics from the firefighting division, major fire losses for the year, causes of fires, classified building fires, losses, and number of buildings, transmission of fire, and miscellaneous alarms, alarms for other than fire, deaths by fire, information on bureaus of instruction and training, construction and maintenance, fire communications, and administration. Several related organizations are given brief mention. Report includes photographs.

WI26. Milwaukee. Health Department. *Report.* (Municipal Bldg., Rm. 112, 841 N. Broadway, Milwaukee 53202) 1892-   . Annual.
From the reports of the various bureaus, divisions, and sections of the health department, the commissioner of health assembles a one-volume report for presentation to the mayor and common council. Major matters for consideration are presented in the introductory report, with detailed statistical and other factual data presented in succeeding pages. The Bureau of Administration includes the divisions of accounting, vital statistics, and health education; the Bureau of Maternal and Child Health includes that division and one of dentistry; the Bureau of Laboratories includes the divisions of bacteriology, chemistry, and virology; and the Bureau of Preventable Diseases and Medical Services includes the divisions of preventable diseases and medical services. There are also bureaus of consumer protection and environmental health, and public health nursing.

WI27. Milwaukee. Ordinances, Local Laws, etc. *Milwaukee Code of Ordinances.* 12th Supplement. Milwaukee: Common Council (Legislative Reference Bureau, City Hall, Rm. 404, 200 E. Wells St., Milwaukee 53202), Vol. 1 1974. 2 vol. Published irregularly since 1847. Title varies. For 12th Supplement, Vol. 1: $40; Vol. 2: price not yet set.
Volume 1 contains general ordinances of the city of Milwaukee; the latest edition (12th Supplement) includes all ordinances passed as of April 9, 1974. Volume 2 contains the building and zoning ordinances of the city; the latest edition includes all ordinances passed as of March 1976. Health, utilities, traffic, safety, morals,

welfare, and in construction, fire prevention, electrical installations, plumbing, and sheet metal work laws are set forth. The Milwaukee City Charter and Milwaukee organization charts are published as separate documents.

WI28. Milwaukee. Police Department. *Annual Report, Milwaukee Police Department.* (749 W. State St., Milwaukee 53233) 1909-1920; 1927-1955; 1957-1973; 1975-   . Annual. Free.
Contains an organization chart of the department, map of police districts, statistics of crimes and offenses, citations and awards of merit to citizens, and financial statistics. Illustrated with photographs.

WI29. Sewerage Commission of the City of Milwaukee. *Annual Report of the Sewerage Commission of the City of Milwaukee, 1974.* (Metropolitan Sewerage Commission of the County of Milwaukee, 700 E. Jones St., Milwaukee 53207) 1914-1974. Annual.
A report of the year's work of the sewerage commission containing many statistics, photographs, and technical illustrations.

WI30. Milwaukee. Water Works. *Annual Report Milwaukee Water Works.* (841 N. Broadway, Milwaukee 53202) 1912-1920; 1954-1975. Free.
A short publication consisting almost entirely of financial statistics. A summary of expenditures, sales, pumpage, and capital improvements is given in the superintendent's comments.

Collections

WI31. Legislative Reference Bureau. City Hall, Rm. 404, 200 E. Wells St., Milwaukee 53202 (414)278-2295.
The bureau is the official depository for city government documents and depository for selected U.S. Census Bureau reports. A clipping file of local newspaper articles on city subjects is maintained, and filed by subject. The Legislative Reference Bureau maintains a collection of over 50,000 titles in monographs, almost 250 titles in periodicals, 12 newspapers, plus microtext materials, pamphlets, maps, and federal, state, and local government documents. The bureau's subject strengths include city planning, public finance, housing, urban affairs, public administration, and employment.

WI32. Milwaukee Public Library. 814 W. Wisconsin Ave., Milwaukee 53233 (414)278-3087. Teletype Service: (910)262-1120.
A newspaper clipping file, chiefly on local subjects is maintained, and filed by subject.

RACINE

Many city departments do not supply the library with copies of annual reports. Others annually publish reports summarizing activities and budget. The Racine Public Library sends copies of all city department publications to Greenwood Press's *Index to Current Urban Documents*. Departments of Racine, Wisconsin which publish annual reports are the building department, fire department, Memorial Hall Commission, parks and recreation department, public library, transportation department, and water department. **Local Newspaper Indexing:** Racine *Journal Times* library indexes local news, local people, state, and national news which has an effect on the community. The index is from 1958 to date. The Racine Public Library (see **WI40**) maintains an abbreviated index of articles dealing with subjects of general local interest only, 1962 to date.

Publications

WI33. Racine. City Clerk. *Common Council Official Proceedings.* 1893- .
Unpaged. Biweekly.
Summary of actions at each common council meeting, including voting by aldermen
on each issue. Published annually in a single volume, arranged by date. Annual
volume is indexed.

WI34. Racine. City Clerk. *Directory of City Officials, Boards, Commissions.*
1926- . Unpaged. Annual.
Lists of names and home addresses of city officials, boards, commissions, and
special committees. Chairmen are indicated; the publication is indexed by name of
agency.

WI35. Racine. City Clerk. *Guide to Racine City Government.* 1971; 1972, 2nd
ed. 36pp.
A manual which explains the operation and administration of the city government.
Included are an administrative chart, aldermanic districts, maps, and organization
of the common council, its rules and actions. Procedure for conduct of city business,
public hearings, and a schedule of meetings of committees, boards, and commissions are also included. A listing and brief description of the function of each city
department and an index of city services complete the booklet.

WI36. Racine. City Planning Commission. *Capital Improvement Program.*
1961- . Annual.
Contains information about capital expenditures for the city, including a summary of
operation expenditures since 1957, summary of funds to be expended in the next
five years, recommended financing and methods of financing, and capital improvements by major city departments.

WI37. Racine. Common Council. *Municipal Code.* 1973. 2 vols. Irregular.
A compilation of ordinances which govern the city of Racine, kept current by
replacement pages; indexed.

WI38. Racine. Office of the Mayor. *Adopted Budget.* 1933-1966; 1967- .
Compiled annually by the comptroller.
Includes overall information on the city budget, comparisons with the previous year
and statistics on sources of income. A summary of expenditures by character and
major object is given. Individual department requests and adopted budgets are given
along with a summary of the function of the departments and comments regarding
reason for budget requests.

WI39. Racine. Office of the Mayor. *Quarterly Report to the Council.* October 2,
1973- . Quarterly.
Reports from 15 city departments compiled by the mayor's office and distributed
to members of the common council. The reports vary in length and scope; many
summarize activities, special projects, problems and future plans of the various
departments; a few are mostly statistical.

Collections

WI40. Racine Public Library. 75 Seventh St., Racine 53403 (414)636-9241.
The collection has a strong emphasis on Racine City and Racine County history; the
library has a complete set of city directories, published since 1850.

WYOMING

General Publications

WY1. Wyoming Association of Municipalities. *Official Municipal Annual.* Cheyenne (200 E. Eighth Ave., Rm. 211, Cheyenne 82001). Annual. 28pp. $5.
Directory of elected and appointed officials for Wyoming municipalities. Arranged by municipality, it includes title and name of office holder only.

CHEYENNE

The city of Cheyenne is an infrequent publisher of municipal documents. The only document published in any true sense is the *City Ordinances.* Other than that the only sources published are a few legally required items (i.e., the budget), but these are often published in the local newspaper, and a few annual reports produced for the city council's use (e.g., the fire department), which are occasionally made available on a very limited basis. Approximately five years ago, several project reports were published as mandated by federal monies.

Collections

WY2. Laramie County Library System. 2800 Central Ave., Cheyenne 82001 (307)634-3561.
The library's document collection is almost nonexistent, but the staff would be willing to help out as best they can. Photocopies of documents are available at a small per page charge.

WY3. Wyoming State Library. Supreme Court and Library Bldg., Cheyenne 82002 (307)777-7281. Teletype Services: TWX (910)949-4787.
The library does not collect municipal documents. However, it should be noted that few state documents are oriented toward cities. Wyoming documents have the county as their basic orientation. Still, municipal information can be extracted from state publications.

LARAMIE

Collections

WY4. Coe Library—Documents Division. The University of Wyoming, P.O. Box 3334, University Station, Laramie 82071 (307)766-2174. Teletype Service: TWX (910)949-4946.
Municipal documents are cataloged and shelved with the regular collection. The University Library does not make an extraordinary effort to collect official Laramie publications. The municipality, however, does not issue many publications.

APPENDIX
County–City Cross-Reference List

Many entries in this volume cite reports and studies at the county level without indicating the major municipality included in the county. By listing the counties for each municipality covered in the book, this list provides access back to the local level.

Alameda Co., CA, *see* Berkeley; Fremont; Oakland
Albany Co., NY, *see* Albany
Albany Co., WY *see* Laramie
Allegheny Co., PA, *see* Pittsburgh
Allen Co., ID, *see* Fort Wayne
Anchorage Co., AK, *see* Anchorage
Anne Arundel Co., MD, *see* Annapolis
Bannock Co., ID, *see* Pocatello
Bernalillo Co., NM, *see* Albuquerque
Bexar Co., TX, *see* San Antonio
Bronx Co., NY, *see* New York City
Broward Co., FL, *see* Fort Lauderdale
Burleigh Co., ND, *see* Bismarck
Cabell Co., WV, *see* Huntington
Caddo Co., LA, *see* Shreveport
Camden Co., NJ, *see* Camden
Cascade Co., MT, *see* Great Falls
Charleston Co., SC, *see* Charleston
Chittenden Co., VT, *see* Burlington
Clark Co., NV, *see* Las Vegas
Clay Co., MO, *see* Kansas City
Cook Co., IL, *see* Chicago
Cumberland Co., ME, *see* Portland
Cuyahoga Co., OH, *see* Cleveland; Parma
Dade Co., FL, *see* Miami
Dallas Co., TX, *see* Dallas
Dane Co., WI, *see* Madison
Davidson Co., TN, *see* Nashville
DeKalb Co., GA, *see* Atlanta
Denver Co., CO, *see* Denver
Douglas Co., NE, *see* Omaha
Durham Co., NC, *see* Durham

Duval Co., FL, *see* Jacksonville
East Baton Rouge Co., LA, *see* Baton Rouge
El Paso Co., CO, *see* Colorado Springs
El Paso Co., TX, *see* El Paso
Erie Co., NY, *see* Buffalo
Escambia Co., FL, *see* Pensacola
Essex Co., NJ, *see* Newark
Fairfield Co., CT, *see* Stamford
Forsyth Co., NC, *see* Winston-Salem
Franklin Co., OH, *see* Columbus
Fresno Co., CA, *see* Fresno
Fulton Co., GA, *see* Atlanta
Genesee Co., MI, *see* Flint
Greene Co., MO, *see* Springfield
Guilford Co., NC, *see* Greensboro
Hamilton Co., OH, *see* Cincinnati
Hampden Co., MA, *see* Springfield
Harris Co., TX, *see* Houston
Harrison Co., MS, *see* Biloxi; Gulfport
Hartford Co., CT, *see* Hartford
Hennepin Co., MN, *see* Bloomington; Minneapolis
Hillsborough Co., FL, *see* Tampa
Hinds Co., MS, *see* Jackson
Honolulu Co., HI, *see* Honolulu
Hudson Co., NJ, *see* Jersey City
Jackson Co., MO, *see* Kansas City
Jefferson Co., AL, *see* Birmingham
Jefferson Co., TX, *see* Beaumont
Johnson Co., KS, *see* Overland Park
Kennebec Co., ME, *see* Augusta
Kent Co., MI, *see* Grand Rapids
Kent Co., RI, *see* Warwick

Kenton Co., KY, *see* Covington
King Co., WA, *see* Seattle
Kings Co., NY, *see* New York City
Lackawanna Co., PA, *see* Scranton
Lake Co., IN, *see* Gary; Hammond
Lancaster Co., NE, *see* Lincoln
Lane Co., OR, *see* Eugene
Laramie Co., WY, *see* Cheyenne
Lehigh Co., PA, *see* Allentown
Leon Co., FL, *see* Tallahassee
Lewis and Clark Co., MT, *see* Helena
Linn Co., IA, *see* Cedar Rapids
Los Angeles Co., CA, *see* Glendale;
   Los Angeles; Torrance
Lubbock Co., TX, *see* Lubbock
Lucas Co., OH, *see* Toledo
Madison Co., AL, *see* Huntsville
Mahoning Co., OH, *see* Youngstown
Maricopa Co., AZ, *see* Mesa; Phoenix;
   Scottsdale; Tempe
Marion Co., IN, *see* Indianapolis
Mecklenburg Co., NC, *see* Charlotte
Mercer Co., NJ, *see* Trenton
Merrimack Co., NH, *see* Concord
Middlesex Co., MA, *see* Cambridge
Milwaukee Co., WI, *see* Milwaukee
Minnehaha Co., SD, *see* Sioux Falls
Missoula Co., MT, *see* Missoula
Mobile Co., AL, *see* Mobile
Monroe Co., NY, *see* Rochester
Montgomery Co., MD, *see* Rockville
Montgomery Co., OH, *see* Dayton
Multnomah Co., OR, *see* Portland
New Castle Co., DE, *see* Newark;
   Wilmington
New Haven Co., CT, *see* New Haven;
   Waterbury
New York Co., NY, *see* New York City
Nueces Co., TX, *see* Corpus Christi
Oklahoma Co., OK, *see* Oklahoma City
Onondaga Co., NY, *see* Syracuse
Orange Co., CA, *see* Huntington Beach;
   Santa Ana
Orange Co., FL, *see* Orlando
Orleans Co., LA, *see* New Orleans
Passaic Co., NJ, *see* Paterson
Pennington Co., SD, *see* Rapid City
Philadelphia Co., PA, *see* Philadelphia
Pierce Co., WA, *see* Tacoma
Pima Co., AZ, *see* Tucson
Polk Co., IA, *see* Des Moines
Potter Co., TX, *see* Amarillo
Providence Co., RI, *see* Providence
Pueblo Co., CO, *see* Pueblo

Pulaski Co., AR, *see* Little Rock
Queens Co., NY, *see* New York City
Racine Co., WI, *see* Racine
Ramsey Co., MN, *see* St. Paul
Richland Co., SC, *see* Columbia
Richmond Co., NY, *see* New York City
Riverside Co., CA, *see* Riverside
Rutland Co., VT, *see* Rutland
Sacramento Co., CA, *see* Sacramento
St. Joseph Co., IN. *see* South Bend
St. Louis Co., MN, *see* Duluth
Salt Lake Co., UT, *see* Salt Lake City
San Bernardino Co., CA, *see* San
   Bernardino
San Diego Co., CA, *see* San Diego
San Francisco Co., CA, *see* San
   Francisco
Sangamon Co., IL, *see* Springfield
San Joaquin Co., CA, *see* Stockton
Schenectady Co., NY, *see* Schenectady
Scott Co., IA, *see* Davenport
Sebastian Co., AR, *see* Fort Smith
Sedgwick Co., KS, *see* Wichita
Shawnee Co., KS, *see* Topeka
Spokane Co., WA, *see* Spokane
Stark Co., OH, *see* Canton
Suffolk Co., MA, *see* Boston
Summit Co., OH, *see* Akron
Tarrant Co., TX, *see* Fort Worth
Travis Co., TX, *see* Austin
Trumbull Co., OH, *see* Youngstown
Tulsa Co., OK, *see* Tulsa
Tuscaloosa Co., AL, *see* Tuscaloosa
Union Co., NJ, *see* Elizabeth
Vanderburgh Co., IN, *see* Evansville
Washoe Co., NV, *see* Reno
Wayne Co., MI, *see* Detroit
Wayne Co., WV, *see* Huntington
Weber Co., UT, *see* Ogden
Westchester Co., NY, *see* Yonkers
Winnebago Co., IL, *see* Rockford
Worcester Co., MA, *see* Worcester
Yellowstone Co., MT, *see* Billings

The following cities have no county
designation:

   Baltimore, MD
   Hampton, VA
   Newport News, VA
   Norfolk, VA
   Portsmouth, VA
   St. Louis, MO
   Virginia Beach, VA
   Washington, DC

SUBJECT INDEX

References are to entry numbers.

Trade and commerce, AL10, AL66, AL74,
AK8, AZ3, AZ19, AZ60, CO15,
CT1, CT8, CT25, CT37, IL26, IN27,
IN38, IN56, IN77, IA2, IA10, KY7, LA1,
LA4, LA9, LA13, MD25, MD57, MA2,
MI19, MN8, MN9, MS10, NV3, NY82,
NY166, NY203, RI4, TX17, TX66,
TX104, TX135, VT9
Traffic, AZ32, CO26, CO35, CT1, IN68,
IA15, MD18, MD44, MN39, NV13,
NY124, NY170, TX109, VT4, WI24
Transportation, US4, AL7, AL54, AL65,
AL74, AL78, AK1, AK21, AZ9, AZ10,
AZ17, AZ21, AZ29, AZ46, CA39, CO8,
CO25, CO30, CO35, CO70, CT6, CT8,
CT32, CT33, CT39, CT50, DC3, DC11,
FL17, GA13, GA14, GA24, GA26, GA38,
GA48, ID5, IL2, IL26, IL32, IL35, IL36,
IN8, IN26, IN36, IN47, IN65, IN68,
IN71, IA10, KY14, LA28, LA35, MD7,
MD18, MD44, MD48, MD57, MD61,
MD68, MD71, MD73, MA25, MI13,
MI20, MN36, MO14, NV3, NV20, NV25,
NJ18, NY7, NY18, NY32, NY39, NY 56,
NY57, NY58, NY105, NY113, NY158,
NY164, NY167, NY170, NY178, NY179,
NY193, NY300, OH27, OH28, OH31,
PA22, TX17, TX20, TX21, TX27, TX61,
TX89, TX90, TX104, TX121, UT15,
UT17, VT6, VT10, VA4, VA31, WI1

Universities and colleges, see Education
and schools
Urban renewal, AZ56, CO43, CO44, CT20,
CT50, GA12, IN24, IN27, MD53, MD61
MI11, NJ27, NM13, NY40, NY63,
NY111, NY112, NY324, NY325, OH21,

OH23, OK15, OK22, PA11, PA15, TX20,
TX131, WV9; see also Planning

Vital statistics, see Population
Voters, see Elections

Wages, see Income
Waste disposal, AZ10, AZ17, AZ21, AZ32,
CO8, GA8, LA25, MN20, OH255, WI24;
see also Sewerage
Water resources, US4, AL29, AL32, AK31,
AZ8, AZ17, AZ21, AZ32, CA39, CO8,
CO20, CO59, CO62, CO70, GA39,
MD59, MI20, MN40, NV31, NY82,
NY95, NY276, NY278, TX104, TX117,
TX121, VT6, WI11, WI30
Welfare, public, AL15, IL22, IN6, IN18, IN47,
IN60, IN80, IA26, LA25, LA32, LA34,
MD1, MN36, MT12, MT19, NJ25, NJ29,
NJ31, NY29, NY32, NY64, NY68,
NY113, NY132, NY133, NY134, NY192,
NY330, OH20, OH60, RI1, TX33, TX43,
TX84, TX121, TX144, VT5
Women, MD2, MN49, NY107, NY267, TX35

Youth and youth services, CO66, CT55,
GA31, MD49, MI13, MN42, NV25,
NY221, NY330, NY337, NY338, PA2,
WI5

Zoning, US4, AL55, AL79, AK20, AR6,
CA15, CA26, CA45, CO16, CT2, CT39,
CT48, GA20, IL40, MD7, MD12, MD26,
NY28, NY100, NY101, NY117, NY150,
NY178, NY223, OH10, PA5, SC8, SC31,
VT3, VT4, VT6